SOLUTIONS MANUAL

TO ACCOMPANY

FINANCIAL ACCOUNTING

AN INTRODUCTION TO CONCEPTS, METHODS, AND USES

NINTH EDITION

CLYDE P. STICKNEY | *Dartmouth College*
ROMAN L. WEIL | *University of Chicago*

D1522971

THE DRYDEN PRESS
A DIVISION OF HARCOURT COLLEGE PUBLISHERS
FORT WORTH   PHILADELPHIA   SAN DIEGO   NEW YORK   AUSTIN   ORLANDO   SAN ANTONIO
TORONTO   MONTREAL   LONDON   SYDNEY   TOKYO

ISBN: 0-03-026969-5

Address for Domestic Orders
The Dryden Press, 6277 Sea Harbor Drive, Orlando, FL 32887-6777
800-782-4479

Address for International Orders
International Customer Service
The Dryden Press, 6277 Sea Harbor Drive, Orlando, FL 32887-6777
407-345-3800
(fax) 407-345-4060
(e-mail) hbintl@harcourtbrace.com

Address for Editorial Correspondence
The Dryden Press, 301 Commerce Street, Suite 3700, Fort Worth, TX 76102

Web Site Address
http://www.harcourtcollege.com

Printed in the United States of America

9 0 1 2 3 4 5 6 7 8   023   9 8 7 6 5 4 3 2

The Dryden Press
Harcourt College Publishers

PREFACE

This book presents answers and solutions for the questions, exercises, problems and cases contained in each chapter of the textbook *Financial Accounting: An Introduction to Concepts, Methods and Uses* Ninth Edition.

If you have any suggestions as to how this book might be improved in subsequent editions, please feel free to bring them to our attention.

C.P.S.

R.L.W.

CONTENTS

SPREADSHEET TEMPLATES

For your convenience, Spreadsheet Templates in Microsoft Excel have been created and are available on disk. To obtain a copy, contact your local Dryden Press/Harcourt College Publishers representative.

Instructors can use the templates with their students on the following problems in each chapter.

Chapter	End of Chapter Exercise or Problem
1	20, 24, 29
2	27, 28, 30
3	38, 40, 42
4	18, 19, 21
5	14, 15, 19
6	18, 27, 31
7	27, 31, 32
8	15, 19, 23
9	26, 33, 34
10	33, 42, 47
11	21, 47, 50
12	30, 34, 35
13	11, 13, 14
14	13, 14, 15

CHAPTER 1

INTRODUCTION TO BUSINESS ACTIVITIES AND OVERVIEW OF FINANCIAL STATEMENTS AND THE REPORTING PROCESS

Questions, Exercises, Problems, and Cases: Answers and Solutions

1.1 The first question at the end of each chapter requires the student to review the important concepts or terms discussed in the chapter. In addition to the definitions or descriptions in the chapter, a glossary appears at the end of the book.

1.2 *Setting Goals and Strategies*: A charitable organization would not pursue profit or increasing wealth as goals. Instead, it would direct its efforts at providing some type of service to particular constituencies.

   Financing: Charitable organizations generally obtain the majority of their financing from contributions, although they may engage in borrowing in some situations. Charitable organizations do not issue common stock or other forms of owners' equity. Because they do not operate for a profit, charitable organizations do not have retained earnings.

   Investing: Charitable organizations may acquire supplies, buildings, equipment and other assets to carry out their charitable activities.

   Operations: A charitable organization might prepare a financial statement each period that compares contributions received with operating expenses. Although such a financial statement might resemble an income statement, the organization would probably not label the difference between contributions received and operating expenses as net income or net loss.

1.3 A balance sheet reports the assets, liabilities, and shareholders' equity of a firm at a moment in time (similar to a snapshot), whereas the income statement and statement of cash flows report amounts for a period of time (similar to a motion picture).

1.4   Revenues measure the increase in net assets (assets minus liabilities) and expenses measure the decrease in net assets from selling goods and providing services. An asset such as inventory generally appears on the balance sheet at acquisition cost while it is held. Thus, the asset valuation remains the same and the firm recognizes no revenue. When the firm sells the inventory, the inventory item leaves the firm and cash or a receivable from a customer comes in. If more assets flow in than flow out, total assets increase and the firm recognizes income (revenue minus expense).

1.5   As Chapter 3 makes clear, firms do not necessarily recognize revenues when they receive cash or recognize expenses when they disburse cash. Thus, net income will not necessarily equal cash flow from operations each period. Furthermore, firms disburse cash to acquire property, plant and equipment, repay debt, and pay dividends. Thus, net income and cash flows usually differ. A profitable firm will likely borrow funds in order to remain in business, but eventually operations must generate cash to repay the borrowing.

1.6   No. The unqualified opinion of the CPA indicates that the presentation is a fair reflection of the financial position and operating results of the firm. Because the accountant bases this opinion on an audit of only a portion of the transactions occurring during the year, the CPA does not vouch for the absolute accuracy of every item in the financial statements. The unqualified opinion has evolved to mean, however, that the firm has made sufficient disclosures in the statements so they are not misleading. This interpretation of the unqualified opinion suggests that the statements are free of gross misrepresentations. In court suits against the independent accountants, where courts have found gross misrepresentation to exist, the principal issue is whether the CPA had reasonable grounds (based on audit tests) to believe that the statements were fairly presented at the time the accountant issued the unqualified opinion.

1.7   A wide range of individuals and entities (creditors, investors, security analysts, governmental agencies) use financial accounting reports for a broad range of purposes. If each firm selected whatever format and content of financial reports it deemed best, the resulting reporting process would probably be incomprehensible to many users. Accounting reports generated for internal management purposes, on the other hand, satisfy the information needs of a more limited set of users. Standardization is, therefore, not as necessary.

1.8   **Advantages**

   1.   Government authorities can enforce their pronouncements by law.

   2.   Firms need maintain only one set of accounting records that serves the needs of both financial and tax reporting.

1.8 continued.

3. Greater uniformity in accounting methods across firms likely results because firms either use the methods prescribed for tax purposes or, where there is a choice of several alternative methods for a particular item, use the method that minimizes the present value of tax payments.

Disadvantages

1. The objectives in setting accounting methods for tax purposes (raising tax revenues) may differ from the objectives for financial reporting (measuring financial position and results of operations).

2. Individuals in the government responsible for setting accounting methods may not have the necessary technical expertise or financial statement user perspective.

3. Political lobbying could dominate the standard-setting process.

1.9 The accounting method would be uniform but the resulting information in the financial statements may not provide uniform measures of financial position or results of operations. If the economic characteristics of firms' activities differ, then different accounting methods may be needed to reflect these differences.

1.10 Accounting standards set in the public sector (that is, by a government agency) become subject to political pressures inherent in a democratic system. Accounting standards set in the private sector become subject to political pressures of various preparer and user groups. Because accounting standards set in the private sector have no enforcement power on their own, private-sector standard-setting bodies must respond to these political pressures by gaining acceptance for their standards.

1.11 We would disagree. Within capital market settings, someone must analyze and interpret financial accounting reports if market prices are to incorporate information from those reports. The principal message of efficient market research is that digestion of such information occurs very quickly. In addition, there are many users and uses of financial accounting reports outside of a capital market setting (lending, antitrust regulation, competitor analysis).

1.12 (Preparing a personal balance sheet.)

There is no distinction between contributed capital and retained earnings, because an individual does not issue common stock. The excess of assets over liabilities is called an individual's _net worth_. The methods used in valuing an individual's assets and liabilities are critical variables in determining net worth. Possibilities include acquisition cost, current replacement cost, current selling price, and others.

1.13   (Classifying financial statement accounts.)

    a. NA.

    b. NI (revenue).

    c. CC.

    d. X.

    e. NA.

    f. CA.

    g. X (a footnote to the balance sheet would probably disclose the lawsuit).

    h. NI (expense).

    i. CA.

    j. CL.

    k. X (not recognized as a gain until the firm sells the land).

    l. X (firms report dividends on the statement of retained earnings).

    m. CL.

    n. NL.

1.14   (Sports Authority; balance sheet relations.)

    a. The **given** (boldface) and missing items appear below (amounts in millions).

	Year 8	Year 9	Year 10	Year 11
Current Assets	$ **306**	$ 312	$ 445	$ 389[b]
Noncurrent Assets	**157**	212	**309**	423
Total Assets	$ 463	$ 524	$ **754**	$ 812
Current Liabilities	$ **197**	$ **228**	$ 269[a]	$ 290
Noncurrent Liabilities	**14**	18	175	**188**
Shareholders' Equity	252	**278**	**310**	**334**
Total Liabilities and Shareholders' Equity	$ 463	$ **524**	$ 754	$ **812**

    [a]$269 = $445 − $176.
    [b]$389 = $290 + $99.

1.14 continued.

b. Noncurrent assets increased as a proportion of total assets, suggesting major new investments in property, plant, and equipment or the acquisition of a firm with heavy investments in property, plant and equipment.

c. The proportion of liabilities (both current and noncurrent) increased while the proportion of shareholders' equity decreased. Sports Authority used debt to finance the acquisition of property, plant and equipment.

1.15 (TJX Cos., Inc.; balance sheet relations.)

a. The **given** (boldface) and missing items appear below (amounts in millions).

	Year 8	Year 9	Year 10	Year 11
Current Assets	**$1,008**	$1,615	**$1,662**	**$1,683**
Noncurrent Assets	592	**1,059**	**899**	927
Total Assets.....................	**$1,600**	$2,674	$2,561	**$2,610**
Current Liabilities.............	$ **720**	$1,206	$1,182	$1,218
Noncurrent Liabilities	**273**	**703**	252	**228**
Shareholders' Equity	607	**765**	**1,127**	1,164
Total Liabilities and Share- holders' Equity...............	$1,600	**$2,674**	$2,561	$2,610

b. Noncurrent assets increased as a percentage of total assets, suggesting investments in property, plant and equipment. TJX Cos., Inc. may have also acquired other firms which had higher proportions of noncurrent assets than TJX Cos., Inc.

c. Total liabilities, particularly noncurrent liabilities, increased as a percentage of total financing, suggesting the use of debt to finance the growth in noncurrent assets.

d. Noncurrent assets decreased as a percentage of total assets, probably because TJX Cos., Inc. sold off some of the noncurrent assets acquired during Year 9.

e. Total liabilities, particularly noncurrent liabilities, decreased as a percentage of total financing, suggesting that TJX Cos., Inc. used some of the cash proceeds from selling noncurrent assets to repay noncurrent liabilities.

1.16   (Procter & Gamble; balance sheet relations.)

a. The **given** (boldface) and missing items appear below (amounts in millions).

	Year 6	Year 7	Year 8	Year 9
Current Assets	$ 8,435	$ 9,366[a]	$ 9,975	$ 9,988
Noncurrent Assets............	12,033	14,659	14,960	15,547
Total Assets......................	$20,468	$24,025	$24,935	$25,535
Current Liabilities.............	$ 6,733	$ 7,642	$ 8,287	$ 8,040[c]
Noncurrent Liabilities	5,999	7,312	9,207	8,663
Contributed Capital...........	1,017	1,149	1,292	1,399
Retained Earnings	6,719	7,922	6,149[b]	7,433[d]
Total Liabilities and Share- holders' Equity...............	$20,468	$24,025	$24,935	$25,535

[a]$7,642 + $1,724 = $9,366.
[b]$7,922 – $656 – $1,117 = $6,149.
[c]$9,988 – $1,948 = $8,040.
[d]$6,149 + $2,524 – $1,240 = $7,433.

b. Procter & Gamble likely acquired another firm. The acquired firm probably has a slightly higher percentage of noncurrent assets than Procter & Gamble. Because the mix of short- versus long-term financing and debt versus equity financing did not change substantially between the two years, either Procter & Gamble used a mix of these types of financing or the acquired firm has a capital structure similar to Procter & Gamble's. The acquisition target in this case was the cosmetics and fragrance business of Revlon.

c. Noncurrent liabilities increased in an amount approximately equal to the decrease in retained earnings. Procter & Gamble operated at a net loss during Year 10. One possible explanation is that the net loss reduced cash, requiring Procter & Gamble to obtain additional financing. The actual explanation in this case is that Procter & Gamble adopted the provisions of Financial Accounting Standards Board *Statement No. 106* and *Statement 109*. The adoptions resulted in a charge against earnings and an increase in noncurrent liabilities.

d. Procter & Gamble was profitable during Year 9. It used a portion of the cash generated by profitable operations to repay short- and long-term financing.

1.17   (Anheuser-Busch; balance sheet relations.)

a. The **given** (boldface) and missing items appear below (amounts in millions).

	Year 6	Year 7	Year 8	Year 9
Current Assets	**$ 1,546**	$ 1,511	**$ 1,466**	$ 1,584
Noncurrent Assets................	9,001	**9,080**	8,998	10,143
Total Assets.........................	**$10,547**	**$10,591**	$10,464	$11,727
Current Liabilities................	**$ 1,489**	$ 1,242	$ 1,432	**$ 1,501**
Noncurrent Liabilities	**4,643**	**4,915**	5,003	6,184
Shareholders' Equity	4,415	**4,434**	4,029	4,042
Total Liabilities and Share-holders' Equity...................	$10,547	$10,591	$10,464	$11,727
Current Assets/Current Liabilities..............................	1.038	1.217	**1.024**	**1.055**

b. The proportion of total assets comprising noncurrent assets increased during the four years, suggesting either additional beer-brewing capacity or additional investments in theme parks. Anheuser-Busch increased the proportion of noncurrent liabilities in the capital structure. It likely used the additional noncurrent liabilities to finance the growth in noncurrent assets.

1.18   (Texas Instruments; balance sheet relations.)

a. The **given** (boldface) and missing items appear below (amounts in millions).

	Year 5	Year 6	Year 7	Year 8
Current Assets	$2,381	**$2,626**	**$3,314**	$ 4,024
Noncurrent Assets................	2,628	2,559	**2,679**	2,965
Total Assets.........................	$5,009	**$5,185**	$5,993	$ 6,989
Current Liabilities................	**$1,568**	$1,662	**$2,001**	$ 2,199
Noncurrent Liabilities	**1,486**	1,576	**1,677**	**1,751**
Contributed Capital	1,189	**1,031**	1,008	**1,127**
Retained Earnings	**766**	**916**	1,307[a]	1,912[b]
Total Liabilities and Share-holders' Equity...................	**$5,009**	$5,185	$5,993	$ 6,989
Current Assets/Current Liabilities..............................	1.52	**1.58**	1.66	**1.83**

[a]$916 + $472 − $81 = $1,307.
[b]$1,307 + $691 − $86 = $1,912.

1.18 continued.

    b.   Although current assets and noncurrent assets increased during the four years, current assets increased faster than noncurrent assets. One possible explanation is that Texas Instruments had unused manufacturing capacity at the beginning of Year 6 which it increasingly used in later years to manufacture inventory and to generate increased sales Thus, inventories and accounts receivable grew faster than property, plant and equipment. The proportion of noncurrent liabilities and contributed capital in the capital structure declined over the four years while the proportion from retained earnings increased. Texas Instruments experienced rapidly increased earnings during the three-year period. It used the assets generated by these earnings to finance the growth in assets. The growth in assets was also financed in part with additional noncurrent liabilities and contributed capital.

1.19   (Olin Corporation, retained earnings relations.)

    a.   The **given** (boldface) and missing items appear below (amounts in millions).

	Year 6	Year 7	Year 8	Year 9
Retained Earnings, Beginning of Year	$ **499**	$ 435	$ **388**	$ **238**
Net Income	**(13)**	**9**	(92)	**91**
Dividends Declared and Paid	**(51)**	**(56)**	**(58)**	**(60)**
Retained Earnings, End of Year	$ 435	$ **388**	$ **238**	$ 269

    b.   The sales of Olin Corporation are cyclical. The economy was apparently in a recession during Year 6, Year 7 and Year 8 and began pulling out of the recession in Year 9.

    c.   A slowly growing but continuous dividend sends a signal to common shareholders that the firm expects to grow and return to profitable operations when the economy pulls out of the recession. Also, shareholders who rely on dividends for their living expenses will probably prefer steady dividends instead of distributions that vary with net income each year.

1.20   (Volvo Group; retained earnings relations.)

a. The changes in retained earnings appear below. **Given** amounts appear in boldface (amounts in millions of Swedish Krona).

	Year 3	**Year 4**	**Year 5**	**Year 6**
Retained Earnings, January 1 ..	**25,634**	30,484	**34,338**	**37,922**
Net Income	**5,665**	**4,940**	4,787	(1,020)*
Dividends	**815**	1,086	**1,203**	**1,203**
Retained Earnings, December 31	30,484	**34,338**	37,922	**35,699**

*Net loss.

b. Volvo Group experienced decreasing amounts of net income over the four years, even operating at a net loss in Year 6. The firm, however, increased or at least maintained its dividends during this period of declining profitability. Thus, retained earnings grew at a declining rate (Year 3 to Year 5) or decreased (Year 6).

1.21   (Home Depot; relating net income to balance sheet changes.)

a.

(Amount in Millions)	**Year 3**	**Year 4**
Retained Earnings, Beginning of Year	$2,579	$3,407
Plus Net Income	938	1,162
Less Dividends Declared and Paid..................	(110)	(139)
Retained Earnings, End of Year......................	$3,407	$4,430

b.

$$\text{Net Income} = \text{Increase in Assets} - \text{Increase in Liabilities} - \text{Increase in Contributed Capital} + \text{Dividends}$$

Year 3

$$\$938 = \$1,988 - \$999 - \$161 + \$110$$

Year 4

$$\$1,162 = \$1,887 - \$726 - \$138 + \$139$$

1.22   (Nestle Group; relating net income to balance sheet changes.)

a.

(Amount in Millions)	Year 5	Year 6
Retained Earnings, Beginning of Year	SF17,096	SF18,439
Plus Net Income	1,960	1,896
Less Dividends Declared and Paid................	(617)	(740)
Retained Earnings, End of Year..................	SF18,439	SF19,595

b.

$$\text{Net Income} = \text{Increase in Assets} - \text{Increase in Liabilities} - \text{Increase in Contributed Capital} + \text{Dividends}$$

Year 5

$$\text{SF1,960} = \text{SF1,996} - \text{SF635} - \text{SF18} + \text{SF617}$$

Year 6

$$\text{SF1,896} = \text{SF231} - \text{SF(}-925\text{)} - \text{SF0} + \text{SF740}$$

1.23   (Dell Computer; income statement relations.)

a. The **given** (boldface) and missing items appear below (amounts are in millions).

	Year 4	Year 5	Year 6
Sales...	**$ 5,296**	**$ 7,759**	**$12,327**
Interest Revenue...............................	**6**	**33**	**52**
Cost of Goods Sold.............................	**(4,229)**	**(6,093)**	(9,605)
Research and Development Expenses..	**(95)**	**(126)**	**(204)**
Marketing and Administrative Expenses.....................................	**(595)**	**(826)**	**(1,202)**
Income Tax Expense	**(111)**	**(216)**	**(424)**
Net Income......................................	$ 272	$ 531	$ 944

b. The common size income statement appears below:

	Year 4	Year 5	Year 6
Sales	100.0%	100.0%	100.0%
Interest Revenue	.1	.4	.4
Cost of Goods Sold	(79.9)	(78.5)	(77.9)
Research and Development Expenses....	(1.8)	(1.6)	(1.6)
Marketing and Administrative Expenses.......................................	(11.2)	(10.7)	(9.8)
Income Tax Expense...........................	(2.1)	(2.8)	(3.4)
Net Income.......................................	5.1%	6.8%	7.7%

The ratio of net income to sales increased steadily during the three years. The cost of goods sold to sales percentage and the marketing and administrative expense to sales percentage both decreased steadily. One possible explanation is that excess demand in compu-

1.23 b. continued.

ter products permitted Dell to raise its selling prices. Another possible explanation is that the increased sales were spread over certain relatively fixed manufacturing, marketing, or administrative expenses, lowering the expense percentages.

1.24   (Circuit City Stores; income statement relations.)

a. The **given** (boldface) and missing items appear below (amounts in millions).

	Year 6	Year 7	Year 8
Sales	**$ 7,029**	$ 7,664	**$ 8,871**
Cost of Goods Sold	**(5,394)**	**(5,903)**	(6,827)
Marketing and Administrative Expenses	**(1,322)**	**(1,511)**	**(1,849)**
Interest Expense	**(25)**	**(30)**	**(27)**
Income Tax Expense	**(108)**	**(84)**	**(64)**
Net Income	$ 180	$ **136**	$ **104**

b. The common size income statement appears below.

	Year 6	Year 7	Year 8
Sales	100.0%	100.0%	100.0%
Cost of Goods Sold	(76.7)	(77.0)	(77.0)
Marketing and Administrative Expenses	(18.8)	(19.7)	(20.8)
Interest Expense	(.4)	(.4)	(.3)
Income Tax Expense	(1.5)	(1.1)	(.7)
Net Income	2.6%	1.8%	1.2%

Circuit City Stores experienced a declining net income to sales percentage during the three-year period. The principal contributing factor was an increase in the marketing and administrative expense to sales percentage. Increased competition may have increased marketing expenditures. Growth in new stores may have increased administrative expenses.

1.25   (Delta Airlines; statement of cash flows relations.)

a.
DELTA AIRLINES
Statement of Cash Flows
(Amounts in Millions)

	Year 2	Year 3	Year 4
Operations:			
Revenues Increasing Cash	$10,519	$12,196	$12,528
Expenses Decreasing Cash	(10,369)	(11,519)	(11,204)
Cash Flow from Operations.................	$ 150	$ 677	$ 1,324
Investing:			
Sale of Property and Equipment	$ 43	$ 87	$ 103
Acquisition of Property and			
Equipment................................	(3,082)	(1,414)	(1,613)
Cash Flow from Investing.................	$(3,039)	$(1,327)	$(1,510)
Financing:			
Increase (Decrease) in Short-term			
Debt	$ 746	$ (801)	$ 0
Increase in Long-term Debt.............	2,313	2,111	975
Increase in Common Stock	0	1,127	0
Decrease in Long-term Debt	(794)	(519)	(547)
Dividends....................................	(89)	(138)	(120)
Cash Flow from Financing.................	$ 2,176	$ 1,780	$ 308
Change in Cash	$ (713)	$ 1,130	$ 122

b.   Although cash flow from operations increased during the three years, its amount was not sufficient to finance acquisition of property and equipment. Delta financed these acquisitions with long-term debt in all three years and with common stock in Year 3.

1.26   (Nike; statement of cash flows relations.)

a.

NIKE, INC.
Statement of Cash Flows
(Amounts in Millions)

	Year 8	Year 9	Year 10
Operations:			
Revenues Increasing Cash	$6,184	$6,087	$9,633
Expenses Decreasing Cash	(5,844)	(5,764)	(9,115)
Cash Flow from Operations................	$ 340	$ 323	$ 518
Investing:			
Acquisition of Property, Plant and			
Equipment...................................	$ (240)	$ (496)	$ (595)
Cash Flow from Investing..................	$ (240)	$ (496)	$ (595)
Financing:			
Proceeds of Bank Borrowing.............	$ 23	$ 388	$ 26
Issue of Common Stock...................	2	69	12
Repurchase of Common Stock	--	--	(170)
Dividends.....................................	(79)	(101)	(127)
Cash Flow from Financing.................	$ (54)	$ 356	$ (259)
Change in Cash...............................	$ 46	$ 183	$ (336)

b. Nike made a larger amount of sales on account during Year 8 and Year 9 than it collected from customers from sales on account (that is, accounts receivable increased). Likewise, Nike manufactured more products than it sold in order to meet growing demand. Thus, cash inflows were less than sales revenues and cash outflows for operations exceeded expenses. The net result was that net income exceeded cash flow from operations. Net income declined significantly between Year 9 and Year 10, suggesting the likelihood of decreased sales. Nike collected more receivables than sales on account and reduced production levels. Thus, cash flow from operations exceeded net income.

1.27   (Relations between financial statements.)

a. $630 + $3,290 − $2,780 = a; a = $1,140.

b. $1,240 + b − $8,290 = $1,410; b = $8,460.

c. $89,000 − c − $0 + $17,600 = $102,150; c = $4,450.

d. $76,200 + $14,200 − d = $83,300; d = $7,100.

1.28 (America Online; preparing a balance sheet and income statement.)

a.

AMERICA ONLINE
Income Statement
For the Year Ended June 30, Year 8

Revenues:	
Sales..	$2,600,000
Interest Revenue...............................	21,000
Total Revenues.............................	$2,621,000
Less Expenses:	
Cost of Goods Sold	$1,678,000
Research and Development Expense	175,000
Selling and Administrative Expense	604,000
Depreciation Expense........................	14,000
Interest Expense................................	58,000
Total Expenses..............................	2,529,000
Net Income..	$ 92,000

b.

AMERICA ONLINE
Comparative Balance Sheet
(Amounts in Thousands)

	June 30, Year 7	June 30, Year 8
Assets		
Current Assets:		
Cash......................................	$ 124,000	$ 631,000
Accounts Receivable.............................	65,000	104,000
Other Current Assets............................	134,000	195,000
Total Current Assets...........................	$ 323,000	$ 930,000
Noncurrent Assets:		
Investments in Securities	$ 277,000	$ 921,000
Property, Plant and Equipment—Net of		
Depreciation	233,000	363,000
Total Noncurrent Assets	$ 510,000	$1,284,000
Total Assets.....................................	$ 833,000	$2,214,000
Liabilities and Shareholders' Equity		
Current Liabilities:		
Accounts Payable to Suppliers..................	$ 68,000	$ 87,000
Other Current Liabilities	485,000	807,000
Total Current Liabilities.......................	$ 553,000	$ 894,000
Long-Term Debt..	140,000	722,000
Total Liabilities	$ 693,000	$1,616,000
Shareholders' Equity:		
Common Stock....................................	$ 647,000	$1,013,000
Retained Earnings (Deficit).....................	(507,000)	(415,000)
Total Shareholders' Equity...................	$ 140,000	$ 598,000
Total Liabilities and Shareholders'		
Equity	$ 833,000	$2,214,000

1.28 continued.

c. Retained Earnings, (Deficit) June 30, Year 7 .... $ (507,000)
   Plus Net Income for Year Ending June 30, Year 8 92,000
   Subtract Dividends for Year Ending June 30, Year 8 0
   Retained Earnings (Deficit), June 30, Year 8 .... $ (415,000)

1.29 (Ben and Jerry's Homemade Ice Cream, Inc.: preparing a balance sheet and income statement.) (Amounts in Thousands)

a.   BEN AND JERRY'S HOMEMADE ICE CREAM, INC.
                          Balance Sheet
             December 31, Year 6, and December 31, Year 7

	Dec. 31, Year 6	Dec. 31, Year 7
Assets		
Current Assets:		
Cash..	$ 796	$ 6,704
Accounts Receivable	5,044	6,940
Inventories..	10,083	9,000
Other Current Assets	518	1,091
Total Current Assets........................	$ 16,441	$ 23,735
Noncurrent Assets:		
Property, Plant and Equipment.................	$ 17,299	$ 19,300
Other Noncurrent Assets........................	559	21
Total Noncurrent Assets	$ 17,858	$ 19,321
Total Assets......................................	$ 34,299	$ 43,056
Liabilities and Shareholders' Equity		
Current Liabilities:		
Accounts Payable	$ 5,219	$ 7,873
Salaries Payable..................................	42	63
Other Current Liabilities	2,623	4,249
Total Current Liabilities.....................	$ 7,884	$ 12,185
Noncurrent Liabilities:		
Bonds Payable (due Year 20)....................	10,313	4,602
Total Liabilities	$ 18,197	$ 16,787
Shareholders' Equity:		
Common Stock.....................................	$ 6,532	$ 12,959
Retained Earnings................................	9,570	13,310
Total Shareholders' Equity..................	$ 16,102	$ 26,269
Total Liabilities and Shareholders' Equity	$ 34,299	$ 43,056

1.29 continued.

b. BEN AND JERRY'S HOMEMADE ICE CREAM, INC.
Income Statement
For Year 7

Revenues:
Sales Revenue... $ 97,005
　　Total Revenue... $ 97,005

Expenses:
Cost of Goods Sold... $ 68,500
Selling Expense.. 16,466
Administrative Expense....................................... 4,798
Interest Expense... 736
Income Tax Expense 2,765
　　Total Expenses .... $ 93,265
Net Income... $ 3,740

c. Retained Earnings, December 31, Year 6..................... $ 9,570
Plus Net Income for Year 7... 3,740
Less Dividends Declared and Paid............................... --
Retained Earnings, December 31, Year 7..................... $ 13,310

d. Ben and Jerry's issued common stock and paid no dividends, despite positive net income for the year. It used cash flow from these activities to repay long-term debt, acquire property, plant and equipment, and increase the balance in the cash account.

1.30   (Wal-Mart Stores, Inc.; preparing a balance sheet and income statement.)

a.
WAL-MART STORES, INC.
Comparative Balance Sheet
December 31, Year 1 and Year 2
(Amounts in Millions)

	Dec. 31, Year 1	Dec. 31, Year 2
Assets		
Current Assets:		
Cash..	$ 20	$ 45
Accounts Receivable..................................	898	900
Merchandise Inventory	11,196	14,393
Total Current Assets..............................	$12,114	$15,338
Noncurrent Assets:		
Land..	$ 2,741	$ 3,036
Equipment (net of accumulated depreciation)..	4,307	4,675
Buildings (net of accumulated depreciation)....	6,128	8,163
Other Noncurrent Assets............................	1,151	1,607
Total Noncurrent Assets	$14,327	$17,481
Total Assets...	$26,441	$32,819
Liabilities and Shareholders' Equity		
Current Liabilities:		
Bank Loan Payable (due Year 2 and Year 3)....	$ 1,646	$ 1,882
Accounts Payable	4,104	5,907
Income Taxes Payable	183	365
Other Current Liabilities	1,473	1,819
Total Current Liabilities..........................	$ 7,406	$ 9,973
Noncurrent Liabilities:		
Bonds Payable (due Year 16).......................	7,960	9,709
Total Liabilities	$15,366	$19,682
Shareholders' Equity:		
Common Stock..	$ 766	$ 769
Retained Earnings.....................................	10,309	12,368
Total Shareholders' Equity.......................	$11,075	$13,137
Total Liabilities and Shareholders' Equity ...	$26,441	$32,819

1.30 continued.

b.

WAL-MART STORES, INC.
Income Statement
For Year 2
(Amounts in Millions)

Revenues:
Sales Revenue.. $ 83,412

Expenses:
Cost of Merchandise Sold .... $ 65,586
Depreciation Expense 1,070
Interest Expense... 706
Other Operating Expenses....................................... 11,788
Income Tax Expense 1,581
    Total Expenses.. $ 80,731
Net Income.. $ 2,681

c.   Retained Earnings, December 31, Year 1....................... $ 10,309
Plus Net Income for Year 2.. 2,681
Less Dividends Declared and Paid during Year 2........... (622)
Retained Earnings, December 31, Year 2....................... $ 12,368

1.31   (ABC Company; relation between net income and cash flows.)

a.

Month	Cash Balance at Beginning of Month	+ Cash Receipts from Customers	− Cash Disbursements for Production Costs	= Cash Balance at End of the Month
January	$ 875	$1,000	$ 750	$1,125
February	1,125	1,000	1,500	625
March	625	1,500	1,875	250
April	250	2,000	2,250	0

The cash flow problem arises because of a lag between cash expenditures incurred in producing goods and cash collections from customers once the firm sells those goods. For example, cash expenditures during February ($1,500) are for goods produced during February and sold during March. Cash is not collected from customers on these sales, however, until April ($2,000). A growing firm must generally produce more units than it sells during a period if it is to have sufficient quantities of inventory on hand for future sales. The cash needed for this higher level of production may well exceed the cash received from the prior period's sales. Thus, a cash shortage develops.

1.31 continued.

b. The difference between the selling price of goods sold and the cost of those goods equals net income for the period. As long as selling prices exceed the cost of the goods, a positive net income results. As the number of units sold increases, net income increases. A firm does not necessarily recognize revenues and expenses in the same period as the related cash receipts and expenditures. Thus, cash decreases, for reasons Part *a*. discusses, even though net income increases.

c. The income statement and statement of cash flows provide information about the profitability and liquidity respectively of a firm during a period. The fact that net income and cash flows can move in opposite directions highlights the need for information from both statements. A firm without sufficient cash will not survive, even if it operates profitably. The balance sheet indicates a firm's asset and equity position at a moment in time. The deteriorating cash position is evident from the listing of assets at the beginning of each month. Examining the cash receipts and disbursements during each month, however, identifies the reasons for the deterioration.

d. Strategies for dealing with the cash flow problem center around (a) reducing the lag between cash outflows to produce widgets and cash inflows from their sale, and (b) increasing the margin between selling prices and production costs.

To reduce the lag on collection of accounts receivable, ABC might:

(1) Provide to customers an incentive to pay faster than 30 days, such as offering a discount if customers pay more quickly or charge interest if customers delay payment.

(2) Use the accounts receivable as a basis for external financing, such as borrowing from a bank and using the receivables as collateral or selling (factoring) the receivables for immediate cash

(3) Sell only for cash, although competition may preclude this alternative.

To delay the payment for widgets, ABC might:

(1) Delay paying its suppliers (increases accounts payable) or borrow from a bank using the inventory as collateral (increases bank loan payable).

1.31 d. continued.

    (2) Reduce the holding period for inventories by instituting a just-in-time inventory system. This alternative requires ordering raw materials only when needed in production and manufacturing widgets only to customer orders. Demand appears to be sufficiently predictable so that opportunities for a just-in-time inventory system seem attractive.

To increase the margin between selling price and manufacturing cost, ABC might:

    (1) Negotiate a lower purchase price with suppliers of raw materials.

    (2) Substitute more efficient manufacturing equipment for work now done by employees.

    (3) Increase selling prices.

The cash flow problem is short-term because it will neutralize itself by June. This neutralization occurs because the growth rate in sales is declining (500 additional units sold on top of an ever-increasing sales base). Thus, the firm needs a short-term solution to the cash flow problem. If the growth rate were steady or increasing, ABC might consider obtaining a more permanent source of cash, such as issuing long-term debt or common stock.

1.32   (Balance sheet and income statement relations.)

    a. Bushels of wheat are the most convenient in this case with the given information. This question emphasizes the need for a common measuring unit.

1.32 continued.

b.

IVAN AND IGOR
Comparative Balance Sheets
(Amounts in Bushels of Wheat)

Assets	Beginning of Period	End of Period	Beginning of Period	End of Period
Wheat	20	223	10	105
Fertilizer	2	--	1	--
Ox	40	36	40	36
Plow	--	--	--	2
Land	100	100	50	50
Total Assets	162	359	101	193
Liabilities and Owners' Equity				
Accounts Payable	--	3	--	--
Owners' Equity	162	356	101	193
Total Liabilities and Owners' Equity	162	359	101	193

Questions will likely arise as to the accounting entity. One view is that there are two accounting entities (Ivan and Igor) to whom the Red Bearded Baron has entrusted assets and required a periodic reporting on stewardship. The "owner" in owners' equity in this case is the Red Bearded Baron. Another view is that the Red Bearded Baron is the accounting entity, in which case financial statements that combine the financial statements for Ivan and Igor are appropriate. Identifying the accounting entity depends on the intended use of the financial statements. For purposes of evaluating the performance of Ivan and Igor, the accounting entities are separate—Ivan and Igor. To assess the change in wealth of the Red Bearded Baron during the period, the combined financial statements reflect the accounting entity.

1.32 continued.

c.

IVAN AND IGOR
Comparative Income Statement
(Amounts in Bushels of Wheat)

	IVAN	IGOR
Revenues	243	138
Expenses:		
Seed	20	10
Fertilizer	2	1
Depreciation on Ox	4	4
Plow	3	1
Total Expenses	29	16
Net Income	214	122

Chapter 1 does not expose students to the concept of depreciation. Most students, however, grasp the need to record some amount of expense for the ox and the plow.

d.

(Amounts in Bushels of Wheat)	IVAN	IGOR
Owners' Equity, Beginning of Period	162	101
Plus Net Income	214	122
Less Distributions to Owner	(20)	(30)
Owners' Equity, End of Period	356	193

e. We cannot simply compare the amounts of net income for Ivan and Igor because the Red Bearded Baron entrusted them with different amounts of resources. We must relate the net income amounts to some base. Several possibilities include:

	IVAN	IGOR
Net Income/Average Total Assets	82.2%	83.0%
Net Income/Beginning Total Assets	132.1%	120.8%
Net Income/Average Noncurrent Assets	155.1%	137.1%
Net Income/Beginning Noncurrent Assets	152.9%	135.6%
Net Income/Average Owners' Equity	82.6%	82.0%
Net Income/Beginning Owners' Equity	132.1%	120.8%
Net Income/Acre	$10.70	$12.20

This question has no definitive answer. Its purpose is to get students to think about performance measurement. The instructor may or may not wish to devote class time at this point discussing which base is more appropriate.

CHAPTER 2

BALANCE SHEET: PRESENTING THE INVESTMENTS AND FINANCING OF A FIRM

Questions, Exercises, Problems, and Cases: Answers and Solutions

2.1 See the text or the glossary at the end of the book.

2.2 Based on the conservatively reported earnings, a shareholder might sell shares of stock based on the assessment that the firm is not performing well. If the economic or "true" earnings of the firm are larger, the shareholder's assessment would result in a poor decision. Or, shareholders might dismiss the management of a firm because they feel the firm is not performing well. It should be emphasized here that the principal objective of accounting reports as currently prepared is to present *fairly* the results of operations and the financial condition of the firm. When doubt exists as to the treatment of a particular item or transaction, accountants tend to select the procedure resulting in the more conservative measurement of earnings.

2.3 The justification relates to the need for a reasonably high degree of objectivity in the preparation of the financial statements. When there is an exchange between a firm and some other entity, there is market evidence of the economic effects of the transaction. The independent auditor verifies these economic effects by referring to contracts, cancelled checks and other documents underlying the transaction. If accounting recognized events without such a market exchange (for example, the increase in market value of a firm's assets), increased subjectivity would enter into the preparation of the financial statements.

2.4 The justification relates to the uncertainty as to the ultimate economic effects of the contracts. One party or the other may pull out of the contract. The accountant may not know the benefits and costs of the contract at the time of signing. Until one party or the other begins to perform under the contract, accounting gives no recognition. Accountants often disclose significant contracts of this nature in the notes to the financial statements.

2.5 Accountants record assets at acquisition cost. Cash discounts reduce acquisition cost and, therefore, the amount recorded for merchandise or equipment.

2.6   a.   The contract between the investors and the construction company as well as cancelled checks provide evidence as to the acquisition cost.

     b.   Adjusted acquisition cost differs from the amount in Part *a.* by the portion of acquisition cost applicable to the services of the asset consumed during the first five years. There are several generally accepted methods of computing this amount (discussed in Chapter 9). A review of the accounting records for the office building should indicate how this amount was calculated.

     c.   There are at least two possibilities for ascertaining current replacement cost. One alternative is to consult a construction company to determine the cost of constructing a similar office building (that is, with respect to location, materials, size). The accountant would then adjust the current cost of constructing a new building downward to reflect the used condition of the five-year old office building. The current replacement cost amount could be reduced by 12.5 percent (= 5/40) if the asset's service potential decreases evenly with age. The actual economic decline in the value of the building during the first five years is likely to differ from 12.5 percent and, therefore, some other rate is probably appropriate. A second alternative for ascertaining current replacement cost is to consult a real estate dealer to determine the cost of acquiring a used office building providing services similar to the building that the investors own. The accountant might encounter difficulties in locating such a similar building.

     d.   The accountant might consult a local real estate dealer to ascertain the current market price, net of transactions cost, at which the investors might sell the building. There is always the question as to whether an interested buyer could be found at the quoted price. The accountant might also use any recent offers to purchase the building received by the investors.

     e.   The accountant measures the present value of the future net cash flows using estimated rental receipts and operating expenses (excluding depreciation) for the building's remaining 35-year life. These cash flows are then discounted to the present using an appropriate rate of interest.

2.7   a.   Liability—Receivable from Supplier or Prepaid Merchandise Orders.

     b.   Liability—Investment in Bonds.

     c.   Asset—Interest Payable.

     d.   Asset—Insurance Premiums Received in Advance.

     e.   Liability—Prepaid Rent.

2.8   (Eli Lilly and Company; asset recognition and valuation.)

   a.   Prepaid Insurance, $12,000,000.

   b.   Deposit on Equipment, $500,000.

   c.   Investment in Securities, $325,000.

   d.   Raw Materials Inventory, $784,000.

   e.   Accounting does not recognize the employment contract, a mutually unexecuted contract, as an asset.

   f.   Marketable Securities, $3,200,000.

   g.   Accounting does not recognize the customer's order, a mutually unexecuted contract, as an asset because no exchange between the buyer and the seller has occurred.

   h.   Raw Materials Inventory, $200,000. Legal rights to use the raw materials have passed to Eli Lilly, creating a legal obligation to make payment.

2.9   (IBM Corporation; asset recognition and valuation.)

   a.   Investment in Bond, $8,000,000.

   b.   Prepaid Rent, $600,000.

   c.   Deposit on Land, $1,000,000.

   d.   Accounting does not recognize the employment contract, a mutually unexecuted contract, as an asset.

   e.   Patent, $1,200,000.

   f.   Accounting does not recognize a patent developed from research and development expenditures by a firm as an asset because of the difficulties in ascertaining whether future benefits existed at the time the firm made the expenditures.

   g.   Accounting does not recognize an asset because an exchange has not yet occurred.

2.10   (General Mills, Inc.; asset recognition and valuation.)

   a. Accounting does not recognize as assets, under generally accepted
       accounting principles, expenditures firms make internally to develop
       new products. Too much uncertainty exists as to the existence and
       valuation of future benefits to justify recognition of an asset.

   b. Contractual Rights to Food Products (or similar creative account
       title), $2,800,000. In contrast to Part *a.*, the exchange between buyer
       and seller of presumably a commercially feasible product permits the
       identification and valuation of future benefits to justify recognition of
       an asset. A thin line appears to distinguish the situation in Part *a.*
       and Part *b.*

   c. Deposit on Land, $1,800,000.

   d. Accounting does not recognize an asset because of the difficulty of
       identifying and measuring any future benefits from these advertising
       expenditures.

   e. Investment in Securities, $3,500,000. The market value of the shares
       of General Mills given in exchange is probably a more reliable
       indicator of value than independent appraisals.

   f. Land, $2,188,000. Acquisition cost includes all expenditures made to
       prepare an asset for its intended use.

2.11   (Office Depot; asset recognition and valuation.)

   a. Prepaid Rent, $120,000; Security Deposit, $130,000.

   b. Leasehold Improvements, $36,500 (= $10,000 + $6,500 + $20,000).
       These expenditures prepare the rented facility for its intended use as
       a retail store.

   c. Equipment or Fixtures, $31,400 [= .98 X $30,000) + $1,200 + $800]. The
       latter two expenditures prepare the display counters for their
       intended use.

   d. Accounting does not recognize an asset for the future services of
       employees.

   e. One might argue that Office Depot will realize many benefits from
       the advertisements in the future after it opens the store. Thus, it
       should recognize an asset for Prepaid Advertising of $1,500. Most
       accountants would argue that any future benefits of the advertising
       are too uncertain to justify recognizing an asset.

2.11 continued.

    f.   Merchandise Inventory $145,600 [= (.98 × $120,000) + $40,000 − $12,000]. One might argue that Office Depot should reduce the acquisition cost of the $28,000 (= $40,000 − $12,000) of merchandise that it has not yet paid for by the 2 percent discount. It is possible, however, that cash discounts are not available on this merchandise. If Office Depot takes advantage of any discounts when it pays for this merchandise, it will reduce the acquisition cost at that time.

2.12   (Asset recognition and valuation.)

    a.

Automobile, List Price	$20,000
Less Cash Discount	(1,600)
Dealer Preparation Charges	350
Sales Tax (.06 × $18,750)	1,125
Name Painted on Truck	190
Total Cost of Delivery Truck (a noncurrent asset)	$20,065
Prepaid Insurance (current asset)	$ 500
Prepaid License Fees (current asset)	$ 125

    b.   This part and the next are designed to stimulate discussion. There is no right answer, although our reading of APB *Opinion No. 29* and the facts of the situation lead us to use $5,200,000, the apparent value of the Microsoft shares. (We recall once a student who answered this question in no uncertain terms that the appraiser's figure was correct. When pressed as to why he picked this answer and why he was so certain, he admitted that he was the son of a real estate appraiser and that appraisers never make mistakes!)

    c.   Here we are more inclined to believe the appraiser rather than the stock market, but we are not unanimous in agreeing on the right answer. Historical cost accounting is not as objective and verifiable as is sometimes thought.

2.13   (Travelers Insurance Company; liability recognition and valuation.)

    a.   Insurance Premiums Received in Advance or Advances from Customers, $6,500,000.

    b.   Accounting normally does not recognize a liability for mutually unexecuted contracts. When the president renders services, a liability arises.

    c.   Legal Fees Payable, $1,200,000.

    d.   Common stock does not meet the definition of a liability because the firm need not repay the funds in a particular amount at a particular time.

2.13 continued.

    e.   Salaries and Commissions Payable, $950,000; Payroll Taxes Payable, $76,000 (= .08 × $950,000).

    f.   The treatment of this item depends on the probability of having to make a cash payment in the future, whose amount and timing of payment the Company can estimate with reasonable accuracy. Most firms do not recognize unsettled lawsuits as liabilities because it is not clear (1) that the firm received benefits in the past, and (2) that the lawsuit will require a future cash payment.

2.14   (Kansas City Royals, Inc.; liability recognition and valuation.)

    a.   Accounting normally does not recognize a liability for mutually unexecuted contracts. When the player renders services, a liability arises.

    b.   Advances from Customers, $2,700,000.

    c.   Bonds Payable, $8,400,000.

    d.   Utilities Payable, $3,400.

    e.   The treatment of this item depends on the probability of having to make a cash payment in the future, whose amount and timing of payment the firm can estimate with reasonable accuracy. Most firms do not recognize unsettled lawsuits as liabilities because it is not clear (1) that the firm has received benefits in the past, and (2) that the lawsuit will require a future cash payment.

    f.   The firm does not recognize a liability for the uniforms until the supplier makes delivery. The $10,000 deposit appears as a Deposit on Uniforms, an asset, on the firm's balance sheet and an Advance from Customers, a liability, on the balance sheet of the supplier.

2.15   (Liability recognition and valuation.)

    a.   Bonds Payable, $10,000,000.

    b.   Accounting normally does not recognize a liability for unexecuted contracts. The $2,000,000 deposit appears as an asset, Deposit on Building, on the college's balance sheet and as a liability, Advance from Customers, on the balance sheet of the construction company.

    c.   Advances from Customers, $1,800,000.

    d.   Accounts Payable, $170,000.

2.15 continued.

  e.   Compensation Payable, $280,000; Payroll Taxes Payable $16,800 (.06 X $280,000).

  f.   The college does not recognize a liability for the grant. Although it receives the benefits of the funds, it incurs no obligation to repay the amount of the grant in the future.

2.16   (Liability recognition and valuation.)

  a.   Accounting does not recognize a liability for the paving work, because there has merely been an exchange of promises for future performance.

  b.   Fees Received in Advance, $400.

  c.   Advances from Customers, $500,000.

  d.   Common stock is not a liability because there is no fixed amount or repayment date.

  e.   Note Payable, $30,000.

  f.   Accounting does not recognize a liability for the reason in Part *a*. above.

  g.   Accounting does not recognize a liability for the reason in Part *a*. above.

  h.   Accounts Payable, $2,500.

2.17   (Balance sheet classification.)

a. 2	f. 2	k. 1		
b. 3	g. 1	l. 1	(if purchased from another firm)	
c. 1	h. 2	4	(if created by the firm)	
d. 4	i. 4	m. 4		
e. 1	j. 2	n. 3		

2.18   (Balance sheet classification.)

a. 3	h. 2
b. 1	i. 1
c. 4	j. 2
d. 1	k. 2
e. 3	l. 1
f. 1	m. 2
g. 1 (if purchased from another firm)	n. 3
4 (if created by the firm)	

2.19   (Brackin Corporation; journal entries for various transactions.)

(1) **October 2**
     Cash.. 9,600,000
        Common Stock.................................   6,000,000
        Additional Paid-in Capital   3,600,000
     Issue of 600,000 shares of $10 par value
     common stock at $16 per share.

(2) **October 3**
     Building.. 3,000,000
        Cash...   300,000
        Note Payable...................................   2,700,000
     Acquisition of building for cash and
     issuance of a note.

(3) **October 8**
     Equipment...   40,000
        Cash...   40,000
     Acquisition of a machine for cash.

(4) **October 15**
     Merchandise Inventory.............................. 130,000
        Accounts Payable..............................   130,000
     Acquisition of merchandise inventory on
     account.

(5) **October 18**
     Prepaid Insurance......................................   800
        Cash...   800
     Prepayment of insurance premium for cover-
     age beginning November 1.

(6) **October 20**
     Cash...   2,200
        Advances from Customers.....................   2,200
     Advance from customers on merchandise to
     be delivered on November 5.

(7) **October 26**
     Accounts Payable   90,000
        Cash...   88,200
        Merchandise Inventory   1,800
     Payment of invoices totaling $90,000 but subject
     to a 2 percent discount for prompt payment.

2.19 continued.

    (8) **October 30**

Accounts Payable	40,000	
Cash		40,000

    Payment of invoices totaling $40,000.

Note: Some students treat the lost discounts of $800 (= .02 × $40,000) as an expense and reduce the book value of merchandise inventory accordingly. We allow this answer as well.

2.20   (Schneider Corporation; journal entries for various transactions.)

    (1)

Cash	500,000	
Common Stock		500,000

    (2)

Land	40,000	
Building	185,000	
Cash		50,000
Mortgage Payable		175,000

    (3)

Equipment	13,200	
Cash		13,200

    (4)

Raw Materials Inventory	8,600	
Accounts Payable		8,600

    (5)

Accounts Payable	900	
Raw Materials Inventory		900

    (6)

Accounts Payable	7,700	
Cash		7,546
Raw Materials Inventory		154

    .98($8,600 − $900) = $7,546.

    (7)

Prepaid Insurance	4,950	
Cash		4,950

    (8)

Patent	8,000	
Cash		8,000

    (9)

Prepaid Rent	1,800	
Cash		1,800

    (10)

Patent	90,000	
Cash		90,000

    (11)

Equipment	2,700	
Cash		250
Account Payable		2,450

    (12)

Equipment	825	
Cash		825

2.21   (Winkle Grocery Store; journal entries for various transactions.)

(1)	Cash..	30,000	
	Common Stock		30,000

(2)	Cash..	5,000	
	Notes Payable..		5,000

(3)	Prepaid Rent..	12,000	
	Cash		12,000

(4)	Equipment..	8,000	
	Cash		8,000

(5)	Merchandise Inventory.............................	25,000	
	Cash		12,000
	Accounts Payable.....................................		13,000

(6)	Cash..	4,000	
	Advances from Customers........................		4,000

(7)	Prepaid Insurance....................................	1,200	
	Cash		1,200

(8)	Prepaid Advertising	600	
	Cash		600

(9) The placing of an order does not give rise to a journal entry because it represents a mutually unexecuted contract.

2.22   (Journal entries for various transactions.)

(1)	Investment in Bonds.................................	103,500	
	Cash		103,500

(2)	Cash..	6,390	
	Insurance Premiums Received in		
	Advance..		6,390

(3)	Land..	15,000	
	Building..	105,000	
	Equipment..	60,000	
	Common Stock—Par Value		144,000
	Additional Paid-in Capital........................		36,000

(4) Accounting makes no entry because an exchange between the buyer and seller has not yet occurred to warrant recognition of either an asset or a liability.

2.22 continued.

(5)	Patent...	7,500	
	Preferred Stock—Par Value........................		6,000
	Additional Paid-in Capital..........................		1,500

(6)	Cash..	650	
	Admission Fees Received in Advance..........		650

(7) No entry is made until accountants establish the amount and timing of payment.

(8)	Accounts Payable..	4,000	
	Merchandise Inventory...............................		4,000

2.23 (Wendy's International, Inc.; journal entries for various transactions.)

(1) The firm does not make an entry for the supplies until it receives them.

(2)	Supplies Inventory	1,600,000	
	Accounts Payable......................................		1,600,000

(3)	Accounts Payable..	40,000	
	Supplies Inventory....................................		40,000

(4)	Accounts Payable..	1,400,000	
	Cash		1,372,000
	Supplies Inventory....................................		28,000

(5)	Accounts Payable..	160,000	
	Cash		160,000

Note: Some students treat the lost discounts of $3,200 (= .02 × $160,000) as an expense and reduce Supplies Inventory accordingly. We allow this answer as well.

(6)	Deposit on Equipment...................................	200,000	
	Cash		200,000

(7)	Equipment..	900,000	
	Deposit on Equipment..............................		200,000
	Cash		700,000

(8)	Equipment..	27,000	
	Cash		27,000

(9)	Receivable from Supplier.............................	22,000	
	Equipment...		22,000

(10)	Cash..	22,000	
	Receivable from Supplier..........................		22,000

2.24   (Effect of transactions on balance sheet equation.)

Transaction Number		Assets	=	Liabilities	+	Shareholders' Equity
(1)		+ $30,000				+ $30,000
	Subtotal	$30,000	=			$30,000
(2)		+ 18,900		+ $18,900		
	Subtotal	$48,900	=	$18,900	+	$30,000
(3)		+ 12,700				
		− 2,000		+ 10,700		
	Subtotal	$59,600	=	$29,600	+	$30,000
(4)		+ 1,800				
		− 1,800				
	Subtotal	$59,600	=	$29,600	+	$30,000
(5)				− 10,700	+	10,700
	Subtotal	$59,600	=	$18,900	+	$40,700
(6)		− 18,900		− 18,900		
	Total	$40,700	=	-0-	+	$40,700

2.25   (Regaldo Department Stores; effect of transactions on balance sheet equation.)

a.

Transaction Number	Cash	+ Inventories	+ Other Assets	= Liabilities	+ Common Stock	+ Retained Earnings
(1)	+Ps 500,000				+Ps 500,000	
(2)	−Ps 24,000		+Ps 24,000			
(3)a						
(4)	−Ps 60,000		+Ps 60,000			
(5)		+Ps 200,000		+Ps 200,000		
(6)		−Ps 8,000		−Ps 8,000		
(7)	−Ps 156,800	−Ps 3,200		−Ps 160,000		
(8)	−Ps 12,000		+Ps 12,000			
	Ps 247,200	+ Ps 188,800	+ Ps 96,000	= Ps 32,000	+ Ps 500,000	+ Ps 0

aAccounting views the ordering of merchandise as a mutually unexecuted contract and, therefore, makes no entry at this time.

2.25 continued.

b.

REGALDO DEPARTMENT STORES
Balance Sheet
January 31, Year 8

Assets

Current Assets:
Cash..	Ps 247,200
Merchandise Inventories...........................	188,800
Prepaid Rent	60,000
Prepaid Insurance...................................	12,000
Total Current Assets........................	Ps 508,000
Patent..	24,000
Total Assets...................................	Ps 532,000

Liabilities and Shareholders' Equity

Current Liabilities:
Accounts Payable....................................	Ps 32,000
Total Current Liabilities....................	Ps 32,000

Shareholders' Equity:
Common Stock...	Ps 500,000
Retained Earnings...................................	0
Total Shareholders' Equity................	Ps 500,000
Total Liabilities and Shareholders' Equity	Ps 532,000

2.26   (T-account entries for various transactions.)

Cash (A)					Merchandise Inventory (A)				Prepaid Insurance (A)	
(1)	240,000	80,000	(2)	(3)	35,000		(4)	3,000	
(5)	20,000	3,000	(4)						
(7)	600	22,000	(6)						
	155,600				35,000			3,000	

Building (A)			Equipment (A)			Accounts Payable (L)		
(2)	500,000		(3)	20,000		(6)	22,000	55,000 (3)
	500,000			20,000				33,000

Note Payable (L)			Advances from Customers (L)			Mortgage Payable (L)	
	20,000 (5)			600 (7)			420,000 (2)
	20,000			600			420,000

Common Stock— Par Value (SE)		Additional Paid-in Capital (SE)	
	100,000 (1)		140,000 (1)
	100,000		140,000

2.27 (Patterson Manufacturing Corporation; T-account entries and balance sheet preparation.)

a.

Cash (A)				Marketable Securities (A)		Receivable from Supplier (A)	
(1) 210,000	5,400	(5)		(14) 95,000		(13) 1,455	
(11) 4,500	350	(6)					
	1,400	(8)					
	58,200	(9)					
	7,000	(12)					
	95,000	(14)					
47,150				95,000		1,455	

Raw Materials Inventory (A)				Prepaid Rent (A)		Land (A)	
(4) 75,000	800	(7)		(8) 1,400		(2) 80,000	
	1,800	(9)					
	1,455	(13)					
70,945				1,400		80,000	

Buildings (A)			Equipment (A)			Patent (A)	
(2) 220,000			(2) 92,000			(3) 28,000	
(12) 60,000			(5) 5,400				
			(6) 350				
280,000			97,750			28,000	

Accounts Payable (L)			Advances from Customers (L)		Mortgage Payable (L)	
(7) 800	75,000	(4)		4,500 (11)		53,000 (12)
(9) 60,000						
	14,200			4,500		53,000

Common Stock Par Value (SE)		Additional Paid-in Capital (SE)	
	150,000 (1)		60,000 (1)
	280,000 (2)		112,000 (2)
	20,000 (3)		8,000 (3)
	450,000		180,000

(10) Because no insurance coverage has yet been provided and no cash has changed hands, the principle of mutual exchange suggests that no asset and no liability be recorded.

2.27 continued.

b.

PATTERSON MANUFACTURING CORPORATION
Balance Sheet
January 31

Assets

Current Assets:

Cash...	$ 47,150	
Marketable Securities.............................	95,000	
Receivable from Supplier	1,455	
Raw Materials Inventory.........................	70,945	
Prepaid Rent[a].....................................	1,400	
Total Current Assets...........................		$ 215,950
Property, Plant, and Equipment (at Acquisition Cost):		
Land..	$ 80,000	
Buildings..	280,000	
Equipment	97,750	
Total Property, Plant, and Equipment...		457,750
Intangibles:		
Patent...		28,000
Total Assets..		$ 701,700

Liabilities and Shareholders' Equity

Current Liabilities:		
Accounts Payable[a]	$ 14,200	
Advances from Customers.......................	4,500	
Total Current Liabilities.......................		$ 18,700
Long-Term Debt:		
Mortgage Payable..................................		53,000
Total Liabilities		$ 71,700
Shareholders' Equity:		
Common Stock—$10 Par Value	$ 450,000	
Additional Paid-in Capital	180,000	
Total Shareholders' Equity...................		630,000
Total Liabilities and Shareholders' Equity		$ 701,700

[a]See discussion of transaction (10) on the preceding page. It is not wrong to show a current asset, Prepaid Insurance, of $400 and an additional $400 in the current liability, Accounts Payable. If that amount is shown, then, of course, the various subtotals and totals will increase by $400.

2.28   (Idaho Products Corporation; T-account entries and balance sheet preparation.)

a.

Cash (A)			Merchandise Inventory (A)			Prepaid License Fees (A)		
(1) 240,000	40,000	(3)	(7) 60,000	1,900	(9)	(8) 1,300		
(2) 50,000	8,000	(4)		800	(12)			
(11) 12,000	1,200	(5)						
	1,800	(6)						
	1,300	(8)						
	30,000	(10)						
	39,200	(12)						
180,500			57,300			1,300		

Land (A)		Buildings (A)		Equipment (A)	
(3) 25,000		(3) 75,000		(4) 46,000	
				(5) 1,200	
				(6) 1,800	
25,000		75,000		49,000	

Patent (A)		Note Payable (L)		Accounts Payable (L)	
(10) 30,000			38,000 (4)	(9) 1,900	60,000 (7)
				(12) 40,000	
30,000			38,000		18,100

Advances from Customers (L)		Preferred Stock (SE)		Common Stock (SE)	
	12,000 (11)		50,000 (2)		100,000 (1)
					25,000 (3)
	12,000		50,000		125,000

Additional Paid-in Capital (SE)	
	140,000 (1)
	35,000 (3)
	175,000

2.28 continued.

b.
IDAHO PRODUCTS CORPORATION
Balance Sheet
April 30

Assets

Current Assets:		
Cash..	$ 180,500	
Merchandise Inventory	57,300	
Prepaid License Fees.............................	1,300	
Total Current Assets.........................		$ 239,100
Property, Plant, and Equipment:		
Land..	$ 25,000	
Buildings..	75,000	
Equipment	49,000	
Total Property, Plant, and Equipment...		149,000
Intangibles:		
Patent..		30,000
Total Assets......................................		$ 418,100

Liabilities and Shareholders' Equity

Current Liabilities:		
Note Payable.......................................	$ 38,000	
Accounts Payable.................................	18,100	
Advances from Customers.....................	12,000	
Total Current Liabilities....................		$ 68,100
Shareholders' Equity:		
Preferred Stock—$100 Par Value	$ 50,000	
Common Stock—$5 Par Value................	125,000	
Additional Paid-in Capital	175,000	
Total Shareholders' Equity.................		350,000
Total Liabilities and Shareholders' Equity		$ 418,100

2.29 (Soybel Corporation; T-account entries and balance sheet preparation.)

a.

Cash (A)				Merchandise Inventory (A)				Prepaid Insurance (A)		
(1)	150,000	220,000	(3)	(5)	75,000	8,000	(6)	(7)	3,200	
(2)	250,000	88,200	(4)							
(8)	900	3,200	(7)							
		64,000	(9)							
	25,500				67,000				3,200	

Land (A)			Buildings (A)			Equipment (A)		
(3)	60,000		(3)	240,000		(4)	88,200	
	60,000			240,000			88,200	

Accounts Payable (L)				Advances from Customers (L)			Mortgage Payable (L)		
(6)	8,000	75,000	(5)		900	(8)		80,000	(3)
(9)	64,000								
		3,000			900			80,000	

Bonds Payable (L)			Common Stock (SE)			Additional Paid-in Capital (SE)		
		250,000	(2)		100,000	(1)		50,000	(1)
		250,000			100,000			50,000	

b.

SOYBEL CORPORATION
Balance Sheet
January 31

Assets

Current Assets:		
Cash..	$ 25,500	
Merchandise Inventory	67,000	
Prepaid Insurance................................	3,200	
Total Current Assets..........................		$ 95,700
Property, Plant and Equipment:		
Land..	$ 60,000	
Buildings..	240,000	
Equipment	88,200	
Total Property, Plant and Equipment....		388,200
Total Assets......................................		$ 483,900

2.29 b. continued.

Liabilities and Shareholders' Equity

Current Liabilities:		
Accounts Payable	$ 3,000	
Advances from Customers	900	
Total Current Liabilities		$ 3,900
Long-Term Debt:		
Mortgage Payable	$ 80,000	
Bonds Payable	250,000	
Total Long-Term Debt		330,000
Total Liabilities		$ 333,900
Shareholders' Equity:		
Common Stock	$ 100,000	
Additional Paid-in Capital	50,000	
Total Shareholders' Equity		150,000
Total Liabilities and Shareholders' Equity		$ 483,900

2.30   (Computer Graphics, Inc.; T-account entries and balance sheet preparation.)

a.

Cash (A)			Supplies Inventory (A)			Prepaid Rent (A)	
(1) 150,000	18,000 (4)		(8) 4,900	98 (10)		(4) 18,000	
(7) 1,500	12,000 (5)		(9) 900				
	900 (9)						
	4,802 (10)						
115,798			5,702			18,000	

Equipment (A)		Software (A)		Patent (A)	
(5) 12,000		(2) 90,000		(3) 1,500	
12,000		90,000		1,500	

Accounts Payable (L)		Advances from Customers (L)		Common Stock (SE)	
(10) 4,900	4,900 (8)		1,500 (7)		100,000 (1)
					60,000 (2)
					1,000 (3)
--	--		1,500		161,000

2.30 a. continued.

```
    Additional Paid-In
     Capital (SE)
    ┌──────────────────────
    │    50,000  (1)
    │    30,000  (2)
    │       500  (3)
    ├──────────────────────
    │    80,500
    │
```

b.

COMPUTER GRAPHICS, INC.
Balance Sheet
May 30

Assets

Current Assets:		
Cash	$ 115,798	
Supplies Inventory	5,702	
Prepaid Rent	18,000	
Total Current Assets		$ 139,500
Noncurrent Assets:		
Equipment	$ 12,000	
Computer Software	90,000	
Patent	1,500	
Total Noncurrent Assets		103,500
Total Assets		$ 243,000

Liabilities and Shareholders' Equity

Current Liabilities:		
Advances from Customers		$ 1,500
Shareholders' Equity:		
Common Stock	$ 161,000	
Additional Paid-in Capital	80,500	
Total Shareholders' Equity		241,500
Total Liabilities and Shareholders' Equity		$ 243,000

2.31   (Blacksmith's Bakery, Inc.; T-account entries and balance sheet preparation.)

a.

	Cash (A)				Supplies Inventory (A)				Prepayments (A)	
(1)	2,000	450	(4)	(7)	390			(6)	800	
(2)	220	580	(5)	(9)	240			(8)	120	
(3)	500	800	(6)							
		390	(7)							
		120	(8)							
	380				630				920	

	Equipment (A)			Accounts Payable (L)			Advances from Customers (L)	
(4)	450				240	(9)	220	(2)
(5)	580				750	(10)		
(10)	750							
	1,780				990		220	

	Common Stock (SE)		Additional Paid-in Capital (SE)	
		2,000 (1)		500 (3)*
		2,000		500

Note: *The chapter does not discuss the correct credit entry for transaction (3). Students should realize that the absence of a repayment obligation precludes recognition of a liability. The principal issue is the appropriate shareholders' equity account. We tend to allow various account titles.

2.31 continued.

b.

BLACKSMITH'S BAKERY, INC.,
Balance Sheet
August 31

Assets

Current Assets:

Cash...	$ 380	
Supplies Inventory.................................	630	
Prepaid Rent..	920	
Total Current Assets..........................		$ 1,930
Noncurrent Assets:....................................		
Equipment...		1,780
Total Assets......................................		$ 3,710

Liabilities and Shareholders' Equity

Current Liabilities:

Accounts Payable....................................	$ 990	
Advances from Customers......................	220	
Total Current Liabilities......................		$ 1,210
Shareholders' Equity:		
Common Stock......................................	$ 2,000	
Additional Paid-in Capital	500	
Total Shareholders' Equity...................		2,500
Total Liabilities and Shareholders' Equity		$3,710

2.32   (Effect of recording errors on balance sheet equation.)

Transaction Number	Assets	=	Liabilities	+	Shareholders' Equity
(1)	U/S $ 8,000		U/S $ 8,000		No
(2)	U/S $15,000		U/S $15,000		No
(3)	No		No		No
(4)	U/S $ 600		U/S $ 600		No
(5)	O/S $ 1,200[a]		No		No
	U/S $ 1,200[a]				
(6)	U/S $ 2,500		No		U/S $ 2,500
(7)	O/S $ 4,000		O/S $ 4,000		No
(8)	O/S $ 5,000[a]		No		No
	U/S $ 5,000[a]				

[a]The response "No" is also acceptable here.

2.33   (Effect of recording errors on balance sheet equation.)

Transaction Number	Assets	=	Liabilities	+	Shareholders' Equity
(1)	U/S $760,000		U/S $760,000		No
(2)	O/S $ 800[a]		No		No
	U/S $ 800[a]				No
(3)	No		No		No
(4)	No		O/S $10,000		U/S $10,000
(5)	U/S $ 900[a]				
	O/S $ 900[a]				
(6)	No		No		No
(7)	O/S $ 2,000		No		O/S $2,000
(8)	O/S $ 3,000[b]		O/S $ 3,000		No

[a]The response "No" is also acceptable here.
[b]Cash is overstated $2,940 and inventory is overstated $60.

2.34   (Effect of recording errors on balance sheet equation.)

Transaction Number	Assets	=	Liabilities	+	Shareholders' Equity
(1)	U/S $8,000		U/S $ 8,000		No
(2)	O/S $3,000		O/S $ 3,000		No
(3)	U/S $ 800		U/S $ 800		No
(4)	O/S $1,000		O/S $ 1,000		No
(5)	U/S $2,500		No		U/S $2,500
(6)	O/S $4,900[a]		No		No
	U/S $4,900[a]				

[a]The response "No" is also acceptable here.

2.35   (Marks and Spenser; balance sheet format, terminology, and accounting methods.)

a.   MARKS AND SPENCER, PLC
                                 Balance Sheet
                             (In Millions of Pounds)

	March 30 Year 4	March 30 Year 5
Assets		
Current Assets:		
Cash...	£ 266	£ 293
Marketable Securities	28	29
Accounts Receivable.............................	192	212
Inventories..	374	351
Prepayments..	134	142
Total Current Assets	£ 994	£ 1,027
Property, Plant and Equipment:..................		
Land and Buildings..............................	£ 1,636[a]	£ 1,733[b]
Equipment	375	419
Total Property, Plant and Equipment	£ 2,011	£ 2,152
Other Noncurrent Assets...........................	£ 212	£ 264
Total Assets.......................................	£ 3,217	£ 3,443
Liabilities and Shareholders' Equity		
Current Liabilities:		
Accounts Payable.................................	£ 187	£ 168
Bank Loans..	100	107
Other Current Liabilities	638	622
Total Current Liabilities......................	£ 925	£ 897
Noncurrent Liabilities:		
Bonds Payable.....................................	£ 565	£ 550
Other Noncurrent Liabilities....................	4	19
Total Noncurrent Liabilities.................	£ 569	£ 569
Total Liabilities	£ 1,494	£ 1,466
Shareholders' Equity:		
Common Stock......................................	£ 675	£ 680
Additional Paid-in Capital	50	69
Retained Earnings................................	998	1,228
Total Shareholders' Equity...................	£ 1,723	£ 1,977
Total Liabilities and Shareholders' Equity....................................	£ 3,217	£ 3,443

[a]£2,094 – £458 = £1,636.
[b]£2,193 – £460 = £1,733.

b.   A close relation exists between the amount of current assets and current liabilities and between noncurrent assets and noncurrent liabilities plus shareholders' equity.

2.36 (United Breweries Group; balance sheet format, terminology, and accounting methods.)

a.
UNITED BREWERIES GROUP
Balance Sheet
(In Millions of Kronor)

	September 30 Year 8	September 30 Year 9
Assets		
Current Assets:		
Cash..	Kr 810	Kr 1,224
Marketable Securities	3,018	3,460
Accounts Receivable.............................	1,413	1,444
Inventories..	1,290	1,393
Prepayments.......................................	317	285
Total Current Assets.........................	Kr 6,848	Kr 7,806
Investments In Securities.........................	422	573
Property, Plant and Equipment[a]................	3,518	3,545
Total Assets....................................	Kr 10,788	Kr 11,924
Liabilities and Shareholders' Equity		
Current Liabilities:		
Accounts Payable..................................	Kr 913	Kr 902
Bank Debt...	619	986
Other Current Liabilities	2,157	2,240
Total Current Liabilities......................	Kr 3,689	Kr 4,128
Bonds Payable.......................................	1,805	1,723
Other Noncurrent Liabilities	1,149	1,425
Total Liabilities	Kr 6,643	Kr 7,276
Shareholders' Equity:		
Common Stock......................................	Kr 976	Kr 976
Retained Earnings.................................	3,169	3,672
Total Shareholders' Equity..................	Kr 4,145	Kr 4,648
Total Liabilities and Shareholders' Equity	Kr 10,788	Kr 11,924

[a]The amounts for this account reflect historical costs instead of current market values as follows:

	As Reported By Company	– Revaluation Reserve	+ As Restated
Property, Plant and Equipment:			
September 30, Year 8..............	Kr3,934	– Kr416	+ Kr3,518
September 30, Year 9..............	Kr4,106	– Kr561	+ Kr3,545

b. Current assets significantly exceed current liabilities, primarily because of the high proportion of current assets that comprises cash and marketable securities. United Breweries has apparently generated substantial cash flow from operations which it has not reinvested in operating assets.

2.37 (Staples, Inc.; interpreting balance sheet changes.)

    a. The principal assets of a retail chain are inventories and retail stores. Merchandise inventories dominate the balance sheet of Staples, in part because some of its retail space is leased from other entities and does not appear in property, plant and equipment. Accounts payable to suppliers of merchandise is the largest current liability. Thus, Staples uses short-term financing to finance short-term assets. The common size percentage for long-term debt is approximately the same as the percentage for property, plant and equipment. Staples, therefore, appears to use long-term financing for long-term assets. The relatively large common size percentage for total shareholders' equity suggests that Staples uses long-term financing to finance both current and noncurrent assets. Such a financing strategy permits Staples to grow both its current and noncurrent assets without needing to repay borrowing in the near term, possibly constraining its ability to grow.

    b. The common size percentage for cash increased significantly between Year 6 and Year 7. The decreased common size percentage for accounts receivable may suggest more stringent credit policies that permitted Staples to collect more quickly from customers. The increased common size percentage for accounts payable may suggest that Staples delayed paying its suppliers, thereby conserving cash.

    c. The percentages in the common size balance sheet are not independent of each other. A decrease in the dollar amount of property, plant and equipment may result in an increasing, decreasing, or stable proportion for this balance sheet item, depending on the changes in other assets.

2.38 (Kroger Company; interpreting balance sheet changes.)

    a. Inventories and property, plant and equipment dominate the asset side of the balance sheet. The mix of short-term financing matches the mix of short-term assets. Kroger Company finances its property, plant and equipment with a mixture of long-term debt and retained earnings. The large proportion for treasury stock suggests a buyback of stock perhaps to defend against an unfriendly takeover.

    b. Kroger Company increased the proportion of long-term debt in its capital structure and generated a negative balance in retained earnings. The most likely explanation for the negative retained earnings is the payment of a dividend to shareholders using the proceeds from the long-term borrowing. These transactions increased the proportion of debt in the capital structure and made Kroger Company a less attractive target for an unfriendly takeover.

2.39   (Relating market value to book value of shareholders' equity.)

(1) **Coke**—One important asset missing from the balance sheet of Coke is the value of its brand names. Coke follows generally accepted accounting principles (GAAP) in expensing the cost of developing and maintaining its brand names each year (for example, product development, quality control, advertising). The future benefits of these expenditures are too difficult to identify and measure with sufficient precision to justify recognizing an asset. Coke also reports its property, plant and equipment at acquisition cost (adjusted downward for depreciation) instead of current market values. Acquisition cost valuations are more objective and easier to audit than current market valuations.

(2) **Bristol**—Bristol engages in research and development to discover new drugs. GAAP requires firms to expense research and development expenditures immediately. The future benefits of these expenditures are too uncertain to justify recognizing an asset. Thus, the value of patents and technologies developed by Bristol, as well as the value of the research scientists employed by Bristol, do not appear on its balance sheet.

(3) **Bankers Trust**—The market-to-book ratio for Bankers is 1.0. Most of the assets and liabilities of Bankers are monetary items and turn over frequently. Thus, the market values and book values closely conform.

(4) **International Paper (IP)**—IP reports its forest lands on the balance sheet at acquisition cost. IP likely acquired the land many years ago. The acquisition cost of the land is considerably less than its current market value. Also, IP follows general industry practice and expenses the annual cost of maintaining its forest lands. Thus, the value of forest lands increases each year as trees grow. The market incorporates this value increase into its price of the common stock of IP even though GAAP does not reflect the value increase on the balance sheet. The value increase is too difficult to measure objectively to justify substituting market values for acquisition cost.

(5) **Disney**—Disney depreciates the cost of film inventory over its expected useful life. Fortunately for Disney and other film production companies, the value of old films has increased in recent years with the growth of cable networks. Thus, the market value of some of Disney's films exceeds their book values. The market-to-book ratio reflects this under valuation. Also, Disney reports its property, plant and equipment at acquisition cost (adjusted downward for depreciation) instead of current market values. The land underlying its theme parks has likely increased in value since the date of acquisition, but the accounting records do not reflect the value increase under GAAP.

2.39 continued.

Some instructors may also wish to use this problem to discuss the term structure of assets and the term structure of liabilities and shareholders' equity, even though the problem requirements do not ask students to discuss this factor.

(1) **Coke**—Coke's current assets are less than its current liabilities. This relation indicates short-term liquidity risk. The high market-to-book ratio suggests that the market value (selling price) of its inventory exceeds the book value, so current assets probably equal or exceed current liabilities at market value. Shareholders' equity represents a higher proportion of long-term financing than long-term debt. One explanation for the relatively low proportion of long-term debt is that Coke is very profitable (suggested by the high market-to-book ratio) and therefore generates most of its needed cash from operations. Further support for the internal generation of cash is the high proportion of retained earnings and significant treasury stock purchases. Another explanation for the relatively low proportion of long-term debt relates to the investments in its bottlers. Chapter 13 discusses the accounting for intercorporate investments. Because Coke owns less than 50 percent of the outstanding common stock of these bottlers, it does not consolidate them. Thus, the assets and the financing of the bottlers are "off balance sheet." These bottlers may carry significantly more long-term debt than Coke.

(2) **Bristol**—The interesting insight from studying Bristol's capital structure is the relatively small proportion of long-term debt. The products of Bristol are subject to technological obsolescence. Competitors could develop technologically superior drugs that would replace those of Bristol in the market. Given this product risk, Bristol probably does not want to add the financial risk that fixed interest and principal payments on debt create.

(3) **Bankers Trust**—Bankers relies heavily on short-term sources for financing, principally deposits and short-term borrowing. Customers can withdraw their funds on no, or very short, notice. Thus, Bankers must maintain a relatively liquid balance sheet. Most of its assets are in cash, short-term marketable securities, and loans. The loans are less liquid than cash and marketable securities but tend to have predictable cash flows. Note that shareholders' equity makes up approximately 5 percent of liabilities plus shareholders' equities. Such a low percentage is common for commercial banks. Banks carry high proportions of liabilities because of the high liquidity of their assets.

2.39 continued.

    (4) **International Paper (IP)**—IP carries a high proportion of noncurrent assets and matches this with a high proportion of long-term financing. IP uses approximately equal proportions of long-term liabilities and shareholders' equity to finance its noncurrent assets. The sales of paper products vary with movements through economic cycles. During recessionary periods, demand slackens and firms reduce prices in order to utilize capital-intensive manufacturing facilities. Paper companies do not want too much debt in their capital structures that could force them into bankruptcy during these times. On the other hand, when the economy is booming, the profits and cash flows of paper companies increase significantly. Firms spread the cost of their capital-intensive plants over larger volumes of output. In these cases, shareholders benefit from debt in the capital structure (a phenomenon known as *financial leverage*, discussed in Chapter 6). Thus, the approximately equal proportions of long-term debt and shareholders' equity reflect these opposing considerations.

    (5) **Disney**—Disney reports a significant excess of current assets over current liabilities. Interpreting this excess involves two opposing considerations. Some of Disney's films continue to generate revenues and cash flows, even though the films carry a zero book value on Disney's books. On the other hand, Disney accumulates the cost of films in process in the inventory account without knowing whether or not the films will be a commercial success. Disney uses a higher proportion of shareholders' equity than long-term debt in its long-term financing structure. Its property, plant and equipment can serve as collateral for long-term borrowing. Its predictable revenue and cash flows from theme parks also argues for a high proportion of long-term debt relative to shareholders' equity. Perhaps Disney did not want to use up its borrowing capacity in case it had the opportunity to make an acquisition (such as Capital Cities/ABC) and needed to borrow to finance the transaction.

2.40   (Relating market value to book value of shareholders' equity.)

    (1) **Merck**—Pharmaceutical firms make ongoing expenditures on research and development (R&D) to develop new products. Some of these expenditures result in profitable new products, while other expenditures do not provide any future benefit. The difficulty encountered in trying to identify whether or not a particular R&D expenditure results in a future benefit has led accounting standard setters to require the immediate expensing of R&D costs in the year incurred. Thus, the valuable patents for pharmaceutical products and the value of potential products in the research pipeline do not appear on the balance sheet of Merck. The market does place a value on these technologies in deciding on an appropriate market price for the firm's stock.

2.40 continued.

Students might suggest approaches that technology firms could follow to measure the value of their technology resources. One approach might be to study the past success record of discovering new technologies For example, if 20 percent of expenditures in the past resulted in valuable technologies, the firm might report 20 percent of the expenditures on R&D each period as an asset. If these new technologies provided benefits for, say, seven years on average, then the firm would amortize the amount recognized as an asset over seven years. An alternative approach would be to use the prices paid recently when acquiring firms purchase target firms that have similar technologies. Each of these approaches involves a degree of subjectivity that has led standard setters to require the immediate expensing of R&D expenditures in the year incurred.

(2) **Nestle**—The products of Nestle carry a high degree of brand recognition, which leads loyal customers to purchase Nestle products on a regular basis and new customers to try its products. The value of the Nestle and its other brand names is created through advertising, quality control, and new product introductions. Nestle follows GAAP in expensing these expenditures each year. Thus, the value of the brand name does not appear on the balance sheet as an asset. If the brand name did appear on the balance sheet, assets and shareholders' equity would be larger and the market-to-book ratio would be closer to 1.0.

One might ask how Nestle might value its brand names if it were permitted to recognize these valuable resources as assets. One approach might be to determine the profit margin (that is, net income divided by sales) that Nestle realizes on sales of its products relative to the profit margin of competitors. Nestle would then multiply the excess profit margin times the number of units expected to be sold in future years to measure its excess profitability. It would then discount the future excess earnings to a present value. An alternative approach is to identify the prices paid recently by firms acquiring other branded consumer products companies to ascertain the approximate price paid for identifiable assets and the portion paid for brand names. Each of these approaches involves a degree of subjectivity and opens the door for firms to cast their balance sheets in the most favorable light possible. Accounting standard setters in most countries recognize this potential source of bias and require firms to expense brand development costs in the year expenditures are made.

(3) **Promodes**—Promodes is the largest grocery store chain in France and likely has some brand name recognition that does not appear on its balance sheet. In addition, the stores of Promodes are valued at acquisition cost adjusted downward for depreciation to date. The land and perhaps the store buildings probably have market values

2.40 continued.

that exceed their book values. Standard setters in most countries require firms to account for land and buildings using acquisition costs instead of current market values because of the subjectivity in the latter valuations. This real estate is probably easier to value than brand names and technological know how because of active real estate markets. Thus, the market-to-book ratio probably reflects brand recognition and undervalued fixed assets.

(4) **Deutsche Bank**—Most of the assets of a commercial bank are reported on the balance sheet at current market values. Marketable securities are revalued to market value at each balance sheet date. Loans receivable are stated net of estimated uncollectibles and should therefore reflect cash-equivalent values. Deposits and short-term borrowing on the liability side of the balance sheet appear at current cash-equivalent values. Thus, the market-to-book ratio should be approximately 1.0. The ratio of 1.7 for Deutsche Bank suggests the presence of intangibles that do not appear on the balance sheet. Possibilities include the size and dominant influence of Deutsche Bank in the German economy, technologically sophisticated information systems, and superior work force. The financial consulting capabilities of its investment banking employees are a valuable resource that does not appear on the balance sheet as an asset.

(5) **British Airways**—The aircraft and ground facilities of British Airways appear at acquisition cost net of depreciation to date. The market values of these fixed assets likely exceed their book values. In addition, British Airways has landing and gateway rights that appear on the balance sheet only to the extent that the firm has paid amounts up front. In most cases, British Airways pays fees periodically as it uses these facilities. Thus, no asset appears on the balance sheet.

(6) **New Oji Paper Co.**—The balance sheet of New Oji Paper Co. includes a high proportion of intercorporate investments in securities and property, plant, and equipment. GAAP in Japan reports these assets at acquisition cost, with plant and equipment adjusted downward for depreciation to date. The market value of land probably exceeds its book value. The market values of securities in Japan have decreased significantly in recent years but may still exceed their book values if the investments were made many years ago. Note that the market-to-book ratio does not exceed 1.0 by as much as the consumer products and pharmaceutical companies with brand recognition.

This exercise also provides an opportunity to discuss various relationships between items in the financial statements.

2.40 continued.

(1) **Merck**—Other noncurrent assets include a substantial amount of goodwill arising from the acquisition of Medco Containment Services. The goodwill represents the excess of the cost of acquiring Medco over the market value of its identifiable assets. One might raise the question as to whether this amount represents an asset with economic value to Merck. This question addresses the issue as to why Merck would pay more for Medco than the market value of its identifiable assets. Medco is a service firm that utilizes information systems. Neither the value of the employees nor the software used in providing these services likely appears on Medco's balance sheet. Thus, some excess purchase price is expected. However, the possibility also exists that Merck overpaid for Medco and the goodwill includes the effect of this overpayment.

Another question related to Merck is why it would use such a small percentage of long-term debt financing. Pharmaceutical firms face product obsolescence and legal liability risks. They tend not to add financial risk from having a high proportion of long-term debt on the balance sheet. Although this exercise does not provide the needed information, Merck is very profitable and generates sufficient cash flow from operations that it does not need much external financing.

A third question related to Merck is the large percentage for other noncurrent liabilities on the balance sheet. This amount includes its healthcare benefit obligation to employees and deferred income taxes. Students generally have not studied these two items sufficiently to generate much discussion.

A fourth question related to Merck is its high proportion of treasury stock. Economic theory would suggest that if the market fairly values a firm prior to a stock buyback, then the market price of the stock should not change. The economic value of the firm should decrease by the amount of cash paid out. The number of shares of common stock outstanding should decline proportionally and the stock price should remain the same. However, the effect of stock buybacks generally is to increase the market price of the stock. One possible explanation for the market price increase is that the market views the buyback as a positive signal by management about the firm's future prospects. Management knows about the firm's future plans and might feel that the market is underpricing the firm, given these future plans. The buyback signals this positive information and the market price increases.

(2) **Nestle**—Nestle, like Merck, has highly predictable cash flows from its brand name products and generates sufficient cash flows in the long term to reduce the need for long-term debt financing. Nestle, however, extends credit to customers and must carry inventory for some period of time before sale. It uses suppliers and short-term borrowing to finance this working capital.

2.40 continued.

    (3) **Promodes**—The majority of the assets of Promodes is short-term receivables and inventories. The majority of its financing is likewise short-term. Thus, firms attempt to match the term structure of their financing to the term structure of their assets.

    (4) **Deutsche Bank**—Deutsche Bank obtains the vast majority of its funds from depositors and short-term borrowing. Such a high proportion of short-term financing might appear risky. However, a large portion of its assets is in highly liquid cash and short-term investments. A large portion is also in loans to businesses and consumers. Although loans are generally not as liquid as cash and investments, they do have predictable cash flows. The large number of borrowers also diversifies the risk of Deutsche Bank on these loans. The low level of risk on the asset side of the balance sheet and the stability of the deposit base means that banks need only a small proportion of shareholders' equity.

    (5) **British Airways**—The majority of the assets of British Airways is in flight and ground support equipment. British Airways matches these long-term assets with long-term financing, either in the form of long-term debt or shareholders' equity. The heavier use of debt financing stems from its lower cost and the availability of the equipment to serve as collateral for the borrowing. Lenders generally prefer that firms have more current assets than current liabilities. The excess current liabilities of British Airways stem from advance sales of airline tickets (appears in Other Current Liabilities). British Airways will satisfy this liability by providing transportation services rather than paying cash. Thus, the net current liability position is not of particular concern.

    (6) **New Oji Paper Co.**—The balance sheet of Oji portrays some relationships that are typical of Japanese companies. First, note the high proportion of investments in securities. Many Japanese companies are part of corporate groups (called "Kieretsus"). The investments in firms in the corporate groups tend to represent 20 percent to 30 percent of these other companies and appear as intercorporate investments on the balance sheet. Secondly, note the relatively high proportion of short-term bank borrowing. Most corporate groups have a commercial bank as a member. This commercial bank is not likely to force a member of the group into bankruptcy if it is unable to repay a loan at maturity. The bank will more likely simply extend the term of the loan. Short-term borrowing is usually less costly than long-term borrowing and helps explain the high proportion of short-term borrowing on the balance sheet.

CHAPTER 3

INCOME STATEMENT: REPORTING THE RESULTS OF OPERATING ACTIVITIES

Questions, Exercises, Problems, and Cases: Answers and Solutions

3.1   See the text or the glossary at the end of the book.

3.2   One factor considered in the accounting period decision is whether a firm has a natural business year upon which to base its accounting period. If a firm's activities are reasonably uniform throughout the year, it does not have a natural business year and, therefore, must choose an "artificial" one. In selecting such a period, a firm probably considers what other firms in its industry do. A large proportion of publicly held firms use the calendar year as their accounting period.

3.3   A natural business year is one beginning with a slack season, followed by a busy period, and ending with a slack season one year later. The ski resort and basketball team both have natural business years. The business of the grocery store is reasonably uniform throughout the year and, therefore, it does not have a natural business year.

3.4   Revenues measure the inflows of net assets from selling goods and providing services. Under the accrual basis of accounting, accountants recognize revenue in the period of sale rather than in the period when the firm receives cash. Under the cash basis of accounting, accountants recognize revenue at the time the firm receives cash.

    Under the accrual basis of accounting, revenue equals cash receipts in the case of cash sales (in contrast to sales on account). Under the cash basis of accounting, they are the same except for receipts from additional financing, such as borrowings from a bank or issuances of bonds or common stock on the market.

3.5   Expenses measure the outflows of net assets used up, or consumed, in the process of generating revenues. Under the accrual basis of accounting, accountants recognize expenses either in the period in which the firm recognizes associated revenues or in the period in which the firm consumes services. The timing of cash disbursements may precede (as in the case of purchasing a machine), coincide with (as in the case of weekly salespersons' salaries), or follow (as in the case of unpaid taxes at year-end) the expense recognition. Under the cash basis of accounting, accountants recognize expenses at the time of the cash expenditure.

3.5 continued.

Under the accrual basis of accounting, expenses equal cash expenditures in the case where goods or services are paid for at the time the firm consumes them. Under the cash basis of accounting, they will be the same except in cases where a firm repays bank loans or redeems long-term bonds or common stock.

3.6 The amount of revenue recognized equals the amount of cash the firm expects to collect from customers. The firm does not necessarily recognize the revenue, however, at the time it receives the cash. It typically recognizes revenue at the time of sale even though it has not yet collected cash from customers. Likewise, the amount of expense recognized equals the cash disbursement made for equipment, materials, labor, and so forth. However, the firm recognizes the expense when it consumes the services of these factor inputs, not when it makes the cash expenditure.

3.7 Accountants treat assets as expired costs, or expenses, when the firm consumes the services of the assets in generating revenues. The initial financing of the asset (for example, outright cash purchase, acquisition on account, acquisition by the issuance of common stock) is irrelevant to when the asset becomes an expense under the accrual basis of accounting. Likewise, the timing of the receipt of cash from customers is not relevant to when accountants recognize revenue under the accrual basis. Accounting recognizes revenue when a firm has performed all, or a substantial portion, of the services to be provided and has received cash, a receivable, or some other asset susceptible to reasonably precise measurement.

3.8 Revenues measure the inflow of net assets from operating activities and expenses measure the outflow of net assets consumed in the process of generating revenues. Thus, recognizing revenues and expenses always involves a simultaneous entry in an asset and/or liability account. Likewise, adjusting entries almost always involve an entry in at least one income statement and one balance sheet account.

3.9 The accountant could record the revenue and expense aspects of transactions during the period and adjustments at the end of the period directly in the Retained Earnings or another shareholders' equity account.

3.10 Revenues and expenses measure the inflows and outflows of net assets from selling goods and providing services for a particular period of time. If the accountant did not close revenue and expense accounts at the end of each period, the revenue and expense amounts of one period would mingle with similar amounts of subsequent periods.

3.11   Before the books are closed, both balance sheet (permanent) and income statement (temporary) accounts have nonzero balances. After the closing of income statement accounts, only the balance sheet accounts have nonzero balances.

3.12   Some events occur that affect the net income and financial position of a firm but for which an external transaction does not occur by the end of a period that signals the need for an entry in the accounting records. For example, a firm uses depreciable assets during the year. Because no external exchange occurs, the use of such depreciable assets is not recorded until the accountant makes adjusting entries. Likewise, workers earn salaries during the last several days of the year but are not paid until early next year. Here, again, no external exchange occurs before year end to trigger recognition of the cost of the labor services in the accounts. The adjusting entry accomplishes this.

3.13   Contra accounts provide disaggregated information concerning the net amount of an asset, liability, or shareholders' equity item. For example, the account, Accounts Receivable Net of Estimated Uncollectible Accounts, does not indicate separately the gross amount of receivables from customers and the estimated amount of the gross receivables that the firm expects to collect. If the firm used a contra account, it would have such information. The alternative to using contra accounts is to debit or credit directly the principal account involved (for example, Accounts Receivable from Customers). This alternative procedure, however, does not permit computation of disaggregated information about the net balance in the account. Note that the use of contra accounts does not affect the total of assets, liabilities, shareholders' equity, revenues, or expenses.

3.14   (JCPenney; revenue recognition.)

a. None.	d. None.
b. $16,940,000.	e. $8,000.
c. $2,925,000.	f. $8,000.

3.15   (Revenue recognition.)

	April	May	June
a.	$6,500	--	--
b.	--	$28,600	--
c.	--	--	$2,200
d.	$ 150	$ 150	$ 150

3.15 continued.

e.	--	$ 150	$ 150
f.	--	--	$ 150

3.16   (Revenue recognition.)

    a. No (Magnavox has not yet delivered the goods).

    b. Yes.

    c. No (this is a financing, not an operating, transaction).

    d. No (NIKE has not identified a customer, set a price, or shipped the goods).

    e. No (the concert will not take place for two weeks).

    f. Yes (the agent has provided the services); the revenue amount is only the commission, however.

    g. Yes (on an accrual basis, accounting recognizes interest as time passes).

    h. No (accounting usually recognizes revenue when a firm sells goods or services).

    i. Yes.

3.17   (Computervision; expense recognition.)

    a. 0 asset; 0 expense.

    b. 0 asset; 0 expense.

    c. 0 asset; 0 expense.

    d. $406,000 asset; 0 expense.

    e. 0 asset; 0 expense.

    f. Reduce assets by $14,000; 0 expense.

    g. $384,160 [= .98($406,000 − $14,000)] cash reduction + $7,840 [= .02($406,000 − $14,000)] inventory reduction.

    h. $115,840 (= $500,000 − $384,160) asset increase; $384,160 (= $406,000 − $14,000 − $7,840) expense.

3.18   (Hewlett-Packard; expense recognition.)

    a. $1,500.   d. $5,500 (= $2,000 + $7,000 – $3,500).

    b. $4,600.   e. $4,000 (= $48,000/12).

    c. $6,500 (= $3,000 + $7,000 –   f. Zero (an expense of April).
         $3,500).

3.19   (Expense recognition.)

	April	May	June
a.	$3,300	--	--
b.	--	$4,500	--
c.	--	--	$1,600
d.	--	$ 200	$ 200
e.	--	--	--
f.	$ 300	$ 300	$ 300

3.20   (Demski Company; income recognition.)

    a.

Cash Equivalent Value of Consideration at Time of Sale		Received $147,000
Less Expenses:		
Cost of Trucks	$125,000	
Preparation Costs	8,000	
Delivery Costs	6,000	
Total Expenses		139,000
Profit on Sale		$ 8,000

    b. Same as *a.* above.

    c. Same as *a.* above.

3.21   (Identifying missing half of journal entries.)

    a. Merchandise Inventory or Finished Goods Inventory decreases because the firm has sold goods.

    b. Sales Revenue increases because of sales.

    c. Cash increases because of collections from customers.

    d. Cash decreases because of payments to creditors.

3.21 continued.

e. Either an inventory account or an expense account increases because of receipts of goods or services.

f. Depreciation Expense increases because an adjusting entry recognizes the expense.

g. Dividends Payable increases because of the dividend; or closing entry for an expense or income summary account showing a loss.

h. Either Insurance Expense increases (period expense) or Work-in-Process Inventory increases (product cost) as a result of an adjusting entry.

i. Cash decreases because a firm pays property taxes.

j. Either Accounts Payable increases or Cash decreases because of acquisition of Inventory.

k. Revenue increases because a firm provides goods or services to customers.

l. Assets increase for the amount of the cash or goods received from supplier.

3.22 (Midland Grocery Stores; asset versus expense recognition.)

a. Supplies Inventory (A)..................................... 430
    Accounts Payable (L)..................................... 430

b. Accounting Expense (SE)............................... 1,500
    Accounts Payable (L)..................................... 1,500

c. Equipment (A).. 14,720
    Accounts Payable (L)..................................... 14,720

d. Supplies Inventory (A)..................................... 450
    Accounts Payable (L)..................................... 450

e. Equipment (A).. 790
    Accounts Payable (L)..................................... 790

f. Organization Expense (SE)............................. 2,000
    Accounts Payable (L)..................................... 2,000

g. No entry.

h. Repair Expense (SE)...................................... 73
    Accounts Payable (L)..................................... 73

i. Utilities Expense (SE) 190
    Accounts Payable (L)..................................... 190

3.23 (Restaurant Supply Company/Wendy's; journal entries for notes receivable and notes payable.)

a. **Year 6**
Dec. 1

Notes Receivable	60,000	
Accounts Receivable		60,000

Dec. 31

Interest Receivable	400	
Interest Revenue		400

$60,000 × .08 × 30/360.

Dec. 31

Interest Revenue	400	
Retained Earnings (or Income Summary)		400

Entry assumes this note is the only one giving rise to interest revenue during the period.

Year 7
March 1

Cash	61,200	
Interest Receivable		400
Interest Revenue		800
Notes Receivable		60,000

b. **Year 6**
Dec. 1

Accounts Payable	60,000	
Notes Payable		60,000

Dec. 31

Interest Expense	400	
Interest Payable		400

Dec. 31

Retained Earnings (or Income Summary)	400	
Interest Expense		400

Entry assumes this note is the only one giving rise to interest expense during the period.

Year 7
March 1

Interest Payable	400	
Interest Expense	800	
Notes Payable	60,000	
Cash		61,200

3.24   (Kelly Services; journal entries for office supply inventories.)

a. **1/1–3/31**

Office Supplies Inventory	137,900	
Accounts Payable		137,900

March 31

Office Supplies Expense	149,200	
Office Supplies Inventory		149,200

$149,200 = $48,700 + $137,900 − $37,400.

b. **1/1–3/31**

Office Supplies Expense	137,900	
Accounts Payable		137,900

March 31

Office Supplies Expense	11,300	
Office Supplies Inventory		11,300

$11,300 = $48,700 − $37,400.

3.25   (Arizona Realty Company; journal entries for rental receipts and payments.)

(Arizona Realty Company)

May 1

Cash	900	
Advances from Tenant		900

May 30

Advances from Tenant	900	
Rent Revenue		900

May 30

Rent Revenue	900	
Income Summary		900

June 1

Cash	1,800	
Advances from Tenant		1,800

June 30

Advances from Tenant	900	
Rent Revenue		900

June 30

Rent Revenue	900	
Income Summary		900

3.25 continued.

July 31

Advances from Tenant..	900	
Rent Revenue...		900

July 31

Rent Revenue...	900	
Income Summary..		900

Aug. 1

Cash..	2,700	
Advances from Tenant..................................		2,700

Aug. 31

Advances from Tenant..	900	
Rent Revenue...		900

Aug. 31

Rent Revenue...	900	
Income Summary..		900

Note: An alternative set of journal entries credits Rent Revenue instead of Advances from Tenant when the firm receives amounts on the first of any month covering rental fees for that month.

(Hagen Consultants)
May 1

Prepaid Rent	900	
Cash...		900

May 30

Rent Expense..	900	
Prepaid Rent...		900

May 30

Income Summary...	900	
Rent Expense..		900

June 1

Prepaid Rent	1,800	
Cash...		1,800

June 30

Rent Expense	900	
Prepaid Rent...		900

June 30

Income Summary...	900	
Rent Expense..		900

3.25 continued.

July 31

Rent Expense	900	
Prepaid Rent...		900

July 31

Income Summary...	900	
Rent Expense..		900

Aug. 1

Prepaid Rent	2,700	
Cash..		2,700

Aug. 31

Rent Expense	900	
Prepaid Rent...		900

Aug. 31

Income Summary...	900	
Rent Expense..		900

Note: An alternative set of journal entries debits Rent Expense instead of Prepaid Rent when the firm pays amounts on the first of any month covering rental fees for that month.

3.26 (Using accumulated depreciation to estimate asset age.)

a. $\dfrac{\$9,000}{\$15,000} \times 10 \text{ years} = 6 \text{ years old.}$

b. $\dfrac{\$8,000}{\$4,000 \text{ per year}} = $ 2 years of accumulated depreciation, suggesting that the asset is two years old.

3.27 (Effect of recording errors on financial statements.)

a. **Actual Entry:**

Prepaid Rent (A)...	1,800	
Cash (A)..		1,800

Correct Entries:

Prepaid Rent (A)...	1,800	
Cash (A)..		1,800

Rent Expense (SE)..	300	
Prepaid Rent (A)...		300

Assets overstated by $300 and shareholders' equity overstated by $300.

3.27 continued.

b. **Actual Entry:**

Administrative Expense (SE).........................	9,000	
Cash (A)...		9,000

Correct Entries:

Equipment (A)...	9,000	
Cash (A)...		9,000

Depreciation Expense (SE)...........................	1,500	
Accumulated Depreciation (XA)..................		1,500

Assets understated by $7,500 and shareholders' equity understated by $7,500.

c. **Actual Entry:**

Cash (A)	1,500	
Rental Fees Received in Advance (L).............		1,500

Correct Entries:

Cash (A)	1,500	
Rental Fees Received in Advance (L).............		1,500

Rental Fees Received in Advance (L)	1,500	
Rent Revenue (SE).....................................		1,500

Liabilities overstated by $1,500 and shareholders' equity understated by $1,500.

d. **Actual Entry:**
None

Correct Entry:

Interest Receivable (A).................................	300	
Interest Revenue (SE).................................		300

Assets understated by $300 and shareholders' equity understated by $300.

e. **Actual Entry:**
None

Correct Entry:

Notes Receivable (A).....................................	250	
Accounts Receivable (A)		250

No effect on assets, liabilities, or shareholders' equity. We also accept assets overstated by $250 and assets understated by $250.

3.27 continued.

    f. **Actual Entry:**

Travel Expenses (SE)	740	
Cash (A)		740

      Correct Entry:

Travel Expenses (SE)	470	
Cash (A)		470

Assets understated by $270 (= $740 − $470) and shareholders' equity understated by $270.

3.28   (Forgetful Corporation; effect of recording errors on financial statements.)

    a. **Actual Entry:**

Cash	1,400	
Sales Revenue		1,400

      Correct Entry:

Cash	1,400	
Advance from Customer		1,400

Liabilities understated by $1,400 and shareholders' equity overstated by $1,400.

    b. **Actual Entry:**

Cost of Goods Sold	5,000	
Cash		5,000

      Correct Entries:

Machine	5,000	
Cash		5,000
Depreciation Expense	500	
Accumulated Depreciation		500

Assets understated by $4,500 and shareholders' equity understated by $4,500.

3.28 continued.

c. **Actual Entry:**
None for accrued interest.

Correct Entry:

Interest Receivable ($2,000 X .12 X 60/360)............	40	
Interest Revenue		40

Assets understated by $40 and shareholders' equity understated by $40.

d. The entry is correct as recorded.

e. **Actual Entry:**
None for declared dividend.

Correct Entry:

Retained Earnings..	1,500	
Dividend Payable		1,500

Liabilities understated by $1,500 and shareholders' equity overstated by $1,500.

f. **Actual Entries:**

Machinery	50,000	
Accounts Payable.....................................		50,000
Accounts Payable..	50,000	
Cash		49,000
Machinery..		1,000
Maintenance Expense	4,000	
Cash		4,000

Correct Entries:

Machinery..	50,000	
Accounts Payable.....................................		50,000
Accounts Payable..	50,000	
Cash		49,000
Machinery..		1,000
Machinery	4,000	
Cash		4,000

Assets understated by $3,000 and shareholders' equity understated by $3,000.

3.29   (K9 Supplies Company; reconstructing accounting records.)

a.

K9 SUPPLIES COMPANY
Balance Sheet
October 31

Assets

Cash...	$ 3,995	
Accounts Receivable..............................	1,510	
Note Receivable......................................	1,500	
Interest Receivable.................................	75	
Merchandise Inventories........................	9,740	
Prepaid Insurance..................................	1,100	
Prepaid License Fee	500	
Total Assets..		$18,420

Liabilities and Shareholders' Equity

Liabilities:		
Accounts Payable...............................	$ 3,620	
Rent Payable.......................................	300	
Total Liabilities		$ 3,920
Shareholders' Equity:		
Common Stock....................................	$12,000	
Retained Earnings.............................	2,500	
Total Shareholders' Equity..............		14,500
Total Liabilities and Shareholders' Equity		$18,420

b.   The cash shortage is $705 (= $3,995 − $3,290).

3.30   (Argenti Corporation; cash versus accrual basis of accounting.)

a. and b.

	a. **Accrual** **Basis**	**b.** **Cash** **Basis**
Sales Revenue..	$ 47,500	$ 40,800[a]
Less Expenses:		
Cost of Merchandise Sold.........................	$ 32,100[b]	--
Payments on Merchandise Purchased	--	$ 34,900
Depreciation Expense..............................	500[c]	--
Payments on Equipment Purchased...........	--	30,000
Utilities Expense....................................	1,610[d]	850
Salaries Expense	4,840[e]	2,250
Rent Expense	2,500	5,000
Insurance Expense..................................	200	2,400
Interest Expense.....................................	100[f]	--
Total Expenses.................................	$(41,850)	$ (75,400)
Net Income (Loss)	$ 5,650	$ (34,600)

[a]$40,800 = $40,000 + $800.
[b]$32,100 = $34,900 + $4,400 − $7,200.
[c]$500 = ($30,000/5)/12.
[d]$1,610 = $850 + $760.
[e]$4,840 = $2,250 + $2,590.
[f]$100 = (.06 × $20,000) × 30/360.

c.   The accrual basis of accounting provides superior measures of operating performance because it matches revenues generated from selling activities during January with the costs incurred in generating that revenue. Note that the capital contribution and bank loan do not give rise to revenue under either basis of accounting because they represent financing, not operating, activities.

3.31   (Management Consultants, Inc.; cash versus accrual basis of accounting.)

a. and b.

	a. Accrual Basis	b. Cash Basis
Consulting Revenue	$ 45,000	$ 39,000
Less Expenses:		
Rental Expense	$ 8,000	$ 8,000
Depreciation Expense	1,250[a]	--
Payments on Equipment Purchased	--	12,000
Utilities Expense	400[b]	350
Salaries Expense	30,000[c]	28,200
Supplies Expense	690[a]	650
Interest Expense	225[e]	--
Total Expenses	$ 40,565	$ 49,200
Net Income (Loss)	$ 4,435	$ (10,200)

[a]$1,250 = ($12,000/4) \times 5/12$.
[b]$400 = $350 + 50.
[c]$30,000 = $28,200 + $1,800$.
[d]$690 = $650 + 40.
[e]$225 = ($6,000 \times .09) \times 5/12$.

c.   See the answer for Problem 3.30, Part *c.* above.

3.32   (J. Hennessey; cash versus accrual basis of accounting.)

a. and b.

	a. Accrual Basis	b. Cash Basis
Sales Revenue	$100,000	$ 86,000
Less Expenses:		
Cost of Merchandise Sold	$ 72,000[a]	--
Payments on Merchandise Purchased	--	$ 76,000
Salaries Expense	21,400[b]	20,000
Utilities Expense	1,620[c]	1,500
Interest Expense	1,200[d]	--
Total Expenses	$ 96,220	$ 97,500
Net Income (Loss)	$ 3,780	$ (11,500)

[a]$72,000 = $84,000 - $12,000$.
[b]$21,400 = $20,000 + $1,400$.
[c]$1,620 = $1,500 + 120.
[d]$1,200 = $10,000 \times .12$.

c.   See the answer for Problem 3.30, Part *c.*

3.32 continued.

d.

HENNESSEY RETAIL STORE, INC.
Balance Sheet
December 31, Year 8

Assets

Cash ($20,000 + $10,000 − $76,000 +$30,000 + $56,000 − $20,000 − $1,500)	$18,500
Accounts Receivable ($70,000 − $56,000)	14,000
Merchandise Inventories ($84,000 − $72,000)	12,000
Total Assets	$44,500

Liabilities and Shareholders' Equity

Accounts Payable—Merchandise Supplies ($84,000 − $76,000)	$ 8,000
Note Payable	10,000
Interest Payable	1,200
Salaries Payable	1,400
Utilities Payable	120
Total Liabilities	$20,720
Common Stock	$20,000
Retained Earnings (see Part *a*.)	3,780
Total Shareholders' Equity	$23,780
Total Liabilities and Shareholders' Equity	$44,500

3.33 (Regaldo Department Stores; work sheet preparation of income statement and balance sheet.)

a. and b.

Cash
Ps 247,200	
+ Ps 62,900 (3)	
− Ps 32,400 (4)	
− Ps 2,700 (5)	
+ Ps 84,600 (6)	
− Ps 234,800 (7)	
Ps 124,800	

Accounts Receivable
+ Ps 194,600 (3)	
− 84,600 (6)	
Ps 110,000	

Inventories
Ps 188,800	
+ Ps 217,900 (2)	
− Ps 162,400 (3)	
− Ps 4,200 (7)	
Ps 240,100	

Prepaid Rent
Ps 60,000	
− Ps 30,000 (11)	
Ps 30,000	

Prepaid Insurance
Ps 12,000	
− Ps 1,000 (12)	
Ps 11,000	

Equipment
Ps 90,000 (1)	
− 1,500 (10)	
Ps 88,500	

Patent
Ps 24,000	
− Ps 400	
Ps 23,600	

Accounts Payable
Ps 32,000	
+ Ps 217,900 (2)	
− Ps 239,000 (7)	
Ps 10,900	

Salaries Payable
+ Ps 6,700 (8)	
Ps 6,700	

Utilities Payable
+ Ps 800 (9)	
Ps 800	

Interest Payable
− Ps 900 (14)	
Ps 900	

Income Tax Payable
+ Ps 5,610 (15)	
Ps 5,610	

Loan Payable
+ Ps 90,000 (1)	
Ps 90,000	

Common Stock
Ps 50,000	
Ps 50,000	

Revenues
+ Ps 257,500 (3) Sales Revenue	
Ps 257,500	

Expenses
− Ps 162,400	(3)	Cost of Goods Sold
− Ps 32,400	(4)	Compensation Expense
− Ps 2,700	(5)	Utilities Expense
− Ps 6,700	(8)	Compensation Expense
− Ps 800	(9)	Utilities Expense
− Ps 1,500	(10)	Depreciation Expense
− Ps 30,000	(11)	Rent Expense
− Ps 1,000	(12)	Insurance Expense
− Ps 400	(13)	Amortization Expense
− Ps 900	(14)	Interest Expense
− Ps 5,610	(15)	Income Tax Expense
Ps 244,410		

3.33 continued.

c.

REGALDO DEPARTMENT STORES
Income Statement
For the Month of February Year 8

Sales Revenue	Ps 257,500
Expenses:	
Cost of Goods Sold	Ps 162,400
Compensation (Ps32,400 + Ps6,700)	39,100
Utilities	3,500
Depreciation	1,500
Rent	30,000
Insurance	1,000
Patent Amortization	400
Interest	900
Total Expenses	Ps 238,800
Net Income before Income Taxes	Ps 18,700
Income Tax Expense at 30 Percent	(5,610)
Net Income	Ps 13,090

d.

REGALDO DEPARTMENT STORES
Balance Sheet
February 28, Year 8

Assets

Cash	Ps 124,800
Accounts Receivable	110,000
Inventories	240,100
Prepaid Rent	30,000
Prepaid Insurance	11,000
Total Current Assets	Ps 515,900
Equipment	88,500
Patent	23,600
Total Assets	Ps 628,000

Liabilities and Shareholders' Equity

Accounts Payable	Ps 10,900
Salaries Payable	6,700
Utilities Payable	800
Interest Payable	900
Income Tax Payable	5,610
Loan Payable	90,000
Total Liabilities	Ps 114,910
Common Stock	Ps 500,000
Retained Earnings	13,090
Total Shareholders' Equity	Ps 513,090
Total Liabilities and Shareholders' Equity	Ps 628,000

3.34   (Miscellaneous transactions and adjusting entries.)

a. **Jan. 31**
    Interest Receivable.. 45
        Interest Revenue   45
    [$18,000 × .06 × (15/360)] = $45.

    Feb. 28
    Interest Receivable.. 90
        Interest Revenue   90
    [$18,000 × .06 × (30/360)] = $90.

    March 15
    Cash.. 18,180
        Interest Receivable....................................   135
        Interest Revenue   45
        Notes Receivable.......................................   18,000

b. **Dec. 31**
    Cost of Goods Sold 570,000
        Merchandise Inventory..............................   570,000
    $620,000 – $50,000 = $570,000.

c. **Jan. 31**
    Rent Receivable.. 1,200
        Rent Revenue   1,200

    Feb. 1
    Cash.. 3,600
        Advances from Tenants............................   2,400
        Rent Receivable   1,200

    Feb. 28
    Advances from Tenants............................... 1,200
        Rent Revenue   1,200

    March 31
    Advances from Tenants............................... 1,200
        Rent Revenue   1,200

d. **July 1**
    Prepaid Rent 12,000
        Cash   12,000

    July 31
    Rent Expense... 2,000
        Prepaid Rent...   2,000
    If the payment on July 1 resulted in a debit to
    the expense account, the adjustment requires a
    credit to the expense account and a debit to the
    prepayment account for $10,000.

3.34 d. continued.

    Aug. 31
    Rent Expense... 2,000
       Prepaid Rent...   2,000

e. **Dec. 1**
    Prepaid Insurance...................................... 11,700
       Cash   11,700

    Dec. 31
    Insurance Expense 925
       Prepaid Insurance...................................   925
    $600 for October and November plus $11,700/36 =
    $325 for December.

f. **Dec. 31**
    Office Supplies on Hand.............................. 20
       Office Supplies Expense............................   20
    To reduce expense for office supplies purchased
    but not used: $420 – $400 = $20.

g. **Dec. 31**
    Depreciation Expense................................. 3,000
       Accumulated Depreciation on Building.........   3,000
    Two months depreciation expense = 1/480 × 2 ×
    ($820,000 – $100,000).

3.35 (Miscellaneous transactions and adjusting entries.)

a. (1) Accounts Payable (L)............................. 6,000
        Notes Payable (L).................................   6,000

    (2) Interest Expense (SE)............................ 50
        Interest Payable (L).............................   50
       [$6,000 × .10 × (30/360)] = $50.

b. (1) Cash (A).. 18,000
        Advances from Customers (L)..............   18,000

    (2) Advances from Customers (L)................. 3,000
        Insurance Revenue (SE)......................   3,000
       ($18,000 × 4/24) = $3,000.

c. (1) Equipment (A)..................................... 40,000
        Cash (A)..   40,000

3.35 c. continued.

    (2) Depreciation Expense (SE)....................... 2,250
          Accumulated Depreciation (XA)............   2,250
         [.25($40,000 − $4,000)/4].

d. (1) Automobile (A)..................................... 24,000
          Cash (A)   24,000

    (2) Depreciation Expense (SE)....................... 3,500
          Accumulated Depreciation (XA)............   3,500
         .5 × [($24,000 − $3,000)/3] = $3,500.

e. (1) Prepaid Rent (A) 12,000
          Cash (A)   12,000

    (2) Rent Expense (SE) 4,000
          Prepaid Rent (A)   4,000

f. (1) Office Supplies Inventory (A).................... 7,000
          Accounts Payable (L)............................   7,000

    (2) Accounts Payable (L) 5,000
          Cash (A)   5,000

    (3) Office Supplies Expense (SE)..................... 5,500
          Office Supplies Inventory (A).................   5,500
         ($7,000 − $1,500) = $5,500.

3.36   (Miscellaneous transactions and adjusting entries.)

a. (1) Cash.. 48,000
          Rental Fees Received in Advance...........   48,000

    (2) Rental Fees Received in Advance 12,000
          Rent Revenue   12,000

b. (1) Notes Receivable................................... 10,000
          Accounts Receivable............................   10,000

    (2) Interest Receivable................................. 50
          Interest Revenue.................................   50
         $10,000 × .06 × 30/360 = $50.

c. (1) Prepaid Insurance................................. 6,600
          Cash..   6,600

3.36 c. continued.

	(2)	Insurance Expense	3,250	
		Prepaid Insurance		3,250
		$500 + (\$6,600 \times 10/24) = \$3,250$.		

Alternate entries for Part c. are:

	(1)	Insurance Expense	500	
		Prepaid Insurance ($6,600 − $500)	6,100	
		Cash		6,600

	(2)	Insurance Expense	2,750	
		Prepaid Insurance		2,750
		$\$6,600 \times 10/24 = \$2,750$.		

| d. | (1) | Repair Expense | 14,900 | |
| | | Cash | | 14,900 |

| | (2) | Repair Expense | 200 | |
| | | Repair Parts Inventory | | 200 |

| e. | (1) | Equipment | 200,000 | |
| | | Cash | | 200,000 |

	(2)	Depreciation Expense	9,000	
		Accumulated Depreciation		9,000
		$(\$200,000 − \$20,000) \times .5/10$.		

| f. | (1) | Prepaid Property Expense | 12,000 | |
| | | Cash | | 12,000 |

    (2) No adjusting entry required because the full amount paid is an expense for Year 3.

3.37 (Sister's Collection Agency; preparation of T-account entries and adjusted trial balance.)

a.

Office Supplies		Common Stock		Office Equipment	
(1) 2,000			10,000 (1)	(2) 6,000	
			10,000 (2)		
Bal. 2,000			20,000 Bal.	Bal. 6,000	

3.37 a. continued.

Cash				Commissions Revenue				Office Salaries Expense			
(1)	8,000	1,500	(4)			600	(3)	(4)	1,500		
(2)	4,000	600	(6)								
(3)	1,200	1,000	(7)								
		2,500	(8)								
Bal.	7,600					600 Bal.		Bal.	1,500		

Accounting System Installation			Accounts Payable, Lyband and Linn				Accounts Payable, Z-Mart Stores			
(5)	800				800	(5)	(6)	600	600	(3)
Bal.	800				800 Bal.				0 Bal.	

Prepaid Rent			Automobile			Installment Contract Payable		
(7)	1,000		(8)	15,000			12,500	(8)
Bal.	1,000		Bal.	15,000			12,500 Bal.	

b.

SISTER'S COLLECTION AGENCY
Trial Balance
January 31, Year 3

Office Supplies	$ 2,000	
Common Stock		$20,000
Office Equipment	6,000	
Cash	7,600	
Commissions Revenue (R)		600
Office Salaries Expense (E)	1,500	
Accounting System Installation	800	
Accounts Payable, Lyband and Linn		800
Prepaid Rent	1,000	
Automobile	15,000	
Installment Contract Payable		12,500
Totals	$33,900	$33,900

3.38 (Kleen Cleaners, Inc.; preparation of T-account entries, adjusted trial balance, income statement, and balance sheet.)

a., b., and d.

Cash				Accounts Receivable				Supplies on Hand			
Bal. 3,400	4,600	(5)		Bal. 15,200	11,200	(2)		Bal. 4,800	5,610	(8)	
(1) 15,000	800	(6)		(1) 4,900				(4) 3,100			
(2) 11,200	10,930	(9)									
Bal. 13,270				Bal. 8,900				Bal. 2,290			

Prepaid Insurance				Equipment				Accumulated Depreciation			
Bal. 1,200	300	(11)		Bal. 65,000					9,680	Bal.	
									2,560	(9)	
Bal. 900				Bal. 65,000					12,240	Bal.	

Accounts Payable				Common Stock				Retained Earnings			
(5) 4,600	7,900	Bal.			20,000	Bal.			40,000	Bal.	
	700	(3)							10,220	(14)	
	3,100	(4)									
	800	(10)									
	7,900	Bal.			20,000	Bal.			50,220	Bal.	

Sales Revenue				Salaries and Wages Expense				Cost of Outside Work			
(12) 65,960	46,060	Bal.		Bal. 26,600	37,530	(13)		Bal. 2,040	2,740	(13)	
	15,000	(1)		(9) 10,930				(3) 700			
	4,900	(1)									
65,960	65,960			37,530	37,530			2,740	2,740		

Advertising Expense				Repairs Expense				Rent Expense			
Bal. 400	700	(13)		Bal. 500	580	(13)		Bal. 1,200	2,000	(13)	
(10) 300				(10) 80				(6) 800			
700	700			580	580			2,000	2,000		

Power, Gas, and Water Expense				Supplies Expense				Depreciation Expense			
Bal. 880	1,300	(13)		(7) 5,610	5,610	(13)		(9) 2,560	2,560	(13)	
(10) 420											
1,300	1,300			5,610	5,610			2,560	2,560		

3.38 a., b., and d. continued.

Insurance Expense		Miscellaneous Expense		Income Summary	
(11) 300	300 (13)	Bal. 2,420	2,420 (13)	(13) 55,740	65,960 (12)
				(14) 10,220	
300	300	2,420	2,420	65,960	65,960

Note: T-account entries (1) through (11) respond to Part *b.*, after which students can perform Part *c.* requirements. T-account entries (12) through (14) respond to Part *d.*, after which students can perform Part *e.* requirements.

c.

KLEEN CLEANERS, INC.
Adjusted Preclosing Trial Balance
March 31, Year 6

Cash	$ 13,270	
Accounts Receivable	8,900	
Supplies on Hand	2,290	
Prepaid Insurance	900	
Equipment	65,000	
Accumulated Depreciation		$ 12,240
Accounts Payable		7,900
Common Stock		20,000
Retained Earnings		40,000
Sales Revenue		65,960
Salaries and Wages Expense	37,530	
Cost of Outside Work	2,740	
Advertising Expense	700	
Repairs Expense	580	
Rent Expense	2,000	
Power, Gas, and Water Expense	1,300	
Supplies Expense	5,610	
Depreciation Expense	2,560	
Insurance Expense	300	
Miscellaneous Expense	2,420	
Totals	$ 146,100	$ 146,100

3.38 c. continued.

KLEEN CLEANERS, INC.
Income Statement
For the Three Months Ended March 31, Year 6

Sales Revenue...		$65,960
Expenses:		
Salaries and Wages Expense	$37,530	
Cost of Outside Work............................	2,740	
Advertising Expense.............................	700	
Repairs Expense	580	
Rent Expense.......................................	2,000	
Power, Gas, and Water Expense	1,300	
Supplies Expense	5,610	
Depreciation Expense	2,560	
Insurance Expense	300	
Miscellaneous Expense..........................	2,420	
Total Expenses...............................		55,740
Net Income for the Quarter		$10,220

e.

KLEEN CLEANERS, INC.
Balance Sheet
March 31, Year 6

Assets

Current Assets:		
Cash...	$13,270	
Accounts Receivable	8,900	
Supplies on Hand..................................	2,290	
Prepaid Insurance................................	900	
Total Current Assets..........................		$25,360
Noncurrent Assets:		
Equipment..	$65,000	
Less Accumulated Depreciation..............	(12,240)	
Total Noncurrent Assets.....................		52,760
Total Assets...................................		$78,120

Liabilities and Shareholders' Equity

Current Liabilities:		
Accounts Payable..................................	$ 7,900	
Total Current Liabilities		$ 7,900
Shareholders' Equity:		
Common Stock......................................	$20,000	
Retained Earnings	50,220	
Total Shareholders' Equity..................		70,220
Total Liabilities and Shareholders'		
Equity...		$78,120

3.39 (Bosworth Computer Repair Services; preparation of T-account entries, adjusted trial balance, income statement, and balance sheet.)

a., b., and d.

Cash			
Bal.	4,800	1,000	(3)
(1)	2,250	240	(4)
(8)	250	150	(5)
		325	(6)
		90	(7)
		1,100	(9)
Bal.	4,395		

Repair Parts Inventory			
Bal.	1,500	450	(11)
Bal.	1,050		

Office Supplies Inventory			
Bal.	200	100	(12)
Bal.	100		

Equipment			
Bal.	5,500		
Bal.	5,500		

Accumulated Depreciation			
		750	Bal.
		75	(13)
		825	Bal.

Accounts Payable			
(3)	1,000	6,250	Bal.
		5,250	Bal.

Common Stock			
		1,250	Bal.
		1,250	Bal.

Retained Earnings			
		3,750	Bal.
		440	(23)
		4,190	Bal.

Repair Revenue			
(14)	2,750	2,250	(1)
		500	(2)
	2,750	2,750	

Accounts Receivable			
(2)	500	250	(8)
Bal.	250		

Prepaid Insurance			
(4)	240	20	(10)
Bal.	220		

Advertising Expense			
(5)	150	150	(15)

Rent Expense			
(6)	325	325	(16)

Telephone Expense			
(7)	90	90	(17)

Salary Expense			
(9)	1,100	1,100	(18)

Insurance Expense			
(10)	20	20	(19)

Repair Parts Expense			
(11)	450	450	(20)

Office Supplies Expense			
(12)	100	100	(21)

3.39 a., b., and d. continued.

Depreciation Expense		Income Summary			
(13) 75	75 (22)	(15)	150	2,750	(14)
		(16)	325		
		(17)	90		
		(18)	1,100		
		(19)	20		
		(20)	450		
		(21)	100		
		(22)	75		
		(23)	440		
			2,750		

Note: T-account entries (1) through (13) respond to Part *b.*, after which students can perform Part *c.* requirements. T-account entries (14) through (22) respond to Part *d.*, after which students can perform Part *e.* requirements.

c.   BOSWORTH COMPUTER REPAIR SERVICES
                    Adjusted Preclosing Trial Balance
                            July 31, Year 8

Cash	$ 4,395	
Repair Parts Inventory	1,050	
Office Supplies Inventory	100	
Equipment	5,500	
Accumulated Depreciation		$ 825
Accounts Payable		5,250
Common Stock		1,250
Retained Earnings		3,750
Repair Revenue		2,750
Accounts Receivable	250	
Prepaid Insurance	220	
Advertising Expense	150	
Rent Expense	325	
Telephone Expense	90	
Salary Expense	1,100	
Insurance Expense	20	
Repair Parts Expense	450	
Office Supplies Expense	100	
Depreciation Expense	75	
Totals	$13,825	$13,825

3.39 c. continued.

BOSWORTH COMPUTER REPAIR SERVICES
Income Statement
For the Month of July, Year 8

Repair Revenue.................................		$2,750
Expenses:		
Advertising Expense	$ 150	
Rent Expense.................................	325	
Telephone Expense..........................	90	
Salary Expense...............................	1,100	
Insurance Expense..........................	20	
Repair Parts Expense......................	450	
Office Supplies Expense...................	100	
Depreciation Expense......................	75	
Total Expenses............................		2,310
Net Income		$ 440

e.
BOSWORTH COMPUTER REPAIR SERVICES
Balance Sheet
July 31, Year 8

Assets

Current Assets:		
Cash..	$4,395	
Accounts Receivable.........................	250	
Repair Parts Inventory.....................	1,050	
Office Supplies Inventory..................	100	
Prepaid Insurance...........................	220	
Total Current Assets....................		$ 6,015
Property, Plant, and Equipment:		
Equipment	$5,500	
Less Accumulated Depreciation	(825)	
Total Property, Plant, and Equipment................................		4,675
Total Assets................................		$10,690

Liabilities and Shareholders' Equity

Current Liabilities:		
Accounts Payable.............................		$ 5,250
Shareholders' Equity:		
Common Stock.................................	$1,250	
Retained Earnings...........................	4,190	
Total Shareholders' Equity...............		5,440
Total Liabilities and Shareholders' Equity		$10,690

3.40 (Jones Shoe Repair Shop, Inc.; preparation of T-account entries, adjusted trial balance, income statement, and balance sheet.)

a., b., and d.

	Cash				Accounts Receivable				Supplies Inventory		
Bal.	6,060	5,800	(5)	Bal.	15,200	18,200	(2)	Bal.	4,800	6,820	(8)
(1)	22,000	1,000	(6)	(1)	14,900			(4)	3,700		
(2)	18,200	11,900	(7)								
Bal.	27,560			Bal.	11,900			Bal.	1,680		

	Prepaid Insurance				Equipment			Accumulated Depreciation			
Bal.	900	400	(11)	Bal.	65,000					11,460	Bal.
										2,820	(9)
Bal.	500			Bal.	65,000					14,280	Bal.

	Accounts Payable				Common Stock				Retained Earnings		
(5)	5,800	6,120	Bal.			15,000	Bal.			47,360	Bal.
		1,200	(3)							23,860	(14)
		3,700	(4)								
		920	(10)								
		6,140	Bal.			15,000	Bal.			71,220	Bal.

	Sales Revenue			Salaries and Wages Expense				Cost of Outside Work			
(12)	82,960	46,060	Bal.	Bal.	26,600	38,500	(13)	Bal.	2,040	3,240	(13)
		22,000	(1)	(7)	11,900			(3)	1,200		
		14,900	(1)								
	82,960	82,960			38,500	38,500			3,240	3,240	

	Advertising Expense				Rent Expense			Power, Gas, and Water Expense			
Bal.	900	1,300	(13)	Bal.	1,200	2,200	(13)	Bal.	880	1,400	(13)
(10)	400			(6)	1,000			(10)	520		
	1,300	1,300			2,200	2,200			1,400	1,400	

	Supplies Expense			Depreciation Expense				Insurance Expense			
(8)	6,820	6,820	(13)	(9)	2,820	2,820	(13)	(11)	400	400	(13)
	6,820	6,820			2,820	2,820			400	400	

3.40 a., b., and d. continued.

Miscellaneous Expense			Income Summary		
Bal. 2,420	2,420 (13)		(13) 59,100	82,960 (12)	
			(14) 23,860		
2,420	2,420		82,960	82,960	

Note: T-account entries (1) through (11) respond to Part *b.*, after which students can perform Part *c.* requirements. T-account entries (12) through (14) respond to Part *d.*, after which students can perform Part *e.* requirements.

c.
JONES SHOE REPAIR SHOP, INC.
Adjusted Preclosing Trial Balance
March 31, Year 2

Cash...	$ 27,560	
Accounts Receivable..............................	11,900	
Supplies Inventory................................	1,680	
Prepaid Insurance.................................	500	
Equipment...	65,000	
Accumulated Depreciation......................		$ 14,280
Accounts Payable..................................		6,140
Common Stock......................................		15,000
Retained Earnings		47,360
Sales Revenue......................................		82,960
Salaries and Wages Expense	38,500	
Cost of Outside Work.............................	3,240	
Advertising Expense..............................	1,300	
Rent Expense..	2,200	
Power, Gas, and Water Expense	1,400	
Supplies Expense	6,820	
Depreciation Expense	2,820	
Insurance Expense.................................	400	
Miscellaneous Expense...........................	2,420	
Totals	$ 165,740	$ 165,740

3.40 c. continued.

JONES SHOE REPAIR SHOP, INC.
Income Statement
For the Three Months Ending March 31, Year 2

Sales Revenue		$82,960
Expenses:		
Salaries and Wages Expense	$38,500	
Cost of Outside Work	3,240	
Advertising Expense	1,300	
Rent Expense	2,200	
Power, Gas, and Water Expense	1,400	
Supplies Expense	6,820	
Depreciation Expense	2,820	
Insurance Expense	400	
Miscellaneous Expense	2,420	
Total Expenses		59,100
Net Income for the Quarter		$23,860

e.

JONES SHOE REPAIR SHOP, INC.
Balance Sheet
March 31, Year 2

Assets

Current Assets:		
Cash	$27,560	
Accounts Receivable	11,900	
Supplies Inventory	1,680	
Prepaid Insurance	500	
Total Current Assets		$41,640
Property, Plant, and Equipment:		
Equipment	$65,000	
Less Accumulated Depreciation	(14,280)	
Total Property, Plant, and Equipment		50,720
Total Assets		$92,360

Liabilities and Shareholders' Equity

Current Liabilities:		
Accounts Payable	$ 6,140	
Total Current Liabilities		$ 6,140
Shareholders' Equity:		
Common Stock	$15,000	
Retained Earnings	71,220	
Total Shareholders' Equity		86,220
Total Liabilities and Shareholders' Equity		$92,360

3.41   (Rybowiak's Building Supplies; preparation of journal entries, T-accounts, adjusted trial balance, income statement, and balance sheet.)

a.   (T): Transaction Entry   (A): Adjusting Entry

(1) (T)	Accounts Receivable............................. Sales Revenue......................................	85,000	 85,000
(2) (T)	Merchandise Inventory......................... Accounts Payable.................................	46,300	 46,300
(3) (T)	Rent Expense.. Cash..	11,750	 11,750
(4) (T)	Salaries Payable................................... Salaries Expense................................... Cash..	1,250 19,350	 20,600
(5) (T)	Cash.. Accounts Receivable............................	34,150	 34,150
(6) (T)	Accounts Payable................................. Cash..	38,950	 38,950
(7) (T)	Miscellaneous Expenses .... Cash..	3,200	 3,200
(8) (A)	Insurance Expense .... Prepaid Insurance.............................. $400/8 months.	50	 50
(9) (A)	Depreciation Expense .... Accumulated Depreciation................... 1/12 X $210,000/10.	1,750	 1,750
(10) (A)	Salaries Expense................................... Salaries Payable.................................	1,600	 1,600
(11) (A)	Interest Expense .... Interest Payable................................. $5,000 X .12 X 30/360.	50	 50
(12) (A)	Cost of Goods Sold............................... Merchandise Inventory .... $68,150 + $46,300 − $77,950.	36,500	 36,500

3.41 continued.

b. and e.

Cash			
Bal.	44,200	11,750	(3)
(5)	34,150	20,600	(4)
		38,950	(6)
		3,200	(7)
Bal.	3,850		

Accounts Receivable			
Bal.	27,250	34,150	(5)
(1)	85,000		
Bal.	78,100		

Merchandise Inventory			
Bal.	68,150	36,500	(12)
(2)	46,300		
Bal.	77,950		

Prepaid Insurance			
Bal.	400	50	(8)
Bal.	350		

Equipment			
Bal.	210,000		
Bal.	210,000		

Accumulated Depreciation			
		84,000	Bal.
		1,750	(9)
		85,750	Bal.

Accounts Payable			
		33,100	Bal.
(6)	38,950	46,300	(2)
		40,450	Bal.

Note Payable			
		5,000	Bal.
		5,000	Bal.

Salaries Payable			
(4)	1,250	1,250	Bal.
		1,600	(10)
		1,600	Bal.

Common Stock			
		150,000	Bal.
		150,000	Bal.

Retained Earnings			
		76,650	Bal.
		10,750	(15)
		87,400	Bal.

Sales Revenue			
(13)	85,000	85,000	(1)

Rent Expense			
(3)	11,750	11,750	(14)

Salaries Expense			
(4)	19,350		
(10)	1,600	20,950	(14)
	20,950		

3.41 b. and e. continued.

Miscellaneous Expenses				Insurance Expense			
(7)	3,200	3,200	(14)	(8)	50	50	(14)

Depreciation Expense				Interest Expense			
(9)	1,750	1,750	(14)	(11)	50	50	(14)

Interest Payable				Cost of Goods Sold			
		50	(11)	(12)	36,500	36,500	(14)
		50	Bal.				

Income Summary			
(14)	74,250	85,000	(13)
(15)	10,750		
	85,000		

c.

RYBOWIAK'S BUILDING SUPPLIES
Adjusted Preclosing Trial Balance
July 31, Year 9

Cash	$ 3,850	
Accounts Receivable	78,100	
Merchandise Inventory	77,950	
Prepaid Insurance	350	
Equipment	210,000	
Accumulated Depreciation		$ 85,750
Accounts Payable		40,450
Note Payable		5,000
Salaries Payable		1,600
Common Stock		150,000
Retained Earnings (September 30)		76,650
Sales Revenue		85,000
Rent Expense	11,750	
Salaries Expense	20,950	
Miscellaneous Expenses	3,200	
Insurance Expense	50	
Depreciation Expense	1,750	
Interest Expense	50	
Interest Payable		50
Cost of Goods Sold	36,500	
Totals	$ 444,500	$ 444,500

3.41 continued.

d.

RYBOWIAK'S BUILDING SUPPLIES
Income Statement
For the Month of July, Year 9

Sales Revenue...		$ 85,000
Less Expenses:		
Cost of Goods Sold	$ 36,500	
Salaries Expense...............................	20,950	
Rent Expense....................................	11,750	
Depreciation Expense.........................	1,750	
Insurance Expense.............................	50	
Interest Expense................................	50	
Miscellaneous Expenses......................	3,200	(74,250)
Net Income		$ 10,750

f.

RYBOWIAK'S BUILDING SUPPLIES
Balance Sheet
July 31, Year 9

Assets

Current Assets:		
Cash...		$ 3,850
Accounts Receivable...........................		78,100
Merchandise Inventory		77,950
Prepaid Insurance.............................		350
Total Current Assets.......................		$ 160,250
Noncurrent Assets:		
Equipment—at Cost	$ 210,000	
Less Accumulated Depreciation	(85,750)	
Total Noncurrent Assets		124,250
Total Assets..................................		$ 284,500

Liabilities and Shareholders' Equity

Current Liabilities:		
Accounts Payable..............................		$ 40,450
Note Payable....................................		5,000
Salaries Payable...............................		1,600
Interest Payable................................		50
Total Current Liabilities..................		$ 47,100
Shareholders' Equity:		
Common Stock..................................		$ 150,000
Retained Earnings.............................		87,400
Total Shareholders' Equity...............		$ 237,400
Total Liabilities and Shareholders' Equity		$ 284,500

3.42   (Reliable Appliance Company; preparation of adjusting entries.)

(1) Depreciation Expense 88
        Accumulated Depreciation 88
    1/12 × ($5,280/5).

(2) Depreciation Expense 500
        Accumulated Depreciation 500
    1/12 × ($24,000/4).

(3) Rent Expense 1,800
        Leasehold 1,800

(4) Accounts Payable 360
        Merchandise Inventory 360

(5) Salaries and Commissions Expense 210
        Salaries and Commissions Payable 210

(6) Advances by Customers 490
        Accounts Receivable 490

(7) Insurance Expense 50
        Prepaid Insurance 50
    $900/18 = $50.

(8) Retained Earnings 2,500
        Dividends Payable 2,500

(9) Merchandise Cost of Goods Sold 37,440
        Merchandise Inventory 37,440
    $99,000 − $360 − $61,200 = $37,440.

3.43   (Williamson Corporation; preparation of adjusting entries.)

(1) Depreciation Expense 6,250
         Accumulated Depreciation 6,250
     ($50,000/8) = $6,250.

(2) Advances from Customers 290
         Sales Revenue 290

(3) Accounts Payable 860
         Accounts Receivable 860

(4) Prepaid Rent 200
         Marketing and Administrative Expenses 200
     ($1,400 – $1,200) = $200.

(5) Marketing and Administrative Expenses 450
         Salaries Payable 450
     ($2,250 – $1,800) = $450.

(6) Merchandise Cost of Goods Sold 94,800
         Merchandise Inventory 94,800
     ($110,000 – $15,200) = $94,800.

(7) Income Tax Expense 1,017
         Income Tax Payable 1,017
     .30[($150,000 + $290) – ($94,800 + $45,600 + $6,250
     – $200 + $450)] = $1,017.

3.44   (Creative Photographers, Inc.; preparation of closing entries.)

a. Revenue—Commercial Photography................ 54,270
    Revenue—Printing Service 14,040
        Advertising Expense.....................................   4,500
        Depreciation Expense—Cameras and Equip-
            ment...   540
        Depreciation Expense—Furniture and Fix-
            tures...   315
        Electricity Expense......................................   900
        Equipment Repairs Expense   540
        Insurance Expense.......................................   990
        Photographic Supplies Expense...................   5,850
        Rent Expense   4,275
        Salaries Expense   32,400
        Telephone Expense   360
        Retained Earnings.......................................   17,640

b.

Revenue—Commercial Photography			Revenue—Printing Service			Advertising Expense		
(1)	54,270	54,270 Bal.	(1)	14,040	14,040 Bal.	Bal.	4,500	4,500 (1)

Depreciation Expense—Cameras and Equipment			Depreciation Expense—Furniture and Fixtures			Electricity Expense		
Bal.	540	540 (1)	Bal.	315	315 (1)	Bal.	900	900 (1)

Equipment Repairs Expense			Insurance Expense			Photographic Supplies Expense		
Bal.	540	540 (1)	Bal.	990	990 (1)	Bal.	5,850	5,850 (1)

Rent Expense			Salaries Expense			Telephone Expense		
Bal.	4,275	4,275 (1)	Bal.	32,400	32,400 (1)	Bal.	360	360 (1)

Retained Earnings		
	42,414	Bal.
	17,640	(1)

3.45 (Prima Company; working backwards to balance sheet at beginning of period.)

PRIMA COMPANY
Balance Sheet
As of January 1, Year 2

Assets

Cash...		$ 11,700
Marketable Securities.....................................		12,000
Accounts Receivable......................................		22,000
Merchandise Inventory		33,000
Prepayments		1,700
Land, Buildings, and Equipment....................	$ 40,000	
Less Accumulated Depreciation	(12,000)	28,000
Total Assets..		$ 108,400

Equities

Accounts Payable..	$ 26,000
Interest Payable..	300
Taxes Payable..	3,500
Notes Payable (6 Percent)	20,000
Capital Stock	50,000
Retained Earnings...	8,600
Total Equities.......................................	$ 108,400

A T-account method for deriving the solution appears below and on the following page. The end-of-year balance appears at the bottom of the T-account. The derived starting balance appears at the top. "p" indicates plug; "c," closing entry.

	Cash					Marketable Securities	
(p)	11,700				(p)	12,000	
(1)	47,000	128,000	(3)		(8)	8,000	
(2)	150,000	49,000	(4)				
		7,500	(5)				
		1,200	(6)				
		5,000	(7)				
		8,000	(8)				
Bal.	10,000				Bal.	20,000	

	Accounts Receivable					Merchandise Inventory		
(p)	22,000				(p)	33,000		
(10)	153,000	150,000	(2)		(9)	127,000	130,000	(11)
Bal.	25,000				Bal.	30,000		

3.45 continued.

Prepayments for Miscellaneous Services

(p)	1,700		
(4)	49,000	47,700	(14)
Bal.	3,000		

Land, Buildings, and Equipment

(p)	40,000	
Bal.	40,000	

Accounts Payable (for Merchandise)

		26,000	(p)
(3)	128,000	127,000	(9)
		25,000	Bal.

Interest Payable

		300	(p)
(6)	1,200	1,200	(15)
		300	Bal.

Taxes Payable

		3,500	(p)
(5)	7,500	8,000	(13)
		4,000	Bal.

Notes Payable

	20,000	(p)
	20,000	Bal.

Accumulated Depreciation

	12,000	(p)
	4,000	(12)
	16,000	Bal.

Capital Stock

	50,000	(p)
	50,000	Bal.

Retained Earnings

		8,600	(p)
(7)	5,000	9,100	(22)
		12,700	Bal.

Sales

		47,000	(1)
(16c)	200,000	153,000	(10)

Cost of Goods Sold

(11)	130,000	130,000	(17c)

Depreciation Expense

(12)	4,000	4,000	(18c)

Taxes Expense

(13)	8,000	8,000	(19c)

Other Operating Expense

(14)	47,700	47,700	(20c)

Interest Expense

(15)	1,200	1,200	(21c)

Income Summary

(17)	130,000	200,000	(16)
(18)	4,000		
(19)	8,000		
(20)	47,700		
(21)	1,200		
(22c)	9,100		

3.46   (Secunda Company; working backwards to the balance sheet at the beginning of the period.)

SECUNDA COMPANY
Cash Receipts and Disbursements Schedule

Receipts:

Collections from Customers		$85,000
Disbursements:		
Suppliers of Merchandise and Other Services	$81,000	
Mortgage...	3,000	
Dividends	10,000	
Interest...	2,000	
Total Disbursements		96,000
Decrease in Cash		$11,000
Cash Balance, January 1		20,000
Cash Balance, December 31		$ 9,000

A T-account method for deriving the solution appears below and on the following page. After Entry (6), we have explained all revenue and expense account changes. Plugging for the unknown amounts determines the remaining, unexplained changes in balance sheet accounts. A "p" next to the entry number designates these entries. Note that the revenue and expense accounts are not yet closed to retained earnings, so dividends account for the decrease in the Retained Earnings account during the year of $10,000.

	Cash					Accounts Receivable		
Bal.	20,000				Bal.	36,000		
(7)	85,000				(1)	100,000	85,000	(7p)
		2,000	(9)					
		81,000	(10)					
		3,000	(11)					
		10,000	(12)					
Bal.	9,000				Bal.	51,000		

	Merchandise Inventory					Prepayments		
Bal.	45,000				Bal.	2,000		
(8p)	65,000	50,000	(2)				1,000	(5)
Bal.	60,000				Bal.	1,000		

	Land, Buildings and Equipment			Cost of Goods Sold		
Bal.	40,000			Bal.	0	
				(2)	50,000	
Bal.	40,000			Bal.	50,000	

3.46 continued.

Interest Expense		
Bal.	0	
(3)	3,000	
Bal.	3,000	

Other Operating Expenses		
Bal.	0	
(4)	2,000	
(5)	1,000	
(6p)	26,000	
Bal.	29,000	

Accumulated Depreciation		
	16,000	Bal.
	2,000	(4)
	18,000	Bal.

Interest Payable		
	1,000	Bal.
(9p)	2,000	3,000	(3)
	2,000	Bal.

Accounts Payable		
	30,000	Bal.
(10p)	81,000	26,000	(6)
	65,000	(8)
	40,000	Bal.

Mortgage Payable		
	20,000	Bal.
(11p)	3,000	
	17,000	Bal.

Capital Stock		
	50,000	Bal.
	50,000	Bal.

Retained Earnings		
	26,000	Bal.
(12p)	10,000	
	16,000	Bal.

Sales		
	0	Bal.
	100,000	(1)
	100,000	Bal.

3.47 (Tertia Company; working backwards to income statement.)

TERTIA COMPANY
Statement of Income and Retained Earnings

Revenues:

Sales...	$ 212,000	
Interest Revenue....................................	700	
Total Revenues		$ 212,700
Expenses:		
Cost of Goods Sold................................	$ 126,500	
Property Tax Expense............................	1,700	
Depreciation Expense	2,000	
Interest Expense....................................	500	
Miscellaneous Expenses	56,800	
Total Expenses................................		187,500
Net Income		$ 25,200
Less Dividends......................................		(2,000)
Increase in Retained Earnings...................		$ 23,200
Retained Earnings, Beginning of Year...........		76,000
Retained Earnings, End of Year		$ 99,200

A T-account method for deriving the solution appears below and on the following pages. Transactions (1) – (9) correspond to the numbered cash transactions information. In transactions (10) – (25), "p" indicates that the figure was derived by a "plug" and "c" indicates a closing entry. The final check is that the debit to close Income Summary in (25) matches the plug in the Retained Earnings account.

Cash					Accounts and Notes Receivable			
Bal.	(a)				Bal.	36,000		
(1)	144,000	114,000	(4)		(10p)	149,000	144,000	(1)
(2)	63,000	5,000	(5)					
(3)	1,000	500	(6)					
		57,500	(7)					
		1,200	(8)					
		2,000	(9)					
Bal.	(b)				Bal.	41,000		

(a) Total debits, $183,000, less specific, known debits, $143,000, equal beginning balance in Cash account of $40,000.

(b) Beginning balance of $40,000 plus increase in cash balance for the year of $27,800 equals ending balance in Cash account of $67,800.

3.47 continued.

Merchandise Inventory			
Bal.	55,000		
(14)	121,000	126,500	(15p)
Bal.	49,500		

Interest Receivable			
Bal.	1,000		
(11p)	700	1,000	(3)
Bal.	700		

Prepaid Miscellaneous Services			
Bal.	4,000		
(7)	57,500	56,300	(12p)
Bal.	5,200		

Building, Machinery, and Equipment			
Bal.	47,000		
Bal.	47,000		

Accounts Payable (Miscellaneous Services)			
		2,000	Bal.
		500	(13p)
		2,500	Bal.

Accounts Payable (Merchandise)			
		34,000	Bal.
(4)	114,000	121,000	(14p)
		41,000	Bal.

Property Taxes Payable			
		1,000	Bal.
(8)	1,200	1,700	(16p)
		1,500	Bal.

Accumulated Depreciation			
		10,000	Bal.
		2,000	(17p)
		12,000	Bal.

Mortgage Payable			
		35,000	Bal.
(5)	5,000		
		30,000	Bal.

Capital Stock			
		25,000	Bal.
		25,000	Bal.

Retained Earnings			
		76,000	Bal.
(9)	2,000	25,200	(25p)
		99,200	Bal.

Sales			
		63,000	(2)
		149,000	(10)
(18c)	212,000	212,000	

Cost of Goods Sold			
(15)	126,500	126,500	(20c)

Interest Expense			
(6)	500	500	(21c)

3.47 continued.

	Interest Revenue				Miscellaneous Expenses	
(19c)	700	700	(11)	(12)	56,300	
				(13)	500	
					56,800	56,800 (22c)

	Property Tax Expense				Depreciation Expense	
(16)	1,700	1,700	(23c)	(17)	2,000	2,000 (24c)

	Income Summary		
(20)	126,500	212,000	(18)
(21)	500	700	(19)
(22)	56,800		
(23)	1,700		
(24)	2,000		
(25c)	25,200		

3.48   (Portobello Co.; reconstructing the income statement and balance sheet.)

PORTOBELLO CO.
Income Statement
For the Year Ended December 31, Year 10

Revenues:
Sales..	$ 227,200
Interest..	300
Total Revenues......................................	$ 227,500

Expenses:
Cost of Goods Sold.....................................	$ 88,000
Depreciation	17,500
Salaries...	75,800
Taxes..	18,000
Insurance	3,000
Consulting..	4,800
Interest...	5,000
Total Expenses......................................	$ 212,100
Net Income	$ 15,400

3.48 continued.

PORTOBELLO CO.
Balance Sheet
December 31, Year 10

Assets

Current Assets:
Cash..		$ 4,700
Accounts Receivable............................		51,000
Merchandise Inventories.....................		40,000
Prepaid Insurance..............................		1,500
Prepaid Salaries		4,000
Prepaid Taxes.....................................		3,000
Total Current Assets........................		$ 104,200
Noncurrent Assets:		
Computer System—at Cost...................	$ 78,000	
Less Accumulated Depreciation	(39,000)	$ 39,000
Delivery Trucks	$ 60,000	
Less Accumulated Depreciation	(4,500)	55,500
Total Noncurrent Assets		94,500
Total Assets.....................................		$ 198,700

Liabilities and Shareholders' Equity

Current Liabilities:
Accounts Payable................................	$ 16,000
Interest Payable..................................	2,000
Dividend Payable................................	3,000
Salaries Payable.................................	1,300
Taxes Payable.....................................	4,000
Consulting Fee Payable.......................	4,800
Advances from Customers...................	1,400
Total Current Liabilities...................	$ 32,500
Note Payable.......................................	60,000
Total Liabilities	$ 92,500
Shareholders' Equity:	
Common Stock....................................	$ 51,000
Retained Earnings..............................	55,200
Total Shareholders' Equity...............	$ 106,200 ·
Total Liabilities and Shareholders'	
Equity	$ 198,700

T-accounts to derive the amounts in the income statement and balance sheet appear on the following pages.

3.48 continued.

Cash					Accounts Receivable			
√	18,600				√	33,000		
(4)	10,900	4,800	(3)		(15)	228,000	210,000	(14)
(14)	210,000	115,000	(5)					
		3,000	(10)					
		85,000	(17)					
		27,000	(19)					
√	4,700				√	51,000		

Notes Receivable					Interest Receivable			
√	10,000				√	600		
		10,000	(4)				600	(4)
√	0				√	0		

Merchandise Inventories					Prepaid Insurance			
√	22,000				√	4,500		
(6)	95,000	88,000	(8)				3,000	(1)
(7)	11,000							
√	40,000				√	1,500		

Prepaid Salaries			Prepaid Taxes		
√	0		√	0	
(17)	4,000		(19)	3,000	
√	4,000		√	3,000	

Computer System (at Cost)			Accumulated Depreciation—Computer System		
√	78,000			26,000	√
				13,000	(13)
√	78,000			39,000	√

Delivery Trucks			Accumulated Depreciation—Delivery Trucks		
√	0			0	√
(9)	60,000			4,500	(12)
√	60,000			4,500	√

3.48 continued.

Accounts Payable			
		36,000	√
(5)	115,000	95,000	(6)
		16,000	√

Notes Payable			
		0	√
		60,000	(9)
		60,000	√

Interest Payable			
		0	√
		2,000	(11)
		2,000	√

Dividend Payable			
		1,800	√
(3)	4,800	6,000	(2)
		3,000	√

Salaries Payable			
		6,500	√
(17)	6,500		
		1,300	(18)
		1,300	√

Taxes Payable			
		10,000	√
(19)	10,000	4,000	(20)
		4,000	√

Consulting Fee Payable			
		0	√
		4,800	(21)
		4,800	√

Advances from Customers			
		600	√
(16)	600	1,400	(15)
		1,400	√

Common Stock			
		40,000	√
		11,000	(7)
		51,000	√

Retained Earnings			
		45,800	√
(2)	6,000	15,400	(31)
		55,200	√

Sales Revenue			
		226,600	(15)
(22)	227,200	600	(16)

Interest Revenue			
(23)	300	300	(4)

Cost of Goods Sold			
(8)	88,000	88,000	(24)

Depreciation Expense			
(12)	4,500		
(13)	13,000	17,500	(25)

Salary Expense			
(17)	74,500		
(18)	1,300	75,800	(26)

Tax Expense			
(19)	14,000		
(20)	4,000	18,000	(27)

3.48 continued.

Insurance Expense				Consulting Expense		
(1)	3,000	3,000	(28)	(21)	4,800	4,800	(29)

Interest Expense				Income Summary		
(10)	3,000			(24)	88,000	227,200	(22)
(11)	2,000	5,000	(30)	(25)	17,500	300	(23)
				(26)	75,800		
				(27)	18,000		
				(28)	3,000		
				(29)	4,800		
				(30)	5,000		
				(31)	15,400		

3.49 Computer Needs, Inc.; reconstructing the income statement and balance sheet.)

a.

Cash				Accounts Receivable		
√	15,600			√	32,100		
(A)	37,500	164,600	(D)	(C)	159,700	151,500	(B)
(B)	151,500	21,000	(G)				
		3,390	(H)				
		4,800	(I)				
		6,000	(J)				
√	4,810			√	40,300		

Inventories				Prepayments		
√	46,700			√	1,500		
(E)	172,100	158,100	(F)	(G)	300		
√	60,700			√	1,800		

Property, Plant and Equipment				Accumulated Depreciation		
√	59,700					2,800	√
(J)	6,000					3,300	(K)
√	65,700					6,100	√

Accounts Payable—Merchandise				Income Tax Payable		
		37,800	√			3,390	√
(D)	164,600	172,100	(E)	(H)	3,390	3,584	(L)
		45,300	√			3,584	√

3.49 a. continued.

Other Current Liabilities		
	2,900	√
(G) 1,700		
	1,200	√

Mortgage Payable		
	50,000	√
(I) 800		
	49,200	√

Common Stock		
	50,000	√
	50,000	√

Retained Earnings		
	8,710	√
(11p)	9,216	(M)
	17,926	√

Sales		
	37,500	(A)
(M) 197,200	159,700	(B)

Cost of Goods Sold		
(F) 158,100	158,100	(M)

Selling & Admin. Expense		
(G) 19,000	19,000	(M)

Depreciation Expense		
(K) 3,300	3,300	(M)

Interest Expense		
(I) 4,000	4,000	(M)

Income Tax Expense		
(L) 3,584	3,584	(M)

COMPUTER NEEDS, INC.
Income Statement
For the Years Ended December 31

	Year 8		Year 9	
	Amounts	Percentages	Amounts	Percentages
Sales............................	$ 152,700	100.0%	$ 197,200	100.0%
Cost of Goods Sold...........	(116,400)	(76.2)	(158,100)	(80.2)
Selling and Adminis-				
tration Expenses.........	(17,400)	(11.4)	(19,000)	(9.6)
Depreciation...................	(2,800)	(1.9)	(3,300)	(1.7)
Interest........................	(4,000)	(2.6)	(4,000)	(2.0)
Income Taxes	(3,390)	(2.2)	(3,584)	(1.8)
Net Income....................	$ 8,710	5.7%	$ 9,216	4.7%

3.49 a. continued.

COMPUTER NEEDS, INC.
Balance Sheet
December 31

	Year 8		Year 9	
	Amounts	Percentages	Amounts	Percentages
Assets				
Cash.............................	$ 15,600	10.2%	$ 4,810	2.9%
Accounts Receivable.......	32,100	21.0	40,300	24.1
Inventories....................	46,700	30.6	60,700	36.3
Prepayments	1,500	1.0	1,800	1.1
Total Current Assets...	$ 95,900	62.8%	$ 107,610	64.4%
Property, Plant and Equipment:				
At Cost....................	$ 59,700	39.0%	$ 65,700	39.3%
Less Accumulated Depreciation..........	(2,800)	(1.8)	(6,100)	(3.7)
Net.........................	$ 56,900	37.2%	$ 59,600	35.6%
Total Assets	$ 152,800	100.0%	$ 167,210	100.0%
Liabilities and Share- holders' Equity				
Accounts Payable— Merchandise..............	$ 37,800	24.8%	$ 45,300	27.1%
Income Tax Payable	3,390	2.2	3,584	2.2
Other Current Liabilities	2,900	1.9	1,200	.7
Total Current Liabil- ities........................	$ 44,090	28.9%	$ 50,084	30.0%
Mortgage Payable...........	50,000	32.7	49,200	29.4
Total Liabilities...........	$ 94,090	61.6%	$ 99,284	59.4%
Common Stock..............	$ 50,000	32.7%	$ 50,000	29.9%
Retained Earnings	8,710	5.7	17,926	10.7
Total Shareholders' Equity.....................	$ 58,710	38.4%	$ 67,926	40.6%
Total Liabilities and Shareholders' Equity.....................	$ 152,800	100.0%	$ 167,210	100.0%

3.49 continued.

b. Although sales increased between Year 8 and Year 9, net income as a percentage of sales declined from 5.7% to 4.7%. The decline occurs primarily as a result of an increase in the cost of goods sold to sales percentage. The increased percentage might suggest (1) increased competition, which forced Computer Needs, Inc. to lower its prices, (2) increased cost of merchandise, which Computer Needs, Inc. could not or chose not to pass on to customers, or (3) a shift in product mix to lower margin products. The percentage is also affected by the estimates made for the December 31, Year 9 balances in Accounts Receivable, Inventories, and Accounts Payable. The following summarizes the effects of an overstatement or understatement of each of these three accounts, assuming the other two accounts are correctly stated, on the cost of goods sold to sales percentage.

December 31, Year 9 Balance Is:	Effect of Cost of Goods Sold to Sales Percentage		
	Numerator	Denominator	Net Effect
Accounts Receivable Overstated...	O	O/S	U/S
Accounts Receivable Understated	O	U/S	O/S
Inventories Overstated	U/S	O	U/S
Inventories Understated	O/S	O	O/S
Accounts Payable Overstated	O/S	O	O/S
Accounts Payable Understated	U/S	O	U/S

Of course, there could be compounding or offsetting errors in each of these three accounts.

The selling and administrative expense to sales percentage declined. Compensation of employees is largely a fixed cost, so the increased sales should permit Computer Needs, Inc. to spread this cost over the larger sales base. The estimate of Accounts Receivable and Other Current Liabilities on December 31, Year 9 also can affect this percentage.

The reduced expense percentage for depreciation reflects the spreading of this fixed cost over a larger sales base. Although depreciation expense increased between Year 8 and Year 9, sales increased by a higher percentage.

The reduced expense percentage for interest likewise results from spreading this fixed cost of a larger sales base. Note that interest expense was the same amount in Year 8 and Year 9. Given that the amount of the loan outstanding decreased, the interest rate on the loan must have increased.

The decreased income tax percentage results from a lower income before taxes to sales percentage. The income tax rate was 28 percent in both years.

3.49 b. continued.

	Year 8		Year 9	
	Amounts	Percentages	Amounts	Percentages
Net Income before Taxes .	$ 12,100	100.0%	$ 12,800	100.0%
Income Tax Expense	(3,390)	(28.0)	(3,584)	(28.0)
Net Income...................	$ 8,710	72.0%	$ 9,216	72.0%

The balance sheet shows a significant decline in cash and a buildup of accounts receivable, inventories, and accounts payable. It is possible that each of these accounts is overstated. The decline in cash, however, is consistent with the buildup of accounts receivable. The buildup of accounts payable is consistent with a buildup in inventories.

3.50   (Interpreting common-size income statements.)

Sales for the three companies grew at a rapid rate during the three-year period as the firms added new stores. The growth rate declined as the base for calculating the growth rate increased. Staples, and to a lesser extent Office Max, gained market share relative to Office Depot.

a. Staples had the highest net income to sales percentage of the three firms. Its advantage lies in a lower cost of goods sold to sales percentage and thereby a higher gross profit percentage. Staples is smaller than Office Depot, so a greater ability to take advantage of quantity discounts would not seem to explain Staples' lower cost of goods sold to sales percentage. Sales revenue grew much more rapidly for Staples than Office Depot (see sales mix data in Exhibit 3.28). Perhaps Staples placed more of its new stores in locations not directly competing with Office Depot and Office Max stores, permitting it to charge somewhat higher prices. However, the similar selling and administrative expense to sales percentages for Staples and Office Depot suggest that their selling prices maybe comparable. If this is the case, then the lower cost of goods sold percentage for Staples may result from more efficient inventory control systems or more higher gross margin products in its sales mix. The similar selling and administrative expense to sales percentages for Staples and Office Depot might also result from the offsetting effects of higher selling prices for Staples but the spreading of relatively fixed administrative expenses over a larger sales base for Office Depot. Dampening Staples' advantage on the net income to sales percentage is a higher interest expense to sales percentage. Staples has apparently used debt to finance its rapid growth in sales. Its relative advantage over Office Depot declined during the two-year period because of the increased borrowing.

3.50 continued.

b. Office Depot and Office Max have similar net income to sales percentages. Office Depot has a lower cost of goods sold to sales percentage than Office Max. Perhaps the larger size of Office Depot permits it to take greater advantage of quantity discounts for merchandise. Office Max offsets its disadvantage on the gross margin percentage by taking on much less debt. The lower level of debt for Office Max might reflect the need to lower its financing costs to offset its disadvantage on the cost of goods sold to sales percentage.

CHAPTER 4

STATEMENT OF CASH FLOWS:
REPORTING THE EFFECTS OF OPERATING,
INVESTING, AND FINANCING ACTIVITIES
ON CASH FLOWS

Questions, Exercises, Problems, and Cases: Answers and Solutions

4.1 See the text or the glossary at the end of the book.

4.2 One can criticize a single income statement using a cash basis of accounting from two standpoints: (1) it provides a poor measure of operating performance each period because of the inaccurate matching of revenues and expenses (see discussion in Chapter 3), and (2) it excludes important investing (acquisitions and sales of long-lived assets) activities and financing (issuance or redemption of bonds or capital stock) activities of a firm that affect cash flow.

4.3 Accrual accounting attempts to provide a measure of operating performance that relates inputs to output without regard to when a firm receives or disburses cash. Accrual accounting also attempts to portray the resources of a firm and the claims on those resources without regard to whether the firm holds the resource in the form of cash. Although accrual accounting may satisfy user's needs for information about operating performance and financial position, it does not provide sufficient information about the cash flow effects of a firm's operating, investing, and financing activities. The latter is the objective of the statement of cash flows.

4.4 The statement of cash flows reports changes in the investing and financing activities of a firm. Significant changes in property, plant, and equipment affect the maturity structure of assets on the balance sheet. Significant changes in long-term debt or capital stock affect both the maturity structure of equities as well as the mix of debt versus shareholder financing.

4.5 The indirect method reconciles net income, the primary measure of a firm's profitability, with cash flow from operations. Some would argue that the relation between net income and cash flow from operations is less evident when a firm reports using the direct method. The frequent use of the indirect method prior to the issuance of FASB *Statement No. 95* also probably explains its continuing popularity.

4.6   The classification in the statement of cash flows parallels that in the income statement, where interest on debt is an expense but payments on the principal amount of the debt are not an expense but a reduction in a liability.

4.7   The classification in the statement of cash flows parallels that in the income statement, where interest on debt is an expense but dividends are a distribution of earnings, not an expense.

4.8   Firms generally use accounts payable directly in financing purchases of inventory and other operating costs. Firms might use short-term bank financing indirectly in financing accounts receivable, inventories, or operating costs or use it to finance acquisitions of noncurrent assets or reductions in long-term financing. Thus, the link between short-term bank financing and operations is less direct and may not even relate to operating activities. To achieve consistency in classification, the FASB stipulates that changes in short-term bank loans are financing activities.

4.9   This is an investing and financing transaction whose disclosure helps the statement user understand why property, plant and equipment and long-term debt changed during the period. Because the transaction does not affect cash directly, however, firms must distinguish it from investing and financing transactions that do affect cash flow.

4.10   Both are correct, but the writer's point is not expressed clearly. Depreciation expense is a charge to operations, but does not require cash. If revenues precisely equal total expenses, there will be a retention of net funds in the business equal to the amount of the depreciation. As long as replacement of the depreciating assets is not necessary, it is possible to finance considerable expansion without resorting to borrowing or the issuance of additional stock.

        The "reader" is correct in saying that depreciation in itself is not a source of cash and that the total cash available would not have increased by adding larger amounts to the depreciation accounts. The source of cash is sales to customers.

        When one considers income tax effects, however, depreciation expenses do save cash because taxable income and, hence, income tax expense using cash are lower than they would be in the absence of depreciation charges.

4.11   The firm must have increased substantially its investment in accounts receivable or inventories or decreased substantially its current liabilities.

4.12   The firm might be capital intensive and, therefore, subtracted substantial amounts of depreciation expense in computing net income. This depreciation expense is added back to net income in computing cash flow from operations. In addition, the firm might have decreased significantly its investment in accounts receivable or inventories or increased its current liabilities.

4.13 The accountant classifies the entire cash proceeds from the equipment sale as an investing activity. Because the calculation of cash flow from operations starts with net income (which includes the gain on sale of equipment), the accountant must subtract the gain to avoid counting cash flow equal to the gain twice, once as an operating activity and once as an investing activity.

4.14 (Amazon.com; calculating and interpreting cash flows.) (Amounts in Thousands)

a. **Year 4**

	Balance Sheet Changes	Operations	Investing	Financing
(Increases) Decreases in Assets				
Marketable Securities	—			
Inventories	$ (554)	$ (554)		
Prepayments	(307)	(307)		
Property, Plant and Equipment (at Cost)	(1,360)		$ (1,360)	
Accumulated Depreciation ...	286	286		
Increases (Decreases) in Liabilities and Shareholders' Equity				
Accounts Payable—Merchandise Suppliers	2,753	2,753		
Other Current Liabilities	2,010	2,010		
Long-Term Debt....................	—			
Common Stock	8,201			$ 8,201
Retained Earnings	(5,777)	(5,777)		
Increase (Decrease) in Cash..................................	$ 5,252	$ (1,589)	$ (1,360)	$ 8,201

4.14 a. continued.

Year 5

	Balance Sheet Changes	Operations	Investing	Financing
(Increases) Decreases in Assets				
Marketable Securities	$ (15,256)		$ (15,256)	
Inventories	(8,400)	$ (8,400)		
Prepayments	(2,977)	(2,977)		
Property, Plant and Equipment (at Cost).....	(15,283)		(15,283)	
Accumulated Depreciation..............................	4,742	4,742		
Increases (Decreases) in Liabilities and Shareholders' Equity				
Accounts Payable—Merchandise Suppliers.......	29,845	29,845		
Other Current Liabilities	7,603	7,603		
Long-Term Debt...............	78,202			$ 78,202
Common Stock	52,675			52,675
Retained Earnings	(27,590)	(27,590)		
Increase (Decrease) in Cash..............................	$ 103,561	$ 3,223	$ (30,539)	$ 130,877

4.14 continued.

b.

AMAZON.COM
Statement of Cash Flows
For Year 4 and Year 5

	Year 4	Year 5
Operations:		
Net Income (Loss)	$ (5,777)	$ (27,590)
Depreciation	286	4,742
(Increase) Decrease in Inventories	(554)	(8,400)
(Increase) Decrease in Prepayments	(307)	(2,977)
Increase (Decrease) in Accounts Payable—		
Merchandise Suppliers	2,753	29,845
Increase (Decrease) in Other Current Lia-		
bilities	2,010	7,603
Cash Flow from Operations	$ (1,589)	$ 3,223
Investing:		
Acquisition of Property, Plant and Equip-		
ment...	$ (1,360)	$ (30,539)
Financing:		
Increase in Long-Term Debt		$ 78,202
Issue of Common Stock...................................	$ 8,201	52,675
Cash Flow from Financing	$ 8,201	$ 130,877
Increase (Decrease) in Cash	$ 5,252	$ 103,561
Cash, Beginning of Year..................................	996	6,248
Cash, End of Year	$ 6,248	$ 109,809

c. Amazon.com operated at a net loss each year. Its cash flow from operations was not as negative as the net loss, and even turned positive in Year 5, because the firm delayed paying its creditors. Note that the increase in accounts payable to merchandise suppliers exceeds the increase in merchandise inventories each year. Cash flow from operations was not sufficient in Year 5 to finance the substantial growth in capital expenditures. Amazon.com used a mixture of long-term debt and common stock to finance these long-term assets. The firm invested a portion of the financing obtained that was not needed during Year 5 in marketable securities, allowing the remaining excess to increase the balance in its cash account. Given its rapid growth, Amazon.com will likely need the excess cash to finance capital expenditures in the near future.

4.15 (Yahoo, Inc.; calculating and interpreting cash flows.)

a. **Year 8**

(Increases) Decreases in Assets	Balance Sheet Changes	Operations	Investing	Financing
Marketable Securities	$ (60,689)		$ (60,689)	
Accounts Receivable	(4,267)	$ (4,267)		
Prepayments	(384)	(384)		
Property, Plant and Equipment (at Cost).....	(3,155)		(3,155)	
Accumulated Depreciation	552	552		
Investment in Securities .	(10,477)		(10,477)	
Increases (Decreases) in Liabilities and Shareholders' Equity				
Accounts Payable	1,086	1,086		
Other Current Liabilities	6,447	6,447		
Common Stock	103,796			$ 103,796
Retained Earnings	(4,659)	(4,659)		
Increase (Decrease) in Cash.............................	$ 28,250	$ (1,225)	$ (74,321)	$ 103,796

Year 9

(Increases) Decreases in Assets	Balance Sheet Changes	Operations	Investing	Financing
Marketable Securities	$ 32,917		$ 32,917	
Accounts Receivable	(5,904)	$ (5,904)		
Prepayments	(5,509)	(5,509)		
Property, Plant and Equipment (at Cost).....	(14,930)		(14,930)	
Accumulated Depreciation	2,554	2,554		
Investment in Securities .	(9,053)		(9,053)	
Increases (Decreases) in Liabilities and Shareholders' Equity				
Accounts Payable	3,605	3,605		
Other Current Liabilities	11,598	11,598		
Common Stock	36,980			$ 36,980
Retained Earnings	(23,267)	(23,267)		
Increase (Decrease) in Cash.............................	$ 28,991	$ (16,923)	$ 8,934	$ 36,980

4.15 continued.

b.

YAHOO, INC.
Statement of Cash Flows
For Year 8 and Year 9

	Year 8	Year 9
Operations:		
Net Income (Loss)	$ (4,659)	$(23,267)
Depreciation	552	2,554
(Increase) Decrease in Accounts Receivable	(4,267)	(5,904)
(Increase) Decrease in Prepayments	(384)	(5,509)
Increase (Decrease) in Accounts Payable	1,086	3,605
Increase (Decrease) in Other Current Liabilities	6,447	11,598
Cash Flow from Operations	$ (1,225)	$(16,923)
Investing:		
Acquisition of Property, Plant and Equipment...	$ (3,155)	$(14,930)
Sale of Marketable Securities	--	32,917
Acquisition of Marketable Securities.............	(60,689)	--
Acquisition of Investment in Securities.........	(10,477)	(9,053)
Cash Flow from Investing	$(74,321)	$ 8,934
Financing:		
Issue of Common Stock....................................	$103,796	$ 36,980
Increase (Decrease) in Cash	$ 28,250	$ 28,991
Cash, Beginning of Year..................................	5,297	33,547
Cash, End of Year..	$ 33,547	$ 62,538

c. Yahoo, Inc. operated at a loss and generated negative cash flow from operations each year. Such operating results are not unusual for a startup company. Although its expenditures on property, plant and equipment increased significantly between the two years, Yahoo, Inc. is not heavily capital intensive. The firm used common stock to finance its growth during the startup phase. The main resources of an internet service provider are its software and customer list, neither of which serve as safe collateral for borrowing. Yahoo, Inc., therefore, did not use long-term borrowing to finance itself. The firm did not need all of the cash immediately to finance operations and capital expenditures. It invested the excess cash in marketable securities and investments in securities. Yahoo, Inc. sold some of its marketable securities during Year 9 to provide cash for conducting its operations.

4.16   (Coca-Cola Company; preparing a columnar work sheet for a statement of cash flows from changes in balance sheet accounts.) (Amounts in Millions)

a.

	Balance Sheet Changes	Operations	Investing	Financing
(Increases) Decreases in Assets				
Accounts Receivable	$ (282)	$ (282)		
Inventories	2	2		
Prepayments	(38)	(38)		
Property, Plant and Equipment (at Cost)	(1,291)		$ 150	
			(1,441)	
Accumulated Depreciation ...	210	290	(80)	
Increases (Decreases) in Liabilities and Shareholders' Equity				
Accounts Payable	347	347		
Short-Term Borrowing..........	411			$ 411
Other Current Liabilities	248	248		
Bonds Payable.......................	195			345
				(150)
Common Stock	(1,104)			(1,104)
Retained Earnings	1,755	2,761		(1,006)
Increase (Decrease) in Cash	$ 453	$ 3,328	$ (1,371)	$ (1,504)

b.   The Coca-Cola Company is a relatively mature and profitable firm. Its cash flow from operations was more than sufficient to finance capital expenditures. It used the excess to pay dividends and repurchase outstanding common stock.

4.17   (Delta Airlines; preparing a statement of cash flows from changes in balance sheet accounts.)

a.   DELTA AIRLINES
                      Statement of Cash Flows
                          For the Year
                      (Amounts in Millions)

Operations:
   Net Income .... $ 303
   Additions:
       Depreciation Expense ($363 + $96)   459
       Loss on Sale of Equipment [$30 – ($151 – $96)]   25
       Decrease in Accounts Receivable   26
       Increase in Accounts Payable   14
   Subtractions:
       Increase in Inventories ....   (11)
       Increase in Prepayments ....   (19)
       Decrease in Other Current Liabilities ....   (32)
Cash Flow from Operations .... $ 765
Investing:
   Sale of Equipment .... $ 30
   Acquisition of Property, Plant and Equipment
       ($1,219 + $151) .... (1,370)
   Acquisition of Securities ....   (345)
Cash Flow from Investing .... $ (1,685)
Financing:
   Increase in Notes Payable .... $ 88
   Increase in Long-term Debt   674
   Decrease in Common Stock ....   (187)
   Dividends Paid ($303 – $186) ....   (117)
Cash Flow from Financing .... $ 458
Net Change in Cash .... $ (462)
Cash, Beginning of Year   530
Cash, End of Year .... $ 68

b.   Cash flow from operations exceeds net income primarily because of the addback for depreciation expense. Cash flow from operations was insufficient to finance acquisitions of investments and plant and equipment so Delta Airlines relied on external borrowing, primarily long-term debt. Delta Airlines also repurchased shares of its common stock during the year, thereby increasing the proportion of debt in its capital structure.

4.18   (Upjohn; calculating and interpreting cash flow from operations.)

a.

Net Income	$ 489[a]
Additions:	
Depreciation Expense	163
Decrease in Accounts Receivable	3
Increase in Accounts Payable	58
Increase in Other Current Liabilities	62
Subtraction:	
Increase in Inventories	(46)
Increase in Prepayments	(195)
Cash Flow from Operations	$ 534

[a]$489 = $3,275 − $163 − $154 − $2,469.

b.   The production of pharmaceutical products is capital intensive. Upjohn reports a significant addback for depreciation, a noncash expense. Cash flow from operations was reduced during the year by a substantial increase in prepayments.

4.19   (L.A. Gear; calculating and interpreting cash flow from operations.)

a.   (Amounts in Millions)

	Year 8	Year 9	Year 10	Year 11
Net Income (Loss)	$ 22	$ 55	$ 31	$ (68)
Depreciation Expense	1	1	3	7
(Inc.) Dec. in Accounts Receivable	(35)	(51)	(56)	48
(Inc.) Dec. in Inventories	(51)	(73)	(21)	20
(Inc.) Dec. in Prepayments	(2)	(13)	(1)	(25)
Inc. (Dec.) in Accounts Payable	7	18	(4)	(15)
Inc. (Dec.) in Other Current Liabilities	12	13	7	7
Cash Flow from Operations	$ (46)	$ (50)	$ (41)	$ (26)

b.   Cash flow from operations is negative during Year 8, Year 9, and Year 10 despite positive earnings for each year because of the increases in accounts receivable and inventories. L.A. Gear, however, did not increase its accounts payable to finance the increased inventories. The negative cash flow from operations during Year 11 results primarily from the net loss from operations. Sales probably declined between Year 10 and Year 11, leading to decreased investment in accounts receivable and inventories and payment of accounts payable. Note that L.A. Gear is not capital intensive, so the depreciation addback is not significant.

4.20   (Kelly Services; calculating and interpreting cash flows.)

a.
KELLY SERVICES
Comparative Statement of Cash Flows
(Amounts in Thousands)

	Year 3	Year 4	Year 5
Operations			
Net Income	$ 39,225	$ 44,559	$ 61,057
Depreciation	13,977	16,614	17,309
(Inc.) Dec. in Accounts Receivable	(32,273)	(39,116)	(59,317)
(Inc.) Dec. in Prepayments	(2,340)	(2,656)	(9,137)
Inc. (Dec.) in Salaries Payable	14,793	14,465	34,460
Inc. (Dec.) in Other Current Liabilities	(21,203)	12,600	20,241
Cash Flow from Operations	$ 12,179	$ 46,466	$ 64,613
Investing			
Acquisition of Property, Plant and Equipment	$(32,449)	$(16,056)	$(18,433)
Decrease in Marketable Securities	31,571	9,614	2,265
Cash Flow from Investing	$ (878)	$ (6,442)	$(16,168)
Financing			
Common Stock Issued	$ 1,617	$ 1,031	$ 373
Dividends Paid	(21,999)	(23,846)	(26,570)
Cash Flow from Financing	$(20,382)	$(22,815)	$(26,197)
Change in Cash	$ (9,081)	$ 17,209	$ 22,248

b.   Net income and cash flow from operations both increased during the three-year period. Cash flow from operations was significantly less than net income during Year 3 but approximately the same in Year 4 and Year 5. Kelly Services repaid other current liabilities during Year 3, lowering cash flow from operations. The relation between Year 4 and Year 5 is typical of a service loan.

Expenditures for property, plant and equipment decreased in Year 4 and Year 5 relative to Year 3. Perhaps Kelly Services made significant expenditures on computer equipment during Year 3. Cash flow from operations was sufficient to finance capital expenditures in Year 4 and Year 5, but not in Year 3. Kelly Services sold marketable securities during Year 3 (as well as Year 4 and Year 5) to fund capital expenditures.

Kelly Services increased its dividends each year as net income increased, but dividends increased more slowly. The excess cash flow increased cash on the balance sheet.

4.21   (American Airlines; working backwards from changes in buildings and equipment account.)

Buildings and Equipment (Original Cost)		Accumulated Depreciation	
Balance, 12/31/Year 3	$16,825	Balance, 12/31/Year 3	$4,914
Outlays in Year 4	1,314	Depreciation in Year 4	1,253
	$18,139		$6,167
Balance, 12/31/Year 4	17,369	Balance, 12/31/Year 4	5,465
Retirements in Year 4........	$ 770	Retirements in Year 4	$ 702

$$\text{Proceeds} = \text{Book Value}$$
$$= \$770 - \$702$$
$$= \$68.$$

4.22   (Largay Corporation; effects of gains and losses from sales of equipment on cash flows.) (Amounts in Thousands)

	a.	b.	c.
Operations:			
Net Income	$ 100	$ 102	$ 98
Depreciation Expense	15	15	15
Gain on Sale of Equipment	--	(2)	--
Loss on Sale of Equipment	--	--	2
Changes in Working Capital Accounts ...	(40)	(40)	(40)
Cash Flow from Operations........................	$ 75	$ 75	$ 75
Investing:			
Sale of Equipment	$ 10	$ 12	$ 8
Acquisition of Buildings and Equipment	(30)	(30)	(30)
Cash Flow from Investing	$ (20)	$ (18)	$ (22)
Financing:			
Repayment of Long-term Debt...............	$ (40)	$ (40)	$ (40)
Change in Cash	$ 15	$ 17	$ 13
Cash, Beginning of Year	27	27	27
Cash, End of Year	$ 42	$ 44	$ 40

4.23   (Effect of various transactions on statement of cash flows.)

If you use transparencies in class, it is effective to flash onto the screen the answer transparency for some problem showing a comprehensive statement of cash flows. Then you can point to the lines affected as the students attempt to answer the question. It helps them by letting them see the possibilities. We use this question for in-class discussion. We seldom assign it for actual homework. A favorite form of question for examinations is to present a schematic statement of cash flows and to ask which lines certain transactions affect and how much. When we use this problem in class, we invariably tell students that it makes a good examination question; this serves to strengthen their interest in the discussion.

a. (1) Decreases by $600; reduces net income through amortization expense.
    (2) Increases by $600; amount of expense is added back to net income in deriving cash flow from operations.
    No effect on net cash flow from operations.

b. The transaction does not appear in the statement of cash flows because it does not affect cash. The firm must disclose information about the transaction in a supplemental schedule or note.

c. (2) Increases by $7,500; operating increase in cash from increase in Accounts Payable.
    (3) Increases by $7,500; operating decrease in cash for increase in inventory.
    The net effect of these two transactions is to leave cash from operations unchanged, because the amounts added and subtracted change in such a way as to cancel out each other.

d. (1) Decreases by $1,500; net income goes down.
    (2) Increases by $1,500; additions go up because inventory, not cash, was destroyed.

e. (2) Increases by $1,450; operating increase in cash reflected by decrease in the amount of Accounts Receivable.
    (9) Increases by $1,450.

f. (6) Increases by $10,000; increase in cash from security issue.
    (9) Increases by $10,000.

g. (4) Increases by $4,500; increase in cash from sale of noncurrent asset.
    (9) Increases by $4,500.

4.24   (The GAP; preparing and interpreting the statement of cash flows using a columnar work sheet.) (Amounts in Millions)

a. **Year 6**

	Balance Sheet Changes	Operations	Investing	Financing
(Increases) Decreases in Assets				
Marketable Securities	$ (46)		$ (46)	
Merchandise Inventories	(96)	$ (96)		
Prepayments	(1)	(1)		
Property, Plant and Equipment (at Cost)	(372)		(372)	
Accumulated Depreciation ...	215	215		
Other Noncurrent Assets	(51)		(51)	
Increases (Decreases) in Liabilities and Shareholders' Equity				
Accounts Payable—Merchandise Suppliers	114	114		
Notes Payable to Banks	18			$ 18
Income Taxes Payable	26	26		
Other Current Liabilities	90	90		
Common Stock	(360)			(360)
Retained Earnings	369	453		(84)
Increase (Decrease) in Cash	$ (94)	$ 801	$ (469)	$ (426)

4.24 a. continued.

Year 7

(Increases) Decreases in Assets	Balance Sheet Changes	Operations	Investing	Financing
Marketable Securities	$ 46		$ 46	
Merchandise Inventories	(154)	$ (154)		
Prepayments	(56)	(56)		
Property, Plant and Equipment (at Cost)	(466)		(466)	
Accumulated Depreciation ...	270	270		
Other Noncurrent Assets	(15)		(15)	
Increases (Decreases) in Liabilities and Shareholders' Equity				
Accounts Payable—Merchandise Suppliers	134	134		
Notes Payable to Banks........	45			$ 45
Income Taxes Payable	(7)	(7)		
Other Current Liabilities	123	123		
Bonds Payable......................	577			577
Common Stock	(524)			(524)
Retained Earnings	455	534		(79)
Increase (Decrease) in Cash...................................	$ 428	$ 844	$ (435)	$ 19

4.24 continued.

b.

THE GAP
Statement of Cash Flows
For Year 6 and Year 7

	Year 6	Year 7
Operations:		
Net Income	$ 453	$ 534
Depreciation	215	270
(Increase) Decrease in Merchandise Inventories ..	(96)	(154)
(Increase) Decrease in Prepayments	(1)	(56)
Increase (Decrease) in Accounts Payable—		
Merchandise Suppliers	114	134
Increase (Decrease) in Income Taxes Payable	26	(7)
Increase (Decrease) in Other Current Liabil-		
ities	90	123
Cash Flow from Operations	$ 801	$ 844
Investing:		
Acquisition of Property, Plant and Equipment	$ (372)	$ (466)
Sale of Marketable Securities	--	46
Acquisition of Marketable Securities	(46)	--
Acquisition of Other Noncurrent Assets	(51)	(15)
Cash Flow from Investing	$ (469)	$ (435)
Financing:		
Increase in Short-Term Borrowing	$ 18	$ 45
Increase in Long-Term Borrowing	--	577
Decrease in Common Stock	(360)	(524)
Dividends	(84)	(79)
Cash Flow from Financing	$ (426)	$ 19
Increase (Decrease) in Cash	$ (94)	$ 428
Cash, Beginning of Year	580	486
Cash, End of Year	$ 486	$ 914

4.24 continued.

c. **Year 6**

	Income Statement Account	+	Operating Balance Sheet Changes	=	Cash Receipts	−	Cash Disbursements	=	Cash Flow from Operations
Sales	$ 5,284				$ 5,284				
Cost of Goods Sold........	(3,285)		$ (96)				$(3,267)		
			114						
Selling and Administrative Expenses........	(1,250)		(1)				(946)		
			215						
			90						
Income Tax Expense....	(296)		26				(270)		
Net Income	$ 453	+	$ 348	=	$ 5,284	−	$(4,483)	=	$ 801

Year 7

	Income Statement Account	+	Operating Balance Sheet Changes	=	Cash Receipts	−	Cash Disbursements	=	Cash Flow from Operations
Sales	$ 6,508				$ 6,508				
Cost of Goods Sold........	(4,022)		$(154)				$(4,042)		
			134						
Selling and Administrative Expenses........	(1,632)		(56)				(1,295)		
			270						
			123						
Income Tax Expense....	(320)		(7)				(327)		
Net Income	$ 534	+	$ 310	=	$ 6,508	−	$(5,664)	=	$ 844

d. Cash flow from operations exceeded net income each year primarily because of the addback for depreciation and the delay in paying Other Current Liabilities. Cash flow from operations was more than sufficient to finance acquisition of property, plant and equipment. The Gap used its excess cash flow during each year to repurchase shares of its common stock. The firm increased its long-term borrowing in Year 7, thereby increasing the balance in its cash account.

4.25 (Circuit City; preparing and interpreting the statement of cash flows using a columnar work sheet.) (Amounts in Millions)

a. **Year 7**

	Balance Sheet Changes	Operations	Investing	Financing
(Increases) Decreases in Assets				
Accounts Receivable	$ (208)	$ (208)		
Merchandise Inventories	(69)	(69)		
Prepayments	8	8		
Property, Plant and Equipment (at Cost)	(209)		$ (209)	
Accumulated Depreciation ...	99	99		
Increases (Decreases) in Liabilities and Shareholders' Equity				
Accounts Payable—Merchandise Suppliers	117	117		
Notes Payable to Banks	(92)			$ (92)
Other Current Liabilities	(71)	(71)		
Bonds Payable	31			31
Common Stock	428			428
Retained Earnings	125	136		(11)
Increase (Decrease) in Cash .	$ 159	$ 12	$ (209)	$ 356

Year 8

	Balance Sheet Changes	Operations	Investing	Financing
(Increases) Decreases in Assets				
Accounts Receivable	$ (66)	$ (66)		
Merchandise Inventories	(19)	(19)		
Prepayments	15	15		
Property, Plant and Equipment (at Cost)	(291)		$ (291)	
Accumulated Depreciation ...	116	116		
Increases (Decreases) in Liabilities and Shareholders' Equity				
Accounts Payable—Merchandise Suppliers	44	44		
Notes Payable to Banks	27			$ 27
Other Current Liabilities	(9)	(9)		
Bonds Payable	(19)			(19)
Common Stock	25			25
Retained Earnings	91	104		(13)
Increase (Decrease) in Cash .	$ (86)	$ 185	$ (291)	$ 20

4.25 continued.

b.
CIRCUIT CITY
Statement of Cash Flows
For Year 7 and Year 8

	Year 7	Year 8
Operations:		
Net Income	$ 136	$ 104
Depreciation	99	116
(Increase) Decrease in Accounts Receivable	(208)	(66)
(Increase) Decrease in Merchandise Inventories	(69)	(19)
(Increase) Decrease in Prepayments	8	15
Increase (Decrease) in Accounts Payable— Merchandise Suppliers	117	44
Increase (Decrease) in Other Current Liabilities	(71)	(9)
Cash Flow from Operations	$ 12	$ 185
Investing:		
Acquisition of Property, Plant and Equipment	$ (209)	$ (291)
Financing:		
Increase (Decrease) in Short-Term Borrowing	$ (92)	$ 27
Increase (Decrease) in Long-Term Borrowing	31	(19)
Increase (Decrease) in Common Stock	428	25
Dividends	(11)	(13)
Cash Flow from Financing	$ 356	$ 20
Increase (Decrease) in Cash	$ 159	$ (86)
Cash, Beginning of Year	44	203
Cash, End of Year	$ 203	$ 117

c.

	Year 7	Year 8
Sales Revenue	$ 7,664	$ 8,871
Less Increase in Accounts Receivable	(208)	(66)
Cash Collected from Customers	$ 7,456	$ 8,805

d.

	Year 7	Year 8
Cost of Goods Sold	$ (5,903)	$ (6,827)
Plus Increase in Inventories	(69)	(19)
Less Increase in Accounts Payable—Merchandise Suppliers	117	44
Cash Collected from Customers	$ (5,855)	$ (6,802)

e.

	Year 7	Year 8
Selling and Administrative Expenses	$ (1,511)	$ (1,849)
Plus Decrease in Prepayments	8	15
Less Increase in Other Current Liabilities	71	9
Plus Depreciation	99	116
Cash Paid to Suppliers of Selling and Administrative Services	$ (1,333)	$ (1,709)

4.25 continued.

 f. Cash flow from operations was significantly less than net income during Year 7, primarily because of a buildup of accounts receivable from customers. Circuit City financed its acquisitions of property, plant and equipment by issuing common stock. Cash flow from operations exceeded net income during Year 8 because of the addback in depreciation and a smaller increase in accounts receivable. Cash flow from operations was not sufficient to finance capital expenditures. Circuit City used cash on hand at the beginning of the year to finance the shortfall.

4.26 (Swan Corporation; preparing and interpreting a statement of cash flows using a columnar work sheet.)

a.

	Balance Sheet Changes	Operations	Investing	Financing
(Increases) Decreases in Assets				
Accounts Receivable	$(12,000)	$(12,000)		
Merchandise Inventories..	(20,000)	(20,000)		
Property, Plant and Equipment	(75,000)		$(75,000)	
Accumulated Depreci- ation	79,000	79,000		
Increases (Decreases) in Liabilities and Shareholders' Equity				
Accounts Payable	(25,000)	(25,000)		
Income Taxes Payable	5,000	5,000		
Bonds Payable...................	(4,000)			$ (4,000)
Common Stock	5,000			5,000
Retained Earnings	50,000	50,000		
Increase (Decrease) in Cash	$ 3,000	$ 77,000	$(75,000)	$ 1,000

4.26 continued.

b.

SWAN CORPORATION
Statement of Cash Flows
For the Current Year

Operations:

Net Income	$50,000	
Additions:		
Depreciation Expense	79,000	
Increase in Income Taxes Payable	5,000	
Subtractions:		
Increase in Accounts Receivable	(12,000)	
Increase in Merchandise Inventories	(20,000)	
Decrease in Accounts Payable	(25,000)	
Cash Flow from Operations		$77,000
Investing:		
Acquisition of Property, Plant, and Equipment		(75,000)
Financing:		
Issue of Common Stock	$ 5,000	
Retirement of Bonds	(4,000)	
Cash Flow from Financing		1,000
Net Change in Cash		$ 3,000
Cash, January 1		12,000
Cash, December 31		$15,000

c. Cash flow from operations was positive and sufficient to finance acquisitions of property, plant and equipment. The firm issued common stock to finance the retirement of long-term debt.

4.27   (Hale Company; preparing and interpreting a statement of cash flows using a T-account work sheet.)

a.

HALE COMPANY
Statement of Cash Flows
For the Year

Operations:		
Net Income	$ 44,000	
Additions:		
Depreciation Expense	54,000	
Increase in Accounts Payable	5,000	
Subtractions:		
Increase in Accounts Receivable	(13,000)	
Increase in Inventory	(11,000)	
Decrease in Interest Payable	(2,000)	
Cash Flow from Operations		$77,000
Investing:		
Sale of Equipment	$ 5,000	
Acquisition of Equipment	(55,000)	
Cash Flow from Investing		(50,000)
Financing:		
Dividends	$(10,000)	
Retirement of Portion of Mortgage Payable	(11,000)	
Cash Flow from Financing		(21,000)
Net Change in Cash		$ 6,000
Cash, January 1		52,000
Cash, December 31		$58,000

4.27 a. continued.

The amounts in the T-account work sheet below are in thousands.

Cash

√		52					

Operations

Net Income	(1)	44	13	(5)	Increase in Accounts Receivable	
Depreciation	(3)	54				
Increase in Accounts Payable	(8)	5	11	(6)	Increase in Inventory	
			2	(9)	Decrease in Interest Payable	

Investing

Sale of Equipment	(4)	5	55	(7)	Acquisition of Equipment

Financing

10	(2)	Dividends	
11	(10)	Payment of Mortgage Payable	

√		58	

Accounts Receivable		Inventory		Land	
√ 93		√ 151		√ 30	
(5) 13		(6) 11			
√ 106		√ 162		√ 30	

Buildings and Equipment (Cost)		Accumulated Depreciation		Accounts Payable	
√ 790			460 √		136 √
(7) 55	15 (4)	(4) 10	54 (3)		5 (8)
√ 830			504 √		141 √

Interest Payable		Mortgage Payable		Common Stock	
	10 √		120 √		250 √
(9) 2		(10) 11			
	8 √		109 √		250 √

4.27 a. continued.

Retained Earnings

		140	√
(2)	10	44	(1)
		174	√

b.
Sales Revenue	$ 1,200,000
Less Increase in Accounts Receivable ($106,000 – $93,000)	(13,000)
Cash Collected from Customers during the Year	$ 1,187,000

c.
Cost of Goods Sold	$ (788,000)
Less Increase in Inventories ($162,000 – $151,000)	(11,000)
Plus Increase in Accounts Payable for Inventory ($141,000 – $136,000)	5,000
Cash Paid to Suppliers of Inventory during the Year	$ (794,000)

d.
Interest Expense	$ (12,000)
Less Decrease in Interest Payable ($8,000 – $10,000)	(2,000)
Cash Paid for Interest during the Year	$ (14,000)

e. Cash flow from operations was sufficient to finance acquisitions of equipment during the year. The firm used the excess cash flow to pay dividends and retire long-term debt.

4.28   (Dickerson Manufacturing Company; preparing and interpreting a statement of cash flows using a T-account work sheet.)

a.   **DICKERSON MANUFACTURING COMPANY**
Statement of Cash Flows
For the Year

Operations:		
Net Income	$ 568,000	
Additions:		
Depreciation	510,000	
Loss on Sale of Machinery	5,000	
Increase in Accounts Payable	146,000	
Increase in Taxes Payable	16,000	
Increase in Short-Term Payables	138,000	
Subtractions:		
Increase in Accounts Receivable	(106,000)	
Increase in Inventory	(204,000)	
Cash Flow from Operations		$ 1,073,000
Investing:		
Sale of Machinery	$ 25,000	
Acquisition of Land	(36,000)	
Acquisition of Buildings and Machinery	(1,018,000)	
Cash Flow from Investing		(1,029,000)
Financing:		
Issue of Common Stock	$ 32,000	
Dividends Paid	(60,000)	
Bonds Retired	(50,000)	
Cash Flow from Financing		(78,000)
Net Change in Cash		$ (34,000)
Cash, January 1		358,000
Cash, December 31		$ 324,000

4.28 a. continued.

The amounts in the T-account work sheet below are in thousands.

Cash

√		358			

Operations

Net Income	(1)	568	106	(5)	Increase in Accounts Receivable
Depreciation Expense	(3)	510			
Loss on Sale of Equipment	(4)	5	204	(6)	Increase in Inventory
Increase in Accounts Payable	(9)	146			
Increase in Taxes Payable	(10)	16			
Increase in Other Short-Term Payables	(11)	138			

Investing

Sale of Machinery	(4)	25	1,018	(7)	Acquisition of Buildings and Machinery
			36	(8)	Acquisition of Land

Financing

Issue of Common Stock	(13)	32	60	(2)	Dividends
			50	(12)	Retirement of Bonds

√		324	

Accounts Receivable

√	946	
(5)	106	
√	1,052	

Inventory

√	1,004	
(6)	204	
√	1,208	

Buildings and Machinery

√	8,678		
(7)	1,018	150	(4)
√	9,546		

Accumulated Depreciation—Buildings and Machinery

		3,974	√
(4)	120	510	(3)
		4,364	√

4.28 a. continued.

Land				Accounts Payable		
√	594				412	√
(8)	36				146	(9)
√	630				558	√

Taxes Payable				Other Short-Term Payables		
		274	√		588	√
		16	(10)		138	(11)
		290	√		726	√

Bonds Payable				Common Stock		
		1,984	√		1,672	√
(12)	50				32	(13)
		1,934	√		1,704	√

Retained Earnings			
		2,676	√
(2)	60	568	(1)
		3,184	√

b. Dickerson Manufacturing Company is heavily capital intensive. Its cash flow from operations exceeds net income because of the depreciation expense addback. Cash flow from operations appears substantial, but so are its expenditures for building and equipment. The firm's relatively low dividend payout rate suggests that it expects large capital expenditures to continue.

4.29 (Vincent Company; preparing an income statement and a statement of cash flows.)

a.
VINCENT COMPANY
Statement of Income and Retained Earnings
for the Year

Sales		$ 1,300,000
Gain on Sale of Equipment		6,000
Total Revenues		$ 1,306,000
Expenses:		
Cost of Goods Sold	$ 910,000	
Selling and Administrative Expenses	428,000	
Depreciation Expense	85,000	
Interest Expense	24,000	
Total Expenses		(1,447,000)
Net Loss for Year		$ (141,000)
Retained Earnings, January 1		176,000
Retained Earnings, December 31		$ 35,000

4.29 continued.

b.

VINCENT COMPANY
Statement of Cash Flows
For the Year

Operations:
Net Loss.. $(141,000)
Additions:
Depreciation 85,000
Decrease in Accounts Receivable 17,000
Decrease in Inventories 14,000
Subtractions:
Gain on Sale of Equipment .... (6,000)
Decrease in Accounts Payable .... (8,000)
Cash Flow from Operations .... $(39,000)
Investing:
Sale of Equipment... $ 70,000
Acquisition of Plant and Equipment .... (60,000)
Cash Flow from Investing 10,000
Financing:
Issue of Long-Term Debt 25,000
Net Change in Cash... $ (4,000)
Cash, January 1... 42,000
Cash, December 31 .... $ 38,000

The amounts in the T-account work sheet below are in thousands.

Cash

√ 42 |

Operations

Depreciation (2) | 85 | 141 | (1) Net Loss
Decrease in Ac- | | 6 | (4) Gain on Sale of
counts Receivable (5) | 17 | | Equipment
Decrease in Inven- | | 8 | (7) Decrease in Ac-
tories (6) | 14 | | counts Payable

Investing

Sale of Equipment (4)ª | 70 | 60 | (3) Acquisition of
| | | Plant and
| | | Equipment

Financing

Issue of Long- | |
Term Debt (8) | 25 |
√ 38 |

4.29 b. continued.

	Accounts Receivable		Merchandise Inventory		Plant and Equipment	
√	130		√ 216		√ 872	
		17 (5)		14 (6)	(3) 60	82 (4)ᵃ
√	113		√ 202		√ 850	

Accumulated Depreciation		Accounts Payable		Long-Term Debt	
	473 √		61 √		250 √
(4)ᵃ 18	85 (2)	(7) 8			25 (8)
	540 √		53 √		275 √

Common Stock		Retained Earnings	
	300 √		176 √
		(1) 141	
	300 √		35 √

ᵃ(4) Journal entry made at time of sale:

Cash...	70,000	
Accumulated Depreciation	18,000	
Plant and Equipment (Cost)		82,000
Gain on Sale of Equipment		6,000

Plug for Cash in this journal entry; plug for $82,000 amount in T-account for Plant and Equipment and for $18,000 amount in T-account for Accumulated Depreciation.

c. Although Vincent Company's heavy capital intensity resulted in a large addback for depreciation expense, its net loss from operations led to negative cash flow from operations. Sales of equipment and the issue of long-term debt provided the cash needed to cover the negative operating cash flow and fund capital expenditures.

4.30   (Clark Corporation; preparing and interpreting a statement of cash flows using a T-account work sheet.)

a.
CLARK CORPORATION
Statement of Cash Flows
For the Current Year

Operations:		
Net Income	$60,000	
Additions:		
Depreciation Expense..	22,000	
Increase in Accounts Payable	17,000	
Increase in Income Taxes Payable.......................	5,000	
Subtractions:		
Increase in Accounts Receivable	(20,000)	
Increase in Merchandise Inventories	(16,000)	
Cash Flow from Operations.....................................		$68,000
Investing:		
Sale of Property, Plant, and Equipment..............	$ 8,000	
Acquisition of Property, Plant, and Equipment..	(80,000)	
Cash Flow from Investing		(72,000)
Financing:		
Issue of Bonds	$10,000	
Dividends Paid	(10,000)	
Cash Flow from Financing		0
Net Change in Cash..		$ (4,000)
Cash, January 1		42,000
Cash, December 31		$ 38,000

4.30 a. continued.

The amounts in the T-account work sheet below are in thousands.

Cash

√	42				

Operations

Net Income	(1)	60	20	(7)	Increase in Accounts Receivable
Depreciation	(6)	22			
Increase in Accounts Payable	(9)	17	16	(8)	Increase in Merchandise Inventories
Increase in Income Taxes Payable	(10)	5			

Investing

Sale of Property, Plant, and Equipment	(5)	8	80	(3)	Property, Plant, and Equipment Acquired for Cash

Financing

Issue of Long-Term Debt for Cash	(11)	10	10	(2)	Dividends

√	38	

Accounts Receivable			
√	146		
(7)	20		
√	166		

Merchandise Inventories			
√	162		
(8)	16		
√	178		

Property, Plant, and Equipment			
√	180		
(3)	80		
(4)	20	14	(5)
√	266		

Accumulated Depreciation			
		62	√
(5)	6	22	(6)
		78	√

Accounts Payable			
		182	√
		17	(9)
		199	√

Income Taxes Payable			
		20	√
		5	(10)
		25	√

4.30 a. continued.

Bonds Payable		Common Stock		Retained Earnings		
	20 √		50 √			196 √
	20 (4)	(2)	10			60 (1)
	10 (11)					
	50 √		50 √			246 √

b. Clark Company generated cash flow from operations slightly in excess of net income. It used the operating cash flow to finance capital expenditures.

4.31 (Quebec Company; preparing a statement of cash flows over a 2-year period using a T-account work sheet.)

a.

QUEBEC COMPANY
Statement of Cash Flows
For Year 2

Operations:		
Net Income	$166,000	
Additions:		
Depreciation Expense..............................	174,000	
Decrease in Merchandise		
Inventories	20,000	
Subtractions:		
Increase in Accounts Receivable	(20,000)	
Decrease in Accounts Payable	(2,000)	
Cash Flow from Operations		$338,000
Investing:		
Sale of Property, Plant, and Equipment.....	$ 88,000	
Acquisition of Property, Plant, and		
Equipment..	(342,000)	
Cash Flow from Investing		(254,000)
Financing:		
Issue of Common Stock..............................	$ 92,000	
Dividends Paid	(80,000)	
Retirement of Bonds	(32,000)	
Cash Flow from Financing		(20,000)
Net Change in Cash.......................................		$ 64,000
Cash, January 1, Year 2		110,000
Cash, December 31, Year 2		$174,000

4.31 a. continued.

Cash

√	110			

Operations

Net Income	(1)	166[a]	20	(6)	Increase in Accounts Receivable
Depreciation	(3)	174			
Decrease in Merchandise Inventories	(7)	20	2	(8)	Decrease in Accounts Payable

Investing

| Sale of Property, Plant, and Equipment | (4) | 88[b] | 342 | (5) | Acquisition of Property, Plant, and Equipment |

Financing

| Issue of Common Stock | (10) | 92 | 80 | (2) | Dividends |
| | | | 32 | (9) | Retirement of Bonds |

√	174	

[a]See footnote a on following page.
[b]See footnote b on following page.

Accounts Receivable			Merchandise Inventories			Property, Plant, and Equipment		
√	220		√	250		√	3,232	
(6)	20				20 (7)	(5)	342	216[b](4)
√	240		√	230		√	3,358	

Accounts Payable			Accumulated Depreciation			Bonds Payable		
		162 √			1,394 √			212 √
(8)	2		(4)	128	174 (3)	(9)	32	
		160 √			1,440 √			180 √

4.31 a. continued.

Common Stock		Retained Earnings	
	754 √		1,290 √
92(10)	(2) 80		166[a](1)
	846 √		1,376 √

[a]$166 = \$1,820 + \$10 - \$740 - \$640 - \$174 - \$110$.

[b]Journal entry made at time of sale:

Cash (Plug)..	88	
Accumulated Depreciation	128	
Property, Plant, and Equipment.................		216

b.

QUEBEC COMPANY
Statement of Cash Flows
For Year 3

Operations:		
Net Income	$ 198,000	
Additions:		
Depreciation Expense............................	192,000	
Loss on Sale of Equipment......................	4,000	
Decrease in Accounts Receivable............	30,000	
Increase in Accounts Payable	6,000	
Subtractions:		
Increase in Merchandise Inventories	(50,000)	
Cash Flow from Operations		$ 380,000
Investing:		
Sale of Property, Plant, and Equipment.....	$ 98,000	
Acquisition of Property, Plant, and		
Equipment......................................	(636,000)	
Cash Flow from Investing		(538,000)
Financing:		
Issue of Bonds	$ 90,000	
Issue of Common Stock...............................	182,000	
Dividends Paid	(94,000)	
Cash Flow from Financing		178,000
Net Change in Cash......................................		$ 20,000
Cash, January 1, Year 3		174,000
Cash, December 31, Year 3		$ 194,000

4.31 b. continued.

The amounts in the T-account work sheet below are in thousands.

Cash

√	174		

Operations

Net Income	(1)	198[a]	50	(7)	Increase in Merchandise Inventories
Depreciation	(3)	192			
Loss on Sale of in Equipment	(5)	4			
Decrease in Accounts Receivable	(6)	30			
Increase in Accounts Payable	(8)	6			

Investing

Sale of Property, Plant, and Equipment	(5)	98[b]	636	(4)	Acquisition of Property, Plant, and Equipment

Financing

Issue of Bonds Payable	(9)	90	94	(2)	Dividends
Issue of Common Stock	(10)	182			
√		194			

[a]See footnote *a* on following page.
[b]See footnote *b* on following page.

Accounts Receivable				Merchandise Inventories				Property, Plant, and Equipment		
√	240			√	230			√	3,358	
		30 (6)	(7)		50		(4)		636	244[b] (5)
√	210			√	280			√	3,750	

Accounts Payable				Accumulated Depreciation				Bonds Payable		
		160	√			1,440	√			180 √
		6 (8)	(5)	142[b]		192 (3)				90 (9)
		166	√			1,490	√			270 √

4.31 b. continued.

Common Stock		Retained Earnings	
	846 √		1,376 √
	182(10) (2)	94	198ᵃ(1)
	1,028 √		1,480 √

ᵃ$198 = $1,940 + $14 − $826 − $602 − $192 − $4 − $132.

ᵇJournal entry made at time of sale:

Cash (Plug)..	98	
Accumulated Depreciation	142	
Loss on Sale of Equipment	4	
Property, Plant, and Equipment.................		244

c. During Year 2, cash flow from operations was more than sufficient to fund capital expenditures and pay dividends. The firm issued common stock and used the proceeds to retire debt and increase the amount of cash on hand. During Year 3, expenditures on property, plant and equipment increased significantly. Operating cash flows were insufficient to fund these capital expenditures and pay dividends, so the firm issued additional bonds and common stock.

4.32 (Quinta Company; working backwards through the statement of cash flows.)

QUINTA COMPANY
Balance Sheet
January 1, Year 5
($ in 000's)

Assets

Current Assets:

Cash..	$ 20	
Accounts Receivable	190	
Merchandise Inventories...............................	280	
Total Current Assets..................................		$490
Land..		50
Buildings and Equipment................................	$ 405	
Less Accumulated Depreciation......................	(160)	245
Investments...		140
Total Assets..		$925

4.32 continued.

Liabilities and Shareholders' Equity

Current Liabilities:
Accounts Payable .... $ 255
Other Current Liabilities 130
    Total Current Liabilities $385
Bonds Payable 60
Common Stock.. 140
Retained Earnings 340
    Total Liabilities and Shareholders'
      Equity $925

Shown below are T-accounts for deriving the solution. Entries (1)—(13) are reconstructed from the statement of cash flows. Changes for the year are appropriately debited or credited to end-of-year balances to get beginning-of-year balances. T-account amounts are shown in thousands.

Cash				Accounts Receivable			Merchandise Inventories	
	20				190			280
(1)	200	30	(4)	(4)	30		(5)	40
(2)	60	40	(5)					
(3)	25	45	(6)					
(7)	40	130	(10)					
(8)	15	200	(13)					
(9)	10							
(11)	60							
(12)	40							
√	25			√	220		√	320

Land				Buildings and Equipment				Investments		
	50				405				140	
		10	(9)	(10)	130	35	(8)			40 (7)
√	40			√	500			√	100	

Accumulated Depreciation				Accounts Payable				Other Current Liabilities		
		160				255				130
(8)	20	60	(2)			25	(3)	(6)	45	
		200	√			280	√			85 √

Bonds Payable			Common Stock			Retained Earnings		
		60			140			340
		40 (12)			60 (11)	(13)	200	200 (1)
		100 √			200 √			340 √

4.33   (RV Suppliers, Inc.; preparing and interpreting the statement of cash flows using the indirect method.)

This problem was adapted from financial statement data of Winnebago Industries for its 1973 and 1974 fiscal years. A statement of cash flows, and T-account work sheets for Year 5 and Year 6, follow.

The Year 5 period for RV Suppliers, Inc., shows results that are typical of those for a growing firm. Although net income is $34,600, cash flow from operations is only $4,000, due primarily to an increase in accounts receivable and inventories. To finance acquisitions of property, plant, and equipment, the firm relied on short-term bank borrowing. Sound financial policy usually dictates the financing of noncurrent assets with long-term debt or capital stock. The market prospects for recreational vehicles were sufficiently poor during this period that the firm was probably unable to tap the long-term credit and equity markets and had to use short-term bank financing.

The Year 6 period shows results that are typical of those for a firm experiencing a business contraction. Because of decreased sales, accounts receivable decreased and the level of inventories decreased. Cash flow generated from the decrease in receivables and inventories was used to pay off accounts payable. Operations was a net user of cash. The firm again financed acquisitions of property, plant, and equipment with short-term bank borrowing. The firm reduced drastically its rate of capital expenditures, however, during Year 6.

4.33 continued.

RV SUPPLIERS, INC.
Statement of Cash Flows
For Year 5 and Year 6

	Year 5	Year 6
Operations:		
Net Income (Loss)	$ 34.6	$ (13.4)
Plus Additions:		
Depreciation Expense	4.8	8.0
Decrease in Accounts Receivable	--	31.4
Decrease in Inventories	--	4.6
Decrease in Prepayments	--	1.8
Increase in Accounts Payable	21.8	--
Increase in Income Taxes Payable	1.2	--
Increase in Other Current Liabilities	2.6	--
Less Subtractions:		
Increase in Accounts Receivable	(26.8)	--
Increase in Inventories	(31.6)	--
Increase in Tax Refund Receivable	--	(5.0)
Increase in Prepayments	(2.6)	--
Decrease in Accounts Payable	--	(36.0)
Decrease in Income Taxes Payable	--	(7.0)
Decrease in Other Current Liabilities	--	(2.4)
Cash Flow from Operations	$ 4.0	$ (18.0)
Investing:		
Sale of Property, Plant, and Equipment	$ .4	$ 5.4
Acquisition of Property, Plant, and Equipment	(48.4)	(12.2)
Cash Flow from Investing	$ (48.0)	$ (6.8)
Financing:		
Bank Borrowing (Net)	$ 42.0	$ 18.0
Net Change in Cash	$ (2.0)	$ (6.8)

4.33 continued.

RV SUPPLIERS, INC.—YEAR 5

Cash

√	14.0		

Operations

(1)	34.6	26.8	(5)
(2)	4.8	31.6	(6)
(9)	21.8	2.6	(7)
(10)	1.2		
(11)	2.6		

Investing

(4)	.4	48.4	(3)

Financing

(8)	42.0		
√	12.0		

Accounts Receivable			Inventories			Prepayments	
√	28.8		√	54.0		√	4.8
(5)	26.8		(6)	31.6		(7)	2.6
√	55.6		√	85.6		√	7.4

Property, Plant, and Equipment (Net)				Bank Note Payable			Accounts Payable	
√	30.2				10.0 √		31.6	√
(3)	48.4	4.8	(2)		42.0 (8)		21.8	(9)
		.4	(4)					
√	73.4				52.0 √		53.4	√

Income Taxes Payable		Other Current Liabilities		Capital Stock	
	5.8 √		4.2 √		44.6 √
	1.2 (10)		2.6 (11)		
	7.0 √		6.8 √		44.6 √

Retained Earnings	
	35.6 √
	34.6 (1)
	70.2 √

4.33 continued.

RV SUPPLIERS, INC.—YEAR 6

Cash

√	12.0		

Operations

(2)	8.0	13.4	(1)
(5)	31.4	5.0	(7)
(6)	4.6	36.0	(10)
(8)	1.8	7.0	(11)
		2.4	(12)

Investing

(4)	5.4	12.2	(3)

Financing

(9)	18.0		
√	5.2		

Accounts Receivable

√	55.6		
		31.4	(5)
√	24.2		

Inventories

√	85.6		
		4.6	(6)
√	81.0		

Tax Refund Receivable

√	.0		
(7)	5.0		
√	5.0		

Prepayments

√	7.4		
		1.8	(8)
√	5.6		

Property, Plant, and Equipment (Net)

√	73.4		
(3)	12.2	8.0	(2)
		5.4	(4)
√	72.2		

Bank Note Payable

		52.0	√
		18.0	(9)
		70.0	√

Accounts Payable

		53.4	√
(10)	36.0		
		17.4	√

Income Taxes Payable

		7.0	√
(11)	7.0		
		0.0	√

Other Current Liabilities

		6.8	√
(12)	2.4		
		4.4	√

Capital Stock

		44.6	√
		44.6	√

Retained Earnings

		70.2	√
(1)	13.4		
		56.8	√

4.34   (Heidi's Hide-Out; inferring cash flows from trial balance data.)

a.   Sales Revenue from Retail Customers .... $ 120,000
    Less Increase in Accounts Receivable from Retail Cus-
      tomers ($8,900 – $8,000) .... (900)
    Plus Increase in Advances from Retail Customers
      ($10,000 – $9,000) .... $ 1,000
    Cash Collected from Retail Customers .... $ 120,100

b.   Rent Expense .... $ (33,000)
    Less Increase in Advances to Landlords ($5,600 –
      $5,000) .... (600)
    Less Decrease in Rent Payable to Landlords ($5,300 –
      $6,000) .... (700)
    Cash Paid to Landlords .... $ (34,300)

c.   Wage Expense .... $ (20,000)
    Less Increase in Advances to Employees ($1,500 –
      $1,000) .... (500)
    Less Decrease in Wages Payable to Employees ($1,800 –
      $2,000) .... (200)
    Cash Paid to Employees .... $ (20,700)

d.   Cost of Retail Merchandise Sold .... $ (90,000)
    Plus Decrease in Inventory of Retail Merchandise
      ($10,000 – $11,000) 1,000
    Less Increase in Advances to Suppliers of Retail Merchan-
      dise ($10,500 – $10,000) .... (500)
    Less Increase in Accounts Payable to Suppliers of Retail
      Merchandise ($7,700 – $8,000) .... (300)
    Cash Paid to Suppliers of Retail Merchandise .... $ (89,800)

4.35   (Digit Retail Enterprises, Inc.; inferring cash flows from balance sheet and income statement data.)

a.   Sales Revenue .... $ 270,000
    Less Increase in Accounts Receivable ($38,000 –
      $23,000) .... (15,000)
    Less Decrease in Advances from Customers ($6,100 –
      $8,500) .... $ (2,400)
    Cash Received from Customers during the Year .... $ 252,600

b.   Cost of Goods Sold .... $(145,000)
    Less Increase in Merchandise Inventory ($65,000 –
      $48,000) .... (17,000)
    Acquisition Cost of Merchandise Purchased during the
      Year .... $(162,000)

4.35 continued.

c.

Acquisition Cost of Merchandise Purchased during the Year (from Part *b.*)	$(162,000)
Plus Increase in Accounts Payable—Merchandise Suppliers ($20,000 – $18,000)	2,000
Cash Paid for Acquisitions of Merchandise during the Year	$(160,000)

d.

Salaries Expense	$ (68,000)
Plus Increase in Salaries Payable ($2,800 – $2,100)	700
Cash Paid to Salaried Employees during the Year	$ (67,300)

e.

Insurance Expense	$ (5,000)
Less Increase in Prepaid Insurance ($12,000 – $9,000)	(3,000)
Cash Paid to Insurance Companies during the Year	$ (8,000)

f.

Rent Expense	$ (12,000)
Plus Decrease in Prepaid Rent ($0 – $2,000)	2,000
Plus Increase in Rent Payable ($3,000 – $0)	3,000
Cash Paid to Landlords for Rental of Space during the Year	$ (7,000)

g.

Increase in Retained Earnings ($11,800 – $11,500)	$ 300
Less Net Income	(9,600)
Dividend Declared	$ (9,300)
Plus Decrease in Dividend Payable ($2,600 – $4,200)	(1,600)
Cash Paid for Dividends during the Year	$ 10,900

h.

Depreciation Expense	$ (20,000)
Plus Increase in Accumulated Depreciation ($35,000 – $20,000)	15,000
Accumulated Depreciation of Property, Plant and Equipment Sold	$ (5,000)
Cost of Property, Plant and Equipment Sold ($100,000 – $90,000)	10,000
Book Value of Property, Plant and Equipment Sold	$ 5,000
Plus Gain on Sale of Property, Plant and Equipment	3,200
Cash Received from Sale of Property, Plant and Equipment	$ 8,200

4.36   (NIKE, Inc.; interpreting the statement of cash flows.)

   a.   NIKE's growth in sales and net income led to increases of account receivable and inventories. NIKE, however, did not increase its accounts payable and other current operating liabilities to help finance the buildup in current assets. Thus, its cash flow from operations decreased.

   b.   NIKE increased its acquisitions of property, plant and equipment to provide the firm with operating capacity to sustain its rapid growth. NIKE also acquired investments in securities of other firms. It is not clear from the statement of cash flows whether the investments represented short-term investments of temporarily excess cash (a current asset) or long-term investments made to develop an operating relation with another firm (noncurrent asset).

   c.   NIKE used cash flow from operations during Year 7 and Year 8 to finance its investing activities. The excess cash flow after investing activities served to repay short- and long-term debt and pay dividends. Cash flow from operations during Year 9 was insufficient to finance investing activities. NIKE engaged in short-term borrowing to make up the shortfall and finance the payment of dividends.

   d.   Operating cash flows should generally finance the payment of dividends. Either operating cash flows or long-term sources of capital should generally finance acquisitions of property, plant and equipment. Thus, NIKE's use of short-term borrowing seems inappropriate. One might justify such an action if NIKE (1) expected cash flow from operations during Year 10 to return to its historical levels, (2) expected cash outflows for property, plant and equipment to decrease during Year 10, or (3) took advantage of comparatively low short-term borrowing rates during Year 9 and planned to refinance this debt with long-term borrowing during Year 10.

4.37   (Boise Cascade; interpreting the statement of cash flows.)

   a.   Forest products companies are capital intensive. Depreciation is therefore a substantial non-cash expense each year. The addback for depreciation converts a net loss each year into positive cash flow from operations. Note that cash flow from operations increased each year as the net loss decreased.

   b.   Boise Cascade had substantial changes in its property, plant and equipment during the three years. It likely built new, more efficient production facilities and sold off older, less efficient facilities.

4.37 continued.

    c. For the three years combined, Boise Cascade reduced its long-term debt and replaced it with preferred stock. The sales of forest products are cyclical. When the economy is in a recession, as apparently occurred during the three years, the high fixed cost of capital-intensive manufacturing facilities can result in net losses. If Boise Cascade is unable to repay debt on schedule during such years, it causes expensive financial distress or even bankruptcy. Firms have more latitude with respect to dividends on preferred stock than interest on debt. Thus, a shift toward preferred stock and away from long-term debt reduces the bankruptcy risk of Boise Cascade. Note that Boise Cascade continued to pay, and even increase, dividends despite operating at a net loss. Most shareholders prefer less rather than more fluctuation in their dividends over the business cycle.

4.38   (Interpreting the statement of cash flow relations.)

American Airlines—Property, plant and equipment comprises a large proportion of the total assets of American Airlines. Depreciation expense is a major expense for the airline. The firm operated at a net loss for the year, but the addback for depreciation resulted in a positive cash flow from operations. Cash flow from operations was not sufficient to fund capital expenditures on new property, plant and equipment. American Airlines is apparently growing since its capital expenditures exceed depreciation expense for the year. The firm financed its capital expenditures in part with cash flow from operations and in part with the issuance of additional long-term debt and capital stock. The net effect of the cash flow from financing is a reduction in liabilities and an increase in capital stock (actually preferred stock). Operating at a net loss increases the risk of bankruptcy. Perhaps American Airlines reduced the amount of debt in its capital structure to reduce fixed payment claims and substituted preferred stock that generally requires dividend payments only when declared by the board of directors.

American Home Products—Because of patent protection, pharmaceutical companies tend to generate relatively high profit margins and significant cash flows from operations. Although the manufacturing process for pharmaceutical products is capital intensive, cash flow from operations is usually sufficient to fund capital expenditures. American Home Products used the excess cash flow to pay dividends and repurchase capital stock. The firm also borrowed short-term funds and invested the proceeds in the acquisition of another business. Borrowing short term to finance investments in long-term assets is usually undesirable, because the firm must repay the debt before the long-term assets generate sufficient cash flow. Perhaps American Home Products needed to borrow short term to consummate the acquisition, with the expectation of refinancing the short-term debt with long-term borrowing soon after the acquisition. Alternatively, American Home Products might have anticipated a decline in long-term rates in the near future and borrowed short term until long-term rates actually declined.

4.38 continued.

Interpublic Group—An advertising agency serves as a link between clients desiring advertising time and space and various media with advertising time and space to sell. Thus, the principal asset of an advertising agency is accounts receivable from clients and the principal liability is accounts payable to various media. Interpublic Group reports an increase in accounts receivable of $66 million and an increase in accounts payable of $59 million. Thus, the firm appeared to manage its receivables/payables position well. Advertising agencies lease most of the physical facilities used in their operations. They purchase equipment for use in designing and producing advertising copy. Thus, they must make some capital expenditures. Cash flow from operations, however, is more than sufficient to finance acquisitions of equipment. Interpublic Group used the excess cash flow plus the proceeds of additional short- and long-term borrowing to pay dividends, repurchase capital stock, and increase cash on the balance sheet.

Proctor & Gamble—Proctor & Gamble's brand names create high profit margins and cash flows from operations. Cash flow from operations is more than adequate to finance capital expenditures. Note that capital expenditures significantly exceed depreciation, suggesting that the firm is still in a growth mode. The firm used the excess cash flow to repay short- and long-term debt and to pay dividends.

Reebok—Cash flow from operations for Reebok is less than net income plus depreciation, a somewhat unusual relationship for a seasoned firm. Reebok increased its accounts receivable and inventories during the year but did not stretch its accounts payable commensurably. The financing section of the statement of cash flows suggests that Reebok might have e used short-term debt to finance some of its working capital needs. Cash flow from operations was still more than sufficient to fund capital expenditures. One explanation for the sufficiency of cash flow from operations to cover capital expenditures is that Reebok is not very capital intensive. The relation between depreciation expense and net income supports this explanation. Reebok outsources virtually all of its manufacturing. Reebok used the excess cash flows from operating and investing activities to pay dividends and repurchase its capital stock.

Texas Instruments—Like American Home Products and Upjohn (discussed later), Texas Instruments invests heavily in technology to create a competitive advantage. Patents and copyrights on computer hardware, software, and other products serve as a barrier to entry by competitors and provide Texas Instruments with an attractive profit margin. Texas Instruments differs from the two pharmaceutical companies with respect to the amount of depreciation relative to net income. Despite generating less than one-half of the net income of American Home Products, Texas Instruments has more than twice the amount of depreciation expense and capital expenditures. Thus, Texas Instruments is likely more capital intensive than the other two technology-

4.38 continued.

based companies. Note that the changes in individual working capital accounts are relatively large, compared to the amount of net income. These relations suggest, although do not prove, that the operations of Texas Instruments grew significantly during the year. Cash flow from operations was sufficient to fund capital expenditures and increase the balance of cash on the balance sheet. Note that Texas Instruments issued capital stock during the year and repaid long-term debt. The amounts involved, however, are small.

The Limited—Current assets and current liabilities dominate the balance sheets of retailers. Thus, working capital management is of particular importance. The Limited increased its current liabilities in line with increases in accounts receivable and inventories. Thus, cash flow from operations approximately equals net income plus depreciation. The Limited invested most of the cash flow from operations in additional property, plant and equipment, the acquisition of other businesses, the repayment of short-term debt, and the payment of dividends.

Upjohn—This problem includes Upjohn primarily to compare and contrast it with American Home Products, also a pharmaceutical company. Both companies generated sufficient cash flow from operations to fund capital expenditures and pay dividends. Upjohn sold a portion of its business during the year and invested the proceeds in marketable securities.

CHAPTER 5

INTRODUCTION TO FINANCIAL STATEMENT ANALYSIS

Questions, Exercises, Problems, and Cases: Answers and Solutions

5.1   See the text or the glossary at the end of the book.

5.2   1.   The firm may have changed its methods of accounting over time.

       2.   The firm may have changed its product lines, production techniques, investment or financing strategies, or even its managerial personnel.

5.3   1.   The firms may use different methods of accounting.

       2.   The firms may pursue different operating, investing, or financing strategies, so that they have different technologies, production techniques, and selling strategies.

5.4   The adjustment in the numerator of rate of return on assets is for the *incremental* effect on *net* income of having versus not having interest expense.   Because interest expense reduces taxable income and, therefore, income taxes otherwise payable, the tax savings from interest expense incrementally affect net income.   The computation of the numerator must, therefore, incorporate this tax effect.

5.5   The first company apparently has a relatively small profit margin and must rely on turnover to generate a satisfactory rate of return.   A discount department store is an example.   The second company, on the other hand, has a larger profit margin and does not need as much turnover as the first company to generate a satisfactory rate of return.

5.6   Management strives to keep its inventories at a level that is neither too low so that it loses sales nor too high so that it incurs high storage costs.   Thus, there is an optimal level of inventory for a particular firm in a particular period and an optimal inventory turnover ratio.

5.7   The rate of return on common shareholders' equity exceeds the rate of return on assets when the latter rate exceeds the return required by creditors and preferred shareholders (net of tax effects).   In this situation, leverage is working to the benefit of the common shareholders. The rate of return on common shareholders' equity will be less than the return on assets when the latter rate is less than the return required by creditors and preferred shareholders. This situation generally occurs during periods of very poor earnings performance.

5.8   This statement suggests that the difference between the rate of return on assets and the aftertax cost of debt is positive but small. Increasing the amount of debt will require a higher interest rate that will eliminate this positive difference and leverage will work to the disadvantage of the common shareholders.

5.9   Financial leverage involves using debt capital that has a smaller aftertax cost than the return a firm can generate from investing the capital in various assets. The excess return belongs to the common shareholders. A firm cannot continually increase the amount of debt in the capital structure without limit. Increasing the debt level increases the risk to the common shareholders. These shareholders will not tolerate risk levels that they consider too high. Also, the cost of borrowing increases as a firm assumes larger proportions of debt. Sooner or later, the excess of the rate of return on assets over the aftertax cost of borrowing approaches zero or even becomes negative. Leverage then works to the disadvantage of the common shareholders.

5.10

	Dec. 31, Year 1	Dec. 31, Year 2
Current Assets	$ 800,000	$ 600,000
Current Liabilities	(400,000)	(240,000)
Working Capital	$ 400,000	$ 360,000
Current Ratio	2:1	2.5:1

5.11   (Cracker Barrel Old Country Store and Outback Steakhouse; calculating and disaggregating rate of return on assets.)

a.   **Cracker Barrel:** $\dfrac{\$104,136 + (1 - .35)(\$3,026)}{\$910,407}$ = 11.7 percent.

   Outback: $\dfrac{\$91,273 + (1 - .35)(\$2,489)}{\$531,312}$ = 17.5 percent.

b.

Rate of Return on Assets	=	Profit Margin Ratio	X	Total Asset Turnover Ratio
Cracker Barrel:				
$\dfrac{\$104,136 + (1 - .35)(\$3,026)}{\$910,407}$	=	$\dfrac{\$104,136 + (1 - .35)(\$3,026)}{\$1,317,104}$	X	$\dfrac{\$1,317,104}{\$910,407}$
11.7 percent	=	8.1 percent	X	1.45
Outback:				
$\dfrac{\$91,273 + (1 - .35)(\$2,489)}{\$531,312}$	=	$\dfrac{\$91,273 + (1 - .35)(\$2,489)}{\$1,151,637}$	X	$\dfrac{\$1,151,637}{\$531,312}$
17.5 percent	=	8.1 percent	X	2.17

5.11 continued.

    c. The analyst might expect Cracker Barrel to have a lower profit margin and a higher asset turnover, given its value pricing policy and the serving of meals all day. Cracker Barrel's profit margin on its restaurants is probably lower than that of Outback. The similar overall profit margins probably result from the ability of Cracker Barrel to generate a higher profit margin on craft items than on its restaurants. The higher asset turnover of Outback may result from locating its restaurants in buildings that were formerly restaurants, perhaps purchasing the properties for lower costs and bypassing zoning and other regulatory costs. Another possible explanation for the faster assets turnover of Outback is that it just serves meals, whereas Cracker Barrel must maintain an inventory of craft items that turn over less rapidly than food.

5.12   (TJX and The GAP; profitability analysis for two types of retailers.)

Company A is the specialty retailer (The GAP) because of its higher profit margin and lower total assets turnover, relative to Company B (TJX).

	Rate of Return On Assets	=	Profit Margin Ratio	X	Total Assets Turnover Ratio
Company A:	$\dfrac{\$533,901 + (1 - .35)(\$0)}{\$2,982,215}$	=	$\dfrac{\$533,901 + (1 - .35)(\$0)}{\$6,507,825}$	X	$\dfrac{\$6,507,825}{\$2,982,215}$
	17.9 percent	=	8.2 percent	X	2.18
Company B:	$\dfrac{\$306,592 + (1 - .35)(\$4,502)}{\$2,585,422}$	=	$\dfrac{\$306,592 + (1 - .35)(\$4,502)}{\$7,389,069}$	X	$\dfrac{\$7,389,069}{\$2,585,422}$
	12.0 percent	=	4.2 percent	X	2.86

5.13   (Gateway 2000 and Sun Microsystems; analyzing accounts receivable for two companies.)

    a.   **Gateway 2000**   **Sun Microsystems**

$$\frac{\$7,866,656}{.5(\$562,154 + \$638,349)} \qquad \frac{\$9,790,840}{.5(\$1,666,523 + \$1,845,765)}$$

$$= 13.1 \text{ Times per Year.} \qquad = 5.6 \text{ Times per Year.}$$

    b. $\dfrac{365}{13.1} = 27.9$ days. $\dfrac{365}{5.6} = 65.2$ days.

5.13 continued.

    c.   Gateway 2000 sells primarily to individuals who pay with credit cards. Gateway 2000 collects these accounts receivable quickly. Sun Microsystems sells to businesses. Customers may require Sun Microsystems to finance their purchases. Customers may also delay paying Sun Microsystems until their computers are set up and working properly. Sun Microsystems may also offer liberal credit terms as an inducement to businesses to purchase its computers.

5.14   (Kellogg; analyzing inventories over three years.)

a.

Year	Numerator	Denominator	Inventory Turnover
6	$3,178	$387	8.21
7	3,123	401	7.79
8	3,270	430	7.60

b.

Year	Numerator	Denominator	Days Inventory Held
6	365	8.21	44.5
7	365	7.79	46.9
8	365	7.60	48.0

c.

Year	Numerator	Denominator	Cost of Goods Sold Percentage
6	$3,178	$7,004	45.4%
7	3,123	6,677	46.8%
8	3,270	6,830	47.9%

    d.   Kellogg experienced a decreasing inventory turnover and an increasing cost of goods sold to sales percentage. Sales declined between Year 6 and Year 7 and increased only 2.3 percent [= ($6,830/$6,677) – 1] between Year 7 and Year 8. Kellogg experienced difficulty moving its products during this period. It might have lowered prices in an effort to sell cereals, leading to an increasing cost of goods sold percentage. The decreasing inventory turnover suggests either that Kellogg did not obtain the increased volume of sales it anticipated from the lower prices or that Kellogg continued to produce cereals at its usual rate to keep its factories open and workers hired, or some combination of the two.

5.15   (Anheuser Busch; analyzing fixed asset turnover over three years.)

a.

Year	Numerator	Denominator	Plant Asset Turnover
3	$10,345	$6,629	1.56
4	10,884	6,986	1.56
5	11,066	7,479	1.48

b.   The fixed asset turnover was flat between Year 3 and Year 4, suggesting that sales of Anheuser Busch increased in line with additions to property, plant and equipment. Anheuser Busch increased its capital expenditures significantly in Year 5 and the fixed asset turnover declined. Firms seldom experience increases in sales immediately when they purchase new fixed assets. Thus, the decline in the fixed asset turnover in Year 5 is not a cause for concern.

5.16   (Circuit City; calculating and disaggregating rate of return on common shareholders' equity.)

a.

Year	Numerator	Denominator	Rate of Return on Common Shareholders' Equity
4	$179	$971	18.4%
5	136	1,339	10.2%
6	104	1,672	6.2%

b.   **Profit margin**

Year	Numerator	Denominator	Profit Margin
4	$179	$7,029	2.5%
5	136	7,664	1.8%
6	104	8,871	1.2%

Total Asset Turnover

Year	Numerator	Denominator	Total Asset Turnover
4	$7,029	$2,265	3.10
5	7,664	2,804	2.73
6	8,871	3,156	2.81

Leverage Ratio

Year	Numerator	Denominator	Leverage Ratio
4	$2,265	$971	2.33
5	2,804	1,339	2.09
6	3,156	1,672	1.89

5.16 continued.

    c.   The rate of return on common shareholders' equity declined steadily during the three-year period. Although Circuit City experienced increased sales, its profit margin probably declined because of increased competition from other superstores (for example, Best Buy) and purchases over the Internet. The total assets turnover declined between Year 4 and Year 5 and increased slightly in Year 6. Circuit City may have opened new stores expecting more growth in sales than it realized. The decreased financial leverage might have resulted from reductions in debt, to increases in common stock, or the retention of earnings. An examination of the financial statements for Circuit City indicates that most of the decreased leverage ratio results from issuing additional common stock.

5.17   (Profitability analysis for three companies.)

a.

	Rate of Return on Assets	=	Profit Margin	X	Total Asset Turnover
Company A:	$\dfrac{\$69}{\$925}$	=	$\dfrac{\$69}{\$1,308}$	X	$\dfrac{\$1,308}{\$925}$
	7.5 percent	=	5.3 percent	X	1.41
Company B:	$\dfrac{\$174}{\$1,449}$	=	$\dfrac{\$174}{\$1,763}$	X	$\dfrac{\$1,763}{\$1,449}$
	12.0 percent	=	9.9 percent	X	1.22
Company C:	$\dfrac{\$359}{\$3,985}$	=	$\dfrac{\$359}{\$3,817}$	X	$\dfrac{\$3,813}{\$3,985}$
	9.0 percent	=	9.4 percent	X	.96

5.17 continued.

b.

	Rate of Return on Common Shareholders Equity	=	Profit Margin	X	Total Assets Turnover	X	Leverage Ratio
Company A:	$\dfrac{\$68}{\$664}$	=	$\dfrac{\$68}{\$1,308}$	X	$\dfrac{\$1,308}{\$925}$	X	$\dfrac{\$925}{\$664}$
	10.2 percent	=	5.2 percent	X	1.41	X	1.39
Company B:	$\dfrac{\$174}{\$745}$	=	$\dfrac{\$174}{\$1,763}$	X	$\dfrac{\$1,763}{\$1,449}$	X	$\dfrac{\$1,449}{\$745}$
	23.4 percent	=	9.9 percent	X	1.22	X	1.94
Company C:	$\dfrac{\$318}{\$1,829}$	=	$\dfrac{\$318}{\$3,817}$	X	$\dfrac{\$3,817}{\$3,985}$	X	$\dfrac{\$3,985}{\$1,829}$
	17.4 percent	=	8.3 percent	X	.96	X	2.18

c. Company A is Starbucks, Company B is Harley Davidson, and Company C is Southwest Airlines. Starbucks typically leases the space for its restaurants and, therefore, has few fixed assets. It sells for cash and, therefore, has few accounts receivable. It will maintain some inventory, but the need for freshness of its foods suggests a rapid turnover. Thus, we would expect Starbucks to have the fastest total assets turnover. Harley Davidson needs fixed assets to manufacture its motor cycles and Southwest Airlines needs aircraft and ground facilities to operate its airline. The smaller profit margin for Starbucks is somewhat of a surprise, given its market price. Competition from other coffee shops and supermarkets with fresh ground coffees probably dampens its profit margin. Starbuck's low leverage ratio reflects its lack of assets to use as collateral for borrowing. The manufacturing of motor cycles is essentially an assembly operation. Thus, Harley Davidson likely needs fewer fixed assets than Southwest Airlines. The larger proportion of fixed assets for Southwest Airlines permits it to have a higher proportion of debt in its capital structure. The slightly higher profit margin of Harley Davidson probably reflects its brand name. Southwest Airlines achieves a relatively high profit margin by spreading its fixed costs over a high volume of business.

5.18   (Profitability analysis for three companies.)

a.

	Rate of Return on Assets	=	Profit Margin	X	Total Asset Turnover
Company A:	$\dfrac{\$2,213}{\$15,002}$	=	$\dfrac{\$2,213}{\$12,504}$	X	$\dfrac{\$12,504}{\$15,002}$
	14.8 percent	=	17.7 percent	X	.83
Company B:	$\dfrac{\$449}{\$8,209}$	=	$\dfrac{\$449}{\$19,139}$	X	$\dfrac{\$19,139}{\$8,209}$
	5.5 percent	=	2.3 percent	X	2.33
Company C:	$\dfrac{\$2,254}{\$39,938}$	=	$\dfrac{\$2,254}{\$22,976}$	X	$\dfrac{\$22,976}{\$39,938}$
	5.6 percent	=	9.8 percent	X	.58

b.

	Rate of Return on Common Shareholders Equity	=	Profit Margin	X	Total Assets Turnover	X	Leverage Ratio
Company A:	$\dfrac{\$2,213}{\$7,444}$	=	$\dfrac{\$2,213}{\$12,504}$	X	$\dfrac{\$12,504}{\$15,002}$	X	$\dfrac{\$15,002}{\$7,444}$
	29.7 percent	=	17.7 percent	X	.83	X	2.02
Company B:	$\dfrac{\$299}{\$2,422}$	=	$\dfrac{\$299}{\$19,139}$	X	$\dfrac{\$19,139}{\$8,209}$	X	$\dfrac{\$8,209}{\$2,422}$
	12.3 percent	=	1.6 percent	X	2.33	X	3.39
Company C:	$\dfrac{\$1,850}{\$18,337}$	=	$\dfrac{\$1,850}{\$22,976}$	X	$\dfrac{\$22,976}{\$39,938}$	X	$\dfrac{\$39,938}{\$18,337}$
	10.1 percent	=	8.1 percent	X	.58	X	2.18

c. Company B is American Stores. Grocery products are commodities. Competition among many grocery store chains for nondifferentiated products drives the profit margin down. Grocery stores compensate for the low profit margin by a high asset turnover. Many grocery products are perishable and firms must turn them over rapidly. The high leverage ratio for Company B might appear strange for a grocery store chain. American Stores uses long-term debt to finance its buildings and supplier financing for its investments.

5.18 c. continued.

The principal difference between Company A and Company C is the profit margin percentages. Disney has brand name recognition which might provide a high profit margin. Pfizer has patents to limit competition for its drugs and drive up its profit margin. Company A is somewhat less asset intensive and carries slightly less debt. Company A is Pfizer and Company C is Disney. Disney's theme parks require heavy investments in fixed assets, which Disney can use for long-term borrowing. Technology risk for Pfizer tends to dampen its desire to take on much long-term debt.

5.19   (Relating profitability to financial leverage.)

a.

Case	Net Income Plus Aftertax Interest Expense[a]	Aftertax Interest Expense[b]	Net Income[c]	Rate of Return on Common Shareholders' Equity
A	$12	$6.0	$ 6	$ 6/$100 = 6%
B	$16	$6.0	$10	$10/$100 = 10%
C	$16	$7.2	$ 8.8	$8.8/$80 = 11%
D	$ 8	$6.0	$ 2	$ 2/$100 = 2%
E	$12	$3.0	$ 9	$ 9/$100 = 9%
F	$10	$3.0	$ 7	$ 7/$100 = 7%

[a]Numerator of the rate of return on assets. In Case A, $12 = .06 \times \$200$.

[b]After tax cost of borrowing times interest-bearing debt. In Case A, $\$6.0 = .06 \times \$100$.

[c]Net income plus after tax interest expense minus after tax interest expense. In Case A, $\$6 = \$12 - \$6$.

b.   Leverage works successfully in Cases B, C, E, and F with respect to total debt. With respect to interest-bearing debt, leverage works successfully in Cases B and C.

5.20   (Company A/Company B; interpreting changes in earnings per share.)

a.   **Company A Earnings
     per Share:**

Year 1 .... $\dfrac{\$100,000}{100,000 \text{ Shares}} = \$1$ per Share.

Year 2 .... $\dfrac{\$100,000}{100,000 \text{ Shares}} = \$1$ per Share.

**Company B Earnings
per Share:**

Year 1 .... $\dfrac{\$100,000}{100,000 \text{ Shares}} = \$1$ per Share.

Year 2 .... $\dfrac{.10 \times (\$1,000,000 + \$100,000)}{100,000 \text{ Shares}} = \$1.10$ per Share.

b.   Company A: No growth.
     Company B: 10 percent annual growth.

c.   Company B: This result is misleading. Comparisons of growth in earnings per share are valid only if firms employ equal amounts of assets in the business. Both the rate of return on assets and on shareholders' equity are better measures of growth performance. Earnings per share results do not, in general (as in this problem), take earnings retention into account.

5.21   (NIKE; calculating and interpreting short-term liquidity ratios.)

a.   **Current Ratio**

Year End	Numerator	Denominator	Current Ratio
5	$2,046	$1,107	1.85
6	2,727	1,467	1.86
7	3,831	1,867	2.05
8	3,533	1,704	2.07

Quick Ratio

Year End	Numerator	Denominator	Quick Ratio
5	$1,269	$1,107	1.15
6	1,608	1,467	1.10
7	2,199	1,867	1.18
8	1,783	1,704	1.05

b.   **Cash Flow from Operations to Current Liabilities Ratio**

Year	Numerator	Denominator	Cash Flow from Operations to Current Liabilities Ratio
6	$340	$1,287.0[a]	26.4%
7	323	1,667.0[b]	19.4%
8	518	1,785.5[c]	29.0%

[a].5($1,107 + $1,467) = $1,287.0.
[b].5($1,467 + $1,867) = $1,667.0.
[c].5($1,867 + $1,704) = $1,785.5.

Accounts Receivable Turnover Ratio

Year	Numerator	Denominator	Accounts Receivable Turnover Ratio
6	$6,471	$1,199.5[a]	5.39
7	9,187	1,550.0[b]	5.93
8	9,153	1,714.0[c]	5.34

[a].5($1,053 + $1,346) = $1,199.5.
[b].5($1,346 + $1,754) = $1,550.0.
[c].5($1,754 + $1,674) = $1,714.0.

5.21 b. continued.

Inventory Turnover Ratio

Year	Numerator	Denominator	Inventory Turnover Ratio
6	$3,907	$ 780.5[a]	5.01
7	5,503	1,135.0[b]	4.85
8	6,066	1,368.0[c]	4.43

[a].5($630 + $931) = $780.5.
[b].5($931 + $1,339) = $1,135.0.
[c].5($1,339 + $1,397) = $1,368.0.

Accounts Payable Turnover Ratio

Year	Numerator	Denominator	Accounts Payable Turnover Ratio
6	$4,208[a]	$ 376.5[d]	11.18
7	5,911[b]	571.0[e]	10.35
8	6,124[c]	636.0[f]	9.63

[a]$3,907 + $931 − $630 = $4,208. [d].5($298 + $455) = $376.5.
[b]$5,503 + $1,339 − $931 = $5,911. [e].5($455 + $687) = $571.0.
[c]$6,066 + $1,397 − $1,339 = $6,124. [f].5($687 + $585) = $636.0.

c. Sales increased 42.0 percent [= ($9,187/$6,471) − 1] between Year 6 and Year 7 but decreased between Year 7 and Year 8. The large increase in sales during Year 7 led NIKE to increase inventories in expectation of still higher sales in the future, causing its inventory turnover to decline. To finance the buildup of inventories, NIKE stretched its creditors, slowing the accounts payable turnover. Cash flow from operations to average current liabilities declined between Year 6 and Year 7, because of the need to finance the inventory buildup. The accounts receivable turnover increased between these years, which increased cash flow from operations. The decline in sales between Year 7 and Year 8 permitted NIKE to collect accounts receivable from Year 7 sales, increasing cash flow from operations. The inventory turnover declined still further, suggesting that the decreased sales caught NIKE by surprise. NIKE again stretched its creditors to help finance the inventories. The cash flow from operations to average current liabilities ratio is consistently below the 40 percent level usually found for healthy companies. The current and quick ratios for NIKE, however, are well above 1.0, suggesting little short-term liquidity risk. The principal short-term liquidity concerns for NIKE are its inventory buildup and the continued stretching of creditors.

5.22 (International Paper Company; calculating and interpreting short-term liquidity ratios.)

a. **Current Ratio**

Year End	Numerator	Denominator	Current Ratio
2	$4,131	$3,727	1.11
3	4,366	4,531	.96
4	4,401	4,009	1.10
5	4,830	4,034	1.20

Quick Ratio

Year End	Numerator	Denominator	Quick Ratio
2	$2,079	$3,727	.56
3	2,086	4,531	.46
4	2,098	4,009	.52
5	2,511	4,034	.62

b. **Cash Flow from Operations to Current Liabilities Ratio**

Year	Numerator	Denominator	Cash Flow from Operations to Current Liabilities Ratio
3	$1,078	$4,129.0[a]	26.1%
4	929	4,270.0[b]	21.8%
5	1,275	4,021.5[c]	31.7%

[a].5($3,727 + $4,531) = $4,129.0.
[b].5($4,531 + $4,009) = $4,270.0.
[c].5($4,009 + $4,034) = $4,021.5.

Accounts Receivable Turnover Ratio

Year	Numerator	Denominator	Accounts Receivable Turnover Ratio
3	$13,598	$1,851.0[a]	7.35
4	13,685	1,858.5[b]	7.36
5	14,966	2,048.5[c]	7.31

[a].5($1,841 + $1,861) = $1,851.0.
[b].5($1,861 + $1,856) = $1,858.5.
[c].5($1,856 + $2,241) = $2,048.5.

5.22 b. continued.

Inventory Turnover Ratio

Year	Numerator	Denominator	Inventory Turnover Ratio
3	$10,987	$1,859.0[a]	5.91
4	11,089	1,981.0[b]	5.60
5	12,028	2,049.5[c]	5.87

[a].5($1,780 + $1,938) = $1,859.0.
[b].5($1,938 + $2,024) = $1,981.0.
[c].5($2,024 + $2,075) = $2,049.5.

Accounts Payable Turnover Ratio

Year	Numerator	Denominator	Accounts Payable Turnover Ratio
3	$11,145[a]	$1,184.5[d]	9.41
4	11,175[b]	1,174.0[e]	9.52
5	12,079[c]	1,146.5[f]	10.54

[a]$10,987 + $1,938 − $1,780 = $11,145.
[b]$11,089 + $2,024 − $1,938 = $11,175.
[c]$12,028 + $2,075 − $2,024 = $12,079.
[d].5($1,110 + $1,259) = $1,184.5.
[e].5($1,259 + $1,089) = $1,174.0.
[f].5($1,089 + $1,204) = $1,146.5.

c. The short-term liquidity risk of International Paper declined slightly over the three year period. The current and quick ratios showed steady improvement. The accounts receivable and inventory turnover ratios changed relatively little, so one must look at current liabilities to understand the reasons for the improvements in the current and quick ratios. The accounts payable turnover ratio increased, indicating that International Paper paid its suppliers more quickly. Also, International Paper reduced its short-term borrowing. The cash flow from operations to average current liabilities ratio decreased between Year 3 and Year 4 but increased between Year 4 and Year 5. The decline between Year 3 and Year 4 is due primarily to reduced profitability in Year 4. Sales were relatively flat between these two years and the profit margin declined. Improved profitability in Year 5 resulted in increased cash flow from operations. The levels of these short-term liquidity ratios suggest that International Paper still has considerable short-term liquidity risk. Its quick ratio is considerably less than 1.0 and its cash flow from operations to average current liabilities ratio is less than the 40 percent commonly found for a financially-healthy firm.

5.23   (Hasbro; calculating and interpreting long-term liquidity ratios.)

a.   **Long-Term Debt Ratio**

Year End	Numerator	Denominator	Long-Term Debt Ratio
1	$ 57	$ 57 + $ 867	6.2%
2	380	380 + 955	28.5%
3	206	206 + 1,106	15.7%
4	200	200 + 1,277	13.5%

Debt-Equity Ratio

Year End	Numerator	Denominator	Debt-Equity Ratio
1	$ 418	$ 418 + $ 867	32.5%
2	995	995 + 955	51.0%
3	977	977 + 1,106	46.9%
4	1,016	1,016 + 1,277	44.3%

b.   **Cash Flow from Operations to Total Liabilities Ratio**

Year	Numerator	Denominator	Cash Flow from Operations to Total Liabilities Ratio
2	$ 120	.5($418 + $ 995)	17.0%
3	230	.5($995 + $ 977)	23.3%
4	217	.5($977 + $1,016)	21.8%

Interest Coverage Ratio

Year	Numerator	Denominator	Times Interest Charges Earned
2	$ 248	$ 43	5.8
3	328	36	9.1
4	370	30	12.3

c.   Hasbro's debt ratios increased as a result of the acquisition of Tonka in Year 2. Hasbro has reduced its debt levels since Year 2. Its cash flow and interest average ratios are at healthy levels, suggesting low long-term solvency risk.

5.24   (American Airlines; calculating and interpreting long-term liquidity ratios.)

    a. **Long-Term Debt Ratio**

Year End	Numerator	Denominator	Long-Term Debt Ratio
4	$3,482	$3,482 + $3,233	51.9%
5	3,095	3,095 + 3,646	45.9%
6	2,503	2,503 + 4,528	35.6%
7	2,319	2,319 + 5,354	30.2%

Debt-Equity Ratio

Year End	Numerator	Denominator	Debt-Equity Ratio
4	$14,090	$14,090 + $3,233	81.3%
5	13,983	13,983 + 3,646	79.3%
6	13,034	13,034 + 4,528	74.2%
7	12,399	12,399 + 5,354	69.8%

    b. **Cash Flow from Operations to Total Liabilities Ratio**

Year	Numerator	Denominator	Cash Flow from Operations to Total Liabilities Ratio
5	$1,996	.5($14,090 + $13,983)	14.2%
6	2,139	.5($13,983 + $13,034)	15.8%
7	2,266	.5($13,034 + $12,399)	17.8%

Interest Coverage Ratio

Year	Numerator	Denominator	Times Interest Charges Earned
5	$1,086	$273	3.98
6	1,331	203	6.56
7	1,447	194	7.46

    c. The debt ratios of American Airlines steadily declined and the cash flow from operations to average total liabilities ratio and the interest coverage ratio steadily increased, suggesting decreasing long-term solvency risk. American Airlines actually decreased the amount of debt during this period. This exercise offers an opportunity to point out that the numbers in the financial statements can give a misleading picture in some cases. During these years American Airlines replaced capital leases on old aircraft with operating leases on new aircraft. If these operating leases were capitalized, the debt ratios would have increased instead of decreased.

5.25   (Effect of various transactions on financial statement ratios.)

Transaction	Rate of Return on Common Shareholders' Equity	Current Ratio	Debt-Equity Ratio
a.	No Effect	(1)	Increase
b.	Increase	Increase	Decrease
c.	No Effect	No Effect	No Effect
d.	No Effect	(1)	Decrease
e.	No Effect	Increase	No Effect
f.	Increase	Decrease	Increase
g.	Decrease	Increase	Decrease
h.	No Effect	Decrease	Increase

(1) The current ratio remains the same if it was one to one prior to the transaction, decreases if it was greater than one, and increases if it was less than one.

5.26   (Effect of various transactions on financial statement ratios.)

Transaction	Earnings per Common Share	Working Capital	Quick Ratio
a.	Increase	Increase	Increase
b.	No Effect	Decrease	Decrease
c.	No Effect	No Effect	Decrease
d.	No Effect	Increase	Increase
e.	No Effect	No Effect	Increase
f.	Decrease	Increase	Decrease

5.27   (Wal-Mart Stores, Inc.; calculating and interpreting profitability and risk ratios.)

a. 1.   Rate of Return on Assets $= \dfrac{\$3,526 + (1 - .35)(\$784)}{.5(\$42,184 + \$48,122)} = 8.9$ percent.

2.   Profit Margin for Rate of Return on Assets $= \dfrac{\$3,526 + (1 - .35)(\$784)}{\$119,299} = 3.4$ percent.

3.   Total Assets Turnover $= \dfrac{\$119,299}{.5(\$42,184 + \$48,122)} = 2.6$ times.

4.   Cost of Goods Sold/Sales $= \dfrac{\$93,438}{\$119,299} = 78.3$ percent.

5.   Selling Administrative Expense/Sales $= \dfrac{\$19,436}{\$119,299} = 16.3$ percent.

6.   Interest Expense/Sales $= \dfrac{\$784}{\$119,299} = .7$ percent.

7.   Income Tax Expense/Sales $= \dfrac{\$2,115}{\$119,299} = 1.8$ percent.

8.   Accounts Receivable Turnover Ratio $= \dfrac{\$119,299}{.5(\$845 + \$976)} = 131.0$ times.

9.   Inventory Turnover Ratio $= \dfrac{\$93,438}{.5(\$15,897 + \$16,497)} = 5.8$ times.

10.   Fixed Asset Turnover $= \dfrac{\$119,299}{.5(\$22,904 + \$26,344)} = 4.8$ times.

11.   Rate of Return on Common Shareholders' Equity $= \dfrac{\$3,526}{.5(\$17,143 + \$18,503)} = 19.8$ percent.

12.   Profit Margin for Return on Common Shareholders' Equity $= \dfrac{\$3,526}{\$119,299} = 3.0$ percent.

5.27 a. continued.

13. Leverage Ratio $= \dfrac{.5(\$42{,}184 + \$48{,}122)}{.5(\$17{,}143 + \$18{,}503)} = 2.5.$

14. Current Ratio $= \dfrac{\$19{,}352}{\$14{,}460} = 1.34.$

15. Quick Ratio $= \dfrac{\$1{,}447 + \$976}{\$14{,}460} = .17.$

16. Cash Flow from Operations to Current Liabilities Ratio $= \dfrac{\$7{,}123}{.5(\$10{,}957 + \$14{,}460)} = 56.0$ percent.

17. Accounts Payable Turnover $= \dfrac{(\$93{,}438 + \$16{,}497 - \$15{,}897)}{.5(\$7{,}628 + \$9{,}126)} = 11.2$ times.

18. Long-Term Debt Ratio $= \dfrac{\$12{,}412}{(\$12{,}412 + \$18{,}503)} = 40.1$ percent.

19. Debt-Equity Ratio $= \dfrac{\$29{,}619}{\$48{,}121} = 61.5$ percent.

20. Cash Flow from Operations to Total Liabilities Ratio $= \dfrac{\$7{,}123}{.5(\$25{,}041 + \$29{,}619)} = 26.1$ percent.

21. Interest Coverage Ratio $= \dfrac{(\$3{,}526 + \$2{,}115 + \$784)}{\$784} = 8.2$ times.

5.27 continued.

b. The rate of return on assets was relatively flat during the last three years, as was the profit margin and assets turnover. The only change of significance with respect to individual expenses is that the cost of goods sold to sales percentage decreased from 78.8 percent in fiscal Year 7 to 78.3 percent in fiscal Year 8, whereas the selling and administrative expense to sales percentage increased from 15.8 percent in fiscal Year 7 to 16.3 percent in fiscal Year 8. Although the changes offset each other, we should attempt to identify the reasons for them. The decreased cost of goods sold percentage might result from three factors: (1) the shift in sales mix away from Sam's Clubs, which have a lower profit margin than Wal-Mart Stores and Wal-Mart Supercenters, (2) the shift in sales mix to the International segment, where the mix of stores may be toward store concepts with a higher gross margin, and (3) improved profit margin in the International segment between fiscal Year 7 and fiscal Year 8. The increased selling and administrative expense to sales percentage may result from (1) expenditures to administer the rapid growth in supercenters and international operations and (2) increasing advertising and other marketing expenditures in light of a more competitive market (for example, consider the growth of Target Stores and the resurgence of K-Mart).

The relatively flat total assets turnover seems inconsistent with the individual asset turnovers. The accounts receivable turnover increased from 108.1 to 131 during the last three years. Note, however, that the days accounts receivable that are outstanding remained at three days. Thus, the increased accounts receivable turnover had little effect on the overall total assets turnover. The inventory turnover ratio increased steadily during the three years. One likely explanation is improved inventory control systems, which reduced the time that merchandise is held Another explanation is that the sales mix shifted toward grocery products that have a faster turnover than non-grocery products. The fixed asset turnover improved slightly. Inventories and fixed assets comprise 89 percent of total assets at the end of fiscal Year 8. Thus, the significant improvement in the inventory turnover ratio and the slight improvement in the fixed asset turnover should result in an increase in the total assets turnover. However, Wal-Mart experienced an increased proportion of cash among total assets in fiscal Year 7 and fiscal Year 8. These assets do not give rise to sales, which is the numerator of the total assets turnover. Thus, a buildup of cash will result in a slowdown of the total assets turnover. The relatively flat total assets turnover results from the offsetting effects of the improved inventory and fixed assets turnover and the dampening effect of the buildup of cash.

5.27 b. continued.

The segment data in Exhibit 5.19 provides additional insight about the operating profitability of Wal-Mart. Note that the profit margins, assets turnovers, and rates of return on assets generally improved in all segments except the Distribution segment. With performance improving in segments comprising approximately 95 percent of sales each year, one wonders why the profitability ratios for the firm as a whole did not improve. Part of the explanation relates to the worsened performance of the Distribution segment. This segment performs the distribution function for Wal-Mart as well as distributes merchandise to other retailers. Given the service role played by this segment relative to the retailing units of Wal-Mart, issues of cost allocations among the segments naturally arise. Is Wal-Mrt allocating an increasing proportion of central corporate costs to the Distribution segment and, thereby, showing improved operating performance in the retailing units? Another explanation for the relatively flat overall company operating performance and the improved segment operating ratios (except the Distribution segment) is that the sales mix shifted toward the lower margin international segment. Although the profit margins, assets turnovers, and rates of return on assets of the International segment improved during the three years, its ratios are generally less than those of the other retailing segments.

c. The rate of return on common shareholders' equity declined between fiscal Year 6 and fiscal Year 7, the result of decreased financial leverage. Wal-Mart reduced the proportion of long-term debt and total liabilities in its capital structure and, thereby, reduced the beneficial effects of financial leverage. The statement of cash flows indicates that Wal-Mart repaid a significant amount of short-term borrowing in fiscal Year 7, accounting in part for the decreased financial leverage. Retained earnings increased as well, which likewise decreases the proportion of liabilities in the capital structure.

The rate of return on common shareholders' equity increased between fiscal Year 7 and fiscal Year 8. The increase is the net result of a slightly improved rate of return on assets and a still further decrease in financial leverage. There was relatively little change in long-term debt between these two years. Wal-Mart also made a significant buyback of its common stock. However, the retention of earnings more than offset the stock buyback and caused shareholders' equity to grow relative to liabilities.

5.27 continued.

    d.   The short-term liquidity risk of Wal-Mart decreased during the three-year period. The reduced number of days that inventory was outstanding provided the firm with cash. The stretching of the number of days that accounts payable were outstanding also provided the firm with cash. Thus, its cash flow from operations to average current liabilities ratio improved, surpassing the 40 percent rate commonly found for financially healthy companies The quick ratio is at a level that would be considered extremely risky for most businesses However, Wal-Mart is essentially a cash business, so it doesn't need a high level of liquid assets to cover current liabilities.

    e.   The long-term solvency risk of Wal-Mart decreased during the three-year period. The debt levels decreased as a result of repaying short-term borrowing in fiscal Year 7 and the retention of earnings in all three years. The cash flow from operations to average total liabilities ratio increased above the 20 percent commonly found for healthy companies in fiscal Year 8 and its interest coverage ratio provides more than adequate protection for lenders.

5.28   (NIKE and Reebok; calculating and interpreting profitability and risk ratios.)

The financial statement ratios on pages 5-24, 5-25, and 5-26 form the basis for the responses to the questions raised.

    a.   Reebok was more profitable than NIKE in Year 11 as judged by both the rate of return on assets (ROA) and the rate of return on common shareholders' equity (ROCE). NIKE has a higher profit margin for ROA but Reebok has a higher assets turnover. The two firms have similar cost of goods sold to sales percentages. When we compare income tax expense to net income before taxes, the two firms have similar effective tax rates. Thus, the differences in the profit margin for ROA relate to selling and administrative expenses. Perhaps Reebok's greater emphasis on fashion relative to NIKE's greater emphasis on performance caused Reebok to spend more heavily on advertising. Also, Reebok's number two position in industry sales could also have led to proportionally greater advertising and promotion expenditures.

        Reebok, however, has a higher total assets turnover. The asset turnover amounts for NIKE for Year 11 are affected by an acquisition made during the year in which NIKE recognized significant goodwill (included in other assets). The acquisition affects each of NIKE's assets and therefore its asset turnovers. Reebok has a slightly higher accounts receivable turnover (55 days versus 68 days for NIKE). The problem gives no clues as to the reason for this difference. The receivables are from distributors and retailers of each firm's products. Perhaps NIKE gives more generous terms as an inducement for attractive shelf space alloca-

5.28 a. continued.

tions. NIKE has a significantly higher inventory turnover ratio. The problem again does not provide information to interpret the reason for the difference in the inventory turnover ratio. NIKE has an arrangement with its manufacturers and customers whereby merchandise is made to order as needed. Thus, NIKE has a higher inventory turnover. Reebok's plant asset turnover is significantly higher than that of NIKE's. Neither company is capital intensive, both subcontracting manufacturing to suppliers in East Asia. Thus, their plant assets relate primarily to administrative facilities. NIKE built a new company headquarters building in the equivalent of Year 9. In addition, NIKE engages more heavily than Reebok in research to improve its performance-driven athletic shoes. The research facilities are included in plant assets.

Reebok also has a higher ROCE than NIKE. Reebok's advantage on ROA is augmented by a larger leverage ratio. Reebok carries higher levels of both long-term debt and total liabilities in its capital structure than NIKE.

b. Neither of these companies carries much short-term liquidity risk. NIKE's short-term liquidity risk increased during Year 11 as a result of borrowing short-term to help finance its acquisition. NIKE's short-term liquidity ratios are less than those of Reebok at the end of Year 11 (except for a slightly faster accounts payable turnover for NIKE). Thus, NIKE appears to carry somewhat more short-term liquidity risk.

c. Neither of these companies carries much long-term solvency risk. The debt ratios are at reasonable levels and the cash flow and interest coverage ratios are quite healthy. Reebok carries a higher proportion of debt in its capital structure and would thus be viewed as having slightly more long-term solvency risk than NIKE.

5.28 continued.

		NIKE	Reebok
1.	Rate of Return on Assets	$\dfrac{\$400 + (1-.35)(\$24)}{.5(\$2,374 + \$3,143)} = 15.1$ percent.	$\dfrac{\$254 + (1-.35)(\$17)}{.5(\$1,392 + \$1,649)} = 17.4$ percent.
2.	Profit Margin for Return on Assets	$\dfrac{\$400 + (1-.35)(\$24)}{\$4,761} = 8.7$ percent.	$\dfrac{\$254 + (1-.35)(\$17)}{\$3,280} = 8.1$ percent.
3.	Total Assets Turnover	$\dfrac{\$4,761}{.5(\$2,374 + \$3,143)} = 1.7$ times per year.	$\dfrac{\$3,280}{.5(\$1,392 + \$1,649)} = 2.2$ times per year.
4.	Cost of Goods Sold to Sales	$\dfrac{\$2,865}{\$4,761} = 60.2$ percent.	$\dfrac{\$1,966}{\$3,280} = 59.9$ percent.
5.	Selling and Administration Expenses to Sales	$\dfrac{\$1,222}{\$4,761} = 25.7$ percent.	$\dfrac{\$889}{\$3,280} = 27.1$ percent.
6.	Interest Expenses to Sales	$\dfrac{\$24}{\$4,761} = .5$ percent.	$\dfrac{\$17}{\$3,280} = .5$ percent.
7.	Income Tax Expenses to Sales	$\dfrac{\$250}{\$4,761} = 5.3$ percent.	$\dfrac{\$154}{\$3,280} = 4.7$ percent.
8.	Accounts Receivable Turnover	$\dfrac{\$4,761}{.5(\$703 + \$1,053)} = 5.4$ times per year.	$\dfrac{\$3,280}{.5(\$457 + \$532)} = 6.6$ times per year.
9.	Inventory Turnover	$\dfrac{\$2,865}{.5(\$470 + \$630)} = 5.2$ times per year.	$\dfrac{\$1,966}{.5(\$514 + \$625)} = 3.5$ times per year.
10.	Plant Asset Turnover	$\dfrac{\$4,761}{.5(\$406 + \$555)} = 9.9$ times per year.	$\dfrac{\$3,280}{.5(\$131 + \$165)} = 22.2$ times per year.

5.28 continued

11. Rate of Return on Common Shareholders' Equity
$$= \frac{\$400}{.5(\$1,741 + \$1,965)} = 21.6 \text{ percent.}$$
$$\frac{\$254}{.5(\$847 + \$990)} = 27.7 \text{ percent.}$$

12. Profit Margin for Return on Common Shareholders' Equity
$$= \frac{\$400}{\$4,761} = 8.4 \text{ percent.}$$
$$\frac{\$254}{\$3,280} = 7.7 \text{ percent.}$$

13. Leverage Ratio
$$= \frac{.5(\$2,374 + \$3,143)}{.5(\$1,741 + \$1,965)} = 1.5.$$
$$\frac{.5(\$1,392 + \$1,649)}{.5(\$847 + \$990)} = 1.7.$$

14. Current Ratio: Beginning of Year
$$= \frac{\$1,770}{\$562} = 3.1.$$
$$\frac{\$1,127}{\$396} = 2.8.$$

End of Year
$$= \frac{\$2,046}{\$1,108} = 1.8.$$
$$\frac{\$1,337}{\$506} = 2.6.$$

15. Quick Ratio: Beginning of Year
$$= \frac{(\$519 + \$703)}{\$562} = 2.2.$$
$$\frac{(\$79 + \$457)}{\$396} = 1.4.$$

End of Year
$$= \frac{(\$216 + \$1,053)}{\$1,108} = 1.1.$$
$$\frac{(\$84 + \$532)}{\$506} = 1.2.$$

16. Cash Flow from Operations to Current Liabilities
$$= \frac{\$255}{.5(\$562 + \$1,108)} = 30.5 \text{ percent.}$$
$$\frac{\$173}{.5(\$396 + \$506)} = 38.4 \text{ percent.}$$

17. Accounts Payable Turnover
$$= \frac{\$2,865 + \$630 - \$470}{.5(\$211 + \$298)} = 11.9 \text{ times per year.}$$
$$\frac{\$1,966 + \$625 - \$514}{.5(\$282 + \$171)} = 9.2 \text{ times per year.}$$

5.28 continued.

18. Long-Term
Debt Ratio:
Beginning of Year
$$= \frac{\$12}{(\$12 + \$1,741)} = .7 \text{ percent.}$$

$$\frac{\$134}{(\$134 + \$847)} = 13.7 \text{ percent.}$$

End of Year
$$= \frac{\$10}{(\$10 + \$1,965)} = .5 \text{ percent.}$$

$$\frac{\$132}{(\$132 + \$990)} = 11.8 \text{ percent.}$$

19. Debt-Equity Ratio:
Beginning of Year
$$= \frac{\$633}{\$2,374} = 26.7 \text{ percent.}$$

$$\frac{\$545}{\$1,392} = 39.2 \text{ percent.}$$

End of Year
$$= \frac{\$1,178}{\$3,143} = 37.5 \text{ percent.}$$

$$\frac{\$659}{\$1,649} = 40.0 \text{ percent.}$$

20. Cash Flow
from
Operations
to Total
Liabilities
$$= \frac{\$255}{.5(\$633 + \$1,178)} = 28.2 \text{ percent.}$$

$$\frac{\$173}{.5(\$545 + \$659)} = 28.7 \text{ percent.}$$

21. Interest
Coverage
Ratio
$$= \frac{\$400 + \$250 + \$24}{\$24} = 28.1 \text{ times.}$$

$$\frac{\$254 + \$154 + \$17}{\$17} = 25.0 \text{ times.}$$

5.29   (Detective analysis—identify company.)

The names of the thirteen companies appear below.

Company Number	Industry	Company Name
1	Grocery Store Chain	Winn-Dixie Stores
2	Public Accounting Partnership	Arthur Andersen & Company
3	Computer Manufacturer	Sun Microsystems
4	Distiller of Hard Liquor	Brown Forman Distillers
5	Department Store Chain	May Department Stores
6	Tobacco Products Company	Philip Morris, Incorporated
7	Soft Drink Company	Coca-Cola Company
8	Steel Manufacturer	Bethlehem Steel Corporation
9	Pharmaceutical Company	Eli Lilly & Company
10	Electric Utility	Consolidated Edison Company of New York
11	Advertising Agency	Interpublic Group of Companies
12	Insurance Company	St. Pauls, Inc.
13	Finance Company	C. I. T. Group Holdings, Inc.

Authors' Clues

1. The problem includes only one partnership. Only partnerships have no federal income tax burden. Company (2) has essentially no income taxes, but otherwise high profits. This suggests that *(2) is the public accounting firm*. The relatively small size of plant and total assets required to do business confirms this reasoning.

2. Utilities, finance companies, and insurance companies have a large investment in assets per dollar of revenue. For the utility, most of those assets are plant; for the insurance company most assets are investments, and for the finance company most assets are receivables. This aids in identifying *(10) as the utility, (13) as the finance company*, and *(12) as the insurance company*. See also Clue 3 below.

3. Steel companies have relatively old plants. We can estimate the age of plant by dividing accumulated depreciation at the end of the year by depreciation charge for the year. Company (8) has accumulated depreciation of about 91 (= 147 − 56). The average age of its assets is about 14.7 years (= 91/6.20). Note how much older this plant is than that of the electric utility whose plant age is only about (208 − 153)/5.97 = 9.2 years old. *Company (8) is the steel company.*

5.29 continued.

4. The drug company and the computer company have relatively high R & D expenses. Patents and relatively long product life cycles permit pharmaceutical companies to earn a higher profit margin than computer companies. *Company (9) is the drug company* and *Company (3) is the computer company.*

5. The advertising agency acts as an agent between media sellers and media buyers. Thus, it should have significant accounts receivable and accounts payable. *Company (11) is the advertising agency.*

6. The grocery chain has relatively large turnover of inventory, and relatively small investment in assets other than inventory relative to the size of sales. Note the low rate of return on sales, but the high rate of return on assets (and shareholders' equity) and the lack of receivables of (1). This points to *Company (1) as the grocery store chain.*

7. The department store chain has relatively large inventories, large inventory turnover (which the manufacturers of products that must age do not), and high receivables. *Company (5) is the department store chain.*

8. This leaves the manufacturers of soft drinks, tobacco products, and hard liquor. The clue we have in mind using here is the amount of aging required by the inventories. Note that the inventory turnover of companies (4), (6), and (7) are as follows:

Company Number	Inventory Turnover per Year
(4)	33.99/23.19 = 1.47 times
(6)	45.37/14.02 = 3.24 times
(7)	40.17/8.54 = 4.70 times

This suggests that (4) has the most aging to do, the hard liquor distiller, (6) shows the next slowest inventory turnover and is the tobacco manufacturer (the somewhat higher inventory turnover than expected occurs because Philip Morris also sells consumer food products). Soft drinks require no aging, therefore, *Company (7) is the soft drink company.*

Note that all of these three companies have relatively high advertising expenses as appropriate for nondurable consumer goods companies.

5.29 continued.

Analysis of Successful Strategies (Compiled by Ellen K. Hochman.)

The students might use one of two strategies to solve this problem. In the first, study the balance sheets and income statements looking for unusual items such as zero or a relatively high balance in an account. Then try to match these "abnormalities" with the type of firm that would exhibit such characteristics. Alternatively, for each industry, begin by determining distinguishing characteristics in terms of account balances that are unusually high or low. Then scan the data for statements with corresponding "unusual" balances.

A. Following the first strategy, it is noted that four firms, (2), (11), (12), and (13), have zero inventory amounts. These probably correspond to the firms which have operating expenses instead of Cost of Goods Sold: the advertising firm, the finance company, the insurance company, and the accounting firm.

    Company (13) also has a large amount of current receivables—it is the *finance company*.

    Company (12) has large Other Assets, probably investments, and high current liabilities—it is the *insurance company*.

    Company (2) pays almost no income taxes—it is a partnership instead of a corporation—it is the *CPA firm*.

    Company (11) is, therefore, the *advertising company*.

B. Two companies, (8) and (10), have large plant and equipment accounts. These are the steel manufacturer and the utility.

    Company (10) has low inventories and a large amount of debt and, therefore, high interest expense—it is the *utility*.

    Company (8) has substantial inventories—it is the *steel manufacturer*.

C. Two companies (3) and (9) have a very large amount of R & D expense. These are the *computer company* and the *pharmaceutical company*. Company (3) has a lower profit margin and faster inventory turnover—it is the *computer company*. Company (9) has a higher profit margin (patent protection and long product life cycle—it is the *pharmaceutical company*.

5.29 continued.

    D. There are five industries remaining: the distiller, the grocery store, the tobacco manufacturer, the department store, and the soft drink bottler.

        Company (1) has very low receivables. Of the industries left, this must be the *grocery store chain* (very few sales on account).

From the data on the remaining companies, (4), (5), (6), and (7), note that Company (5) has the largest current receivables. This is the *department store*, since it carries its own receivables.

    It is very difficult to identify the remaining three companies. Tobacco products and distilled products require aging. Thus, the inventories for these firms are larger and turn over more slowly than for the soft drink company. This suggests Company (7) as the *soft drink company*. Distilled liquor turns over more slowly than tobacco products. This suggests Company (4) as the *distiller* and Company (6) as the *tobacco products company*.

Following the second strategy, the following list was compiled. [An asterisk (*) designates characteristics which were particularly useful in identifying the companies.]

5.29 continued.

Industry	Expected Characteristics	Company Number
Finance Company	*High receivables No inventory High other assets (investments) No (low?) plant and equipment	13
Public Accounting Firm	*No (low?) income taxes (a partnership) No inventory No advertising Low (no?) R & D	2
Insurance Company	*High current liabilities (to pay claims) *High assets—other (investment of premiums) No inventory Substantial current receivables (insurance premiums)	12
Electric Utility	*High plant and equipment *Large debt (financed with bonds) Low inventory (fuel)	10
Steel Manufacturer	*Large plant—but not as large as the utility No advertising	8
Advertising Agency	*Large accounts receivable and accounts payable No inventory Low plant and equipment No advertising No R & D	11
Pharmaceutical Company	*High R & D *Highest Profit Margin Medium plant and equipment Medium advertising	9
Computer Company	*High R & D *Lower profit margin than Company (9)	3
Grocery Store	*Low net income as a percentage of sales *Low receivables (few credit sales) Low advertising Low plant and equipment	1
Department Store	*High receivables No R & D Substantial inventory	5

The logic to identify the remaining three companies, the distiller, the soft drink company, and the tobacco manufacturer, is the same as used in the first strategy.

5.30   (International Paper Company; interpreting profitability and risk ratios.)

   a.   The main reason for the decrease in the cost of goods sold to sales percentage from 80.0 percent in Year 8 to 75.4 percent in Year 9 is the increase in sales volume of 32.3 percent. This is a very capital-intensive company, with significant fixed manufacturing costs. With the greater volume, fixed costs are spread over more units, lowering the unit cost. We also may presume from the increased demand that IPC enjoyed a more favorable marketing climate, enabling price increases, a more profitable sales mix, etc. Finally, the faster inventory turnover should be noted. This typically results in lower carrying costs and obsolescence costs.

   b.   Two interacting factors explain the decrease in plant asset turnover from 1.67 in Year 9 to 1.33 in Year 10. On the one hand, the rate of sales growth slows from 32.3 percent to 1.7 percent. Thus, the numerator essentially is flat. On the other hand, the denominator continues to increase, as International Paper Company expands its productive capacity. Capital expenditures' growth drops from 69.2 percent to 16.7 percent but still is substantially greater than sales growth.

   c.   Financial leverage was favorable in Year 10 as evidenced by the fact that the rate of return on common equity of 5.1 percent exceeded the rate of return on assets of 3.6 percent. International Paper Company earns more on its non-common capital (liabilities and preferred stock, if any) than the cost of that capital; the excess goes to the benefit of the common equity.

   d.   The reason for the decrease in the current ratio from 1.21 in Year 9 to 1.02 in Year 10 must be that current liabilities have grown relatively more than current assets. The evidence points toward a growth in current assets—cash continues to grow and the turnover of both receivables and inventory slows. The days accounts payable that are outstanding have increased, which increases current liabilities. Also suggestive of an increase in current liabilities is the decrease in the quick ratio.

   e.   The decrease in cash flow from operations to total liabilities from 16.3 percent in Year 9 to 9.9 percent in Year 10 is very substantial and is explained primarily by a significant slowing of cash flow from operations. Sales growth has declined from 32.3 percent to 1.7 percent, and the profit margin is down from 8.2 percent to 4.7 percent. Also slowing the cash flow from operations is that the turnover of both receivables and inventory has slowed, resulting in added investment of operating flows in these current assets.

5.31   (The Limited; interpreting profitability and risk ratios.)

   a. The decreased cost of goods sold to sales percentage probably results from the shift in sales mix from the less profitable women's brands to the more profitable intimate brands. We cannot conclude for sure, because the profit margins of these business segments reflect subtractions for both cost of goods sold and selling and administrative expenses.

   b. The increased selling and administrative expense to sales percentage might reflect increased advertising to stimulate sales. The growth rate in sales declined during the three years. Another possibility is that The Limited overstaffed its stores, which is suggested by the decrease in sales per employee.

   c. The sale of accounts receivable to another company beginning in Year 7 means that The Limited will carry less accounts receivable on its balance sheet and, thereby, increase its accounts receivable turnover.

   d. The increase in the fixed asset turnover results from two factors. The Limited experienced increased sales per square foot during the three-year period, indicating greater productivity of its stores. The Limited also slowed its growth rate in new stores, which means that more of its stores have been open for more than one year and, therefore, have generated a full year of sales.

   e. The rate of return on common shareholders' equity exceeded the rate of return on assets in each year, indicating that financial leverage worked to the advantage of the common shareholders The rate of return on funds obtained from creditors exceeded the cost of the debt. The common shareholders receive the benefit of the excess return. The Limited took increased advantage of financial leverage during the three-year period as its rate of return on assets increased and the proportion of debt in the capital structure increased.

   f. One possible explanation is that the cost of debt decreased during the three-year period. Perhaps The Limited carries variable interest rate debt and benefited from decreased interest rates. The Limited might also have refinanced higher interest rate debt with lower interest rate debt. Another possible explanation for the increased debt ratios is that The Limited repurchased shares of its outstanding common stock. Coupling such a buyback with lower interest rate debt would explain the seeming inconsistency.

   g. The most likely explanation is the sale of accounts receivable beginning in Year 7. The Limited gets its cash more quickly, which will increase cash flow from operations. The debt ratios increased between Year 6 and Year 7, so the explanation for the increased cash flow ratios must be in the numerator rather than the denominator of these ratios.

5.32   (Wal-Mart Stores, Inc.; preparing pro forma financial statements.)

   a.   See attached pro forma financial statements and related financial ratios.

   b.   The statement of cash flows suggests several explanations for the deficit in cash. First, note that cash flow from operations is insufficient to finance capital expenditures. One possible explanation is the large increases in inventories that reduce cash flow from operations, particularly relative to the increase in inventories in Year 8. An examination of the financial statement ratios indicates that inventories are projected to turn over 6.0 times per year, which exceeds the turnover of 5.8 times experienced in Year 8 and is considerably faster than the inventory turnover of previous years. Thus, the increases in inventories do not seem unreasonable. Second, capital expenditures are projected to grow 14 percent per year, whereas sales are projected to grow only 12 percent per year. The rationale for the different growth rates is that Wal-Mart will continue to grow the number of superstores and engage in international acquisitions. Slowing down the growth rate in capital expenditures will solve the cash flow problem, but one must ask if this is reasonable. The growth rate in property, plant and equipment has exceeded the growth rate in sales during the preceding five years. A third possibility is that the projections do not assume a fast enough growth in long-term debt. Although we assume that long-term debt will grow at the growth rate in property, plant and equipment, long-term debt at the end of fiscal Year 8 of $12,412 is much less than property, plant and equipment of $26,344. Growing both amounts at 14 percent will result in an increasing gap between the two amounts. One possibility is to grow long-term debt faster than property, plant and equipment. Growing long-term debt at 1.5 times the growth rate in property, plant and equipment will solve the cash deficit problem. Another possibility is to grow common stock sufficiently to solve the cash flow problem. This approach, however, requires a very large increase in common stock. Still another possibility is to reduce the assumed growth rate in dividends. However, a growth rate in dividends of just 10 percent will not solve the cash flow problem. Still another possibility is to assume a lower interest rate. The average interest rate on borrowing during fiscal Year 8 was 5.9 percent. Perhaps an interest rate closer to 6 percent makes more sense. However, reducing the assumed interest rate to 6 percent will not solve the cash flow problem.

5.32 a. continued.

The following pro forma financial statements were generated by a spreadsheet program that rounds to many decimal places. Rounding causes some of the sub-totals and totals to differ from the sum of the amounts that comprise them.

WAL-MART STORES
PRO FORMA INCOME STATEMENT
YEAR ENDED JANUARY 31

	Year 8	Year 9	Year 10	Year 11	Year 12
Sales Revenue:	$ 119,299	$ 133,615	$ 149,649	$ 167,607	$ 187,719
Expenses:					
Cost of Goods Sold...	$ 93,438	$ 104,888	$ 117,474	$ 131,571	$ 147,360
Marketing and Administration....	19,436	22,046	24,692	27,655	30,974
Interest.................	784	965	1,003	1,056	1,081
Income Taxes........	2,115	2,115	2,397	2,710	3,073
Total Expense......	$ 115,773	$ 130,014	$ 145,567	$ 162,992	$ 182,487
Net Income..............	$ 3,526	$ 3,601	$ 4,082	$ 4,614	$ 5,232
Dividends.................	(611)	(733)	(880)	(1,056)	(1,267)
Increase in Retained Earnings..............	$ 2,915	$ 2,868	$ 3,202	$ 3,558	$ 3,965

Assumptions:

Growth Rate of Sales..	12.0%	
Cost of Goods Sold......	78.5%	of sales
Marketing and Administration..........	16.5%	of sales
Interest Expense........	7.0%	of interest bearing debt
Income Tax Rate	37.0%	of income before income taxes
Dividends.................	20.0%	growth rate

5.32 a. continued.

WAL-MART STORES
PRO FORMA BALANCE SHEET
JANUARY 31

	Year 8	Year 9	Year 10	Year 11	Year 12
Cash	$ 1,447	$ 650	$ (337)	$ (1,288)	$ (3,715)
Accounts Receivable...	976	1,093	1,224	1,371	1,536
Inventories	16,497	18,477	20,694	23,177	25,958
Prepayments.............	432	484	542	607	680
Total Current Assets................	$ 19,352	$ 20,703	$ 22,123	$ 23,867	$ 24,459
Property, Plant and Equipment............	26,344	30,032	34,237	39,030	44,494
Other Assets	2,426	2,717	3,043	3,408	3,817
Total Assets...........	$ 48,122	$ 53,452	$ 59,402	$ 66,305	$ 72,771
Accounts Payable.......	$ 9,126	$ 10,304	$ 11,458	$ 12,916	$ 14,382
Notes Payable............	0	0	0	0	0
Current Portion— Long Term Debt	1,141	1,039	815	2,018	52
Other Current Liabilities..............	4,193	4,696	5,260	5,891	6,598
Total Current Liabilities..........	$ 14,460	$ 16,040	$ 17,532	$ 20,825	$ 21,032
Long-Term Debt.........	12,412	12,965	13,851	13,490	15,319
Other Noncurrent Liabilities..............	2,747	3,077	3,446	3,859	4,322
Total Liabilities....	$ 29,619	$ 32,081	$ 34,829	$ 38,174	$ 40,674
Common Stock	$ 224	$ 224	$ 224	$ 224	$ 224
Additional Paid-in Capital.................	585	585	585	585	585
Retained Earnings.....	17,694	20,562	23,764	27,322	31,288
Total Shareholders' Equity	$ 18,503	$ 21,371	$ 24,573	$ 28,131	$ 32,097
Total Liabilities and Share- holders' Equity.....	$ 48,122	$ 53,452	$ 59,402	$ 66,305	$ 72,771

(See Following Page for Assumptions)

5.32 a. continued.

(Assumptions for Pro Forma Balance Sheet)

Assumptions:

Cash	PLUG				
Accounts Receivable...	Sales Growth Rate				
Inventory.................	Sales Growth Rate				
Prepayments.............	Sales Growth Rate				
Property, Plant and Equipment............	14.0% Growth Rate				
Other Assets	Sales Growth Rate				
Accounts Payable Turnover..............	11.0				
Merchandise Purchases.................		106,867	119,691	134,054	150,141
Average Payables.......		9,715	10,881	12,187	13,649
Notes Payable............		0	0	0	0
Other Current Liabilities..............	Sales Growth Rate				
Long-Term Debt.........	Property, Plant and Equipment Growth Rate				
Other Noncurrent Liabilities..............	Sales Growth Rate				
Common Stock, APIC....................	0.0% Growth Rate				

5.32 a. continued.

WAL-MART STORES
PRO FORMA CASH FLOW STATEMENT
FOR THE YEAR ENDED JANUARY 31

Cash Flow Statement	Year 8	Year 9	Year 10	Year 11	Year 12
Operations:					
Net Income.............	$ 3,526	$ 3,601	$ 4,082	$ 4,614	$ 5,232
Depreciation...........	1,634	1,863	2,124	2,421	2,760
Other....................	0	330	369	414	463
(Inc.)/Dec. in Accounts Receivable....................	(78)	(117)	(131)	(147)	(165)
(Inc.)/Dec. in Inventory....................	(365)	(1,980)	(2,217)	(2,483)	(2,781)
(Inc.)/Dec. in Prepayments............	(64)	(52)	(58)	(65)	(73)
Inc./(Dec.) in Accounts Payable.....	1,048	1,178	1,153	1,458	1,467
Inc./(Dec.) in Other Current Liabilities....................	1,422	503	564	631	707
Cash Flow from Operations..............	$ 7,123	$ 5,327	$ 5,885	$ 6,843	$ 7,610
Investing:					
Acquisition of Property, Plant and Equipment....	$ (2,636)	$ (5,551)	$ (6,328)	$ (7,214)	$ (8,224)
Other Investing.......	(1,785)	(291)	(326)	(365)	(409)
Cash Flow from Investing................	$ (4,421)	$ (5,842)	$ (6,654)	$ (7,579)	$ (8,633)
Financing:					
Inc./(Dec.) in Short-Term Borrowing..	$ 0	$ 0	$ 0	$ 0	$ 0
Inc./(Dec.) in Long-Term Borrowing..	(101)	451	662	842	(137)
Inc./(Dec.) in Common Stock...........	(1,569)	0	0	0	0
Dividends...............	(611)	(733)	(880)	(1,056)	(1,267)
Other Financing.....	143	0	0	0	0
Cash Flow from Financing..............	$ (2,138)	$ (282)	$ (218)	$ (214)	$ (1,404)
Change in Cash.........	$ 564	$ (797)	$ (987)	$ (951)	$ (2,427)
Cash, Beginning of Year......................	883	1,447	650	(337)	(1,288)
Cash, End of Year......	$ 1,447	$ 650	$ (337)	$ (1,288)	$ (3,715)

(See Following Page for Assumptions)

5.32 a. continued.

(Assumptions for Pro Forma Cash Flow Statement)

Assumptions:

Depreciation Growth Rate......................	Same as Property, Plant, and Equipment
Other Operating Add-backs	Change in Noncurrent Liabilities
Other Investing Cash Flows....................	Change in Other Noncurrent Assets

WAL-MART STORES
PRO FORMA FINANCIAL RATIOS

	Year 9	Year 10	Year 11	Year 12
Rate of Return on Assets........	8.3%	8.4%	8.4%	8.5%
Profit Margin for ROA...........	3.2%	3.2%	3.2%	3.2%
Total Assets Turnover	2.6	2.7	2.7	2.7
Cost of Goods Sold/Sales.........	78.5%	78.5%	78.5%	78.5%
Marketing and Administrative Expenses/Sales............	16.5%	16.5%	16.5%	16.5%
Interest Expense/Sales	0.7%	0.7%	0.6%	0.6%
Income Tax Expense/Sales.....	1.6%	1.6%	1.6%	1.6%
Accounts Receivable Turnover Ratio.............................	129.2	129.2	129.2	129.2
Inventory Turnover Ratio.......	6.0	6.0	6.0	6.0
Plant Assets Turnover Ratio...	4.7	4.7	4.6	4.5
Rate of Return on Common Equity..............................	18.1%	17.8%	17.5%	17.4%
Profit Margin for ROCE	2.7%	2.7%	2.8%	2.8%
Leverage Ratio.....................	2.5	2.5	2.4	2.3
Current Ratio.......................	1.29	1.26	1.15	1.16
Quick Ratio	0.11	0.05	0.00	−0.10
Cash Flow from Operations/ Current Liabilities.............	34.9%	35.1%	35.7%	36.4%
Accounts Payable Turnover Ratio.............................	11.0	11.0	11.0	11.0
Long-Term Debt Ratio............	37.8%	36.0%	32.4%	32.3%
Debt-Equity Ratio..................	60.0%	58.6%	57.6%	55.9%
Cash Flow from Operations/ Total Liabilities	17.3%	17.6%	18.7%	19.3%
Interest Coverage Ratio	6.9	7.5	7.9	8.7

5.33   (W. T. Grant Company; case analysis of bankruptcy.)

We begin discussion of this case by placing the following headings on the board:

Major Contributing Factors	Relevant Ratios or Measures	Questionable Policies

We then have the students list all of the contributing factors they found in preparing their solutions. Their list tends to be lengthy, particularly if they consulted other sources in preparing their solutions. We then have the student that suggested each factor indicate which ratios or other measures he or she used in forming the conclusions. We finish the discussion by listing questionable policies in light of Grant's worsening financial condition in the few years before bankruptcy.

Contributing Factors
1. Operations were a net user of cash in each of the years analyzed. In only two of the years during Grant's last decade did operations provide (net) cash. Grant simply lost its ability to generate cash internally. Students should be pushed as to the reason for Grant's inability to generate cash from operations. Possibilities include:

    a. A decreasing profit margin, resulting in smaller amounts of potential cash flow from each sales transaction. The decreasing profit margin percentage between 1972 and 1975 results from both an increase in the cost of goods sold to sales percentage and increasing interest expense.

    b. A buildup of accounts receivable. The data do not support this explanation because the accounts receivable turnover increased during the period under study. However, data from 1965 to 1971 show a dramatic *decrease* in the accounts receivable turnover. Grant instituted a credit card system during this period. Extremely liberal credit extension and collection policies resulted in a significant buildup of receivables during the late 1960s and a drain on cash. Grant failed to provide adequately for estimated uncollectible accounts as the large catch-up provision in 1975 attests.

    c. A buildup of inventories. The decreasing inventory turnover supports this explanation. Since 1965, the inventory turnover decreased from 4 times to 3 times a year. The decrease is largely due to a change in product mix to furniture and appliances.

5.33 continued.

2. Financing Strategies—Grant relied heavily on short-term bank loans for much of its needed cash during the period under study. It used this financing to carry receivables and inventories. As these assets built up, the firm required more and more bank loans. The significant increases in interest rates that occurred in the early 1970s made such financing more difficult. The two long-term bond issues were used primarily to obtain funds for store equipment. Grant leased most of its store space (which was not required to be shown on the balance sheet at that time).

Questionable Policies

1. Liberal extension and collection policies on credit sales.

2. Switch to furniture and large appliances.

3. Switch to larger stores.

4. Continued payment of dividends.

5. Continued purchases of Grant's own common stock.

6. Continued investments in securities.

CHAPTER 6

RECEIVABLES AND REVENUE RECOGNITION

Questions, Exercises, Problems, and Cases: Answers and Solutions

6.1   See the text or the glossary at the end of the book.

6.2   The allowance method, because it reports bad debt expense during the period of the sale, not during the later period(s) when the specific accounts become uncollectible.

6.3   The direct write-off method matches the loss from an uncollectible account with revenue of the period when a particular account becomes uncollectible.   The allowance method matches the loss from an uncollectible account with revenue of the period of the sale that later gave rise to an uncollectible account.

6.4   a.   A firm with stable sales (both volume and price) and a constant proportion of uncollectible accounts will likely report similar amounts for bad debt expense each period.

        b.   The direct write-off method should always result in larger amounts for accounts receivable-net on the balance sheet than the allowance method.

6.5   a.   This statement is valid. Most businesses ought not to set credit policies so stringent that they have no uncollectible accounts. To do so would require extremely careful screening of customers, which is costly, and the probable loss of many customers who will take their business elsewhere. So long as the revenues collected from credit sales exceed the sum of both selling costs and the cost of goods sold on credit, then the firm should not be concerned if some percentage of its accounts receivable are uncollectible.

        b.   If a business liberalizes its credit policy by granting to a group of customers, who were not previously granted this privilege, the right to buy on account, it can find that its net revenues from the new credit customers exceed the cost of goods sold to them and the selling expenses of executing the sales. The extension of credit to new customers can increase net income even though it results in more uncollectible accounts.

6.5 continued

    c. When the net present value of the receipts from selling to new customers is larger than the net present value of the costs of putting goods into their hands.

6.6   If a firm computes the Bad Debt Expense figure at the end of the accounting period but writes off specific accounts receivable during the period as information about uncollectible accounts becomes available, then the Allowance for Uncollectibles will have a debit balance whenever the amount of accounts written off during the period exceeds the opening credit balance in the Allowance account. Firms prepare balance sheets only after making adjusting entries. Both the Bad Debt Expense and the Allowance for Uncollectibles accounts must be made current with appropriate adjusting entries before preparing the balance sheet. Because the Allowance for Uncollectibles account is an asset contra, it will always show a credit (or perhaps a zero) balance after making adjusting entries.

6.7   Manufacturing firms typically do not identify a customer or establish a firm selling price until they sell products. Thus, these firms do not satisfy the criteria for revenue recognition while production is taking place. In contrast, construction companies usually identify a customer and establish a contract price before construction begins. In addition, the production process for a manufacturing firm is usually much shorter than for a construction firm. The recognition of revenue at the time of production or at the time of sale does not result in a significantly different pattern of income for a manufacturing firm. For a construction company, the pattern of income could differ significantly.

6.8   Under the installment method, accountants recognize proportionate parts of the costs incurred as expenses each period as they recognize proportionate parts of the selling price as revenues. Under the cost-recovery-first method, costs match dollar-for-dollar with revenues until revenues equal total costs. Thus, the income patterns differ because of the *expense* recognition pattern, not the revenue recognition pattern.

6.9   Under both the installment method and the cash basis of accounting, accountants recognize revenue when the firm receives cash. The installment method recognizes expenses in the same period as the associated revenues. The cash basis recognizes expenses when the firm makes cash expenditures.

6.10   Application of the installment method requires a reasonably accurate estimate of the total amount of cash the firm expects to receive from customers. The cost-recovery-first method does not require such an estimate.

6.11 Accountants are more concerned with the objectivity or reliability of income data than are economists. Accountants are responsible for measuring and auditing income amounts and, therefore, require objective measures of wealth changes. Such evidence usually takes the form of market transactions.

6.12 The user of the financial statements must identify the reason for the decline in the quality of earnings. Does the measurement of revenues and expenses for a particular business require numerous estimates? Is there evidence that the firm has used the inherent flexibility in the measurement of revenues and expenses to its advantage? Is the declining quality of earnings due to unusual or nonrecurring items which the financial statement user can exclude when assessing operating profitability? In some cases the financial statement user can adjust net income to eliminate the source of the decreasing earnings quality; in other cases, such adjustments are not possible.

6.13 (Kesler Company; journal entries for the allowance method.)

a. **Year 6**

Bad Debt Expense	8,400	
Allowance for Uncollectible Accounts		8,400
.02 × $420,000 = $8,400.		

Allowance for Uncollectible Accounts	1,200	
Accounts Receivable		1,200

Year 7

Bad Debt Expense	9,600	
Allowance for Uncollectible Accounts		9,600
.02 × $480,000 = $9,600.		

Allowance for Uncollectible Accounts	7,000	
Accounts Receivable		7,000

Year 8

Bad Debt Expense	11,000	
Allowance for Uncollectible Accounts		11,000
.02 × $550,000 = $11,000.		

Allowance for Uncollectible Accounts	9,700	
Accounts Receivable		9,700

b. Yes. Uncollectible accounts arising from sales of Years 6, 7 and 8 total $28,800, which equals 1.99 percent (= $28,800/$1,450,000) of total sales on account during the three year period.

6.14   (Emmons Corporation; journal entries for the allowance method.)

a. **Dec. 31**

Bad Debt Expense...	45,000	
Allowance for Uncollectible Accounts...........		45,000

.03 × $1,500,000 = $45,000.

Allowance for Uncollectible Accounts..............	2,300	
Accounts Receivable..................................		2,300

Year 2

Bad Debt Expense...	54,000	
Allowance for Uncollectible Accounts...........		54,000

.03 × $1,800,000 = $54,000.

Allowance for Uncollectible Accounts..............	22,100	
Accounts Receivable..................................		22,100

Year 3

Bad Debt Expense...	72,000	
Allowance for Uncollectible Accounts...........		72,000

.03 × $2,400,000 = $72,000.

Allowance for Uncollectible Accounts..............	38,000	
Accounts Receivable..................................		38,000

b. No. The actual loss experience is 2 percent (= $113,800/$5,700,000) of sales on account for sales during Years 1 through 3.

6.15   (Pandora and Milton; Allowance method: reconstructing journal entry from events.)

a. **Pandora**

Bad Debt Expense...	2,900	
Allowance for Uncollectibles		2,900

Write-off of $2,200 + Ending Balance of Allowance of $5,000 – Beginning Balance of $3,500 – Collection of $800 = $2,900.

6.15 continued.

b.

Accounts Receivable		Allowance for Uncollectible Accounts	
√ 15,200,000			1,400,000 √
(see below)			(see below)
√ 17,600,000			1,550,000 √

Accounts Receivable	75,000,000	
Sales..		75,000,000

$750,000 is 1 percent of sales; sales = $750,000/.01.

Bad Debt Expense	750,000	
Allowance for Uncollectible Accounts..............		750,000

Allowance for Uncollectible Accounts.................	600,000	
Accounts Receivable......................................		600,000

$1,400,000 + $750,000 − $1,550,000 = $600,000.

Cash...	71,400,000	
Accounts Receivable......................................		71,400,000

$15,200,000 + $75,000,000 − $600,000 − $17,600,000 = $72,000,000.

6.16 (Seward Corporation; reconstructing events when using the allowance method.)

Cash		Accounts Receivable		Allowance for Uncollectible Accounts	
		√ 82,900			8,700 √
(4) 231,200		(1) 240,000	4,400 (3)	(3) 4,400	4,800 (2)
			231,200 (4)		
		√ 87,300			9,100 √

Bad Debt Expense		Sales	
--			--
(2) 4,800			240,000 (1)
√ 4,800			240,000

(1) Sales on account.
(2) Provision for estimated uncollectible accounts.
(3) Write off of actual uncollectible accounts.
(4) Collection of cash from customers for sales on account.

6.17 (Logue Corporation; reconstructing events when using the allowance method.)

Cash		Accounts Receivable				Allowance for Uncollectible Accounts		
		√ 115,900						18,200
(4) 422,000		(1) 450,000	21,100	(2)	(2)	21,100		
			422,100	(3)				
		√ 122,700				√	2,900	
								27,000 (4)
								24,100 √

Bad Debt Expense		Sales	
--			--
			450,000 (1)
(4) 27,000			450,000 √

(1) Sales on account.
(2) Write off of actual uncollectible accounts during year.
(3) Collection of cash from customers for sales on account.
(4) Provision for estimated uncollectible accounts on December 31. $.06 \times \$450,000 = \$27,000$.

6.18 (Dove Company; aging accounts receivable.)

Bad Debt Expense 3,700
    Allowance for Uncollectible Accounts..............   3,700
To adopt auditor's suggestion that total allowance
now be $20,900 [(= .005 \times \$400,000) + (.01 \times \$90,000)$
$+ (.10 \times \$40,000) + (.70 \times \$20,000)]$. $\$20,900 - \$17,200$
$= \$3,700$.

6.19 (Rorke Company; aging accounts receivable.)

Allowance for Uncollectible Accounts.................. 6,250
    Bad Debt Expense..   6,250

The Allowance account requires a balance of $\$29,750 = (.005 \times \$700,000) + (.01 \times \$225,000) + (.10 \times \$90,000) + (.30 \times \$50,000)$. The adjusting entry *reduces* the Allowance account by $\$6,250 (= \$36,000 - \$29,750)$ and reduces Bad Debt Expense for the period by the same amount.

6.20   (Reconstructing events from journal entries.)

    a. Estimated bad debt expense for the period is $2,300 using the allowance method.

    b. A firm writes off specific customers' accounts totaling $450 as uncollectible under the allowance method.

    c. A firm writes off specific customers' accounts totaling $495 as uncollectible under the direct write-off method.

6.21   (Home and Office Depot; effects of transactions involving suppliers and customers on cash flows.)

    a. $118,450 = $120,000 − ($8,600 − $8,000) + ($750 − $700) + ($10,000 − $9,000) − $2,000

                     = $120,000 − $600 + $50 + $1,000 − $2,000

    b. $85,100 = $85,000 − ($7,500 − $7,000) + ($10,400 − $10,000) + ($11,200 − $11,000)

                  = $85,000 − $500 + $400 + $200

6.22   (Bechtel Construction Company; percentage-of-completion and completed contract methods of income recognition.)

Percentage-of-Completion Method

Year	Degree of Completion		Revenue	Expense	Income
1	$ 800,000/$3,200,000	= 25.0%	$1,000,000	$ 800,000	$ 200,000
2	$1,920,000/$3,200,000	= 60.0%	2,400,000	1,920,000	480,000
3	$ 480,000/$3,200,000	= 15.0%	600,000	480,000	120,000
			$4,000,000	$3,200,000	$ 800,000

Completed Contract Method

Year	Revenue	Expense	Income
1	--	--	--
2	--	--	--
3	$ 4,000,000	$3,200,000	$ 800,000
	$ 4,000,000	$3,200,000	$ 800,000

6.23   (JMB Realty Partners; installment and cost-recovery-first methods of income recognition.)

Installment Method

Year	Revenue	Percentage of Selling Price	Expense	Income
1	$ 25,000	25%	$15,000	$10,000
2	25,000	25%	15,000	10,000
3	25,000	25%	15,000	10,000
4	25,000	25%	15,000	10,000
	$ 100,000		$60,000	$40,000

Cost-Recovery-First Method

Year	Revenue	Expense	Income
1	$ 25,000	$ 25,000	-0-
2	25,000	25,000	-0-
3	25,000	10,000	15,000
4	25,000	-0-	25,000
	$ 100,000	$ 60,000	$40,000

6.24   (Revenue recognition for various types of businesses.)

We have found this question to be an excellent one for class discussion because it forces the student to think about both revenue *and* expense timing and measurement questions. It also generates active student interest. We have found it helpful to begin consideration of each item by drawing a time line similar to that in Figure 6.1 and appropriately labeling it. Some of the items are relatively obvious while others require more discussion.

a.   Time of sale.

b.   Probably as work progresses using the percentage-of-completion method. Students normally assume the sale is to the United States Government. We ask them if it would make any difference if the sale was to a relatively weak government in Africa or South America. This question gets at the issue of whether the amount of cash the firm will receive is subject to reasonably accurate estimation.

c.   Probably as the firm collects cash using the installment method.

d.   At the time of sale.

6.24 continued.

e. At the time the firm picks citrus products and delivers them to customers. We ask students if their response would change if the citrus farm had a five-year contract at a set price to supply a particular quantity of citrus products to a citrus processor. The issue here is whether, given uncertainties about future weather conditions, the citrus grower will be able to make delivery on the contract.

f. AICPA *Statement of Position 79-4* stipulates that the firm should not recognize revenue until it meets all of the following conditions:

1. The firm knows the sales price.

2. The firm knows the cost of the film or can reasonably estimate the loss.

3. The firm is reasonably assured as to the collectibility of the selling price.

4. A licensee has accepted the film in accordance with the license agreement.

5. The film is available (that is, the licensee can exercise the right to use the film and all conflicting licenses have expired).

Revenue recognition from the sale of rights to the television network is appropriate as soon as the firm meets these conditions even though the license period is three years. The firm cannot recognize revenues from the sale of subsequent rights to others until the three-year licensing period has expired. An important question in this example is when to recognize the production costs as an expense. Should the firm recognize all of the costs as an expense on the initial sale to the television network? Or, should it treat some portion of the costs as an asset, matched against future sales of license rights? Most accountants would probably match all of the costs against revenue from the television network license agreement, unless the firm has signed other license agreements for periods beginning after the initial three-year period at the same time as the television license agreement.

g. At the time of sale of each house to a specific buyer.

h. At the time of sale to a specific buyer at a set price. This will vary, depending on who owns the whiskey during the aging process. We pose the following situation: Suppose a particular whiskey producer has an on-going supplier relationship with a whiskey distributor. The quantity purchased by the distributor and the price set depend

6.24 h. continued.

on supply and demand conditions at the time aged whiskey is brought to the market. The supplier always purchases some minimum quantity. When should the firm recognize revenue? This question gets at the issue of measuring revenue in a reasonably objective manner. You may also want to discuss the following other wrinkle. Suppose the whiskey producer doubles capacity. The firm cannot sell any of the whiskey produced from this new capacity for six years. What should the firm do with the costs of this new capacity?

i. As time passes and the firm lets borrowers use funds.

j. The alternatives here are (1) as customers make reservations, (2) as customers make some formal commitments to confirm their reservations, or (3) as the agency receives cash from commissions. The second alternative is probably best. However, past experience may provide sufficient evidence as to the proportion of reservations that customers ultimately confirm to justify earlier recognition.

k. At the completion of the printing activity.

l. The issue here is whether to recognize revenue when the firm sells stamps to food stores or when customers turn in the stamps for redemption. One might argue for revenue recognition at the time of sale of the stamps, since the seller must have some estimate of the redemption rate in setting the price for the sale of the stamps.

m. At the time the wholesaler delivers food products to stores.

n. The issue here is whether to recognize revenue while the livestock is growing. A grower of timber faces a similar issue. For the reasons Part h. above discusses, it is probably best to await the time of delivery to a specific customer at an agreed upon price.

o. Probably during each period in a manner similar to the percentage-of-completion method. In practice firms use several methods.

6.25   (Whirlpool Corporation; analyzing changes in accounts receivable.)

a.

	Year 5		Year 6		Year 7	
(1) Sales on Account						
Accounts Receivable..	4,008.7		4,179.0		4,314.5	
Sales Revenue		4,008.7		4,179.0		4,314.5
(2) Provision for Estimated Uncollectible Accounts						
Bad Debt Expense......	6.0		17.7		11.5	
Allowance for Uncollectible Accounts............		6.0		17.7		11.5
(3) Write Off of Actual Bad Debts						
Allowance for Uncollectible Accounts..	5.8[a]		17.0[b]		10.4[c]	
Accounts Receivable...............		5.8		17.0		10.4

[a]$2.4 + $6.0 - $2.6 = $5.8.
[b]$2.6 + $17.7 - $3.3 = $17.0.
[c]$3.3 + $11.5 - $4.4 = $10.4.

	Year 5		Year 6		Year 7	
(4) Collection of Cash from Customers						
Cash....................	3,988.8[d]		4,098.8[e]		4,206.9[f]	
Accounts Receivable.................		3,988.8		4,098.8		4,206.9

[d]$249.4 + $4,008.7 - $5.8 - $263.5 = $3,988.8.
[e]$263.5 + $4,179.0 - $17.0 - $326.7 = $4,098.8.
[f]$326.7 + $4,314.5 - $10.4 - $423.9 = $4,206.9.

b.

	Year 5	Year 6	Year 7

(1)

$$\frac{\text{Bad Debt Expense}}{\text{Sales on Account}} \quad \frac{\$6.0}{\$4,008.7} = .15\% \quad \frac{\$17.7}{\$4,179.0} = .42\% \quad \frac{\$11.5}{\$4,314.5} = .27\%$$

(2)

$$\frac{\text{Allowance for Uncollectible Accounts}}{\text{Accounts Receivable Gross}} \quad \frac{\$2.6}{\$263.5} = .99\% \quad \frac{\$3.3}{\$326.7} = 1.01\% \quad \frac{\$4.4}{\$423.9} = 1.04\%$$

6.25 continued.

c. It does not appear that Whirlpool Corporation uses the percentage-of-sales method to provide for estimated uncollectibles because the ratio of bad debt expense to sales on account varies significantly over the three-year period. The firm appears to maintain a relatively constant ratio of allowance for uncollectible accounts as a percentage of accounts receivable. This suggests that Whirlpool Corporation increases its provision in years when charge offs increase (such as Year 6) and vice versa.

6.26 (May Department Stores; analyzing changes in accounts receivable.)

a.

(Amounts in Millions)	Year 9	Year 10	Year11	Year 12
Allowance for Uncollectable Accounts, Beginning of Year.......	$ 47	$ 61	$ 66	$ 84
Plus Bad Debt Expense...................	57	64	82	96
Less Accounts Written Off (Plug)	(43)	(59)	(64)	(81)
Allowance for Uncollectable Accounts, End of Year................	$ 61	$ 66	$ 84	$ 99

b.

	Year 9	Year 10	Year11	Year 12
Accounts Receivable, Gross at Beginning of Year.....................	$1,592	$2,099	$2,223	$2,456
Plus Sales on Account[a]...................	5,181	6,137	6,713	7,293
Less Accounts Written Off..............	(43)	(59)	(64)	(81)
Less Cash Collections from Credit Customers (Plug)......................	(4,631)	(5,954)	(6,416)	(7,061)
Accounts Receivable, Gross at End of Year..................................	$2,099	$2,223	$2,456	$2,607

[a]Total Sales × (Credit Sales ÷ Total Sales Percentage).

c.

Total Sales/Average Accounts Receivable, Net:	Year 9	Year 10	Year11	Year 12
$8,330/.5($1,545 + $2,038)..........	4.65			
$9,456/.5($2,038 + $2,157)..........		4.51		
$10,035/.5($2,157 + $2,372)........			4.43	
$10,615/.5($2,372 + $2,508)........				4.35

d.

Credit Sales/Average Accounts Receivable, Net:	Year 9	Year 10	Year11	Year 12
$5,181/.5($1,545 + $2,038)..........	2.89			
$6,137/.5($2,038 + $2,157)..........		2.93		
$6,713/.5($2,157 + $2,372)..........			2.96	
$7,293/.5($2,372 + $2,508)..........				2.99

6.26 continued.

    e. The accounts receivable turnover ratio based on total sales decreases because of the increasing proportion of credit sales in total sales. The increasing accounts receivable turnover ratio based on credit sales results from actions that cause customers to pay more quickly. Examples include increased finance charges on unpaid balances, reduced repayment period on credit sales, and more stringent controls on the granting of credit.

6.27   (Pins Company; reconstructing transactions affecting accounts receivable and uncollectible accounts.)

    a. $192,000 Dr. = $700,000 − $500,000 − $8,000.

    b. $6,000 Cr. = (.02 × $700,000) − $8,000.

    c. $21,000 = $10,000 + $11,000.

    d. $16,000 = $6,000 + $10,000.

    e. $676,000 = $192,000 + $800,000 − $16,000 − $300,000.

    f. $289,000 = $300,000 − $11,000.

6.28   (Nordstrom; decision to extend credit to a new class of customers.)

Gross Margin on New Sales:	a.	b.
a. .30 × $10,000; b. .30 × $7,000	$3,000	$2,100
Less: Uncollectibles (.07s × $10,000)	(700)	(700)
Selling Expenses	(1,100)	(1,100)
Contribution to Profits	$1,200	$ 300

    a. Nordstrom will be $1,200 better off.

    b. Nordstrom will be $300 better off.

6.29   (Hanrahan Company; decision to extend credit: working backwards to uncollectible rate.)

Gross Margin on New Sales (.20 × $20,000)		$ 4,000
Less: Uncollectibles on Total Sales (.03 × $270,000)	$ 8,100	
Previous Amount of Uncollectibles (.02 × $250,000)	(5,000)	
Increase in Uncollectibles		(3,100)
Less Selling Expenses		(300)
Incremental Contribution to Profits		$ 600

Percentage Uncollectible: $3,100/$20,000 = 15.5 percent.

6.30 (Effect of errors involving accounts receivable on financial statement ratios.)

	Rate of Return on Assets	CFO/ Average Current Liabilities	Debt Equity Ratio
a. Bad Debt Expense......... X	$\frac{O/S}{O/S} = O/S$	$\frac{NO}{NO} = NO$	$\frac{NO}{O/S} = U/S$
Allowance for Uncollectible Accounts...... X			
b. Allowance for Uncollectible Accounts...... X	$\frac{NO}{NO} = NO$	$\frac{NO}{NO} = NO$	$\frac{NO}{NO} = NO$
Accounts Receivable........ X			
c. Advances from Customers...... X	$\frac{NO}{O/S} = U/S$	$\frac{NO}{O/S} = U/S$	$\frac{O/S}{O/S} = O/S$
Accounts Receivable........ X			

Note: This problem asks only for the net effect of each error on the three financial ratios. The journal entries and the numerator and denominator effects appear to show the reason for the net effect.

6.31   (General Electric Company; income recognition for nuclear generator manufacturer.)

a.1.   Percentage-of-Completion Method

Year	Incremental Percentage Complete	Revenue Recognized	Expenses Recognized	Net Income
2	42/120 (.35)	$ 70,000,000	$ 42,000,000	$28,000,000
3	54/120 (.45)	90,000,000	54,000,000	36,000,000
4	24/120 (.20)	40,000,000	24,000,000	16,000,000
Total.....	120/120 (1.00)	$ 200,000,000	$ 120,000,000	$80,000,000

2.   Completed Contract Method

Year	Revenue Recognized	Expenses Recognized	Net Income
2	-0-	-0-	-0-
3	-0-	-0-	-0-
4	$200,000,000	$120,000,000	$80,000,000
Total....	$200,000,000	$120,000,000	$80,000,000

3.   Installment Method

Year	Cash Collected (= Revenue)	Fraction of Cash Collected	Expenses (= Fraction X Total Cost)	Net Income
2	$ 20,000,000	1/10	$ 12,000,000	$ 8,000,000
3	100,000,000	5/10	60,000,000	40,000,000
4	80,000,000	4/10	48,000,000	32,000,000
Total......	$ 200,000,000	1.00	$120,000,000	$80,000,000

4.   Cost-Recovery-First Method

Year	Cash Collected (= Revenue)	Expenses Recognized	Net Income
2	$ 20,000,000	$ 20,000,000	-0-
3	100,000,000	100,000,000	-0-
4	80,000,000	-0-	$80,000,000
Total.....	$ 200,000,000	$120,000,000	$80,000,000

b.   The percentage-of-completion method probably provides a better measure of performance over the life of the contract because each period receives a portion of the net income from the contract. General Electric's original estimates of the cost of the contract were correct. Also, the periodic payments from the Consolidated Edison suggest that General Electric will probably collect cash in the amount of the contract price.

6.32 (Clinton Construction Company; income recognition for a contractor.)

a.1. Percentage-of-Completion Method

Year	Incremental Percentage Complete	Revenue Recognized	Expenses Recognized	Net Income
1	20/100 (.20)	$ 24,000,000	$ 20,000,000	$ 4,000,000
2	30/100 (.30)	36,000,000	30,000,000	6,000,000
3	35/100 (.35)	42,000,000	35,000,000	7,000,000
4	15/100 (.15)	18,000,000	15,000,000	3,000,000
Total.......	100/100 (1.00)	$120,000,000	$100,000,000	$20,000,000

2. Completed Contract Method

Year	Revenue Recognized	Expenses Recognized	Net Income
1	-0-	-0-	-0-
2	-0-	-0-	-0-
3	-0-	-0-	-0-
4	$ 120,000,000	$100,000,000	$20,000,000
Total....	$ 120,000,000	$100,000,000	$20,000,000

3. Installment Method

Year	Cash Collected (= Revenue)	Percentage of Cash Collected	Expenses (= Percentage x Total Cost)	Net Income
1	$ 24,000,000	.20	$ 20,000,000	$ 4,000,000
2	30,000,000	.25	25,000,000	5,000,000
3	30,000,000	.25	25,000,000	5,000,000
4	36,000,000	.30	30,000,000	6,000,000
Total......	$120,000,000	1.00	$100,000,000	$20,000,000

4. Cost-Recovery-First Method

Year	Cash Collected (= Revenue)	Expense Recognized	Net Income
1	$ 24,000,000	$ 24,000,000	-0-
2	30,000,000	30,000,000	-0-
3	30,000,000	30,000,000	-0-
4	36,000,000	16,000,000	$20,000,000
Total.....	$ 120,000,000	$100,000,000	$20,000,000

b. The percentage-of-completion method probably gives the best measure of Clinton's performance each year under the contract. The original estimates of costs on the contract turned out to be correct. Also, the periodic cash collections suggest that the firm will probably collect cash in the amount of the contract price.

6.33   (J. C. Spangle; point-of-sale versus installment method of income recognition.)

a.

	Year 8	Year 9
Sales..	$ 200,000	$ 300,000
Expenses:		
Cost of Goods Sold*............................	$ 120,000	$ 186,000
All Other Expenses	32,000	44,000
Total Expenses	$ 152,000	$ 230,000
Net Income..	$ 48,000	$ 70,000
*Beginning Inventory	$ 0	$ 60,000
Purchases....................................	180,000	240,000
Goods Available	$ 180,000	$ 300,000
Ending Inventory..........................	(60,000)	(114,000)
Cost of Goods Sold	$ 120,000	$ 186,000

Cost of Goods Sold/Sales:
  Year 8--$120,000/$200,000 = 60 percent.
  Year 9--$186,000/$300,000 = 62 percent.

b.

	Year 8	Year 9
Collections from Customers	$ 90,000	$ 230,000
Expenses:		
Merchandise Cost of Collections*..........	$ 54,000	$ 140,400
All Other Expenses	32,000	44,000
Total Expenses	$ 86,000	$ 184,400
Net Income..	$ 4,000	$ 45,600

	Year 8	Year 9
*Calculation:		
Merchandise Cost of Collections:		
Of Goods Sold:		
In Year 8, 60 percent of $90,000	$ 54,000	
In Year 9, 60 percent of $110,000.....		$ 66,000
Of Goods Sold in Year 9:		
62 percent of $120,000		74,400
	$ 54,000	$ 140,400

	Year 8	Year 9
An Alternative Presentation Would Be:		
Realized Gross Margin	$ 36,000	$ 89,600
All Other Expenses........................	32,000	44,000
Net Income	$ 4,000	$ 45,600

6.34   (Pickin Chicken; revenue recognition for a franchise.)

a.

Year	Pickin Chicken, Inc.	Country Delight, Inc.
2	$400,000 (= $50,000 × 8)	$ 160,000 (= $20,000 × 8)
3	250,000 (= $50,000 × 5)	148,000 (= $20,000 × 5 + $6,000 × 8)
4	0	78,000 (= $6,000 × 13)
5	0	78,000 (= $6,000 × 13)
6	0	78,000 (= $6,000 × 13)
7	0	78,000 (= $6,000 × 13)
8	0	30,000 (= $6,000 × 5)
Total..	$ 650,000	$ 650,000

b. The issue here is whether sufficient uncertainty exists regarding the amount the firm will ultimately collect to justify postponing revenue recognition until the time of collection. The casualty rate among franchisees has been very high and has led some accountants to argue that the installment method is the appropriate basis for revenue recognition.

6.35   (Income recognition for various types of businesses.)

a. **Amgen**—The principal income recognition issue for Amgen is the significant lag between the incurrence of research and development expenditures and the realization of sales from any resulting products. Biotechnology firms are a relatively new industry and therefore have few commercially feasible products. Thus, research and development expenditures will likely represent a significant percentage of revenues, as is the case for Amgen. More established technology firms, such as pharmaceuticals, have established products as well as products in the pipeline and therefore research and development expenditures represent both a smaller and a more stable percentage of revenues. GAAP requires biotechnology firms to expense research and development expenditures in the year incurred.

Brown Forman—The principal revenue recognition issue for Brown Forman is whether it should recognize the increase in value of hard liquors while they are aging (that is, revalue the liquors to market value each year) or wait until the liquors are sold at the end of the aging process. Most accountants would argue that the market values of aging liquors are too uncertain prior to sale to justify periodic revaluations and revenue recognition. Brown Forman should include in the cost of the liquor inventory not only the initial production costs but also the cost incurred during the aging process. In this way, the firm can match total incurred costs with revenues generated at the time of sale.

6.35 a. continued.

Deere—Deere faces issues of revenue recognition with respect to both the sale of farm equipment to dealers and the provision of financing services. The concern with respect to the sale of farm equipment to dealers is the right of dealers to return any unsold equipment. If dealers have no right of return, then recognition of revenue at the time of sale is appropriate. If dealers can return any equipment discovered to be faulty prior to sale and the amount of such returns is reasonably predictable, then Deere can reduce the amount of revenue recognized each year for estimated returns. If dealers can return any unsold equipment, then delaying recognition of revenue until the dealer sells the equipment is appropriate. Deere should match the cost of manufacturing the equipment against the sales revenue. Deere reports research and development expense in its income statement. Given the farm equipment industry, one wonders about what proportions of these expenditures Deere makes to enhance existing products versus to develop new products. Although contrary to GAAP, one can make the case that Deere should capitalize and amortize expenditures on new products.

Deere should accrue revenue from financing (interest) and insurance (premiums) services over time. To achieve matching, Deere should capitalize and amortize any initial administrative costs to check customer credit quality and prepare legal documents.

Fluor—The appropriate timing of revenue recognition for Fluor depends on the basis for pricing its services. If the fee is fixed for any particular construction project, then Fluor should recognize the fee in relation to the degree of completion of the construction project. If the fee is a percentage of total construction costs incurred on the project, then Fluor should recognize revenue in relation to costs incurred. If the fee is a percentage of the costs incurred by Fluor (salaries of their employees working on the project), then it should recognize revenue in relation to the incurrence of these costs. It seems clear that a percentage of completion method of revenue recognition is more appropriate than the completed contract method.

Golden West—Golden West should recognize interest revenue from home mortgage loans as time passes. It should provide for estimated uncollectible accounts each year. The uncollectible amount should reflect the resale value of homes repossessed. The more difficult question relates to recognition of revenue from points. One possibility is to recognize the full amount in the initial year of the loan. The rationale for such a procedure is that the points cover administrative costs of setting up the loan. Both the points and the administrative costs would be recognized in full in the initial year of the loan. An alternative view is that the points effectively reduce the

6.35 a. continued.

amount lent by the savings and loan company and increase its yield beyond the stated interest rate. This view suggests that Golden West amortize the points over the term of the loan and match against this revenue amortization of the initial administrative costs to set up the loan. Golden West should recognize interest expense on deposits as time passes. There is no direct relation between interest expense on deposits and interest revenue from loans so Golden West matches interest expense to the period it is incurred.

Merrill Lynch—The principal income recognition issue for Merrill Lynch is whether it should report financial instruments held as assets and liabilities at their acquisition cost or their current market value. These assets and liabilities generally have easily measured market values. They are typically held for short periods of time (days or weeks). Thus, one can argue that use of current market values is appropriate. However, we are still left with the question as to whether the unrealized gain or loss should flow through to the income statement immediately or wait until realization at the time of sale. The argument for immediate recognition is that Merrill Lynch takes short-term financing and investing positions for short-term returns. Its income statement should reflect its operating performance during this period. The case for not recognizing the unrealized gains and losses is that they could reverse prior to realization and, in any case, will be realized very soon. Merrill Lynch should recognize revenue from fee-based services as it provides the services.

Rockwell—The absence of research and development expense from the income statement suggests that Rockwell charges all such costs to specific contracts. These costs become expenses as Rockwell recognizes revenue from the contracts. The multi-year nature of its contracts and the credit quality of the U.S. government suggests use of the percentage-of-completion method of income recognition. One difficulty encountered in applying the percentage-of-completion method is that Rockwell's contracts for projects such as the space shuttle get continually renewed. This procedure makes it difficult to identify a single contract price and accumulate costs for a single contract, which the percentage-of-completion method envisions.

b. **Amgen**—Amgen realized the highest profit margin of the seven companies. Its biotechnology products are protected by patents. It therefore maintains a monopoly position. Note that the cost of manufacturing its products is a small percent of revenues. Amgen's major cost is for research and development. Sales of its existing products are not only sufficient to cover its high, on-going research work but to provide a substantial profit margin as well. Its relatively low revenue to assets percentage is somewhat unexpected,

6.35 b. continued.

given that its major "assets" are patents and research scientists. The reason for this low percentage (reason not provided in the case) is that cash and marketable securities comprise approximately 25 percent of its assets. These assets generated a return of approximately 3 percent during the year. This rate of return decreased the overall ratio of revenues to assets for Amgen.

Brown Forman—Brown Forman realized the third highest profit margin among the seven companies. If one views the excise taxes as a reduction in revenues rather than as an expense, its profit margin is 10.4 percent [= 8.8%/(100.0% − 15.4%)]. Concerns about excess alcoholic drinking in recent years have resulted in some exodus of companies from the industry, leaving the remaining companies with a larger share of a smaller market. The products of Brown Forman carry brand name recognition, permitting the firm to obtain attractive prices.

Deere—Deere's relatively low profit margin reflects (1) weaknesses in the farming industry in recent years, which puts downward pressure on margins, and (2) decreased interest rates, which lowers profit margins. The revenue-to-assets percentage of Deere reflects its capital-intensive manufacturing operations and the low interest rate on outstanding loans to dealers and customers.

Fluor—The low profit margin of Fluor reflects the relatively low value added of construction services. It may also reflect recessionary conditions when construction activity is weak and profit margins are thin.

Golden West—The 12 percent profit margin seems high, relative to interest rates in recent years. Recall though that Golden West pays short-term interest rates on its deposits but obtains long-term interest rates on its loans. An upward-sloping yield curve provides a positive differential. Also, the existence of shareholders' equity funds in the capital structure means that Golden West has assets earning returns for which it recognizes no expense in its income statement (that is, firms do not recognize an expense for the implicit cost of shareholders' funds). Note also that the ratio of revenue to assets is only .1. Thus, the assets of Golden West earned a return of only 1.2 percent (= 12.0% × .1) during the year.

Merrill Lynch—The lower profit margin for Merrill Lynch relative to Golden West reflects in part the fact that both the investments and financing of Merrill Lynch are short term. Merrill Lynch, however, realizes revenue from fee-based services. Firms like Merrill Lynch can differentiate these services somewhat and realize attractive profit margins. However, such services have been quickly copied by competitors in recent years, reducing the profit margins accordingly.

6.35 b. continued.

> **Rockwell**—Rockwell's profit margin is in the middle of the seven companies. Factors arguing for a high profit margin include Rockwell's technological know-how and its role in long-term contracts with the U.S. government. Factors arguing for a lower profit margin include cutbacks in defense expenditures and excess capacity in the aerospace industry.

6.36   (Boston Chicken, Inc.; analyzing revenue recognition from franchising—franchise fees, lease rentals, software sales.)

I. Case Objectives

   A. Apply the criteria for revenue recognition to a restaurant franchiser.
   B. Examine the concept of the reporting entity in light of operating relationships between a franchiser and its franchisees.
   C. Assess the profitability and risk of a rapidly-growing franchiser.

II. Responses to Case Questions

   a. The criteria for the recognition of revenue are: (1) a firm has provided all or a substantial portion of the services it expects to perform for customers, and (2) the firm has received either cash, a receivable, or some other asset capable of reasonably precise measurement. The application of these criteria to each of the sources of revenue of Boston Chicken follows.

   Development Fee—The area developer makes a $5,000 cash payment at the time of signing a development agreement for each store to be developed. At this time, Boston Chicken debits Cash and credits Deferred Franchise Revenue. When each store opens, Boston Chicken recognizes the development fee as revenue by debiting Deferred Franchise Revenue and crediting Development Fee Revenue. One might argue that Boston Chicken should recognize the development fee as revenue at the time of signing the development agreement. At this time Boston Chicken and the area developer have agreed on a schedule of stores to be opened, the development fee has been set, and the area developer has paid the nonrefundable fee. It does not appear that Boston Chicken must provide substantial future services in return for this development fee. Thus, a case could be made for recognizing the development fee at the time of signing the development agreement. Recognition of the development fee as revenue at the time of signing, however, may subject Boston Chicken to criticism from the investment community that it inflates the number of stores to be developed just to increase revenues. The latter may explain the decision to delay the recognition of the development fee as revenue until an actual store opens.

6.36 a. continued.

Initial Franchise Fee—The area development agreement establishes the initial franchise fee at $35,000 per store. The area developer pays $5,000 of this amount at the time of signing the agreement and the remaining $30,000 when the store opens or later. The opening of a store gives the franchisee the right to use the Boston Chicken name from that time forward in that particular location. The only issue with respect to the first criteria for revenue recognition is whether Boston Chicken must provide substantial future services after opening. Boston Chicken does provide on-going operating services, such as menu planning, advertising, information processing, etc. Other fees cover these additional services. Thus, it appears that Boston Chicken has provided most of the services related to the initial franchise fee at the time of opening. The last issue is the collectibility of the remaining $30,000 of the initial franchise fee. A failure of franchisees to pay this fee at the time of opening would result in a buildup of accounts receivable on the balance sheet relative to revenues. Dividing developer and franchise revenues (excluding interest on area developer financing) by average accounts receivable yields an accounts receivable turnover of 3.8 [= $11,551/.5($859 + $5,202)] times for Year 13, 4.8 [= $43,603/.5($5,202 + $13,002)] times for Year 14, and 4.1 [= $74,662/.5($13,002 + $23,059)] times for Year 15. These turnover rates indicate an average collection period between 76.2 days and 95.8 days. Although the turnover rates have varied somewhat over time, the rapid rate of turnover does not indicate an unreasonable buildup of accounts receivable.

One must be careful interpreting these accounts receivable turnover rates, however, for two reasons. First, accounts receivable includes amounts due for a variety of items (for example, initial franchisee fees, royalty fees, software fees). The average collection period of approximately 90 days may result from a 30-day collection period for on-going operating revenues, such as royalties and software fees, and a much longer collection period for the initial franchise fee. Second, one should examine changes in the allowance for uncollectible accounts account to study the pattern of provisions and writeoffs. The amounts appear below, in thousands.

Year	Balance, Beginning of Year	Bad Debt Expense for Year	Accounts Written Off	Balance, End of Year
Year 13	$ 77	$ 321	$ 75	$ 323
Year 14	323	187	264	246
Year 15	246	797	--	1,043

6.36 a. continued.

Bad debt expense as a percentage of revenues from developers and franchisees (other than interest on area developer loans) was 2.8 percent (=$321/$11,551) in Year 13, .4 percent (=$187/$43,603) in Year 14, and 1.1 percent (= $797/$74,662) for Year 15. The balance in the allowance account as a percentage of gross accounts receivable at the end of each year was 8.2 percent [= $77/($859 + $77)] for Year 12, 5.8 percent [= $323/($5,202 + $323)] for Year 13, 1.9 percent [= $246/($13,002 + $246)] for Year 14, and 4.3 percent [= $1,043/$23,059 + $1,043) for Year 15. It appears that Boston Chicken might have understated its provision for bad debts in Year 14 but caught up a bit in Year 15. Also, it seems strange that the firm would not have written off any accounts as uncollectible during Year 15. Thus, although the accounts receivable turnover ratio does not indicate a major problem with collecting accounts receivable, the analysis of changes in the allowance account suggests some possible control problems. One would also like to have data on uncollectible accounts for other franchisers.

Royalties—The royalty rate is 5 percent of gross revenues of each franchisee. The average collection period for accounts receivable of approximately 90 days suggests that Boston Chicken collects the royalty and other fees quarterly on average. The use of integrated computer hardware and software across stores eases the measurement of the royalty fee. Thus, recognizing the royalty fee as the stores generate revenue seems appropriate.

Interest on Loans to Area Developers—Boston Chicken recognizes interest revenue on loans "as earned," which presumably means with the passage of time. Providing financing to the area developers and franchisees and allowing them to repay the loan at a later time represent the services provided by Boston Chicken. The amount of interest is a specified percentage of the outstanding loan based on a floating rate established by the Bank of America Illinois. The interest is payable "currently." Thus, recognition of the interest revenue as time passes appears appropriate.

It might be useful to point out that most of the amounts in the notes receivable accounts represent area developer and franchisee loans. The lending and repayment of the principal amounts of these loans flow through the notes receivable accounts and the investing section of the statement of cash flows. Interest earned on these notes increases the notes receivable accounts and cash collected for interest reduces notes receivable. This interest appears in the statement of cash flows as an operating activity. The fact that the amounts reported for

6.36 a. continued.

cash inflows and outflows related to new loans and repayments of existing loans in the statement of cash flows exactly equal the net change in the notes receivable accounts suggests that Boston Chicken collects the interest currently.

At this point we ask: Of what significance is the fact that Boston Chicken has a zero balance in the Allowance for Loan Losses account as it relates to notes receivable? One interpretation is that the area developers and franchisees are doing so well and Boston Chicken is monitoring their activities so closely that no uncollectible accounts are anticipated. On the other hand, the area's developers and franchisees have operated so far at a net loss, have a negative net worth, and have loans that require a balloon payment at the end of four or five years. Thus, Boston Chicken appears to incur some risks of nonpayment that may not surface for several years. If such losses materialize, then its current income is probably overstated because of a failure to provide for estimated uncollectible accounts. Given that notes receivable represent the largest asset of Boston Chicken, the quality of its current earnings is a bit suspect.

Real Estate Service and Leasing Fees—Boston Chicken assists franchisees in selecting sites and coordinating construction of new stores, for which it receives a real estate fee. The notes to the financial statements indicate that Boston Chicken recognizes this fee "when earned." This disclosure is unclear as to whether the earning process occurs as construction proceeds (a percentage-of-completion method of income recognition) or when the store is complete (a completed contract method of income recognition). Given the use of a standard store architecture, it is likely that the construction process takes only months to complete. Thus, recognizing the real estate fee under either method should produce similar results. As discussed above, the absence of a buildup in accounts receivable suggests that the Company has collected this fee soon after providing the services. Thus, its revenue recognition method for real estate service fees seems appropriate.

Boston Chicken recognizes lease revenues on equipment leased to franchisees on a straight line basis over the lease period. Providing these rental services represents the services provided by Boston Chicken. Uncollected amounts would result in a buildup in accounts receivable, which did not occur. Thus, recognizing this revenue with the passage of time seems appropriate.

6.36 a. continued.

This may be a good point to ask: Will the assets being leased appear on the balance sheet of Boston Chicken or the franchisee? Students have not yet been exposed to the operating and capital lease methods of accounting. We use this as an opportunity to introduce the concept that leased assets do not necessarily appear on the balance sheet of the firm using the assets in its operations. Boston Chicken accounts for these leases as operating leases, although it does not disclose sufficient information to determine why these leases do not qualify as capital leases.

Software License and Maintenance Fees—Boston Chicken recognizes software license fees when software is placed in service at each store. It recognizes software maintenance fees "as earned," which presumably means either with the passage of time or the provision of software services. The disclosures in the notes do not indicate how the Company distinguishes the services that relate to each of these sources of revenue. Given that software is continually updated, the opportunity exists to price these two services in such a way as to accelerate or delay the recognition of revenue as the Company may deem appropriate. Thus, there appears to be some fuzziness in the time of recognizing software fees as revenues.

Summary of Revenue Recognition—A key factor in concluding that Boston Chicken recognizes revenues appropriately is that it receives cash quickly from its area developers and franchisees. The fact that Boston Chicken provides loans to these entities clouds the picture, somewhat, as to whose funds are really being used to make these cash payments. The fact that Boston Chicken does not report a balance in its allowance for loan losses on notes receivable may be interpreted in two ways: (1) Boston Chicken monitors the financial condition of its area developers and franchisees so closely that collectibility of the loans is not expected to be a problem, or (2) Boston Chicken recognizes its ultimate vulnerability to uncollected loans and wants to portray an image of having the situation well in control. Only time will tell which interpretation is correct.

b. The use of non-owned area developers and franchisees, instead of company-owned entities, permits Boston Chicken to report positive income during the development phase, a time when it needs capital to finance development of its network of stores. The area developers and franchisees have operated at a net loss and have negative net worth. If these entities had been company-owned, Boston Chicken would likewise probably have had negative net income and net worth.

6.36 b. continued.

We raise this question: If you were an investor in Boston Chicken, could you separate the activities of Boston Chicken from its area developers and franchisees? Does not the success of Boston Chicken depend on the success of the area developers and franchisees? We use these questions to motivate a discussion of the appropriate reporting entity: Boston Chicken or Boston Chicken consolidated with its area developers and franchisees. Current GAAP requires a majority voting interest for consolidation. Thus, consolidation is not now allowed. Proposed FASB rules require a control criterion, independent of ownership percentage. One might argue that Boston Chicken maintains substantial control over its area developers and franchisees. Boston Chicken sets forth area development plans, helps in site selection and construction, provides financing, and provides menu planning and other operating support activities. Furthermore, some managers of Boston Chicken and their families have an equity interest in certain area developers and franchisees, suggesting even more extensive control.

We also raise the question: Is there anything unethical about managers of Boston Chicken or their families having an equity interest in the area developers? One view is that there is no ethical problem since Boston Chicken discloses the nature and extent of related party involvements and indicates that the arrangements are essentially arms length. A related view is that these managers have an incentive for both Boston Chicken and the area developers to be successful, so there is no conflict of interest. An alternative view is that the related party arrangements provide an opportunity for conflicts of interest to arise. The disclosures are not sufficient to determine what proportion of the area developers and franchisees are controlled by management and their families. These managers probably have a higher ownership percentage in the area developers than they do in Boston Chicken, thus providing an incentive to redirect profits towards the area developers. The reimbursement of Boston Chicken for a portion of general and administrative expenses suggests that these managers spend some of their time working in their own area development. The related party transactions involving aircraft provide further evidence of a pattern of mixing personal and business interests. Even if unethical actions have not occurred, there is at least the appearance of possible ethical conflicts.

6.36 continued.

c. Boston Chicken might argue that advertising and promotion is an activity related to the *operation* of stores, not to the development of a franchise network. This expense should therefore appear on the income statements of the area developers and franchisees, not that of Boston Chicken. Running the advertising fee through revenues of Boston Chicken and the cost of advertising through advertising expense would not change net income as long as the revenue and expense amounts were the same. Boston Chicken discloses, however, that the expenditures exceed the amounts collected by $9.6 million at the end of Year 15. Thus, including the amounts in the income statement of Boston Chicken would reduce its net income.

We again address the question of control. Boston Chicken apparently designs the advertising and promotion campaigns, both nationally and locally. The fact that it has spent more than it has collected suggests that Boston Chicken controls this marketing function. Under the new FASB proposal, Boston Chicken would likely have to consolidate this activity.

d. Exhibit 6.11 in the case indicates that Boston Chicken experienced an increased profit margin, a decreased assets turnover, and a variable rate of return on assets during the last three years.

The increased profit margin results from decreases in the cost of goods sold, salaries and benefits, and administrative expense percentages but is offset by increases in the interest expense and income tax expense percentages. The decreases in the cost of goods sold percentage must be interpreted in light of the decreasing proportion of company-owned stores. We should relate cost of goods sold to revenues from company-owned stores. The amounts are as follows:

Year 13: $11,287/$29,849 = 37.8%
Year 14: $15,876/$40,916 = 38.8%
Year 15: $19,737/$51,566 = 38.3%

Thus, the cost of goods sold in company-owed stores has not changed significantly during the three-year period. The decreased percentages for salaries and benefits and for administrative expenses probably reflect economies of scale as the largely fixed cost of the Company's administrative organization gets spread over a larger number of stores and, therefore, revenue base. The increased interest expense percentage results from additional borrowing to finance the rapid expansion of stores (that is, through loans to franchisees).

6.36 d. continued.

The increased income tax expense percentage probably results from using up net operating loss carryforwards.

The decreasing assets turnover is the result of (1) increasing notes receivable on the balance sheet, which generate an asset turnover equal to the rate of interest on the notes, (2) a decreasing fixed asset turnover, the result of acquiring restaurant equipment leased to franchisees prior to receiving a full year of lease revenues immediately after stores open, and (3) a buildup of cash on the balance sheet on December 31,Year 15 from additional long-term borrowing.

The rate of return on assets increased between Year 13 and Year 14 but decreased between Year 14 and Year 15. The rate of return on common shareholders' equity followed a similar path as ROA. The leverage ratio increased between Year 13 and Year 14 with additional long-term borrowing. Although long-term borrowing increased still further in Year 15, so did profitability (retained earnings), so the leverage ratio did not change much in that year.

There are no particular negative warning signals among the risk ratios. The cash flow to liabilities ratios are at healthy levels and the coverage ratios are quite adequate. The debt levels increased between Year 13 and Year 14 but the firm is generating sufficient cash to service this debt. Note the statement of cash flows reports an addback to net income for zero coupon financing, indicating that some of the interest expense does not require a current cash outflow. Thus, the interest coverage ratio for Year 15 is higher than indicated in Exhibit 6.11.

CHAPTER 7

INVENTORIES: THE SOURCE OF OPERATING PROFITS

Questions, Exercises, Problems, and Cases: Answers and Solutions

7.1 See the text or the glossary at the end of the book.

7.2 The underlying principle is that acquisition cost includes all costs required to prepare an asset for its intended use. Assets provide future services. Costs that a firm must incur to obtain those expected services add value to the asset. Accountants therefore include such costs in the acquisition cost valuation of the asset.

7.3 Depreciation on manufacturing equipment is a product cost and remains in inventory accounts until the firm sells the manufactured goods. Depreciation on selling and administrative equipment is a period expense, because the use of such equipment does not create an asset with future service potential.

7.4 Both the Merchandise Inventory and Finished Goods Inventory accounts include the cost of completed units ready for sale. A merchandising firm acquires the units in finished form and debits Merchandise Inventory for their acquisition cost. A manufacturing firm incurs direct material, direct labor, and manufacturing overhead costs in transforming the units to a finished, salable condition. The Raw Materials Inventory and Work-in-Process Inventory accounts include such costs until the completion of manufacturing operations. Thus, the accountant debits the Finished Goods Inventory account for the cost of producing completed units. The accountant credits both the Merchandise Inventory and Finished Goods Inventory accounts for the cost of units sold and reports them as current assets on the balance sheet.

7.5 The accountant allocates the total income (cash inflow minus cash outflow) over the periods between purchase and sale. The inventory valuation method dictates this allocation. The acquisition cost valuation method allocates all of the income to the period of sale. A current cost valuation method allocates holding gains and losses to the periods when a firm holds inventory and an operating margin (sales minus replacement cost of goods sold) to the period of sale. A lower-of-cost-or-market valuation allocates holding losses to the periods when a firm holds inventory and holding gains plus operating margins to the period of sale.

7.6   Income increases in the year of change because of the recognition of the unrealized holding gains. Cost of goods sold in the next year will increase by the same amount, so that income in the second year will be less by the same amount as it was greater in the year of change. Over long enough time spans, accounting income equals cash inflows minus cash outflows; the valuation method affects the timing of income recognition, not its amount.

7.7

a. A periodic inventory system assumes that the difference between (1) units in beginning inventory plus units purchased during the period and (2) units in the ending inventory count were either sold or lost to shrinkage. The periodic inventory system cannot identify the portion sold versus the portion lost to shrinkage.

b. A perpetual inventory system maintains records to indicate the number of units that should be in ending inventory. Firms using a perpetual system must take a physical count, as in a periodic system, to verify that the expected number is actually on hand. Any difference between expected and actual amounts represents a loss from shrinkage.

c. Perpetual inventory systems are cost effective when a firm has a small number of large-value items because accounting can easily trace and record individual inventory purchases and sales. When a firm has a large number of small-value items, such individual tracing of inventory flows is costly; periodic inventory systems are usually more cost effective in this case.

d. Customer goodwill and loyalty are more critical for some businesses than others. Customers who find a firm "out of stock" of a needed item may never return to give the firm another chance. For such businesses, being out-of-stock is costly. The firm's inventory system should provide the necessary information to ensure adequate levels of inventory at all times. Perpetual inventory systems provide such information. The cost of an "out of stock" condition is less costly for other firms, so that the extra cost of a perpetual system may exceed the expected benefits.

7.8   **Periodic**:   *a., e., f.* (but this is changing), *g., i.* You can tell the story of the salad oil scandal, see below, in *e.* if you choose. With product bar codes and automatic scanners, use of perpetual methods increases.

         Perpetual: *b., c., d., h.* If, however, the automated production line need not close down in case of stockouts (an unusual case), then periodic for Part *c.*

7.8 continued.

The salad oil scandal was recounted by Earl K. Littrell in *Management Accounting*, July 1980, page 61, and August 1980, page 63, as follows:

Those unfamiliar with field warehousing can quickly grasp the basic ideas involved. A company surrenders control of its inventory storage facility to an independent warehousing company. Based on its count, the warehousing company issues receipts representing the quantity of goods in storage at that facility. By carefully checking inventory movement and by frequent audits, the warehousing company keeps the receipts in line with the goods on hand. Meanwhile, since the receipt may be pledged as collateral or sold, it passes through many hands and eventually is sold to a company wishing to take possession of the goods. The holder presents the receipt at the warehouse and hauls away the goods.

Creating Oil from Air
In the late 1950s, Allied Crude Vegetable Oil Refining Corp. had vegetable oil stored in its tanks. It entered into field warehousing agreements with several warehousing companies. By late 1963, warehouse receipts for almost two billion pounds of vegetable oil were outstanding, even though the tanks contained only 130 million pounds of vegetable oil. The nonexistent 1.8 billion pounds of oil were worth about $175 million, thus making this case the first nine-figure swindle in decades.

The various warehousing companies kept pads of their blank warehouse receipts on Allied's premises in an unlocked cabinet in the office of an Allied employee. It was simple to steal and forge these blank warehouse receipts. By November 1963, about $40 million in forged warehouse receipts were outstanding.

Most of the other 1.4 billion pound overstatement involved deceiving auditors about just how much oil was actually in the tanks. Tank contents were customarily measured by climbing the 42-foot tank and measuring the distance between the tank top and the liquid surface with a tape measure. If the tape read 15 feet, that meant there were 27 vertical feet of liquid in the tank. It was customary for an employee to operate the tape and call out the tape measure to a warehouse company employee. It was also customary for employees to short the measure by 10 to 20 feet, creating between a fourth to a half tank of oil out of air, and apparently this went undiscovered by the auditors prior to November 1963.

One device for overstating quantity of oil on hand was simply to add water to the tanks. The oil floated on top of the water, and an observer looking through the observation port at the top of the tank would see oil. The fact that there might only be two feet of oil on top of 35 feet of water could not be discerned readily. Curiously, as early as 1959, the warehousing companies had strong evidence from an

7.8 continued.

anonymous informer and from the U.S. Department of Agriculture that the tanks contained an unusually large amount of water. Inexplicably, the warehousing companies did not follow through on this information.

One of the more ingenious devices employed by Allied Crude Vegetable Oil Refining Corp. was to weld a vertical pipe a few feet in diameter directly underneath the observation port in a tank. This pipe then could be filled with oil or with water with oil floated on top, and an observer could have no idea that the rest of the tank was actually empty. This device is in the same class as the nail manufacturing company that nailed empty nail barrels to the floor of its warehouse. For several years, auditors recorded the barrels as full since they were unable to lift them.

Allied's tank farm had a capacity that was much less than two billion pounds of oil, and it was only natural that some nonexistent tanks were on Allied's books. This meant that the tank numbers on the tanks were repainted often, depending on just which tanks the auditors wished to see. In addition to these phantom tanks, Allied was counting at least seven tanks that were in unusable condition and at least 24 tanks leased to petroleum companies that had contained gasoline throughout the period Allied was in business.

These devices apparently were sufficient to take care of the weekly audit performed by the warehousing company. Occasionally, a more thorough audit would be done by an independent accounting firm or some other independent agency. Since these outside audits were done at a more leisurely pace, usually taking at least two weeks, they permitted an additional inventory trick. That is, the auditors apparently failed to station anyone to observe the pumps, and Allied was able to keep pumping the oil from tank to tank, just ahead of the auditors.

While there were some other fraudulent activities involved, such as a blatant check-kiting scheme for some $3 million, this caper basically was an inventory fraud of the first magnitude. Considering the financial losses and other fallout from the salad oil swindle, this incident served as a very expensive lesson in inventory accounting and auditing.

7.9   Accounting reports cost flows, not flows of physical quantities. Cost flow assumptions trace costs, not physical flows of goods. With specific identification, management manipulates cost flows by controlling goods flows.

7.10   Rising Purchase Prices:
        Higher Inventory Amount: FIFO
        Lower Inventory Amount: LIFO

        Falling Purchase Prices:
        Higher Inventory Amount: LIFO; LIFO results in a constant inventory
                                    amount so long as quantities do not
                                    change.
        Lower Inventory Amount: FIFO; FIFO results in an even lower
                                    inventory than does the weighted-average
                                    assumption.

7.11   a. Higher cost of goods sold amount: LIFO
            Lower cost of goods sold amount: FIFO

        b. Higher cost of goods sold amount: FIFO
            Lower cost of goods sold amount: LIFO

7.12   LIFO provides cost of goods sold closer to current costs than does FIFO
        so long as inventory quantities do not decrease and a firm does not
        liquidate old LIFO layers. Some would say, then, that LIFO does provide
        more meaningful income data when quantities do not decrease. The
        LIFO balance sheet always reflects older costs than does the FIFO
        balance sheet.

7.13   a. FIFO typically uses older acquisition costs for cost of goods sold than
            LIFO (except during a period of dipping into a LIFO layer), whereas
            LIFO uses older acquisition costs for ending inventory than FIFO.
            The larger the rate of change in the acquisition cost of inventory
            items, the more the older costs will differ from current costs and the
            larger will be the difference in cost of goods sold and ending
            inventory values between FIFO and LIFO.

        b. As the rate of inventory turnover increases, purchases during a
            period comprise an increasing proportion of cost of goods sold for
            that period under both FIFO and LIFO and differences in the
            beginning or ending inventory values under FIFO and LIFO play a
            decreasing role. Because purchases are the same regardless of the
            cost flow assumption, cost of goods sold under FIFO and LIFO
            should not differ significantly (unless the firm experienced dips into
            old LIFO layers).

        c. The inventory turnover ratio relates cost of goods sold to average
            inventories. A faster inventory turnover means a smaller level of
            inventories in the denominator relative to cost of goods sold in the
            numerator. The difference between FIFO and LIFO amounts in the
            denominator depends on the age of a firm's LIFO layers and the rate
            of change in the cost of inventory items since the firm adapted LIFO.
            These latter items relate to the passage of time rather than to the
            rate of turnover within a period of time.

7.14   The steel company, as long as equal rates of price increase occur for both firms' purchases. (If prices decline or increase at differing rates, then a different answer could result.) The larger the inventory turnover, the smaller the ratio of ending inventory to cost of goods sold. The smaller the percentage variation in ending inventory, the smaller the percentage variation in cost of goods sold, because the sum of the two must equal the cost of goods available (= beginning inventory + purchases). Because the retailer has the larger inventory turnover, it will have the smaller percentage variation in cost of goods sold by switching.

7.15   Dipping into an old LIFO layer may not be within a firm's control, such as when shortages prevent the firm from replacing a particular raw material. A dip may be partially within a firm's control, such as when a labor strike by employees forces the firm to reduce its finished goods inventory. A dip may be fully within a firm's control, such as when it delays purchases toward the end of the period in an effort to decrease cost of goods sold and increase net income.

7.16   Firms that maintain a relatively constant relation between the replacement cost of inventory items and selling prices will show a constant operating margin percentage (that is, operating margin/sales) each period. The operating margin will be the same under FIFO and LIFO. Both firms also include a realized holding gain or loss in their gross margins. The realized holding gain or loss reflects the change in the replacement cost of inventory items between the time of acquisition and the time of sale. The assumed holding period for FIFO is longer than for LIFO. Thus, FIFO likely includes more price changes (both increases and decreases) in the realized holding gain or loss than LIFO. If prices change at a constant rate and in a constant direction, then both FIFO and LIFO produce a smooth gross margin trend over time. If either the rate or direction of price change varies over time, FIFO more fully reflects these variations in the gross margin than LIFO.

7.17   Assuming a period of rising purchase prices, the firm might prefer to report higher earnings to shareholders and give up the tax savings that LIFO provides. Management's compensation often uses reported earnings as a base in its computation. Management obtains higher compensation by reporting higher earnings under FIFO. The firm might be experiencing operating difficulties and need to report higher earnings to keep shareholders happy. We question the rationality of such thinking but don't doubt that such reasoning occurs.

        The firm might be experiencing decreasing prices (costs) for its inventory items and obtain the maximum tax benefits by using FIFO. Note, however, that the Internal Revenue Code does not preclude a firm from using FIFO for tax purposes and LIFO for financial reporting. This combination minimizes taxes but maximizes earning reported to shareholders.

7.17 continued.

If prices are not changing much or if inventory turns over rapidly, then FIFO and LIFO do not differ significantly in terms of their effects on earnings or balance sheet amounts. The record keeping costs and fears of dipping into very old LIFO layers might lead a firm to use FIFO under these circumstances.

7.18   The firm saved taxes in earlier years when it created its LIFO layers and must pay the taxes in the year that it dips. It has at least delayed paying the taxes relative to FIFO, even if it must pay the same amount of taxes over time under both cost flow assumptions. Thus, the present value of the taxes saved under LIFO exceeds the present value under FIFO.

If tax rates were to rise dramatically during the period of the dip, the higher tax rate might overwhelm the effect of interest rates. Suppose the interest rate is 10 percent per period. Assume LIFO defers $100 at the end of Period 1, which the firm repays at the end of Period 3. The tax deferral is worth $21 [= (1.10 × 1.10 × $100) − $100]. If the income tax rate has increased by more than 21 percent between the end of Period 1 and the end of Period 3, then the deferral will not have saved present value dollars.

7.19   (Trembly Department Store; identifying inventory cost inclusions.)

a.	Purchase Price	$ 300,000
b.	Freight Cost	13,800
c.	Salary of Purchasing Manager	3,000
d.	Depreciation, taxes, Insurance and Utilities on Warehouse	27,300
e.	Salary of Warehouse Manager	2,200
f.	Merchandise Returns	(18,500)
g.	Cash Discounts Taken	(4,900)
	Acquisition Cost	$ 322,900

The underlying principle is that inventories should include all costs required to get the inventory ready for sale. The purchase of the inventory items (items a., c., f., and g.) provides the physical goods to be sold, the freight cost (item b.) puts the inventory items in the place most convenient for sale, and the storage costs (items d. and e.) keep the inventory items until the time of sale. Economists characterize these costs as providing form, place, and time utility, or benefits. Although accounting theory suggests the inclusion of each of these items in the valuation of inventory, some firms might exclude items c., d., e., and g. on the basis of lack of materiality.

7.20   (Identifying product costs and period expenses.)

a.	1 (Product Cost)	g.	1	m.	2
b.	2 (Period Expense)	h.	1	n.	2
c.	1	i.	1	o.	1
d.	1	j.	1	p.	2
e.	1	k.	2	q.	2
f.	2	l.	2		

7.21   (Identifying product costs, period expenses, and assets.)

a.	1 (Period Expense)	g.	3
b.	2 (Product Cost)	h.	2
c.	3 (Other Balance Sheet)	i.	1
d.	1	j.	1
e.	2	k.	2
f.	1		

7.22   (Raw materials inventory transactions.)

a. The relation among the four items is:

Beginning Raw Materials Inventory	+	Purchases of Raw Materials	–	Raw Materials Used	=	Ending Raw Materials Inventory
Year 2: $19,500	+	$87,600	–	$84,300	=	w

w = $22,800.

Year 3: $22,800	+	$93,700	–	x	=	$28,700

x = $87,800.

Year 4: $28,700	+	y	–	$87,600	=	$36,000

y = $94,900.

Year 5: $36,000	+	$98,200	–	$91,600	=	z

z = $42,600.

7.22 continued.

    b.   Purchases exceeded usage each period, causing the amount in the Raw Materials Inventory account to increase each year. One possible explanation is that inventory quantities remained the same but purchase prices increased each year. The raw materials added to inventories cost more than those used. A second explanation is that inventory quantities increased while purchase prices remained the same. Perhaps the firm anticipated higher production levels than actually realized and purchased raw materials to support this higher level of production. Alternatively, the firm may have anticipated increased prices or shortages for raw materials and purchased sufficient quantities before these events occurred. Finally, the increase in the Raw Materials Inventory account may result from both price and quantity increases, a combination of the explanations above.

7.23   (Work-in-process inventory transactions.)

    a.   The relationship among the six items is:

Beginning Work-in-Process Inventory	+	Raw Materials Used	+	Direct Labor Costs Incurred	+	Mfg. Overhead Costs Incurred	−	Cost of Units Completed	=	Ending Work-in-Process Inventory

Year 4: $67,900 + $247,800 + $242,600 + $87,100 − $575,200 = a; a = $70,200.

Year 5: $70,200 + $260,190 + $254,730 + $91,455 − b = $72,615; b = $603,960.

Year 6: $72,615 + $156,115 + c + $87,600 − $426,670 = $42,500; c = $152,840.

Year 7: $42,500 + d + $275,110 + $96,100 − $607,340 = $77,000; d = $270,630.

    b.   This firm experienced a substantial decline in the level of its manufacturing operations during Year 6. An examination of the components of manufacturing costs (raw material, direct labor, and overhead) during Year 7 relative to Year 5 indicates a higher than proportional increase in direct labor costs. Perhaps a labor strike curtailed operations in Year 6. The final compensation settlement increased wage rates in Year 7.

7.24 (Finished goods inventory transactions.)

a. The relationship among the four items is:

	Beginning Finished Goods Inventory	+	Cost of Units Completed	–	Cost of Goods Sold	=	Ending Finished Goods Inventory
Year 6:	$48,900	+	$460,700	–	$455,200	=	w
	w = $54,400.						
Year 7:	$54,400	+	$515,980	–	x	=	$69,660
	x = $500,720.						
Year 8:	$69,660	+	y	–	$560,800	=	$91,920
	y = $583,060.						
Year 9:	$91,920	+	$664,690	–	$634,000	=	z
	z = $122,610.						

b. The cost of units completed exceeded the cost of units sold each year, causing the Finished Goods Inventory account to increase. The cost of units sold increased at an increasing rate, suggesting growing sales levels. The firm likely continued to increase production each year to provide sufficient goods to satisfy these increasing sales levels. An alternative explanation is that manufacturing costs increased each year, but the firm experienced a lag between the incurrence of the cost in manufacturing and the recognition of this cost as an expense (that is, at the time of sale).

7.25 (The Proctor & Gamble Company; income computation for a manufacturing firm.)

Sales..	$ 33,434
Less Cost of Goods Sold	(19,600)
Less Marketing and Administrative Expenses....................	(9,655)
Income before Income Taxes..	$ 4,179
Income Tax Expense at 35%	(1,463)
Net Income..	$ 2,716

7.26 (Rockwell International Corporation; income computation for a manufacturing firm.)

Sales..	$ 11,123
Less Cost of Goods Sold	(8,675)
Less Marketing and Administrative Expenses....................	(1,409)
Less Interest Expense..	(100)
Income before Income Taxes...	$ 939
Income Tax Expense at 35%	(329)
Net Income..	$ 610
Work-in-Process Inventory, October 1................................	$ 850
Plus Manufacturing Costs Incurred during Year...............	8,771
Less Work-in-Process Inventory, September 30....................	(920)
Cost of Goods Completed during Year..............................	$ 8,701
Plus Finished Goods Inventory, October 1	330
Less Finished Goods Inventory, September 30.....................	(356)
Cost of Goods Sold..	$ 8,675

7.27 (Colt Real Estate Development Corporation; effect of inventory valuation basis on net income.)

a.

	Parcel A	Parcel B
(1) Acquisition Cost		
Year 6:...	--	--
Year 7: ($24,600 – $9,000).................	$ 15,600	--
Year 8: ($19,700 – $9,000).................	--	$ 10,700
Total.......................................	$ 15,600	$ 10,700
(2) Current Cost		
Year 6: ($16,700 – $9,000);		
($8,500 – $9,000)...........................	$ 7,700	$ (500)
Year 7: ($24,600 – $16,700);		
($14,400 – $8,500).........................	7,900	5,900
Year 8: ($19,700 – $14,400)..............	--	5,300
Total.......................................	$ 15,600	$ 10,700
(3) Lower of Cost or Market		
Year 6: ($8,500 – $9,000)	--	$ (500)
Year 7: ($24,600 – $9,000).................	$ 15,600	--
Year 8: ($19,700 – $18,500)...............	--	$ 11,200
Total.......................................	$ 15,600	$ 10,700

7.27 continued.

b. The three inventory valuation methods report the same total income for the three years combined, equal to cash inflows minus cash outflows for each parcel. The acquisition cost basis allocates all of the income to the year of sale. The current cost basis allocates a portion of the income to each period while the firm holds the land. The lower-of-cost-or-market method allocates holding gains to the period of sale but unrealized holding losses to the period when inventory values decline.

7.28 (Duggan Company; over sufficiently long spans, income is cash in less cash out; cost basis for inventory.)

a. **Lower of Cost or Market:**

	Year 1	Year 2	Year 3
Sales.................................	$ 200,000	$ 300,000	$ 400,000
Inventories, January 1	--	$ 50,000	$ 65,000
Purchases.........................	$ 210,000	271,000	352,000
Goods Available for Sale......	$ 210,000	$ 321,000	$ 417,000
Less Inventories, December 31.................................	(50,000)	(65,000)	(115,000)
Cost of Goods Sold	$ 160,000	$ 256,000	$ 302,000
Gross Profit on Sales	$ 40,000	$ 44,000	$ 98,000

b. **Acquisition Cost:**

	Year 1	Year 2	Year 3
Sales.................................	$ 200,000	$ 300,000	$ 400,000
Inventory, January 1..........	--	$ 60,000	$ 80,000
Purchases.........................	$ 210,000	271,000	352,000
Gain Available from Sale....	$ 210,000	$ 331,000	$ 432,000
Less Inventory, December 31.................................	(60,000)	(80,000)	(115,000)
Cost of Goods Sold	$ 150,000	$ 251,000	$ 317,000
Gross Profit on Sales	$ 50,000	$ 49,000	$ 83,000

c. The lower-of-cost-or-market basis recognizes lower income in years when prices are falling. However, when that trend is reversed, it produces higher reported income figures than the cost basis. Over long enough time periods, income is constant, equal to cash inflows minus cash outflows. Compare the total gross profit over all three years, a constant $182,000.

7.29 (Cypres; When goods available for sale exceed sales, firms can manipulate income even when they use specific identification.)

	Revenue	− Cost of Goods Sold	= Gross Margin
a. FIFO Cost Flow:	200 × $600 = $120,000	100 × $300 + 100 × $400 = $70,000	$50,000
b. Minimum Income:	200 × $600 = $120,000	100 × $400 + 100 × $350 = $75,000	$45,000
c. Maximum Income:	200 × $600 = $120,000	100 × $300 + 100 × $350 = $65,000	$55,000

7.30 (Harris Company; computations involving different cost flow assumptions.)

	Pounds	a. FIFO	b. Weighted Average	c. LIFO
Goods Available for Sale.........	13,500	$65,925	$65,925	$ 65,925
Less Ending Inventory...........	(2,500)	(13,075)[a]	(12,208)[c]	(11,350)[e]
Goods Sold..........................	11,000	$52,850[b]	$53,717[d]	$ 54,575[f]

[a]$(2,000 \times \$5.25) + (500 \times \$5.15) = \$13,075.$
[b]$(1,500 \times \$4.50) + (4,000 \times \$4.60) + (2,500 \times \$4.90) + (3,000 \times \$5.15) = \$52,850.$
[c]$(\$65,925/13,500) \times 2,500 = \$12,208.$
[d]$(\$65,925/13,500) \times 11,000 = \$53,717.$
[e]$(1,500 \times \$4.50) + (1,000 \times \$4.60) = \$11,350.$
[f]$(2,000 \times \$5.25) + (3,500 \times \$5.15) + (2,500 \times \$4.90) + (3,000 \times \$4.60) = \$54,575.$

7.31 (Moon Company; computations involving different cost flow assumptions.)

	Pounds	a. FIFO	b. Weighted Average	c. LIFO
Goods Available for Sale.........	41,000	$128,700	$128,700	$128,700
Less Ending Inventory...........	(12,500)	(37,830)[a]	(39,238)[c]	(40,430)[e]
Goods Sold..........................	28,500	$ 90,870[b]	$ 89,462[d]	$ 88,270[f]

[a]$(9,200 \times \$3.00) + (3,300 \times \$3.10) = \$37,830.$
[b]$(8,600 \times \$3.25) + (12,300 \times \$3.20) + (7,600 \times \$3.10) = \$90,870.$
[c]$\$128,700/41,000 = \$3.139; 12,500 \times \$3.139 = \$39,238.$
[d]$28,500 \times \$3.139 = \$89,462.$
[e]$(8,600 \times \$3.25) + (3,900 \times \$3.20) = \$40,430.$
[f]$(9,200 \times \$3.00) + (10,900 \times \$3.10) + (8,400 \times \$3.20) = \$88,270.$

7.32   (Benton Company; over sufficiently long time spans, income equals cash inflows minus cash outflows; cost flow assumptions.)

a.   FIFO

Year	Revenue			–	Cost of Goods Sold		=	Income
1	7,000 × $25 =	$	175,000		7,000 × $20 =	$ 140,000		$ 35,000
2	10,000 × $28 =		280,000		8,000 × $20 =	$ 160,000		
					2,000 × $22 =	44,000		
						$ 204,000		76,000
3	12,000 × $30 =		360,000		10,000 × $22 =	$ 220,000		
					2,000 × $24 =	48,000		
						$ 268,000		92,000
4	15,000 × $33 =		495,000		8,000 × $24 =	$ 192,000		
					7,000 × $26 =	182,000		
						$ 374,000		121,000
Totals.................			$1,310,000			$ 986,000		$ 324,000

b.   LIFO

Year	Revenue			–	Cost of Goods Sold		=	Income
1	7,000 × $25 =	$	175,000		7,000 × $20 =	$ 140,000		$ 35,000
2	10,000 × $28 =		280,000		10,000 × $22 =	$ 220,000		60,000
3	12,000 × $30 =		360,000		10,000 × $24 =	$ 240,000		
					2,000 × $22 =	44,000		
						$ 284,000		76,000
4	15,000 × 33 =		495,000		7,000 × $26 =	$ 182,000		
					8,000 × $20 =	160,000		
						$ 342,000		153,000
Totals.................			$1,310,000			$ 986,000		$ 324,000

c.   Over the four-year period, income is the same—cash inflows minus cash outflows—independent of the cost flow assumption. The cost flow assumption affects the timing of income recognition and this may well matter: it affects the timing of income tax payments, potential management bonuses, and potential violation of covenants in borrowing instruments and other contracts with outsiders, including labor contracts.

7.33   (Barnard Corporation; effect of LIFO on financial statements over several periods.)

a. **Year**   **Ending Inventory**

  3   2,000 × $4,00 .... $ 8,000

  4   (2,000 × $4.00) + (2,800 × $4.40)................ $20,320

  5   (2,000 × $4.00) + (2,800 × $4.40) +
              (1,200 × $4.75)................................ $26,020

  6   (2,000 × $4.00) + (1,800 × $4.40) $15,920

  7   (2,000 × $4.00) + (1,800 × $4.40) +
              (1,700 × $5.85)................................ $25,865

b.

Year	Revenue				−	Cost of Goods Sold		=	Income
3	6,000 ×	$5.00 =	$ 30,000			6,000 × $4.00 =	$ 24,000		$ 6,000
4	8,200 ×	5.50 =	45,100			8,200 × $4.40 =	$ 36,080		9,020
5	10,800 ×	5.94 =	64,152			10,800 × $4.75 =	$ 51,300		12,852
6	17,200 ×	6.65 =	114,380			15,000 × $5.32 =	$ 79,800		
						1,200 × $4.75 =	5,700		
						1,000 × $4.40 =	4,400		
							$ 89,900		24,480
	18,300 ×	$7.32 =	133,956			18,300 × $5.85 =	$107,055		26,901
Totals................			$387,588				$308,335		$ 79,253

c.

Year	Income	Sales	Rate of income To Sales
3	$ 6,000	$ 30,000	20.0%
4	9,020	45,100	20.0%
5	12,852	64,152	20.0%
6	24,480	114,380	21.4%
7	26,901	133,956	20.0%

d. Barnard Corporation attempts to maintain a constant relation between replacement costs and selling prices. This relation held for each year. The income to sales percentage increased during Year 6, however, because the firm dipped into LIFO layers of earlier years. The firm matched selling prices during Year 6 with acquisition costs of Year 5 and Year 4, inflating the income to sales percentage.

7.34   (Chan Company; reconstructing financial statement data from information on effects of liquidations of LIFO layers.)

    a. $8. Cost of goods sold was $900,000 lower than it would have been had the firm maintained inventories at 200,000 units. The average cost of the 50,000 units removed from the beginning inventory was $18 (= $900,000/50,000 units) less than current cost: $26 − $18 = $8.

    b. $1,000,000. Derived as follows: $8 × 50,000 units = $400,000 decline in inventory during the year. Beginning inventory must have been $400,000 + $600,000 (ending inventory) = $1,000,000.

7.35   (EKG Company; LIFO provides opportunity for income manipulation.)

    a. Largest cost of goods sold results from producing 70,000 (or more) additional units at a cost of $22 each, giving cost of goods sold of $1,540,000.

    b. Smallest cost of goods sold results from producing no additional units, giving cost of goods sold of $980,000 [= ($8 × 10,000) + ($15 × 60,000)].

    c.

	Income Reported	
	Minimum	**Maximum**
Revenues ($30 × 70,000)	$2,100,000	$2,100,000
Less Cost of Goods Sold	(1,540,000)	(980,000)
Gross Margin	$ 560,000	$1,120,000

7.36   (Sears; analysis of annual report; usage of LIFO.)

    a. Reported pretax income would have been higher by $230 million (= $670 million − $440 million).

    b. After taxes, net income would increase $230 million × .66 = $151.8 million. $151.8/$606.0 = .25; so net income would be 25 percent larger than shown, or $757.8 million.

7.37   (Boise Cascade; identifying quantity and price changes.)

    a. Inventory quantities increased during Year 10 because ending inventory for Year 10 exceeded ending inventory for Year 9. Thus, Boise Cascade added a new LIFO layer. Replacement cost decreased during Year 10 because the excess of current cost over LIFO cost decreased during the year, despite an increase in quantities.

    b. Inventory quantities decreased during Year 11 because ending inventory for Year 11 is less than ending inventory for Year 10. Thus, Boise Cascade dipped into its Year 10 LIFO layer. Replacement cost increased during Year 11 because the excess of current cost over LIFO cost increased during the year, despite a decrease in quantities.

7.38 (Giles Computer Store; separating operating margin from holding gains.)

	FIFO	LIFO
a.		
Beginning Inventory (200 × $300)	$ 60,000	$ 60,000
Purchases (2,500 × $400)	1,000,000	1,000,000
Goods Available for Sale	$ 1,060,000	$ 1,060,000
Less Ending Inventory:		
(400 × $400)	(160,000)	
(200 × $300) + (200 × $400)		(140,000)
Cost of Goods Sold	$ 900,000	$ 920,000
b.		
Revenues (2,300 × $800)	$ 1,840,000	$ 1,840,000
Less Cost of Goods Sold	(900,000)	(920,000)
Gross Margin on Sales	$ 940,000	$ 920,000
c.		
Revenues	$ 1,840,000	$ 1,840,000
Less Replacement Cost of Goods Sold (2,300 × $400)	(920,000)	(920,000)
Operating Margin	$ 920,000	$ 920,000
Realized Holding Gains:		
Replacement Cost of Goods Sold	$ 920,000	$ 920,000
Less Historical Cost of Goods Sold	(900,000)	(920,000)
Realized Holding Gain	20,000	-0-
Gross Margin on Sales	$ 940,000	$ 920,000
d.		
Unrealized Holding Gains:		
Replacement Cost of Ending Inventory (400 × $500)	$ 200,000	$ 200,000
Less Historical Cost of Ending Inventory:		
(400 × $400)	(160,000)	
(200 × $300) + (200 × $400)		(140,000)
Unrealized Holding Gains	40,000	60,000
Total Realized Gross Margin and Unrealized Holding Gains	$ 980,000	$ 980,000

7.38 continued.

    e. The equality is not a coincidence. The choice of cost flow assumption does not affect the increase in wealth during a period. The choice affects only the amount of reported income. When unrealized gains are added to reported, realized gains, income is independent of the cost flow assumption for inventory.

7.39   (Warren Company; effect of inventory errors.)

a.	None.	f.	Understatement by $1,000.
b.	None.	g.	Understatement by $1,000.
c.	Understatement by $1,000.	h.	None.
d.	Overstatement by $1,000.	i.	None.
e.	Overstatement by $1,000.		

7.40   (Soft-Touch, Inc.; preparation of journal entries and income statement for a manufacturing firm.)

a. (1) Raw Materials Inventory 66,700
          Accounts Payable................................. 66,700

    (2) Work-in-Process Inventory...................... 63,900
          Raw Materials Inventory 63,900

    (3) Work-in-Process Inventory...................... 175,770
        Selling Expenses 19,200
        Administrative Expenses 22,500
          Cash... 217,470

    (4) Work-in-Process Inventory...................... 16,200
        Selling Expenses 3,100
        Administrative Expenses 2,200
          Accumulated Depreciation.................... 21,500

    (5) Work-in-Process Inventory...................... 18,300
        Selling Expenses 5,600
        Administrative Expenses 4,100
          Cash... 28,000

    (6) Finished Goods Inventory 270,870
          Work-in-Process Inventory................... 270,870

    (7) Accounts Receivable.............................. 350,000
          Sales... 350,000

    (8) Cost of Goods Sold................................. 268,670
          Finished Goods Inventory 268,670
        $38,000 + $270,870 − $40,200 = $268,670.

7.40 continued.

b.

SOFT-TOUCH, INC.
Income Statement
For the Month of January

Sales..		$ 350,000
Less Expenses:		
Cost of Goods Sold................................	$ 268,670	
Selling	27,900	
Administrative	28,800	(325,370)
Net Income...		$ 24,630

Note: Instead of using a functional classification of expenses (that is, selling, administrative), classification by their nature (salary, depreciation, other operating) is acceptable.

7.41 (Famous Horse Garment Factory; preparation of journal entries and income statement for a manufacturing firm.)

a. (1)
Raw Materials Inventory	245,400	
Accounts Payable.................................		245,400

(2)
Work-in-Process Inventory......................	238,400	
Raw Materials Inventory		238,400

(3)
Work-in-Process Inventory......................	175,200	
Selling Expenses....................................	37,800	
Administrative Expenses.........................	54,800	
Cash..		267,800

(4)
Work-in-Process Inventory......................	29,400	
Selling Expenses....................................	4,800	
Administrative Expenses.........................	5,800	
Accumulated Depreciation....................		40,000

(5)
Work-in-Process Inventory......................	36,400	
Selling Expenses....................................	14,600	
Administrative Expenses.........................	8,800	
Cash..		59,800

(6)
Finished Goods Inventory	468,000	
Work-in-Process Inventory...................		468,000

(7)
Accounts Receivable...............................	650,000	
Sales...		650,000

7.41 a. continued.

    (8) Cost of Goods Sold..................................... 474,000

              Finished Goods Inventory......................   474,000

            $146,000 + $468,000 − $140,000 = $474,000.

b.

FAMOUS HORSE GARMENT FACTORY
Income Statement
For the Month of January
(In Hong Kong Dollars)

Sales...		$ 650,000
Less Expenses:		
Cost of Goods Sold................................	$ 474,000	
Selling...	57,200	
Administrative.....................................	69,400	(600,600)
Net Income...		$ 49,400

Note: Instead of using a functional classification of expenses (that is, selling, administrative), classification by their nature (salary, depreciation, other operating) is acceptable.

7.42   (Parkhurst Company; flow of manufacturing costs through the accounts.)

    a.   The cost of raw materials used is $402,700. The cost of factory supplies used is $25,600.

    b.   The cost of units completed during July is $789,500.

    c.   The cost of units sold during July is $793,000.

The derivation of the amounts in Parts *a., b.,* and *c.* above appear in the T-accounts following.

Raw Materials Inventory				Factory Supplies Inventory			
Bal.	53,900			Bal.	8,700		
(1)	397,400	402,700	(2)*	(3)	26,100	25,600	(4)*
Bal.	48,600			Bal.	9,200		

7.42 continued.

Work-in-Process Inventory				Finished Goods Inventory			
Bal.	73,200			Bal.	49,200		
(2)	402,700						
(4)	25,600						
(5)	294,900	789,500	(10)*	(10)	789,500		
(6)	12,200					793,000	(11)*
(7)	3,600						
(8)	47,300						
(9)	4,800						
Bal.	74,800			Bal.	45,700		

Cost of Goods Sold				Cash or Various Liabilities			
(11)	793,000					397,400	(1)
						26,100	(3)
						294,900	(5)
						12,200	(6)
						3,600	(7)

Prepaid Rent				Accumulated Depreciation			
		4,800	(9)			47,300	(8)

*Amount is calculated by plugging.

7.43   (Oak Ridge Industries; flow of manufacturing costs through the accounts.)

a.   The cost of raw materials used is $89,400.

b.   The cost of units completed and transferred to the finished goods storeroom is $183,700.

c.   Net income is $26,300 (= $250,000 – $182,400 – $41,300).

The derivation of the amounts in Parts a., b., and c. above appear in the T-accounts following.

Raw Materials Inventory				Work-in-Process Inventory			
	25,300				78,100		
(1)	91,300	89,400	(2)*	(2)	89,400		
				(3)	72,400	183,700	(6)*
				(4)	3,100		
				(5)	17,600		
	27,200				76,900		

7.43 continued.

Finished Goods Inventory				Cost of Goods Sold			
	38,400			(7)	182,400		
(6)	183,700	182,400	(7)*				
	39,700						

Accumulated Depreciation				Sales			
		17,600	(5)			250,000	(8)

Selling and Administrative Expenses			Other Accounts			
(9)	41,300		(8)	250,000	91,300	(1)
					72,400	(3)
					3,100	(4)
					41,300	(9)

*Amount derived by plugging.

7.44 (Wilmington Chemical Company; preparing T-account entries, income statement, and balance sheet for a manufacturing firm.)

a., b., and c.

Cash				Accounts Receivable			
Bal.	580,800	60,000	(4)	(10)	510,900	495,000	(11)
(11)	495,000	446,010	(5)				
		105,570	(13)				
Bal.	464,220			Bal.	15,900		

Raw Materials Inventory				Work-in-Process Inventory			
Bal.	28,800	253,200	(3)	(2)	222,000	422,625	(9)
(1)	242,400			(3)	253,200		
				(5)	9,000		
				(5)	4,380		
				(5)	39,600		
				(6)	180		
				(7)	1,800		
				(8)	1,200		
Bal.	18,000			Bal.	108,735		

7.44 a., b., and c. continued.

Finished Goods Inventory			
(9)	422,625	334,125	(15)
Bal.	88,500		

Office Supplies Inventory			
(13)	2,400	1,200	(14)
Bal.	1,200		

Prepaid Insurance			
(5)	14,400	1,200	(8)
Bal.	13,200		

Factory Equipment			
Bal.	204,000		
(4)	168,000		
(6)	3,600		
Bal.	375,600		

Accumulated Depreciation			
		1,800	(7)
		1,800	Bal.

Accounts Payable			
(5)	210,000	33,600	Bal.
		242,400	(1)
		3,780	(6)
		69,780	Bal.

Equipment Contract Payable			
		108,000	(4)
		108,000	Bal.

Wages Payable			
(5)	168,630	222,000	(2)
(13)	41,445	93,000	(12)
(13)	41,325		
		63,600	Bal.

Capital Stock			
		780,000	Bal.
		780,000	Bal.

Retained Earnings			
		62,175	(18)
		62,175	Bal.

Sales Revenue			
(17)	510,900	510,900	(10)

Cost of Goods Sold			
(15)	334,125	334,125	(16)

Sales Salaries Expense			
(12)	46,200	46,200	(16)

Office Salaries Expense			
(12)	46,800	46,800	(16)

Advertising Expense			
(13)	10,800	10,800	(16)

Office Rent Expense			
(13)	3,300	3,300	(16)

7.44 a., b., and c. continued.

	Miscellaneous Office Expenses				Miscellaneous Selling Expenses		
(13)	2,100	2,100	(16)	(13)	4,200	4,200	(16)

	Office Supplies Expense				Income Summary		
(14)	1,200	1,200	(16)	(16)	448,725	510,900	(17)
				(18)	62,175		
					510,900		

d.

WILMINGTON CHEMICAL COMPANY
Statement of Income and Retained Earnings
For the Month of October

Sales...		$ 510,900
Less Operating Expenses:		
Cost of Goods Sold..................................	$ 334,125	
Sales Salaries Expense............................	46,200	
Office Salaries Expense...........................	46,800	
Advertising Expense.............................	10,800	
Office Rent Expense...............................	3,300	
Miscellaneous Office Expenses	2,100	
Miscellaneous Selling Expenses..............	4,200	
Office Supplies Expense	1,200	
Total Operating Expenses....................		(448,725)
Net Income..		$ 62,175
Retained Earnings, October 1.....................		-0-
Retained Earnings, October 31...................		$ 62,175

7.44 continued.

e.

WILMINGTON CHEMICAL COMPANY
Balance Sheet
October 31

Assets

Current Assets:

Cash	$ 464,220	
Accounts Receivable	15,900	
Raw Materials Inventory	18,000	
Work-in-Process Inventory	108,735	
Finished Goods Inventory	88,500	
Office Supplies Inventory	1,200	
Prepaid Insurance	13,200	
Total Current Assets		$ 709,755

Noncurrent Assets:

Factory Equipment	$ 375,600	
Less Accumulated Depreciation	(1,800)	
Total Noncurrent Assets		373,800
Total Assets		$ 1,083,555

Liabilities and Shareholders' Equity

Liabilities:

Accounts Payable	$ 69,780	
Equipment Contract Payable	108,000	
Wages Payable	63,600	
Total Liabilities		$ 241,380

Shareholders' Equity:

Capital Stock	$ 780,000	
Retained Earnings	62,175	
Total Shareholders' Equity		842,175
Total Liabilities and Shareholders' Equity		$ 1,083,555

7.45   (Hartison Corporation; detailed comparison of various choices for inventory accounting.)

	FIFO	LIFO	Weighted Average
Inventory, 1/1/Year 1................	$ 0	$ 0	$ 0
Purchases for Year 1...............	25,600	25,600	25,600
Goods Available for Sale During Year 1.............................	$ 25,600	$ 25,600	$ 25,600
Less Inventory, 12/31/Year 1.....	(6,400)[1]	(5,000)[2]	(5,565)[3]
Cost of Goods Sold for Year 1.....	$ 19,200	$ 20,600	$ 20,035
Inventory, 1/1/Year 2................	$ 6,400 [1]	$ 5,000 [2]	$ 5,565 [3]
Purchases for Year 2...............	42,600	42,600	42,600
Goods Available for Sale During Year 2.............................	$ 49,000	$ 47,600	$ 48,165
Less Inventory, 12/31/Year 2.....	(5,400)[4]	(3,000)[5]	(4,661)[6]
Cost of Goods Sold for Year 2.....	$ 43,600	$ 44,600	$ 43,504

[1]$(400 \times \$13) + (100 \times \$12) = \$6,400$.
[2]$500 \times \$10 = \$5,000$.
[3]$(\$25,600/2,300) \times 500 = \$5,565$.
[4]$300 \times \$18 = \$5,400$.
[5]$300 \times \$10 = \$3,000$.
[6]$(\$48,165/3,100) \times 300 = \$4,661$.

a. $19,200.   d. $43,600.
b. $20,600.   e. $44,600.
c. $20,035.   f. $43,504.

g.

	Cost of Goods Sold for Two Years
FIFO	$62,800
LIFO	65,200

The FIFO cost flow assumption results in reported pretax income which is higher by $2,400 (= $65,200 − $62,800) over the two-year period. After taxes, the difference is reduced to .60 × $2,400 = $1,440.

h. Management might prefer to report the higher net income from FIFO of $1,440. To do so, however, requires $960 (= .40 × $2,400) of extra income tax payments currently that could be postponed until Hartison Corporation dips further into its January Year 1 purchases. We think management should use LIFO for tax purposes and, because financial reports must conform to tax reporting, in this case the firm should use LIFO for financial reporting.

7.46   (Hartison Corporation; continuation of preceding problem introducing current cost concepts.)

a.

	FIFO	**LIFO**	**Weighted Average**
Sales (1,800 × $18)	$ 32,400	$ 32,400	$ 32,400
Less Cost of Goods Sold at Average Current Replacement Cost (1,800 × $12)	(21,600)	(21,600)	(21,600)
Operating Margin..............	$ 10,800	$ 10,800	$ 10,800
Realized Holding Gain:			
Cost of Goods Sold at Current Replacement Cost.	$ 21,600	$ 21,600	$ 21,600
Less Cost of Goods Sold at Acquisition Cost..........	(19,200)	(20,600)	(20,035)
Total Realized Holding Gain...............	$ 2,400	$ 1,000	$ 1,565
Conventional Gross Margin...............................	$ 13,200	$ 11,800	$ 12,365
Unrealized Holding Gain:			
Ending Inventory at Current Replacement Cost (500 × $14)	$ 7,000	$ 7,000	$ 7,000
Less Ending Inventory at Acquisition Cost..........	(6,400)	(5,000)	(5,565)
Total Unrealized Holding Gain	$ 600	$ 2,000	$ 1,435
Less Unrealized Holding Gain at Beginning of Period.........................	--	--	--
Total Profit Including Holding Gain[a]	$ 13,800	$ 13,800	$ 13,800

[a]Total of operating margin, realized holding gain, and unrealized holding gain.

7.46 continued.

b.

	FIFO	LIFO	Weighted Average
Sales (2,800 × $24)	$ 67,200	$ 67,200	$ 67,200
Less Cost of Goods Sold at Average Current Replacement Cost (2,800 × $16)	(44,800)	(44,800)	(44,800)
Operating Margin..............	$ 22,400	$ 22,400	$ 22,400
Realized Holding Gain:			
Cost of Goods Sold at Current Replacement Cost.	$ 44,800	$ 44,800	$ 44,800
Less Cost of Goods Sold at Acquisition Cost..........	(43,600)	(44,600)	(43,504)
Total Realized Holding Gain................	$ 1,200	$ 200	$ 1,296
Conventional Gross Margin................................	$ 23,600	$ 22,600	$ 23,696
Unrealized Holding Gain:			
Ending Inventory at Current Replacement Cost (300 × $18)	$ 5,400	$ 5,400	$ 5,400
Less Ending Inventory at Acquisition Cost..........	(5,400)	(3,000)	(4,661)
Total Unrealized Holding Gain	$ 0	$ 2,400	$ 739
Less Unrealized Holding Gain at Beginning of Period (see Part a.)...........	(600)	(2,000)	$ (1,435)
Increase (Decrease) in Unrealized Holding Gain during Year 2.................	$ (600)	$ 400	$ (696)
Total Profit Including Holding Gain........................	$ 23,000	$ 23,000	$ 23,000

c.

		FIFO	LIFO	Weighted Average
Operating Margin	—Year 1..	$ 10,800	$ 10,800	$ 10,800
	—Year 2..	22,400	22,400	22,400
Realized Holding Gain—				
Year 1	....	2,400	1,000	1,565
Year 2	....	1,200	200	1,296
Unrealized Holding Gain at the End of Year 2	....	0	2,400	739
Total Profit Including Holding Gain	....	$ 36,800	$ 36,800	$ 36,800

7.47   (Burton Corporation; detailed comparison of various choices for inventory accounting.)

	FIFO	LIFO	Weighted Average
Inventory, 1/1/Year 1................	$ 0	$ 0	$ 0
Purchases for Year 1................	14,400	14,400	14,400
Goods Available for Sale During Year 1.............................	$ 14,400	$ 14,400	$ 14,400
Less Inventory, 12/31/Year 1	(3,000)[1]	(2,000)[2]	(2,400)[3]
Cost of Goods Sold for Year 1.....	$ 11,400	$ 12,400	$ 12,000
Inventory, 1/1/Year 2................	$ 3,000 [1]	$ 2,000 [2]	$ 2,400 [3]
Purchases for Year 2................	21,000	21,000	21,000
Goods Available for Sale During Year 2.............................	$ 24,000	$ 23,000	$ 23,400
Less Inventory, 12/31/Year 2	(5,000)[4]	(6,200)[5]	(5,850)[6]
Cost of Goods Sold for Year 2.....	$ 19,000	$ 16,800	$ 17,550

[1] $200 \times \$15 = \$3,000$.
[2] $200 \times \$10 = \$2,000$.
[3] $(\$14,400/1,200) \times 200 = \$2,400$.
[4] $500 \times \$10 = \$5,000$.
[5] $(200 \times \$10) + (300 \times \$14) = \$6,200$.
[6] $(\$23,400/2,000) \times 500 = \$5,850$.

a. $11,400.   d. $19,000.
b. $12,400.   e. $16,800.
c. $12,000.   f. $17,550.

g. FIFO results in higher net income for Year 1. Purchase prices for inventory items increased during Year 1. FIFO uses older, lower purchase prices to measure cost of goods sold, whereas LIFO uses more recent, higher prices.

h. LIFO results in higher net income for Year 2. Purchase prices for inventory items decreased during Year 2. LIFO uses more recent, lower prices to measure cost of goods sold, whereas FIFO uses older, higher prices.

7.48   (Burton Corporation; continuation of preceding problem introducing current cost concepts.)

a.

	FIFO	LIFO	Weighted Average
Sales (1,000 × $25)	$ 25,000	$ 25,000	$ 25,000
Less Cost of Goods Sold at Average Current Replacement Cost (1,000 × $14)	(14,000)	(14,000)	(14,000)
Operating Margin..............	$ 11,000	$ 11,000	$ 11,000
Realized Holding Gain:			
Cost of Goods Sold at Current Replacement Cost.	$ 14,000	$ 14,000	$ 14,000
Less Cost of Goods Sold at Acquisition Cost..........	(11,400)	(12,400)	(12,000)
Total Realized Holding Gain..............	$ 2,600	$ 1,600	$ 2,000
Conventional Gross Margin	$ 13,600	$ 12,600	$ 13,000
Unrealized Holding Gain:			
Ending Inventory at Current Replacement Cost (200 × $16)	$ 3,200	$ 3,200	$ 3,200
Less Ending Inventory at Acquisition Cost..........	(3,000)	(2,000)	(2,400)
Total Unrealized Holding Gain.......	$ 200	$ 1,200	$ 800
Total Profit Including Holding Gain[a]	$ 13,800	$ 13,800	$ 13,800

[a]Total of operating margin, realized holding gain, and unrealized holding gain.

7.48 continued.

b.

	FIFO	LIFO	Weighted Average
Sales (1,500 × $22)	$ 33,000	$ 33,000	$ 33,000
Less Cost of Goods Sold at Average Current Replacement Cost (1,500 × $12)	(18,000)	(18,000)	(18,000)
Operating Margin..............	$ 15,000	$ 15,000	$ 15,000
Realized Holding Gain:			
Cost of Goods Sold at Current Replacement Cost.	$ 18,000	$ 18,000	$ 18,000
Less Cost of Goods Sold at Acquisition Cost..........	(19,000)	(16,800)	(17,550)
Total Realized Holding Gain (Loss).....	$ (1,000)	$ 1,200	$ 450
Conventional Gross Margin................................	$ 14,000	$ 16,200	$ 15,450
Unrealized Holding Gain:			
Ending Inventory at Current Replacement Cost (500 × $10)	$ 5,000	$ 5,000	$ 5,000
Less Ending Inventory at Acquisition Cost..........	(5,000)	(6,200)	(5,850)
Total Unrealized Holding Gain (Loss)	$ 0	$ (1,200)	$ (850)
Less Unrealized Holding Gain at Beginning of Period (see Part a.)..........	(200)	(1,200)	(800)
Increase (Decrease) in Unrealized Holding Gain during Year 2.................	$ (200)	$ (2,400)	$ (1,650)
Total Profit Including Holding Gain........................	$ 13,800	$ 13,800	$ 13,800

		FIFO	LIFO	Weighted Average
c.	Operating Margin—Year 1..	$ 11,000	$ 11,000	$ 11,000
	—Year 2..	15,000	15,000	15,000
	Realized Holding Gain (Loss)			
	Year 1	2,600	1,600	2,000
	Year 2	(1,000)	1,200	450
	Unrealized Holding Gain at the End of Year 2	0	(1,200)	(850)
	Total Profit Including Holding Gain (Loss)..	$ 27,600	$ 27,600	$ 27,600

7.49 (Whitimore Corporation; effect of FIFO and LIFO on gross margin over several periods.)

a.

Year	Revenue			−	Cost of Goods Sold	=	Gross Margin
5	3,600 × $15.00 =	$ 54,000			3,600 × $10 = $ 36,000		$ 18,000
6	8,000 × $18.00 =	144,000			(400 × $10) + (7,600 × $12) = 95,200		48,800
7	5,500 × $16.50 =	90,750			(1,400 × $12) + (4,100 × $11) = 61,900		28,850
8	10,000 × $15.00 =	150,000			(1,900 × $11) + (8,100 × $10) = 101,900		48,100

b.

Year	Revenue			−	Cost of Goods Sold	=	Gross Income
5	3,600 × $15.00 =	$ 54,000			3,600 × $10 = $ 36,000		$ 18,000
6	8,000 × $18.00 =	144,000			8,000 × $12 = $ 96,000		48,000
7	5,500 × $16.50 =	90,750			5,500 × $11 = $ 60,500		30,250
8	10,000 × $15.00 =	150,000			(9,000 × $10) + (500 × $11) + (500 × $12) = $101,500		48,500

c.

		Change in Gross Margin		Change in Sales
		FIFO	LIFO	
Year 6:	[($48,800/$18,000) − 1]	+171.1%		
	[($48,000/$18,000) − 1]		+166.7%	
	[($144,000/$54,000) − 1]			+166.7%
Year 7:	[($28,850/$48,800) − 1]	−40.9%		
	[($30,250/$48,000) − 1]		−37.0%	
	[($90,750/$144,000) − 1]			−37.0%
Year 8:	[($48,100/$28,850) − 1]	+66.7%		
	[($48,500/$30,250) − 1]		+60.3%	
	[($150,000/$90,750) − 1]			+65.3%

d. Whitimore Corporation consistently sets selling prices at 50 percent above replacement costs. Because LIFO uses more current acquisition costs to measure cost of goods sold than FIFO, LIFO's gross margin changes tend to track changes in sales. FIFO uses older acquisition costs to measure cost of goods sold. The gross margin under FIFO each period includes a larger realized holding gain or holding loss than LIFO, resulting in greater fluctuations in reported earnings. An exception to the generalization that LIFO tends to result in smother changes in gross margin each year than FIFO may occur when a LIFO firm dips into an old LIFO layer. Whitimore Corporation dipped into its LIFO layers during Year 8 but, in this case, its percentage change in the gross margin under LIFO is still less than under FIFO.

7.50   (The Back Store; dealing with LIFO inventory layers.)

a. 200,000 units sold in Year 30 − 10,000 units purchased in Year 30 included in the 12/31/Year 30 inventory = 190,000 units.

b.
Revenue (300,000 Units @ $15)	$4,500,000
Replacement Cost of Goods Sold (300,000 Units @ $10)	3,000,000
Operating Margin on Sales	$1,500,000

(Assume the average purchase price during Year 31, $10 was the average replacement cost during the year.)

c.
Replacement-cost Cost of Goods Sold (Average)		$3,000,000
Less Acquisition Cost:		
250,000 × $10	$2,500,000	
10,000 × $9	90,000	
20,000 × $6	120,000	
20,000 × $3	60,000	2,770,000
Realized Holding Gain		$ 230,000

Thus: $1,500,000 + $230,000 = $1,730,000 (conventional gross margin).

d.
Conventional Gross Margin		$1,730,000
Unrealized Holding Gain:		
Replacement Cost at Period-End: 40,000 × $11	$ 440,000	
Acquisition Cost: 40,000 × $3	(120,000)	320,000
Less: Unrealized Holding Gain in Beginning Inventory:		
Replacement Cost on 12/31/Year 30: 90,000 × $8	$ 720,000	
Inventory Cost on 12/31/Year 30	390,000	(330,000)
Economic Profit		$1,720,000

e.
Operating Margin on Sales		$1,500,000
Less Acquisition Cost at FIFO:		
210,000 × $10	$2,100,000	
90,000 × $9	810,000	
	$2,910,000	
Less: Replacement Cost (Average)	(3,000,000)	90,000
Conventional Gross Margin (FIFO)		$1,590,000

7.51   (Burch Corporation; reconstructing underlying events from ending inventory amounts [adapted from CPA examination].)

a. Down. Notice that lower of cost or market is lower than acquisition cost (FIFO); current market price is less than cost.

b. Up. FIFO means last-in, still-here. The last purchases (FIFO = LISH) cost $44,000 and the earlier purchases (LIFO = FISH) cost $41,800. Also, lower-of-cost-or-market basis shows acquisition costs which are greater than or equal to current cost.

c. LIFO Cost. Other things being equal, the largest income results from the method that shows the largest *increase* in inventory during the year.

$$\begin{aligned} \text{Margin} \;=\;& \text{Revenues} - \text{Cost of Goods Sold} \\ =\;& \text{Revenues} - \text{Beginning Inventory} - \text{Purchases} + \text{Ending Inventory} \\ =\;& \text{Revenues} - \text{Purchases} + \text{Increase in Inventory}. \end{aligned}$$

Because the beginning inventory in Year 1 is zero, the method with the largest closing inventory amount implies the largest increase and hence the largest income.

d. Lower of Cost or Market. The method with the "largest increase in inventory" during the year in this case is the method with the smallest decrease, because all methods show declines in inventory during Year 2. Lower of cost or market shows a decrease in inventory of only $3,000 during Year 2—the other methods show larger decreases ($3,800; $4,000).

e. Lower of Cost or Market. The method with the largest increase in inventory: $10,000. LIFO shows a $5,400 increase while FIFO shows $8,000.

f. LIFO Cost. The lower income for all three years results from the method that shows the smallest increase in inventory over the three years. Because all beginning inventories were zero under all methods, we need merely find the method with the smallest ending inventory at Year 3 year-end.

g. FIFO lower by $2,000. Under FIFO, inventories increased $8,000 during Year 3. Under lower of cost or market, inventories increased $10,000 during Year 3. Lower of cost or market has a bigger increase—$2,000—and therefore lower of cost or market shows a $2,000 larger income than FIFO for Year 3.

7.52 (Wilson Company; LIFO layers influence purchasing behavior and provide opportunity for income manipulation.)

Cost per Pound	Layer	Beginning Inventory Cost ($000)	+ Purchases Cost ($000)	-Ending Inventory Pounds	Ending Inventory Cost ($000)	= Cost of Goods Sold ($000)
a. (Controller)	Year 1	$ 60.0	---	2,000	$ 60.0	---
	Year 6	9.2	---	200	9.2	---
	Year 7	19.2	---	400	19.2	---
7,000 @	Year 10	72.8	---	1,400	72.8	---
$62/lb.	Year 11	---	$434.0	---	---	434.0
		$161.2	$434.0	4,000	$161.2	$434.0
b. (Purchasing	Year 1	$ 60.0	---	600	$ 18.0	$ 42.0
Agent)	Year 6	9.2	---	---	---	9.2
	Year 7	19.2	---	---	---	19.2
3,600 @	Year 10	72.8	---	---	---	72.8
$62/lb.	Year 11	---	$223.2	---	---	223.2
		$161.2	$223.2	600	$ 18.0	$366.4

c.
Controller's Policy COGS $62/lb.	$ 434.00
Less Purchasing Agent's COGS	(366.40)
Controller's Extra Deductions	$ 67.60
Tax Rate: 40 Percent	X .40
Controller's Tax Savings	$ 27.04
Controller's Extra Cash Costs for Inventory: 3,400 @ $10/lb.	$ 34.00

d. Follow the purchasing agent's advice. The controller's policy does save taxes but not as much in taxes as the extra inventory costs.

7.52 continued.

e. To maximize income for Year 11, liquidate all our LIFO inventory layers, 4,000 lbs. with total cost $161,200, and purchase only 3,000 lbs. at $62 each during Year 11. To minimize income, acquire 7,000 lbs. at $62 each.

Policy	Cost of Goods Sold for Year 11
Minimum Income:	
7,000 lbs. × $62	$434,000[a]
Maximum Income:	
4,000 lbs. of Old Layer	(161,200)
3,000 lbs. at $62	(186,000)
Income Spread before Taxes	$ 86,800
Taxes at 40 Percent	(34,720)
Income Spread after Taxes	$ 52,080

By manipulating purchases of expensium, Wilson Company reports aftertax income anywhere in the range from $50,000 (by following the controller's policy) up to $102,080 (= $50,000 + $52,080) by acquiring only 3,000 lbs. and liquidating all LIFO layers.

7.53 (Deere & Company; interpreting disclosures relating to LIFO inventories.) (Amounts in Millions)

a. $20.8/(1 − .34) = $31.5 smaller.

b. .34 × $31.5 = $10.7 million.

c. .34[($1,885.0 − $760.9) − ($1,941.0 − $872.0)] = $18.7.

d. .34($1,885.0 − $760.9) = $382.2. Deere's actual tax savings is larger than $$382.2 because the income tax rate in earlier years exceeded 34 percent.

7.54 (Sankyo and Eli Lily; comparing gross margins using FIFO and LIFO cost flow assumptions.)

a. and b.

	Sankyo Average	Eli Lily LIFO	Eli Lily FIFO
Sales	¥516,750	$ 6,452.4	$ 6,452.4
Cost of Goods Sold	(260,225)	(1,959.0)	(1,937.2)[a]
Gross Margin	¥256,525	$ 4,493.4	$ 4,515.2
Gross Margin Percentage	49.6%	69.6%	70.0%

[a]$1,959.0 + $88.9 − $110.7 = $1,937.2.

7.54 continued.

c. Eli Lily outperformed Sankyo during the current year in terms of profitability regardless of the cost flow assumption used. During periods of inflation and increasing inventory quantities, one would expect a lower gross margin percentage using LIFO than using FIFO. Thus, Lily's higher gross margin than Sankyo using LIFO understates its degree of superior profitability relative to the gross margins computed using FIFO. The gross margin percentage for Lily using a weighted average cost flow assumption would presumably be between the amounts computed under LIFO and FIFO, still superior to that for Sankyo.

d. and e.

	Sankyo Average	Eli Lily LIFO	Eli Lily FIFO
Cost of Goods Sold	¥ 260,225	$1,959.0	$1,937.0
Average Inventories:			
.5(¥79,186 + ¥86,347)	¥ 82,766.5		
.5($938.4 + $1,103.0)		$1,020.7	
.5($938.4 + $88.9 + $1,103.0 + $110.7).....................			$1,120.5
Inventory Turnover............	3.1	1.9	1.7

f. Sankyo turns its inventory over more quickly than Lily, regardless of the cost flow assumption used in the calculations. The inventory turnover of Lily based on the reported amounts (LIFO) overstates the likely physical turnover.

7.55 (E. I. duPont de Nemours & Company; analysis of disclosures from published financial reports on effects of changing from average cost to LIFO.)

a. $378.2 [= 249.6/(1.00 − .34)] million. LIFO cost of goods sold was larger by $378.2 million, implying aftertax decrease in income of that amount multiplied by one minus the income tax rate.

b. The costs accumulated in earlier years enter cost of goods sold. In times of rising prices, such as those duPont faced, this means that the older costs are less than current costs, decreasing costs of goods sold and increasing income.

c. $61.2 [= 40.4/(1.00 − .34)] million decrease in cost of goods sold.

d. The income tax rules impose a penalty for changing cost-flow assumptions for inventory and require LIFO conformity. duPont would have had to repay, perhaps in installments, all of its tax savings from the preceding year. Also, attesting auditors must approve changes in accounting policies, and it is hard to persuade them that switching back and forth between policies has any purpose other than income manipulation.

7.55 continued.

    e. $27.2 [= .34 × ($490 − $410)] million.

    f.   Because of LIFO conformity rules and a company's preference for low tax payments, involving real cash flows, over the wish to report higher income in its financial statements. Also, the company may believe that LIFO reports better "matching" in years when no liquidations of LIFO layers occur.

7.56   (Bethlehem Steel; assessing the effect of LIFO versus FIFO on financial statements.) (Amounts in Millions)

a.

	Year 9	Year 10	Year 11
Cost of Goods Sold: LIFO....	$4,399.1	$4,327.2	$4,059.7
Plus Excess of FIFO Cost over LIFO Values, Beginning of Year...................	530.1	562.5	499.1
Less Excess of FIFO Cost over LIFO Values, End of Year.............................	(562.5)	(499.1)	(504.9)
Cost of Goods Sold: FIFO....	$4,366.7	$4,390.6	$4,053.9

b.

Cost of Goods Sold/Sales	Year 9	Year 10	Year 11
LIFO: $4,399.1/$5,250.9	83.8%		
$4,327.2/$4,899.2		88.3%	
$4,059.7/$4,317.9			94.0%
FIFO: $4,366.7/$5,250.9	83.2%		
$4,390.6/$4,899.2		89.6%	
$4,053.9/$4,317.9			93.9%

    c.   Inventory quantities increased during Year 9 (LIFO ending inventory exceeds LIFO beginning inventory) but it is difficult to conclude for sure the direction of the change in manufacturing costs. It appears, however, that manufacturing costs increased during the year because cost of goods sold using LIFO exceeds cost of goods sold using FIFO. Inventory quantities increased again during Year 10 but it appears that manufacturing costs decreased, resulting in a higher cost of goods sold using FIFO than using LIFO. Clues that manufacturing costs decreased include (1) the excess of FIFO cost over LIFO values declined during Year 10, despite an increase in inventory quantities, and (2) ending inventory using FIFO is less that beginning inventory using FIFO, despite an increase in inventory quantities. Inventory quantities decreased during Year 11 but it appears that manufacturing costs increased. The principal clue for the latter conclusion is that the excess of FIFO

7.56 c. continued.

cost over LIFO values increased during the year, despite a decrease in inventory quantities. The slightly higher cost of goods sold percentage using LIFO results from using higher manufacturing costs toward the end of Year 11 as well as dipping into the Year 10 LIFO layer priced at the higher manufacturing cost at the beginning of Year 10.

d.

Inventory Turnover Ratio	Year 9	Year 10	Year 11
LIFO: $4,399.1/.5($369.0 + $410.3)	11.3		
$4,327.2/.5($410.3 + $468.3)		9.9	
$4,059.7/.5($468.3 + $453.4)			8.8
FIFO: $4,366.7/.5($899.1 + $972.8)	4.7		
$4,390.6/.5($972.8 + $967.4)		4.5	
$4,053.9/.5($967.4 + $958.3)			4.2

e. The inventory turnover ratio for LIFO includes current cost data in the numerator and old cost data in the denominator, whereas this ratio under FIFO includes somewhat out-of-date cost data in the numerator and a mixture of out-of-date and current cost data in the denominator. The mismatching of cost data is less severe for FIFO than for LIFO because of the very old LIFO layers. Thus, the inventory turnover ratio using FIFO probably more accurately measures the actual rate of inventory turnover.

f.

Inventory Turnover Ratio	Year 8	Year 9	Year 10	Year 11
LIFO: $1,439.8/$870.1	1.65			
$1,435.2/$838.0		1.71		
$1,203.2/$831.4			1.45	
$957.8/$931.0				1.03
FIFO: $1,439.8 + (.66 X				
$530.1)/$870.1	2.06			
$1,435.2 + (.66 X				
$562.5)/$838.0		2.16		
$1,203.2 + (.66 X				
$499.1/)/$831.4			1.84	
$957.8 + (.66 X				
$504.9)/$931.0				1.39

7.56 continued.

    g. The current ratio decreased between Year 9 and Year 11, suggesting increased short-term liquidity risk. The current ratio using a FIFO cost-flow assumption for inventories probably reflects better the potential of current assets to cover current liabilities because the FIFO inventory values use more recent cost data. The current ratio using FIFO inventory values still exceeds 1.0 at the end of Year 11, suggesting that short-term liquidity risk is not yet at a serious level. However, the sharp decrease during the three-year period coupled with a slower inventory turnover (see Part *d.* above) raise doubts about the future.

    Note: The annual report indicates that the decreased current ratio occurs primarily because of reductions in cash that Bethlehem Steel Company needed to help finance its deteriorating operating position.

7.57   (General Motors Corporation; analysis of financial statement ratios affected by cost flow assumptions.)

    a. Let w and x denote current liabilities at the ends of Year 2 and Year 1, respectively. Then,

$$w = \frac{\$14,043}{1.13} = \$12,427 \qquad\qquad x = \frac{\$13,714}{1.09} = \$12,582.$$

Let y and z denote the excess of FIFO over LIFO ending inventories for Year 2 and Year 1, respectively. If FIFO were used, then cash amounts required for income taxes would have been higher so that after tax (assuming a 34-percent rate), current assets would increase net by $(1.00 - .34)$ times the FIFO excess.

Year 2

$$\frac{\$14,043 + (1.00 - .34)y}{\$12,427} = 1.21$$

$$.66y = (1.21 \times \$12,427) - \$14,043 = \$994$$
$$y = \$994/.66 = \$1,506.$$

Year 1

$$\frac{\$13,714 + (1.00 - .34)z}{\$12,582} = 1.18$$

$$.66z = (1.18 \times \$12,582) - \$13,714 = \$1,133$$
$$z = \$1,717.$$

7.57 continued.

b. Cash flow was *reduced* by $72 million. The excess of FIFO over LIFO inventories *decreased* by $211 (= $1,717 – $1,506) million during Year 2. Therefore, FIFO pretax income is *less* than LIFO pretax income by $211 million. With income taxes computed at 34 percent, LIFO required extra income taxes (and, presumably, cash) of $72 (= .34 X $211) million.

c. Since GM adopted LIFO, LIFO pretax income has been less than FIFO pretax income by $1,717 million and, assuming an income tax rate of 34 percent, has saved cumulative income taxes of $584 (= .34 X $1,717) million.

7.58 (British Petroleum Company; calculating operating margins and realized holding gains.)

a. (Amounts in Millions of British Pounds)

	Year 8	Year 9	Year 10	Year 11
Sales	£ 25,922	£ 29,641	£ 33,039	£ 32,613
Replacement Cost of Goods Sold	(19,330)	(22,095)	(24,655)	(25,117)
Operating Margin	£ 6,592	£ 7,546	£ 8,384	£ 7,496
Realized Holding Gain: Replacement Cost of Goods Sold	£ 19,330	£ 22,095	£ 24,655	£ 25,117
Acquisition Cost of Goods Sold	(19,562)	(21,705)	(24,178)	(25,746)
Total	£ (232)	£ 390	£ 477	£ (629)
Gross Margin	£ 6,360	£ 7,936	£ 8,861	£ 6,867

b. **Operating Margin/Sales**

£6,592/£25,922	25.4%			
£7,546/£29,641		25.5%		
£8,384/£33,039			25.4%	
£7,496/£32,613				23.0%

Gross Margin/Sales

£6,360/£25,922	24.5%			
£7,936/£29,641		26.8%		
£8,861/£33,039			26.8%	
£6,867/£32,613				21.1%

7.58 continued.

    c.   BP's operating margin to sales percentage fluctuates less than its gross margin to sales percentage. Perhaps BP provides the replacement cost of goods sold data to show the financial community that it prices its products at a relatively constant markup on replacement cost (except for Year 11). Variations in the gross margin percentage result from varying rates of change in oil prices over which BP has little, if any, control. The effects of these variations appear in realized holding gains and losses. Although BP's operating margin to sales percentage decreased in Year 11, the rate of decrease is not as large as the decrease in the gross margin to sales percentage. BP was able to almost maintain its historical operating margin percentage, despite decreases in petroleum costs.

        In years when significant increases in oil prices occur because of problems in the Middle East, these disclosures permit BP to show that most of the increase in its gross margin results from realized holding gains instead of increased operating margin. By including these disclosures each year, even when oil prices do not change much, BP educates the financial community regarding the effect of factors outside of its control on profitability.

7.59   (Olin Corporation; interpreting inventory disclosures.)

    a. $2,161 + (\$501 - \$320) - (\$474 - \$329) = \$2,197$.

    b.   The quantities of inventory items increased since Olin Corporation added a new LIFO layer during the year (that is, the ending inventory under LIFO exceeds the beginning inventory under LIFO).

    c.   The cost of inventory items decreased during the year. One clue is that the cost of goods sold under FIFO exceeds that under LIFO. A second clue is that the excess of FIFO over LIFO inventory at the end of the year is less than at the beginning of the year despite an increase in quantities.

    d.   LIFO: $\$2,161/.5(\$320 + \$329) = 6.7$.
        FIFO: $\$2,197/.5(\$501 + \$474) = 4.5$.

    e.   The difference in the rate of inventory turnover occurs because LIFO uses old costs in computing inventory amounts whereas FIFO uses more up-to-date costs. Both cost flow assumptions use relatively recent costs in the numerator of the ratio, although those for LIFO are more up-to-date.

7.59 continued.

    f.   The amount for purchases in the numerator of the accounts payable turnover ratio should not differ between LIFO and FIFO, unless the firm accelerates purchases or production at the end of a year to avoid dipping into its LIFO layers. The average balance for accounts payable in the denominator of the ratio should not differ between LIFO and FIFO, unless the extra income taxes paid under FIFO (rising prices) or LIFO (falling prices) constrains a firm's ability to repay its suppliers.

CHAPTER 8

PLANT, EQUIPMENT, AND INTANGIBLE ASSETS: THE SOURCE OF OPERATING CAPACITY

Questions, Exercises, Problems, and Cases: Answers and Solutions

8.1   See the text or the glossary at the end of the book.

8.2   Maintenance services provided for selling and administrative activities appear as expenses of the current period. Maintenance services provided for manufacturing activities accumulate in Work-in-Process and Finished Goods Inventory accounts. These costs become expenses in the period of sale. Expenditures from any of these activities that increase the service life or service potential of assets beyond that originally expected increase the assets' depreciable base. Such expenditures become expenses as the firm recognizes depreciation during future years.

8.3   Generally accepted accounting principles use acquisition costs in the valuation of most assets. Accounting gives no recognition to the fact that some firms can acquire a particular asset for a lower price than other firms can acquire it. Part of the explanation relates to measuring the relevant cost savings. There is seldom a single, unique alternative price. Additionally, accounting views firms as generating income form using assets in operations, not from simply purchasing them.

The income effect of both recording procedures is a net expense of $250,000, the cash outflow to self-construct the warehouse. The generally accepted procedure recognizes $250,000 as depreciation expense over the life of the warehouse. The unacceptable procedure recognizes revenue of $50,000 upon completion of the warehouse and depreciation expense of $300,000 over the life of the warehouse.

8.4   a. Over the life of the project, income is cash-in less cash-out. Capitalizing and then amortizing interest versus expensing it affects the timing but not the total amount of income. Capitalizing interest defers expense from the construction period to the periods of use, increasing income in the early years of construction and decreasing it in the periods of use, when depreciation charges are larger.

8.4 continued.

    b.   The "catch-up" described in the preceding part is indefinitely delayed. Reported income in each year increases by the policy of capitalizing interest. When the self-construction activity declines, then the reported income declines as a result of reduced capitalization of interest, but not before.

8.5   a.   If the life of an asset is shorter than the accounting period (or that portion of the period remaining after the purchase of the asset), depreciation, as an accounting measurement problem, disappears. The difficulties increase as it becomes necessary to spread the cost of an asset over a number of periods of time. If the accounting period were ten years, fewer items would have to be spread, or "depreciated." If no asset lasted more than a year or two, accountants could make even annual depreciation calculations with considerable accuracy.

    b.   Depreciation accounting allocates the cost of long-lived assets to the periods of use in an orderly, reasonable manner. Charging depreciation does not "provide funds" for the firm. Selling the firm's products to customers provides funds.

8.6   a.   Depreciation life is: $100,000/$10,000 per year = 10 years.

            Age of the asset is: $60,000 accumulated depreciation charge divided by $10,000 depreciation per year = 6 years.

    b.   Age of the asset in years = accumulated depreciation at the end of a year divided by depreciation charge for the year.

8.7   Depreciation for years prior to the change in estimate is larger or smaller than it would have been if the firm had originally used the revised estimate. Depreciation for the current and future years is also smaller or larger than it would be if the firm corrected for the original misestimate retroactively. Thus, depreciation in no year of the assets' service life will show the appropriate depreciation for the actual depreciable life of assets.

8.8   The small amounts of certain expenditures often do not justify the record keeping cost of capitalization and amortization. Firms therefore expense all expenditures below a certain threshold amount.

8.9   The relevant question to apply generally accepted accounting principles is whether the expenditure maintained the originally expected useful life or extended that useful life. Firms should expense, as maintenance or repairs, expenditures that maintain the originally expected five-year life. In this case, the expenditure both maintains and extends the useful life. A portion of the expenditure should appear as an expense immediately (perhaps two-thirds) and a portion (perhaps one-third) should increase the depreciable base for the asset.

8.10   Accounting views sales of plant assets as peripheral to a firm's principal business activities. Revenues and expenses from a firm's principal business activities appear as sales revenue and cost of goods sold. Accounting nets the revenues and expenses from peripheral activities to show only the gain or loss.

8.11   Total expenses equal total cash expenditures. Full costing delays the recognition of expenses relative to successful efforts costing, but ultimately all expenditures to search for mineral resources become expenses.

8.12   Some critics of the required expensing of research and development (R & D) costs argue that there is little difference to justify the different accounting treatments. One possible explanation for the different treatment is the greater tangible nature of mineral resources relative to most R & D expenditures. Yet, some R & D expenditures result in tangible prototypes or products. Another possible explanation for the difference is the established market for most mineral resources versus the more unknown market potential for R & D expenditures.

8.13   Critics of the required expensing of research and development (R & D) costs argue that there is little rationale to justify the different accounting. One difference between the two cases is that firms make R & D expenditures for an uncertain future result (that is, the possibility of a patent), whereas less uncertainty exists for the purchase of a completed patent. A market transaction between an independent buyer and seller establish the existence and value of future benefits in the case of a purchased patent. Similar expenditures for R & D simply establish that a firm has made an expenditure.

8.14   (Classifying expenditure as asset or expense.)

   a. Expense.

   b. Expense.

   c. Expense.

   d. Asset (noncurrent).

   e. Expense.

   f. Expense or asset (noncurrent).

   g. Product cost (current asset).

   h. Equipment (noncurrent asset).

   i. Expense.

8.14 continued.

      j.   Ore deposit (noncurrent asset).

      k.   Prepayment (current asset).

      l.   Marketable securities (current asset).

      m. Product cost (current asset).

      n.   Asset (noncurrent).

      o.   Asset (noncurrent). Copyrights need not be expensed as developed.

8.15   (Bolton Company; cost of self-constructed assets.)

Land			Factory Building			
	70,000		(1)	200,000	7,000	(7)
(14)	2,000		(2)	12,000		
√	72,000		(3)	140,000		
			(5)	6,000		
			(8)	10,000		
			(9)	8,000		
Office Building			(10)	3,000[a]		
	20,000		(11)	8,000[b]		
(4)	13,000		(13)	4,000		
√	33,000		(15)	1,000[a]		
			√	385,000		
Site Improvements						
(12)	5,000					
√	5,000					

[a]The firm might expense these items. It depends on the rationality of the firm's "self-insurance" policy.

[b]The firm might prorate these items in part to the remodeling of the office building.

Item (6) is omitted because of *SFAS No. 34*.

Item (16) is omitted because no arm's length transaction occurred in which the firm earned a profit.

8.16   (New Hampshire Wood Stove Company; cost of self-developed product.)

The first four items qualify as research and development costs which the firm must expense in the year incurred. It might appear that the firm should capitalize the cost of the prototype because it acquires the prototype from an external contractor. However, completion of a prototype does not signify a viable product. Purchasing the prototype externally versus constructing it internally does not change the accounting.

The firm should capitalize the legal fees to register and establish the patent as part of the cost of the patent. The firm might consider this cost as sufficiently immaterial to warrant treatment as an asset and expense it immediately.

The firm should capitalize the cost of the castings and amortize them over the expected useful life of the wood stove product.

8.17   (Samson Chemical Company; amount of interest capitalized during construction.)

a.   Average Construction = ($40,000,000 + $60,000,000)/2 = $50,000,000.

Relevant Loans	Interest Anticipated
$ 30,000,000 at .10	$3,000,000
20,000,000 at .08	1,600,000
$ 50,000,000	$4,600,000

b.   Interest Expense... 8,600,000
          Interest Payable...   8,600,000
      $30,000,000 × .10 + $70,000,000 × .08.

      Construction in Process................................ 4,600,000
          Interest Expense..   4,600,000

c.   Interest Expense... 8,600,000
          Interest Payable...   8,600,000
      $30,000,000 × .10 + $70,000,000 × .08.

      Construction in Process................................ 1,000,000
          Interest Expense..   1,000,000
      $10,000,000 × .10 = $1,000,000.

8.18   (Nebok Company; capitalizing interest during construction.) (Amounts in Thousands)

    a.   Weighted average interest rate: $5,480/.5($51,500 + $49,700) = 10.83 percent.

        Weighted average balance in Construction in Process: .5($23,186 + $68,797) = $45,992.

        Interest Capitalized: .1083 × $45,992 = $4,981.

    b.

Interest Expense...	5,480	
Interest Payable...		5,480
Construction in Process................................	4,981	
Interest Expense......................................		4,981

    c.

Income before Interest Expense and Income Taxes...	$ 16,300
Interest Expense ($5,480 – $4,981)..............................	(499)
Income before Income Taxes	$ 15,801
Income Tax Expense at 34 Percent..............................	(5,372)
Net Income...	$ 10,429

    d. $16,300/$499 = 32.67 times.

    e. $16,300/$5,480 = 2.97 times.

    f.   The interest coverage ratio in Part e. indicates the interest that the firm must pay and therefore provides a better measure for assessing risk.

8.19   (Galeway Motors; calculations for various depreciation methods.)

	Year 1	Year 2	Year 3
a. Straight-Line Method .... ($29,600 – $2,600)/6 = $4,500.	$4,500	$4,500	$4,500
b. Sum-of-the-Years'-Digits Method........................ (6 × 7)/2 = 21 sum-of-the-years'-digits.	$7,714	$6,429	$5,143
c. Declining-Balance Method .. 33 percent rate.	$9,768	$6,545	$4,385
d. Production Method............. $27,000/30,000 = $.90 per hour.	$4,050	$4,500	$4,950

8.20 (Luck Delivery Company; calculations for various depreciation methods.)

a.

Depreciation Charge (Straight-Line)

Year 8	$ 6,000 (30,000/5)
Year 9	6,000
Year 10	6,000
Year 11	6,000
Year 12	6,000
	$30,000

b.

Depreciation Charge (Double-Declining-Balance)

Year 8	$12,000	($30,000 X .40)
Year 9	7,200	($18,000 X .40)
Year 10	4,320	($10,800 X .40)
Year 11	3,240	($6,480/2)
Year 12	3,240	(balance)
	$30,000	

c.

Depreciation Charge (Sum-of-the-Years'-Digits)

Year 8	$10,000	($30,000 X 5/15)
Year 9	8,000	($30,000 X 4/15)
Year 10	6,000	($30,000 X 3/15)
Year 11	4,000	($30,000 X 2/15)
Year 12	2,000	($30,000 X 1/15)
	$30,000	

d.

ACRS (5-Year Class)

Year 8	$ 6,000	(= $30,000 X .20)
Year 9	9,600	(= $30,000 X .32)
Year 10	5,760	(= $30,000 X .192)
Year 11	3,450	(= $30,000 X .115)
Year 12	3,450	(= $30,000 X .115)
Year 13	1,740	(= $30,000 X .058)
	$30,000	

e.

Depreciation Charge (Sum-of-the-Years'-Digits)

Year 8	3/4 X	$10,000		=	$ 7,500
Year 9	3/4 X	$ 8,000	+ 1/4 X $10,000 =		8,500
Year 10	3/4 X	$ 6,000	+ 1/4 X $ 8,000 =		6,500
Year 11	3/4 X	$ 4,000	+ 1/4 X $ 6,000 =		4,500
Year 12	3/4 X	$ 2,000	+ 1/4 X $ 4,000 =		2,500
Year 13			1/4 X $ 2,000 =		500
					$30,000

8.21   (Calculations for various depreciation methods.)

	Year 1	Year 2	
a.	$10,000	$10,000	($450,000 − $50,000)/40 = $10,000.
b.	$22,000	$19,800	($220,000 × 2/20) = $22,000; ($198,000 × 2/20) = $19,800.
c.	$20,000	$16,000	($80,000 − $20,000) × 5/15 = $20,000; ($80,000 − $20,000) × 4/15 = $16,000.
d.	$18,750	$15,937.50	$125,000 × 1.5/10 = $18,750; $106,250 × 1.5/10 = $15,937.50.
e.	$ 3,333	$ 3,333	($24,000 − $4,000)/6 = $3,333.
f.	$ 4,800	$ 7,680	$24,000 × .20 = $4,800; $24,000 × .32 = $7,680.

8.22   (United Express; production or use depreciation.)

a. ($22,600 − $2,600)/100,000 miles = $.20 per mile.

	Miles at $.20 Each	Depreciation Charge
Year 6......................	14,000 Miles	$ 2,800
Year 7......................	34,000 Miles	6,800
Year 8......................	32,000 Miles	6,400
	80,000 Miles	$ 16,000

b. **June 16, Year 9**

Depreciation Expense....................................	3,600	
Accumulated Depreciation		3,600

18,000 (= 98,000 − 80,000) miles at $.20 per mile =
$3,600. Accumulated Depreciation is now
$19,600 (= $.20 × 98,000 miles).

Cash..	2,600	
Accumulated Depreciation............................	19,600	
Loss on Sale of Truck......................................	400	
Truck...		22,600

8.23   (Fast Pace Shipping Company; revision of estimated service life changes depreciation schedule.)

Summary of the depreciation charges under the two methods:

	a. Straight-Line	b. Sum-of-the-Years'-Digits
Year 7	$ 3,600[a]	$ 6,545[c]
Year 8	3,600[a]	5,891[d]
Year 9	4,800[b]	6,733[e]
Year 10...........................	4,800[b]	5,610[f]
	$16,800	$24,779

[a]($40,000 – $4,000)/10 = $3,600.
[b]($40,000 – $3,600 – $3,600 – $4,000)/6 = $4,800.
[c][($40,000 – $4,000) × 10/55] = $6,545.
[d][($40,000 – $4,000) × 9/55] = $5,891.
[e]($40,000 – $6,545 – $5,891 – $4,000) × 6/21 = $6,733.
[f]($40,000 – $6,545 – $5,891 – $4,000) × 5/21 = $5,610.

8.24   (Fort Manufacturing Corporation; journal entries for revising estimate of life.)

a. Work-in-Process Inventory............................   600
        Accumulated Depreciation   600
    ($45,000 – $1,800)/144 = $300 per month.

b. Work-in-Process Inventory............................   3,600
        Accumulated Depreciation   3,600
    12 × $300 = $3,600.

c. Depreciation to 1/1/Year 15 = 62 × $300 = $18,600.
    Remaining depreciation = $45,000 – $18,600 – $960 = $25,440.
    Remaining life = 168 months – 62 months = 106 months as of 1/1/Year 15.
    Depreciation charge per month = $25,440/106 = $240.

    Work-in-Process Inventory............................   2,880
        Accumulated Depreciation   2,880

d. By March 31, Year 20, the machine has been on the new depreciation schedule for Year 15 through Year 19 plus 3 months or 63 months altogether. Accumulated depreciation is $18,600 + (63 × $240) = $15,190; $18,600 + $15,120 = $33,720.

    Book value is $45,000 – $33,720 = $11,280; loss is $1,280.

    Journal entries are:

8.24 d. continued.

Work-in-Process Inventory..............................	720	
Accumulated Depreciation		720

3 × $240 = $720; to bring depreciation up to date as of 3/31/Year 20.

Cash...	10,000	
Accumulated Depreciation.............................	33,720	
Loss on Disposal of Machinery........................	1,280	
Machinery...		45,000

8.25   (Neptune Equipment Corporation; retirement of plant assets.)

a.

	Depreciation Charge for the Year	Accumulated Depreciation at July 1
Year 4—Year 5	$2,000	$ 2,000
Year 5—Year 6	2,000	4,000
Year 6—Year 7	2,000	6,000
	$6,000	

b. **9/30/Year 7**

Work-in-Process Inventory..............................	500	
Accumulated Depreciation		500

3 months' depreciation since 6/30/Year 7: $2,000/4 = $500.

9/30/Year 7

Cash on Hand..	2,700	
Accumulated Depreciation.............................	6,500	
Loss on Sale of Machinery.............................	400	
Machinery...		9,600

$6,000 + $500 = $6,500.

c. **12/31/Year 7**

Work-in-Process Inventory..............................	1,000	
Accumulated Depreciation		1,000

6 months' depreciation since 6/30/Year 7: $2,000/2 = $1,000.

12/31/Year 7

Cash on Hand..	2,700	
Accumulated Depreciation.............................	7,000	
Machinery...		9,600
Gain on Sale of Machinery..........................		100

$6,000 + $1,000 = $7,000.

8.26   (Wilcox Corporation; working backwards to derive proceeds from disposition of plant assets.)

Cost of Equipment Sold:	$400,000 + $230,000 − $550,000 = $80,000.
Accumulated Depreciation on Equipment Sold:	$180,000 + $50,000 − $160,000 = $70,000.
Book Value of Equipment Sold:	$80,000 − $70,000 = $10,000.
Proceeds of Sale:	$10,000 + $4,000 = $14,000.

8.27   (Checker's Pizza Company; use of a single asset account or separate asset accounts affects classification of expenditures as repairs or improvements.)

a.

	Expenses			
Single Asset Account	Depreciation Truck	Engine	Repairs	Total
Year 1	$ 4,500	---	---	$ 4,500
Year 2	4,500	---	$ 5,000	9,500
Year 3	4,500	---	---	4,500
Year 4	4,500	---	---	4,500
Totals......	$ 18,000		$ 5,000	$ 23,000

b.

Separate Asset Accounts				
Year 1	$ 3,250[a]	$ 2,500[b]	---	$ 5,750
Year 2	3,250	2,500	---	5,750
Year 3	3,250	2,500	---	5,750
Year 4	3,250	2,500	---	5,750
Totals.......	$ 13,000	$ 10,000		$ 23,000

[a]($18,000 − $5,000)/4.   [b]$5,000/2.

8.28   (Journal entries to correct accounting errors.)

a. Depreciation Expense   375
        Accumulated Depreciation   375
    $3,000 × .25 × 6/12 = $375.

    Accumulated Depreciation............................   1,875
    Loss on Disposal of Equipment......................   325
        Store Equipment   2,200
    $3,000 × .25 × 2.5 = $1,875. $3,200 + $3000 − $4,000
    = $2,200.

b. Accumulated Depreciation............................   5,000
        Truck   5,000

8.28 continued.

    c.   Depreciation Expense...   60
            Accumulated Depreciation.........................   60
           $1,200 \times .10 \times 6/12 = \$60$.

           Accumulated Depreciation...........................   270
             Theft Loss...   270
           $1,200 \times .10 \times 27/12 = \$270$.

8.29   (Boston Can Corporation; journal entries for depreciable asset transactions.)

3/31/Year 6
Depreciation Expense...   350
    Accumulated Depreciation...............................   350
$(\$12,000 - \$800)/8 = \$1,400$ per year; $3/12 \times \$1,400 = \$350$.

3/31/Year 6
Cash..   4,000
Accumulated Depreciation.....................................   7,350
Loss on Sale..   650
    Machinery (Old)..   12,000
$(\$1,400 \times 5) + \$350 = \$7,350$.

Machinery (New)..   16,000
    Notes Payable...   6,000
    Cash..   10,000

12/31/Year 6
Interest Expense..   450
    Interest Payable...   450
$\$6,000 \times .10 \times 9/12 = \$450$.

Depreciation Expense...   1,125
    Accumulated Depreciation...............................   1,125
$(\$16,000 - \$1,000)/10 = \$1,500$ per year; $9/12 \times \$1,500 = \$1,125$.

8.30   (Effects of transactions on statement of cash flows.)

   a.   The journal entry to record this transaction is as follows:

Cash..	3,000	
Accumulated Depreciation..............................	6,000	
Loss on Sale of Machine.................................	1,000	
Machine..		10,000

   The debit to the Cash account means that Line (9) increases by
   $3,000. Sales of plant assets are investing transactions, so Line (4)
   increases by $3,000. The loss on the sale reduces net income, so Line
   (1) decreases by $1,000. Because we show the full cash proceeds of
   $3,000 on Line (4), we must offset the effect of the $1,000 reduction on
   Line (1). Thus, Line (2) increases by $1,000. The net effect of the
   entries on Lines (1) and (2) is zero.

   b.   The journal entry to record this transaction is as follows:

Cash..	5,000	
Accumulated Depreciation..............................	6,000	
Machine..		10,000
Gain on Sale of Machine...............................		1,000

   The debit to the Cash account means that Line (9) increases by
   $5,000. Sales of plant assets are investing transactions, so Line (4)
   increases by $5,000. The gain on the sale increases net income, so
   Line (1) increases by $1,000. Because we show the full cash proceeds
   of $5,000 on Line (4), we must offset the effect of the $1,000 increase
   on Line (1). Thus, Line (3) increases by $1,000. The net effect of the
   entries on Lines (1) and (3) is zero.

   c.   The journal entry to record this transaction is as follows:

Machine (New)...	8,000	
Accumulated Depreciation (Old)......................	6,000	
Machine (Old)..		10,000
Cash...		4,000

   The credit to the Cash account reduces Line (9) by $4,000.
   Acquisitions of plant assets are investing transactions, so Line (5)
   increases by $4,000. Because this entry does not involve an income
   statement account, there is no effect on the Operating section of the
   statement of cash flows.

   d.   The journal entry to record this transaction is as follows:

Loss from Fire...	50,000	
Accumulated Depreciation..............................	40,000	
Warehouse..		90,000

8.30 d. continued.

Because this entry does not involve an entry to the Cash account there is no effect on Line (9). The loss from the fire reduces net income, so Line (1) decreases by $50,000. We must offset this loss if the net effect on Line (9) is to be zero. Thus, Line (2) increases by $50,000 for the loss that does not use cash.

e. The journal entry to record this transaction is as follows:

Loss from Fire...	60,000	
Inventory...		60,000

This entry does not involve a debit or credit to the Cash account so Line (9) is not affected. The loss from the fire reduces net income, so Line (1) decreases by $60,000. We must offset this loss if the net effect on Line (9) is to be zero. Thus, Line (2) increases by $60,000 for the decrease in inventories.

8.31   (Allocation of cost in basket purchases.)

a.

Land—East Tract..	16,200	
Land—West Tract..	10,800	
Cash..		27,000

To record purchase and legal fees.

If both offers were *bona fide*, then the land appears to be worth $30,000 in separate five-acre plots; 18/30 of the cost of the land is allocated to the east half and 12/30 to the west half.

Cash..	18,000	
Land—East Tract...................................		16,200
Gain on Sale of Land		1,800

b.

Land—East Tract..	10,800	
Land—West Tract..	16,200	
Cash..		27,000

Cash..	15,000	
Loss on Sale of Land	1,200	
Land—West Tract...................................		16,200

The value of the land as two plots ($25,000) appears to be less than its value as one plot ($27,000). The firm recognizes a loss of $1,200 on the sale of the West Tract. Conservatism suggests the recognition of another $800 loss on the East Tract.

8.32   (Intellicorp, Inc.; basket purchase and in-process R&D.)   (Dollar Amounts in Thousands.)

a.   In-process R&D allocated $4,800.

	Year of Acquisition	Subsequent Years
Other Income	$ 1,700	$ 2,600
Charge at Acquisition for In-Process R&D	(4,800)	0
Net Income	$ (3,100)	$ 2,600 [A]

b.   In-process R&D allocated $2,700.

Goodwill is $2,100 (= $4,800 – $2,700) and is amortize over ten years at the rate of $210 (= $2,100/10 years) per year.

	Year of Acquisition	Subsequent Years
Other Income	$ 1,700	$ 2,600
Charge at Acquisition for In-Process R&D	(2,700)	0
Amortization of Goodwill	(210)	(210)
Net Income	$ (1,210)	$ 2,390 [B]

c.   Income would have been larger by a factor of 1.088 (= [A]/[B]) or by 9 percent had the original accounting been allowed.

When the analyst uses a P/E ratio to estimate a market value, a multiplicative operation, the 9-percent difference will carry through to the final valuation.
   So, we an see that the change in the accounting for in-process R&D affects the analyst's valuation by about 9 percent.

8.33   (Deutsch Lufthansa AG; depreciation calculations affect net income; working backwards to derive depreciable assets' costs.)

The improvements in pretax income is DM 280 million marks:

First Six Months Pretax Loss	DM 542 million marks
First Nine months Pretax Loss	262
Loss Reduction in Third Quarter	DM 280 million marks

Let C = Cost of aircraft.
Then $[.75(C - .05C)/10)] - [.75(C - .15C/12] = 280$ million marks
C = 15,450 million marks.

(See following page for **Proof**)

8.33 continued.

Proof

		Amounts in Millions of Deutsch Marks	
		Old Calculations	New Calculations
(1)	Depreciation Lives in Years	10	12
(2)	Salvage Value Percentage of Cost	.05	.15
(3)	Depreciation Cost	15,450.0	15,450.0
(4)	Salvage Value = [2] × [3]	772.5	2,317.5
(5)	Cost Less Salvage	14,677.5	13,132.5
(6)	Depreciation for Year = [5] ÷ [1]	1,467.8	1,094.4
(7)	Depreciation for Nine Months = [6] × .75	1,100.8	820.8
(8)	Depreciation Savings for Nine Months = [7] Old − [7] New	280.0	

8.34 (American Airlines; effect on net income of changes in estimates for depreciable assets.)

Income has been about $180 million (= .06 × $3 billion) per year.

Reconciliation of Plant Data:

Airplanes Cost...	$ 2,500,000,000
Less Salvage Value (10%)...................................	250,000,000
Depreciable Basis...	$ 2,250,000,000
Divided by 10-Year Life Equals Yearly Depreciation Charges...	$ 225,000,000
Times 4 Years Equals Accumulated Depreciation...........	$ 900,000,000
Plus Net Book Value	1,600,000,000
Airplanes Cost...	$ 2,500,000,000

New Depreciation Charge:

Net Book Value..	$ 1,600,000,000
Less Salvage Value (12% of Cost)	300,000,000
Depreciation Basis..	$ 1,300,000,000
Divided by 10 (= 14 − 4) Years Equals Revised Yearly Depreciation Charge	$ 130,000,000

Increase in Pretax Income:

Old Depreciation Charges......................................	$ 225,000,000
New Depreciation Charges	130,000,000
	$ 95,000,000
Multiplied by (1 − tax rate) = 1 − .34 = .66..................	× .66
Increase in Aftertax Income....................................	$ 62,700,000

Income will rise by about 35 percent (= $62.7/$180.0).

8.35   (Cord Manufacturing Company; composite depreciation versus individual-item depreciation.)

a.

Machine Tool (1)	Percentage of Joint Cost (2)	Cost Allocated to Total (2) x $72,000 (3)	Cost to Renovate and Install	Total Cost to Be Capitalized
A	33.3%	$ 24,000	$1,500	$ 25,500
B	44.4%	32,000	2,400	34,400
C	22.2%	16,000	2,000	18,000
	100.0%[a]	$ 72,000	$5,900	$ 77,900

[a]Amounts above do not sum to 100% due to rounding.

b.   **Year 1**

Work-in-Process Inventory.............................	13,050	
Accumulated Depreciation—Tool A..............		4,250
Accumulated Depreciation—Tool B		4,300
Accumulated Depreciation—Tool C		4,500

$25,500/6 = $4,250; $34,400/8 = $4,300; $18,000/4 = $4,500.

Year 5

Work-in-Process Inventory.............................	8,550	
Accumulated Depreciation—Tool A..............		4,250
Accumulated Depreciation—Tool B		4,300

Year 8

Work-in-Process Inventory.............................	4,300	
Accumulated Depreciation—Tool B		4,300

c. $77,900/8 = $9,737.50 per year.

d.   Assumption of a.. The cumulative depreciation charges are always larger. Thus, the cumulative taxable income and tax payments would be smaller until the tenth year. The present value of the tax payments would be less for any positive interest rate.

8.36 (The Mead Corporation; interpreting disclosures regarding plant assets.)

a. Property, Plant and Equipment...................... 315.6

  Cash.. 315.6

  Depreciation Expense.................................... 188.1

  Accumulated Depreciation............................ 188.1

  Cash (Given)... 38.7

  Loss on Sale of Property, Plant and Equipment (Plug).. 19.9

  Accumulated Depreciation ($1,803.7 + $188.1 − x = $1,849.3; x = $142.5)............................... 142.5

  Property, Plant and Equipment ($3,824.0 + $315.6 − x = $3,938.5; x = $201.1).............. 201.1

b. .5($3,824.0 + $3,938.5)/$188.1 = 20.6 years.

c. .5($1,803.7 + $1,849.3)/$188.1 = 9.7 years.

d. $4,557.5/.5($2,020.3 + $2,089.2) = 2.2.

e. $4,557.5/.5($1,013.8[a] + $1,108.0[b]) = 4.3.

  [a]$3,824.0 − $2,810.2 = $1,013.8.
  [b]$3,938.5 − $2,830.5 = $1,108.0.

8.37 (PepsiCo; interpreting disclosures regarding income taxes.)

a. Property, Plant and Equipment...................... 2,253.2

  Cash.. 2,253.2

  Depreciation Expense.................................... 1,200.0

  Accumulated Depreciation............................ 1,200.0

  Cash... 55.3

  Accumulated Depreciation ($5,394.4 + $1,200.0 − x = $6,247.3; x = $347.1)............................... 347.1

  Property, Plant and Equipment ($14,250.0 + $2,253.2 − y = $16,130.1; y = 373.1)............ 373.1

  Gain on Sale of Property, Plant and Equipment (Plug)...................................... 29.3

b. .5($14,250.0 + $16,130.1)/$1,200.0 = 12.7 years.

c. .5($5,394.4 + $6,247.3)/$1,200.0 = 4.9 years.

d. $28,472.4/.5($8,855.6 + $9,882.8) = 3.0.

8.37 continued.

   e. $\$28,472.4/.5(\$7,231.2^a + \$8,393.4^b) = 3.6$.

       $^a\$14,250.0 - \$7,018.8 = \$7,231.2$.
       $^b\$16,130.1 - \$7,736.7 = \$8,393.4$.

8.38   (Grand Met; accounting for plant asset revaluations.)

   a.   **December 31, Year 3 to Year 5**

Depreciation Expense	10,000	
Accumulated Depreciation		10,000

       £10,000 = £50,000/5.

   b.   **January 1, Year 6**

Equipment	5,000	
Revaluation Allowance		5,000

Current Market Value	£ 25,000
Book Value: £50,000 − (£10,000 × 3)	(20,000)
	£ 5,000

   c.   **December 31, Year 6 and Year 7**

Depreciation Expense	10,000	
Revaluation Allowance	2,500	
Accumulated Depreciation		12,500

       £2,500 = £5,000/2.

   d.   The revaluation and subsequent depreciation of the revaluation had no effect on net income. At the end of Year 7 just prior to removing the equipment form the books, the accounts appear as follows:

Equipment (£50,000 + £5,000)	£ 55,000
Accumulated Depreciation (£10,000 × 5) + (£2,500 × 2)	55,000
Revaluation Allowance [£5,000 − (£2,500 × 2)]	-0-

8.39 (Consumer Products Company; capitalizing versus expensing advertising costs: effects on financial statements and rate of return.)

a. Rate of Return on Assets Assuming Advertising Costs Are Expensed in the Year Incurred:

Year	Other Income	Revenue from Advertising Campaign	Expenses for Advertising Campaign	Net Income	Payments to Owner	Addition to (Subtraction from) Total Assets	Total Assets End of Year	Rate of Return
1	$ 45,000	---	$(24,000)	$ 21,000	$ 45,000	$(24,000)	$276,000	7.61%
2	45,000	$ 10,000	---	55,000	47,000	8,000	284,000	19.37%
3	45,000	10,000	---	55,000	47,000	8,000	292,000	18.84%
4	45,000	10,000	---	55,000	47,000	8,000	300,000	18.33%
	$180,000	$ 30,000	$(24,000)	$186,000	$186,000	$ -0-		

b. Rate of Return on Assets Assuming Advertising Costs Are Capitalized:

Year	Other Income	Revenue from Advertising Campaign	Expenses for Advertising Campaign	Net Income	Payments to Owners	Addition to (Subtraction from) Total Assets	Total Assets End of Year	Rate of Return
1	$ 45,000	---	$ (8,000)	$ 45,000	$ 45,000	$ -0-	$300,000	15.00%
2	45,000	$ 10,000	(8,000)	47,000	47,000	-0-	300,000	15.67%
3	45,000	10,000	(8,000)	47,000	47,000	-0-	300,000	15.67%
4	45,000	10,000	(8,000)	47,000	47,000	-0-	300,000	15.67%
	$180,000	$ 30,000	$(24,000)	$186,000	$186,000	$ -0-		

c. Management has made the right decision to pursue the campaign. We know that the advertising campaign was profitable from our answer to Part b. above. We think the accounting in Part b. is better than in Part a., but not all accountants would agree. Most, in fact, would require expensing as in Part a. above.

8.40   (General Mills; expensing versus capitalizing advertising costs for firm advertising every year.)

	Year 1	Year 2	Year 3	Year 4
a. Expense Costs as Incurred				
Other Income.................	$ 30,000	$30,000	$30,000	$ 30,000
Additional Income from Advertising:				
First Year's Ads......	36,000	36,000	36,000	
Second Year's Ads...		36,000	36,000	36,000
Third Year's Ads.....			36,000	36,000
Fourth Year's Ads...				36,000
Advertising Expense.......	(90,000)	(90,000)	(90,000)	(90,000)
Net Income (Loss)...........	$(24,000)	$12,000	$48,000	$ 48,000

	Year 1	Year 2	Year 3	Year 4
b. Capitalize and Amortize Over 3 Years (Including Year of Occurrence)				
Other Income.................	$ 30,000	$ 30,000	$ 30,000	$ 30,000
Additional Income from Advertising:				
First Year's Ads......	36,000	36,000	36,000	
Second Year's Ads...		36,000	36,000	36,000
Third Year's Ads.....			36,000	36,000
Fourth Year's Ads...				36,000
Advertising Amortization Expense:				
First Year's Ads......	(30,000)	(30,000)	(30,000)	
Second Year's Ads...		(30,000)	(30,000)	(30,000)
Third Year's Ads.....			(30,000)	(30,000)
Fourth Year's Ads...				(30,000)
Net Income...................	$ 36,000	$ 42,000	$ 48,000	$ 48,000
Advertising Asset on Balance Sheet:				
First Year's Ads......	$ 60,000	$ 30,000		
Second Year's Ads...		60,000	$ 30,000	
Third Year's Ads.....			60,000	$ 30,000
Fourth Year's Ads...				60,000
Total...........................	$ 60,000	$ 90,000	$ 90,000	$ 90,000

8.40 continued.

c. The expensing policy leads to higher expenses, lower income, and lower asset totals in the first two years. After that, the two policies are the same. When the firm ceases to advertise, the policy of expensing will show higher income in the two years when the benefits of prior advertising continue, but there are no matching expenses. There are no expenses under Policy (1), but Policy (2) continues to show amortization expense.

d. The income under the two policies will continue to be the same if there is no growth or change in policy. Policy (2) will show a lower rate of return on total assets and a lower rate of return on stockholders' equity than will Policy (1) because the asset and equity totals are larger under Policy (2) than under Policy (1). When there is growth in advertising amounts over time and corresponding growth in income, Policy (2) will always appear worse than will Policy (1).

8.41 (Ross Laboratories; valuation of brand name.) (Dollar amounts in millions.)

		Part a.	Part b.
(1)	Operating Margin..	$ 600.0	$ 600.0
	Employed Physical Capital $500.0		
	Subtract Pretax Profit on Physical Capital Required at 10 (Part *a*.) or 20 (Part *b*.)..............	(50.0)	(100.0)
(2)	Profit Generated by Brand............................	$ 550.0	$ 500.0
	Subtract Income Taxes at 40 Percent	(220.0)	(200.0)
(3)	Net Brand Profits	$ 330.0	$ 300.0
	Multiply by Aftertax Capitalization Factor......	12.0	8.0
(4)	Estimate of Brand Value.............................	$3,960.0	$2,400.0

8.42   (May Department Stores; improvements versus repairs or maintenance.)

a. **January 2**
Building (or Entrances) 28,000
   Cash 28,000
To record cost of new entrances.

December 31
Depreciation Expense 24,000
   Accumulated Depreciation on Building 24,000
$24,000 = 1/7 \times [(\$800,000 - \$660,000 + \$28,000)] =$
$1/40 \times \$800,000 + 1/7 \times \$28,000.$

b. **January 2**
Loss 28,000
   Building (or Accumulated Depreciation on
    Building) 28,000
Recognize loss from destruction.

Building (or Accumulated Depreciation on
   Building) 28,000
   Cash 28,000
To recognize cost of new entrance facilities.

These two entries are equivalent to, and could be replaced by:

Loss 28,000
   Cash 28,000

December 31
Depreciation Expense 20,000
   Accumulated Depreciation 20,000
Depreciation for year on remaining $140,000
over 7 years = $800,000/40 years.

c. Same as *b*. above.

d. The authors split on this one. Some favor the treatment in Part *a*., while others favor the treatment in Part *b*. or Part *c*.. Those favoring Part *a*. point to the voluntary nature of the decision to replace the entrances rather than to close down. Presumably society as a whole benefits from use of handicapped-accessible entrances or else regulations would not require them. If future benefits to society as a whole result and the firm decides to make the expenditure, an asset results which the firm will depreciate over its estimated service life. It would be improper, some say, to charge the entire cost of making future operations possible to this year. They cite the enormous expenditures for antipollution equipment as being similar.

8.42 d. continued.

Those favoring the treatment in Part *b*. argue that regulators require this expenditure to maintain the service potential of the building assets at the same level as before passage of the law. They see no essential difference between the economic effects of destruction by natural disaster (Part *b*.), man-made disaster (Part *c*.), and another form of man-made "disaster" (Part *d*.). It may seem antisocial to say that the passage of a law results in damage no different from vandalism, but the economic consequences to the owner of the business are the same as in Parts *c*. and *d*., and so they urge immediate expensing. They agree that the enormous expenditures for antipollution equipment are also a loss (at least to the degree that costs exceed firm-specific benefits) even though most firms do not expense such items.

The holders of the opposing (capitalize) view see a significant difference between natural (or man-made) disasters and democratic social decision, which they view as not being "man-made disasters."

e. If you believe that Part *d*. is like Part *a*., then so is Part *e*. like Part *a*.. If you believe that Part *d*. is like Parts *b*. and *c*., then the loss here should be only $21,000 (= $28,000 − $7,000). Depreciation expense for each of the last seven years is $21,000 [= ($140,000 + $7,000)/7 years].

8.43 (Epstein Company; accounting for intangibles.)

a. The issue here is the length of the amortization period. In spite of the fact that the company plans to make and sell indefinitely, the fair market value of $100,000 attached to the property right is allocable only to the next three years of use. After that, anyone can use the patent. Thus, we would amortize this patent over three years.

b. The same problem and reasoning above leads us to use a five-year life.

c. The amortization period here is theoretically indefinite, but APB *Opinion No. 17* does not permit a period longer than forty years.

d. In Year 2, we should debit expense and credit asset for the diminution in the value of the trade secret. This amount will be hard to estimate. The auditor may argue that the secret has lost all of its value and will require the write off of the remaining book value.

8.43 continued.

e. The firm should capitalize the film as an asset and write it off over its economic life. This is an easy statement to make, but the estimate of life might be as short as three years or as long as the firm sells thyristors, which appears to be the indefinite future. The firm will pick a number and be prepared to give in to the auditor who asks for a shorter life. Management will lack any sound arguments as to what the life should be. We would argue only with the immediate expensing of the film's cost.

Sheldon L. Epstein, former patent counsel of Brunswick Corporation, suggested this question to us. His reaction to the above answers is as follows:

a. The trademark registration is simple proof of ownership in the United States which the company could renew again and again for twenty-year periods. Because trademark rights will continue to exist as long as the company properly uses the mark, the amortization period is theoretically infinite. However, APB *Opinion No. 17* requires that the amortization period be no longer than 40 years. In the event that the company discontinues the use of the mark or loses the exclusive right to use the mark, the firm should write off the unamortized amount in the year in which the event occurs. Where the company owns a foreign trademark, the right to exclusive use may be dependent on a valid registration, and loss or expiration of the registration could require complete amortization in the year when such an event occurs. Note that trademarks receive a different accounting treatment from that given patents because trademarks can have an infinite life while patents expire on a known date.

b. The design patent grants the company the right to exclude others from manufacturing, using or selling the same or similar containers for 5 years. After that, anyone is free to copy the design. Therefore, the privilege of exclusivity diminishes with time and the value should be amortized over the remaining life of the patent.

c. I agree with your answer.

d. I agree with your answer but with the caveat that its value depends on what the competitor does with its knowledge of the trade secret. If it does nothing, then there is little or no loss of value. If it uses it for the purpose of competition, then its value diminishes by the present value of anticipated lost profits and the accountant should recognize the value lost in the year the event occurs. If a competitor publishes the trade secret, then all of its value is lost.

8.43 continued.

   e. The answer is generally correct; however, note that the accounting treatment for copyrights lies somewhere between that used for patents and that used for trademarks. Under the copyright law, it is possible for the copyright to extend for periods well beyond 40 years or for a substantially shorter period (as would be the case for an old work). The important point is to ask what the remaining life of the exclusive privilege is and, in the case of a work licensed by the company from an individual, when the right reverts to the author (35 years). For example, copyrights in new works last for the life of the author plus 50 years except for anonymous or pseudonymous works for which the period is the first of 75 years from publication or 100 years from creation. For older works, many will expire on December 31, 2002; however, there are a number of exceptions.

8.44   (Capitalizing versus expensing; if capitalized, what amortization period?)

   a. If the firm makes this expenditure to secure future benefits, then there is an argument for capitalizing it. The entries would be:

Building (or Fire Escapes)............................. 28,000
   Cash   28,000
To capitalize improvements.

Depreciation Expense..................................... 4,000
   Accumulated Depreciation   4,000
One year's amortization of improvements based
on a seven-year life.

A somewhat more logical view is that the firm made the expenditure to maintain the service potential that it had planned previously. It obtains no additional benefits beyond those planned. See the discussion in Problem 8.42 above. The expenditure is a result of new legislation, so this view results in the following entry at the time the law is passed:

Loss from New Legislation............................. 28,000
   Building (or Accumulated Depreciation)   28,000
To recognize loss.

When the expenditure is made, the entry is:

Building (or Fire Escapes)............................. 28,000
   Cash   28,000
To capitalize expenditure for fire escapes.

8.44 a. continued.

This second treatment results in immediate recognition of the loss, and subsequent depreciation of the building improvements and fire escapes is the same as before the law was passed.

b. Building... 1,050,000
    Investment in General Electric Stock............   100,000
    Gain on Disposal of Investment...................   950,000

In the case of widely traded stock, the stock market valuation is probably a better guide than is the appraisal value of a single building.

c. Building... 1,000,000
    Investment in Small Timers Stock................   100,000
    Gain on Disposal of Investment...................   900,000

For thinly traded issues, the appraisal value of the building may be a more reliable guide. Many people think that investors cannot sell large blocks of such stock at once, except at a discount from the quoted price per share. We would not argue with the same answer as Part *b.* above.

d. Garages... 18,000
    Cash   18,000
To capitalize improvements to garages.

Depreciation Expense.................................... 900
    Accumulated Depreciation...........................   900
$18,000/20 years = $900 per year.

The useful life of the improvements in this case is likely to be as long as the useful lives of the garages. A case can be made, however, for amortization over five or ten years.

e. See the glossary at *reserve-recognition accounting*.

Successful-Efforts Accounting Would Be:

Drilling Expense... 9,000,000
Oil Well 1,000,000
    Cash...   10,000,000

Full-Cost Accounting Would Be:

Oil Well 10,000,000
    Cash...   10,000,000

8.44 e. continued.

Reserve-Recognition Accounting Would Be:

Oil Well	40,000,000	
Cash..		10,000,000
Revenue from Successful Exploration		
Efforts..		30,000,000

Reserve-recognition accounting provides the most up-to-date or current valuation for the oil well. However, because accountants generally base asset valuations on acquisition cost, the choice is between successful-efforts and full costing. The principal argument for full costing is that firms must incur the costs of many dry holes in order to find a few productive holes. The cost of the dry holes is, therefore, a cost of finding productive ones and capitalization is appropriate. The principal argument for successful-efforts costing is that firms capitalize expenditures leading to future benefits (productive hole) but expense expenditures not creating future benefits (dry holes), consistent with the usual accounting for assets and expenses.

f. Advertising Expense	400,000	
Cash		400,000

Firms generally immediately expense expenditures on advertising. Theoretically, the firm should capitalize some portion of the expenditures as an asset because the company probably would not spend on advertising unless it expected future benefits. However, firms seldom follow the more theoretically sound procedure in practice due to the difficulty of identifying and measuring the future benefits.

g. Research Expense...	1,500,000	
Cash		1,500,000

This is the treatment required by FASB *Statement No. 2*, although we criticize it. The company has a proven record of success with its research and it would not continue the research expenditures unless it expected future benefits. Capitalization of these benefits on the balance sheet and subsequent amortization is at least a theoretically superior treatment.

8.44 continued.

h. Charitable Contribution (Expense)................... 250,000
     Cash 250,000

Although some indirect future benefit may come to the company, it is too indefinite to justify recognition. We wonder, though, if companies give away money without some expectation of future benefit.

i. Machine Tools.. 6,000,000
     Cash 6,000,000
To set up asset account.

Depreciation of Machine Tools (a production
     cost) 2,000,000
         Machine Tools...................................... 2,000,000
Amortize over 3 years, the life of the automobile model. An alternative entry debits the Inventory account.

The tools will be obsolete in three years; their physical life of six years is irrelevant. For some reason, automobile manufacturers do not show accumulated depreciation on special tools in published statements; credits appear to go directly to the asset account.

j. (Dollar Amounts in Millions)

Start of Year
Plant Assets (Airbuses) 100
     Cash 100
To record purchase of airplanes.

Plant Assets (Spare Parts)............................ 20
     Cash 20
To record spare parts as plant assets, not as inventory. This is the point of the question. Because the spare parts are giving up their future benefits as the firm uses the airplanes, we treat their cost as plant assets. At the end of the useful life of the airplanes, the spare parts will be worthless. We think they should be depreciated over the life of the airplanes, not accounted for like an inventory of parts which the firm can use in various alternative ways. Nothing in the chapter alerts the student to this treatment and many, if not most, will set up the asset as inventory.

8.44 j. continued.

(Dollar Amounts in Millions)

End of Year

Depreciation Expense...	12	
Accumulated Depreciation		12

Depreciation on plant assets for 1/10 of useful life costing $120 (= $100 + $20) in total. This treatment is consistent with that described in the preceding entry.

Whether or not the instructor or students agree with us, the point is worth discussing. Is the cost of spare parts acquired solely for use with a plant asset and therefore treated like plant assets or like inventory?

k. (Dollar Amounts in Millions)

End of Year

Depreciation Expense.....................................	12	
Accumulated Depreciation		12

The entry made for the same reason as in the preceding question. We think the following entries, which result from treating the spare parts as inventory, are wrong:

Depreciation Expense.....................................	10	
Accumulated Depreciation		10

Repair Expense...	1	
Spare Parts Inventory		1

8.45 (Recognizing and measuring impairment losses.)

a. The loss occurs because of an adverse action by a governmental entity. The undiscounted cash flows of $50 million are less than the book value of the building of $60 million. An impairment loss has therefore occurred. The market value of the building of $32 million is less than the book value of $60 million. Thus, the amount of the impairment loss is 28 million (= $60 million − $32 million). The journal entry to record the impairment loss is (in millions):

Loss from Impairment....................................	28	
Accumulated Depreciation.............................	20	
Building..		48

8.45 a. continued.

This entry records the impairment loss, eliminates the accumulated depreciation, and writes down the building to its market value of $32 million (= $80 − $48).

b. The undiscounted cash flows of $70 exceed the book value of the building of $60 million. Thus, no impairment loss occurs according to the definition in FASB *Statement No. 121*. An **economic** loss occurred but GAAP does not permit it to be recognized.

c. The loss arises because the accumulated costs significantly exceed the amount originally anticipated. The undiscounted future cash flows of $22 million exceed the book value of the building of $25 million. Thus, an impairment loss has occurred. The impairment loss recognized equals $9 million (= $25 million − $16 million). The journal entry is (in millions):

Loss from Impairment................................... 9
    Construction in Process............................. 9

d. The loss occurs because of a significant decline in the market value of the patent. FASB *Statement No. 121* requires the accountant to combine the patent and goodwill in measuring the loss. The undiscounted future cash flows of $18 million are less than the book value of the patent and goodwill of $34 million (= $20 + $14). Thus, an impairment loss occurred. The amount of the loss is $22 million (= $34 million − $52 million). The journal entry to record the loss is:

Loss from Impairment................................... 22
    Goodwill.. 14
    Patent.. 8

Statement No. 121 requires the reduction of goodwill to zero before a firm writes down the identifiable intangible asset (patent) in the amount of the impairment loss.

e. The loss occurs because of a significant change in the business climate for Chicken Franchisees. One might question whether this loss is temporary or permanent. Evidence from previous similar events (for example, Tylenol) suggests that consumers soon forget or at least forgive the offending company. The FASB reporting standard discusses but rejects the use of a permanency criterion in identifying impairment losses. Thus, an impairment loss occurs in this case because the future undiscounted cash flows of $6 million from the franchise rights exceed the book value of the franchise rights of $10 million. Note that Chicken Franchisees must separate the cash flows associated with the preparing and selling of chicken in its physical facilities from the cash flows associated with the

8.45 e. continued.

Chicken Delight franchise name. The amount of the impairment loss is $7 million (= $10 million – $3 million). The journal entry is (in millions):

Impairment Loss...	7	
Franchise Rights..		7

This entry assumes that Chicken Franchisees does not use an Accumulated Amortization account.

8.46 (Ormes Company; preparing statement of cash flows.) A T-account work sheet for Ormes Company for Year 2 appears after the statement of cash flows.

ORMES COMPANY
Statement of Cash Flows
For Year 2

Operations:		
Net Income...	$ 60,000	
Addbacks and Additions:		
Bad Debt Expense....................................	20,000	
Depreciation Expense	39,000	
Loss on Sale of Equipment....................	8,000	
Amortization Expense.........................	15,000	
Increase in Accounts Payable...............	27,000	
Subtractions:		
Gain on Sale of Patent	(125,000)	
Increase in Accounts Receivable	(29,200)	
Increase in Inventories	(25,000)	
Cash Flow from Operations.........................		$ (10,200)
Investing:		
Sale of Patents......................................	$ 125,000	
Sale of Property, Plant and Equipment......	10,000	
Acquisition of Patent.............................	(75,000)	
Acquisition of Property, Plant and Equip-		
ment..	(62,900)	
Cash Flow from Investing..........................		(2,900)
Financing:		
Common Stock Issued	$ 43,900	
Dividends..	(25,000)	
Cash Flow from Financing		18,900
Change in Cash..		$ 5,800
Cash, Beginning of Year 2		25,700
Cash, End of Year 2....................................		$ 31,500

Supplementary Information

Ormes Company issued $30,000 of its common stock in the acquisition of property, plant and equipment during Year 2.

8.46 continued.

Cash

	√	25,700		

Operations

(1)	60,000	125,000	(5)
(7)	20,000	29,200	(9)
(11)	39,000	25,000	(10)
(12)	8,000		
(13)	15,000		
(14)	27,000		

Investing

(5)	125,000	62,900	(3)
(12)	10,000	75,000	(6)

Financing

(15)	43,900	25,000	(2)

	√	31,500		

Accounts Receivable				Allowance for Uncollectable Accounts			
√	120,000					2,400	√
(9)	29,200	19,200	(8)	(8)	19,200	20,000	(7)
√	130,000					3,200	√

Inventory			Property, Plant and Equipment			
√	175,000		√	247,300		
(10)	25,000		(3)	62,900	40,000	(12)
			(4)	30,000		
√	200,000		√	300,200		

Accumulated Depreciation				Patents		
		78,000	√			
(12)	22,000	39,000	(11)	(6)	75,000	
		95,000	√	√	75,000	

Solutions

8.46 continued.

Accumulated Amortization			Accounts Payable		
--				155,000	√
	15,000	(13)		27,000	(14)
	15,000	√		182,000	√

Common Stock			Retained Earnings			
	100,000	√			232,600	√
	30,000	(4)	(2)	25,000	60,000	(1)
	43,900	(15)				
	173,900	√			267,600	√

8.47   (Caterpillar Tractor Company; analysis of financial statement disclosure of effects of depreciation policy.)

(Dollar Amounts in Millions)

a.   **Year 3:** $\$418 = \$505 - [(\$4,020 - \$3,339) - (\$3,894 - \$3,300)]$
        $= \$505 - \$87.$

Year 2: $\$357 = \$448 - [(\$3,894 - \$3,300) - (\$3,431 - \$2,928)]$
        $= \$448 - \$91.$

b.   Assets would be larger by $681 (= $4,020 − $3,339); retained earnings would be larger by $409 [= (1.00 − .40) X $681]; and income tax expense would have been larger by $272 (= .40 X $681). Presumably these would have been paid in cash or would appear in the Income Taxes Payable account or some combination of both. Probably the extra cash payments would not merely reduce the end-of-year cash balances, but would have been raised with some form of financing. This presumption arises because we assume that Caterpillar always maintains the minimum cash balances required to run its business. If it could get along with $207 less cash, then it would be doing so now. Thus, we cannot be sure of all the changes in the balance sheet that would occur if the depreciation policy were different.

8.48 (Pasteur Company: Straight-line depreciation is probably too "conservative"; it usually writes off an asset's cost faster than future benefits disappear.)

a.

PATTERN OF EXPIRATION OF FUTURE BENEFITS MEASURED
AS THE NET PRESENT VALUE OF FUTURE CASH FLOWS

Asset Cost $33,522 and Has 5-Year Life
Discount Rate = 15 Percent per Year

Beginning of Year (1)	Years Remaining (2)	Present Value of Remaining Cash Flows (3)	Percentage of Present Value of Cash Flows Remaining (4)	Percentage of Loss in Value During Preceding Year (5)	Straight-line Depreciation for Preceding Year (6)
1	5	$33,522	100%		
2	4	28,550	85	15%	20%
3	3	22,832	68	17	20
4	2	16,257	48	20	20
5	1	8,696	26	22	20
6	0	-0-	0	26	20
Totals.........				100%	100%

8.48 continued

b.

ENTRIES IN TABLE SHOW CASH FLOWS MULTIPLIED BY DISCOUNT FACTOR

	Cash Flow	Discount Factors				
		1 Year .86957	2 Years .75614	3 Years .65752	4 Years .57175	5 Years .49718
Year 1	$ 11,733	$ 10,203				
Year 2	10,727	$ 9,328	8,111			
Year 3	9,722	$ 8,454	7,351	6,392		
Year 4	8,716	$ 7,579	6,590	5,731	4,983	
Year 5	7,710	$ 6,704	5,830	5,069	4,408	3,833
Diagonal Sum = Present Value of Remaining Cash Flows at Start of Year........		$ 6,704	$ 13,409	$ 20,113	$ 26,818	$ 33,522
		5	4	3	2	1

Beginning of Year (1)	Years Remaining (2)	Cash Flow End of Year (3)	Depreciation in Proportion to Undiscounted Cash Flows (4)	Present Value of Remaining Cash Flows (5)	Percentage of Initial Cash Flows Remaining (6)	Percentage of Loss in Value During Preceding Year (7)
1	5	$11,733		$33,522	100%	
2	4	10,727	24%	26,818	80	20%
3	3	9,722	22	20,113	60	20
4	2	8,716	20	13,409	40	20
5	1	7,710	18	6,704	20	20
	0	0	16	0	0	20
Totals........		$48,608	100%			100%

Note that to achieve straight-line depreciation for present value, cash flows need to be accelerated.

8.48 continued.

    c. Because many projects give their major cash flows in later years, straight-line appears to be more conservative than the rate of disappearance of present value of future cash flows.

8.49   (General Electric Company; analysis of financial statements to compute the change in property and plant assets required to sustain sales growth.)

This case shows both the ordinary use of the asset turnover ratios and the danger of analyzing average, rather than marginal, effects. Refer to Schedule 8.1 which reproduces the text exhibit and adds two more columns showing the incremental sales per dollar of incremental investment in plant, Column (11), and in total assets, Column (12).

The *marginal* effects differ strikingly from the *average* effects. Whereas the total asset turnover indicates that one dollar of sales requires $.70 of total assets, the incremental analysis indicates that one dollar of sales requires $.80 (= $1.00/$1.25) of total assets for *new* sales. Whereas, the fixed asset turnover indicates that one dollar of sales requires $.20 of plant, the incremental analysis indicates that one dollar of sales requires $.65 (= $1.00/$1.55) of new plant for *new* sales.

The implications for financing decisions are that to generate $2.7 billion of new sales, GE will need $2.2 (= .80 X $2.7) billion of new financing, not $1.9 billion, and that GE will raise $1.8 (= $.65 X $2.7) billion, not $540 million, of this amount in long-term financing for investment in plant and equipment. Although incremental analysis indicates that total financing requirements increase by only 15 percent over average analysis, the amounts of long-term financing are roughly triple the amounts suggested by average turnover analysis.

Students learn in the microeconomics and managerial accounting courses the importance of marginal analysis, but we can make the same point in the financial accounting course.

In more advanced financial analysis courses, where you can assume that the students have studied multiple regression tools, you can discuss the results of regressing changes in sales, Column (3), on plant and equipment additions, Column (6), and change in total assets, Column (8). The results of two regressions are as follows:

I. ΔSales = $\hat{a}$ + $\hat{b}\Delta$Plant + $\hat{c}\,\Delta$Assets
           Coefficients: 549   1.08   0.02
           t-statistics: 1.06   1.56   0.03
           Adjusted R^2 =   .39

II. ΔSales = $\hat{a}$ + $\hat{b}\Delta$Plant
           Coefficients: 558   1.10
           t-statistics: (1.38)   (3.07)
           Adjusted R^2 =   .46

Schedule 8.1
GENERAL ELECTRIC COMPANY
Data on Sales, Plant/Equipment, and Total Assets
(Dollars in Millions)

| | | | Plant and Equipment | | | Total Assets | | Sales Per Dollar of Assets Turnover Ratios | | Incremental Sales Per Dollar of Incremental Investment | |
| | | Dollar Change from Preceding Year (3) | Balance Sheet Total Net of Accumulated Depreciation December 31 (4) | Dollar Change from Preceding Year (5) | New Acquisitions for Year (6) | Balance Sheet Total December 31 (7) | Dollar Change from Preceding Year (8) | Fixed Assets (9) | Total Assets (10) | Fixed Assets = (3) / (6) (11) | Total Assets = (3) / (8) (12) |
Year (1)	Sales (2)										
12	$ 27,240	$ 2,281	$ 6,844	$ 1,064	$ 2,025	$20,942	$2,431	4.32	1.38	1.13	.94
11	24,959	2,498	5,780	1,167	1,948	18,511	1,867	4.80	1.42	1.28	1.34
10	22,461	2,807	4,613	590	1,262	16,644	1,608	5.20	1.42	2.22	1.75
9	19,654	2,135	4,023	439	1,055	15,036	1,339	5.17	1.37	2.02	1.59
8	17,519	1,822	3,584	228	823	13,697	1,647	5.05	1.36	2.21	1.11
7	15,697	1,592	3,356	175	740	12,050	1,309	4.80	1.38	2.15	1.22
6	14,105	187	3,181	565	588	10,741	1,372	4.87	1.40	.32	.14
5	13,918	1,973	2,616	255	813	9,369	1,045	5.59	1.57	2.43	1.89
4	11,945	1,471	2,361	224	735	8,324	922	5.31	1.52	2.00	1.60
3	10,474	917	2,137	111	501	7,402	514	5.03	1.47	1.83	1.78
2	9,557	723	2,026	277	711	6,888	688	5.06	1.46	1.02	1.05
1	8,834		1,749		685	6,199					

Columns (2), (4), (6), (7): taken from annual reports.

Columns (3), (5), (8): amount for a given year computed by subtracting amount for preceding year from amount for given year, using data in preceding column.

Column (9) = $.5 \times \dfrac{\text{Column (2)}}{[\text{Column (4)} + \text{Column (4), preceding year}]}$.

Column (10) = $.5 \times \dfrac{\text{Column (2)}}{[\text{Column (7)} + \text{Column (7), preceding year}]}$.

8.50   (AOL; effect of capitalizing versus expensing on reported income.)

a. Assets are resources that have the potential for providing a firm with a future economic benefit. The resources recognized as assets are those

   - for which the firm has acquired rights to their future use as a result of a past transaction or exchange, and

   - for which the firm can measure or quantify the future benefits with a reasonable degree of precision.

Generally accepted accounting principles treat expenditures that do not qualify as assets as expenses in the period of the expenditure. The case that AOL might make to its independent auditors for its policy of capitalizing and amortizing subscriber acquisition costs includes the following:

1. The capitalized costs are those that relate to identifiable prospects only. The future benefit to the firm is the subscription revenue that AOL will receive from these customers.

2. AOL has made direct expenditures for identifiable subscriber acquisition materials (printing, production and shipping of starter kits) or incurred specifically identifiable costs for direct marketing programs (direct marketing response cards or mailing lists).

The capitalized costs include only direct costs, not indirect costs that the Company would have to allocate on some possibly questionable basis. These direct costs incurred serve as a measure of the minimum future benefits to be received.

The instructor might then ask students to evaluate these arguments. Some points to consider follow.

1. One wonders how AOL determines who is a "specific identifiable prospect." The yield rate on direct market response cards and mailing lists is generally very small. Predicting the yield rate on a new product such as online services is even more difficult.

2. One wonders how and when AOL determines that a subscriber acquisition expenditure is on a specific identifiable prospect versus on all others that receive the solicitation.

3. One wonders how AOL determines the total expected revenues relating to a particular advertising expenditure.

4. The amortization period of 24 months suggests that any benefits of such expenditures are short-lived.

8.50 a. continued.

5. One suspects that AOL capitalizes and subsequently amortizes subscriber acquisition costs, instead of expensing them in the year incurred, in order to increase earnings during its high growth phase. AOL must obtain capital to sustain its rapid growth. It can use debt financing for fixed assets but must generally use equity financing to build a customer base and develop its technology. Positive and growing earnings will likely make the firm more attractive to potential investors and lower its financing costs.

b. The changes in the Deferred Subscriber Acquisition Costs account for the Year 3 to Year 6 fiscal years appear below:

| | Fiscal Year Ended June 30: | | | |
	Year 3	Year 4	Year 5	Year 6
Balance, Beginning of Year.............................	$ 3,243	$ 6,890	$ 26,392	$ 77,229
Plus Expenditures during the Year from the Statement of Cash Flows.........	10,685	37,424	111,761	363,024
Less Amortization during the Year from the Statement of Cash Flows.........	(7,038)	(17,922)	(60,924)	(126,072)
Balance, End of Year..........	$ 6,890	$26,392	$ 77,229	$314,181

This analysis shows the significant difference between the amount of subscriber acquisition costs incurred and the amount amortized. The amounts amortized represent an increasing percentage of total marketing costs reported in Exhibit 10 of the case through fiscal Year 5 (72.2 percent in fiscal Year 3, 76.1 percent in fiscal Year 4, 79.1 percent in fiscal Year 5), but this percentage decreased to 59.3 percent in fiscal Year 6.

c. Research and development costs and software development costs incurred prior to the time of developing a commercially feasible product are expensed in the period incurred. Thus, the accounting is the same. The rationale for immediate expensing is the uncertainty of future benefits to justify recognition of an asset. The different accounting occurs after identification of a commercially feasible product. If the product is software, firms must capitalize and amortize the costs. If the product is anything else, firms must expense expenditures in the year incurred. The rationale for the different treatments seems obscure to us. Computer software has physical substance whereas other technologies often do not. There appears to be a thin line here that drives the required accounting.

8.50 continued.

d. The changes in the Deferred Product Development Costs account for the Year 3 to Year 6 fiscal years appear below:

	Fiscal Year Ended June 30:			
	Year 3	Year 4	Year 5	Year 6
Balance, Beginning of Year...........................	$ 2,876	$ 3,915	$ 7,912	$ 18,914
Plus Expenditures on Product Development during the Year..............	1,831	5,132	13,011	32,631
Less Amortization of Product Development Costs from Notes.............	(792)	(1,135)	(2,009)	(7,250)
Balance, End of Year..........	$ 3,915	$ 7,912	$ 18,914	$ 44,295

The expenditures on product development significantly exceed amortization. Unlike subscriber acquisition costs, amortization of product development costs are a decreasing percentage of total product development expenses each year in Exhibit 10 (27.2 percent in fiscal Year 3, 22.9 percent in fiscal Year 4, 15.6 percent in fiscal Year 5, and 13.5 percent in fiscal Year 6).

The instructor might ask students why AOL classifies expenditures on deferred subscriber acquisition costs as an operating activity but expenditures on deferred product development costs as an investing activity in its statement of cash flows. Both expenditures result in an increase in a noncurrent asset. Both expenditures relate directly to the principal operating activities of the firm. We think that both expenditures should appear in the operating section of the statement of cash flows. Classifying the deferred development costs as an investing instead of an operating activity increases cash flow from operations. It is interesting to note that prior to the Year 5 fiscal year, AOL also classified deferred subscriber acquisition costs as an investing activity, thereby inflating cash flow from operations. Note that the portion of expenditures on both subscriber acquisition costs and product development cost that AOL expenses immediately in the year incurred appear in the operating section of the statement of cash flows.

e. The immediate expensing of amounts allocated to in-process technologies in a corporate acquisition is consistent with the required expensing of such expenditures when incurred internally. In both cases there is no evidence of a commercially feasible product. The accounting for developed technologies is different however. If a firm acquires a developed technology externally, it must capitalize and subsequently amortize the expenditure. If a

8.50 e. continued.

firm develops the same technology internally, it must expense the costs of development each period. If the technology is computer software, a firm can capitalize costs incurred subsequent to establishing commercial feasibility. The amount capitalized in the case of internally-developed software will be less than if it purchased the developed technology externally. These differences in the accounting for (1) internally-developed versus externally-purchased technologies, and (2) software technologies versus other technologies makes the analysis of technology companies more difficult.

f.

	Fiscal Year Ended June 30:			
	Year 3	Year 4	Year 5	Year 6
Operating Income as Reported	$ 1,925	$ 4,608	$ (19,294)	$ 65,243
Increase in Subscriber Acquisition Costs:				
Year 3: $10,685 – $7,038	(3,647)			
Year 4: $37,424 – $17,922		(19,502)		
Year 5: $111,761 – $60,924			(50,837)	
Year 6: $363,024 – $126,072				(236,952)
Increase in Product Development Costs:				
Year 3: $1,831 – $792	(1,039)			
Year 4: $5,132 – $1,135		(3,997)		
Year 5: $13,011 – $2,009			(11,002)	
Year 6: $32,631 – $7,250				(25,381)
Elimination of Charge for Acquired Research & Development			50,335	16,981
Revised Operating Income	$ (2,761)	$ (18,891)	$ (30,798)	$ (180,109)

8.50 continued.

g. Schedule 8.2 of this teaching note presents common size operating income statements for AOL for the Year 3 to Year 6 fiscal years. The revised income statement in Schedule 8.2 indicates that AOL operated at an increasing loss during the last four fiscal years. Most expense to sales percentages remained relatively flat except for marketing expenses. Although online revenues per subscriber have increased during the last three years, the cost of obtaining new subscribers continues to escalate. The number of subscribers at each fiscal year end does not permit us to assess how much turnover of subscribers occurred each year. We can relate marketing expenditures to the increase in the number of subscribers each year to see how much more AOL has spent to obtain and retain subscribers. The calculations are as follows:

Fiscal Year	Incremental Subscribers	Marketing Expenditures	Marketing Expenditure per Incremental Subscriber	Marketing Expenditure per Average[a] Subscriber
Year 4	903 − 303 = 600	$ 43,050	$ 71.75	$ 71.39
Year 5	3,005 − 903 = 2,102	127,901	60.85	65.46
Year 6	6,198 − 3,005 = 3,193	449,662	140.83	97.72

[a]Average of number of subscribers at beginning and end of the year.

Thus competition for subscribers appears to be the key driver for profitability in this industry. The outlook for AOL does not appear particularly promising.

8.50 g. continued.

Schedule 8.2

Common Size Operating Income Statements for America Online
As Reported and As Restated
(Amounts in Thousands)

	Year Ended June 30							
As Reported	Year 3		Year 4		Year 5		Year 6	
Revenues...........	$ 51,984	100.0%	$ 115,722	100.0%	$ 394,290	100.0%	$1,093,854	100.0%
Cost of Revenues ..	(28,820)	(55.5)	(69,043)	(59.7)	(229,724)	(58.3)	(627,372)	(57.4)
Marketing.........	(9,745)	(18.7)	(23,548)	(20.3)	(77,064)	(19.5)	(212,710)	(19.4)
Product Development...........	(2,913)	(5.6)	(4,961)	(4.3)	(12,842)	(3.3)	(53,817)	(4.9)
Administrative ...	(8,581)	(16.5)	(13,562)	(11.7)	(41,966)	(10.6)	(110,653)	(10.1)
Acquired Research & Development...........	--	--	--	--	(50,335)	(12.8)	(16,981)	(1.6)
Amortization of Goodwill.........	--	--	--	--	(1,653)	(.4)	(7,078)	(.6)
Operating Income.	$ 1,925	3.7%	$ 4,608	4.0%	$ (19,294)	(4.9)%	$ 65,243	6.0%
As Revised								
Revenues...........	$ 51,984	100.0%	$ 115,722	100.0%	$ 394,290	100.0%	$1,093,854	100.0%
Cost of Revenues ..	(28,820)	(55.5)	(69,043)	(59.7)	(229,724)	(58.3)	(627,372)	(57.4)
Marketing.........	(13,392)	(25.7)	(43,050)	(37.2)	(127,901)	(32.4)	(449,662)	(41.1)
Product Development...........	(3,952)	(7.6)	(8,958)	(7.7)	(23,844)	(6.1)	(79,198)	(7.3)
Administrative ...	(8,581)	(16.5)	(13,562)	(11.7)	(41,966)	(10.6)	(110,653)	(10.1)
Amortization of Goodwill.........	--	--	--	-	(1,653)	(.4)	(7,078)	(.6)
Operating Income.	$ (2,761)	(5.3)%	$ (18,891)	(16.3)%	$ (30,798)	(7.8)%	$ (180,109)	(16.5)%

CHAPTER 9

LIABILITIES: INTRODUCTION

Questions, Exercises, Problems, and Cases: Answers and Solutions

9.1   See the text or the glossary at the end of the book.

9.2   a. Yes; amount of accrued interest payable.

   b. Yes. In spite of the indefiniteness of the time of delivery of the goods or services and the amount, the balance sheet reports a liability in the amount of the cash received.

   c. No; accounting does not record executory promises.

   d. Yes; at the present value, calculated using the yield rate at the time of issue, of the remaining coupon and principal payments.

   e. Yes; at the expected, undiscounted value of future service costs arising from all sales made prior to the balance sheet date. The income statement includes warranty expense because of a desire to match all expenses of a sale with the sale; presumably one reason the firm sold the product was the promise of free repairs. When recognizing the expense, the accountant credits a liability account to recognize the need for the future expenditures.

   f. No. If the firm expected to lose a reasonably estimable amount in the suit, then it would show an estimated liability.

   g. Yes, assuming statutes or contracts require the restoration. The present value of an estimate of the costs is the theoretically correct answer, but many accountants would use the full amount undiscounted.

   h. No; viewed as executory.

   i. Airlines should recognize an expense and a liability for the estimated costs of providing the free flight during the periods when customers use flight services at regular fares. The airlines argue that they incur virtually no incremental cost for the free flight because the customer uses otherwise unused capacity. Thus, the airlines do not recognize an obligation for their frequent flyer programs.

9.3   The store should recognize the loss as soon as it is probable that it has incurred a liability and it can reasonably estimate the amount of the loss. Whether the store recognizes a loss at the time of the injury on July 5, Year 6, depends on the strength of the case the store feels it has against the customer's claims. If the floor was wet because a broken bottle had remained on the floor for several hours and was not cleaned up, then the store may feel it is probable that it has incurred a liability. If, on the other hand, the customer fell while running down a dry, uncluttered aisle while trying to shop quickly, then the store may feel that it is probable that it has not incurred a liability. Attorneys, not accountants, must make these probability assessments.

If the store does not recognize a loss at the time of the injury, the next most likely time is June 15, Year 7, when the jury renders its verdict. Unless attorneys for the store feel that it is highly probable that the court will reverse the verdict on appeal, the store should recognize the loss at this time.

If attorneys feel that the grounds for appeal are strong, then the next most likely time is on April 20, Year 8, when the jury in the lower court reaches the same verdict as previously. This is the latest time in this case at which the store should recognize the loss. If the store had recognized a loss on June 15, Year 7, it would recognize only the extra damage award in Year 8.

9.4   The expected value of the liability is $90,000 in both cases (.90 × $100,000 = $90,000; .09 × $1 × 1,000,000 = $90,000). Accounting would probably report the liability from the lawsuit as $100,000 and the liability for the coupons as $90,000. This inconsistency seems curious since the two situations differ only with respect to the number of possible outcomes (that is, all or nothing with respect to the lawsuit, whereas the coupon redemption rate conceivably ranges from one to one million).

9.5   Suppliers often grant a discount if customers pay within a certain number of days after the invoice date, in which case this source of funds has an explicit interest cost. Suppliers who do not offer discounts for prompt payment often include an implicit interest change in the selling price of the product. Customers in this second category should delay payment as long as possible because they are paying for the use of the funds. Firms should not delay payment to such an extent that it hurts their credit rating and raises their cost of financing.

9.6   The school should accrue the salary in ten monthly installments of $36,000 each at the end of each month, September through June. It will have paid $30,000 at the end of each of these months, so that by the end of the reporting year, it reports a current liability of $60,000 [= $360,000 − (10 × $30,000)].

9.7   There are two principal explanations. First, the obligation to customers in the event the firm does not publish the magazines is $45,000. Second, recognition of a liability of $32,000 requires a remaining credit of $13,000 to some other account. Recognizing the $13,000 as income is inappropriate because the publisher has not yet rendered the required services. Including the $13,000 is some type of Deferred Income account (a liability) has the same effect on total liabilities as reporting the Advance from Customers at $45,000.

9.8   It is cheaper (and, therefore, more profitable) to repair a few sets than to have such stringent quality control that the manufacturing process produces zero defectives. An allowance is justified when firms expect to have warranty costs. Manufacturers of TV sets for space travel or heart pacemakers should strive for zero defects.

9.9   **Similarities:** The accountant makes estimates of future events in both cases. The accountant charges the cost of estimated uncollectibles or warranties to income in the period of sale, not in the later period when specific items become uncollectible or break down. The income statement reports the charge against income as an expense in both cases, although some accountants report the charge for estimated uncollectibles as a revenue contra (and we prefer it that way).

       Differences: The balance sheet account showing the expected costs of future uncollectibles reduces an asset account, while that for estimated warranties appears as a liability.

9.10   The coupon rate and par value of the bonds, the market rate of interest, and the market's opinion of the firm as a borrower. If the coupon rate is 8 percent, the market rate is 12 percent and the market views the firm as a relatively poor credit risk, the bonds will sell at a price to yield say, 15 percent. This means that the firm will receive less than the par value of the bonds it issues. We are told that when bonds are brought to the market, the investment banker attempts to set the coupon rate so the bonds will sell close to par.

9.11   a.   Par value and face value are always synonymous.

       b.   Par value appears on the bond certificate and serves as the base for computing the periodic coupon interest payment. The book value is the same as the par value whenever the market-required interest rate on the date of issue equals the coupon interest rate. The book value will exceed the par value when the coupon rate exceeds the market rate at the time of issue. The par value will exceed the book value when the market rate exceeds the coupon rate at the time of issue.

9.11 continued.

    c. Book value equals the present value of future cash flows on a bond discounted at the market-required interest rate at the time of issue. Current market value equals the present value of future cash flows on a bond discounted at the interest rate the market currently requires to induce purchase of the bond. The book value exceeds the current market value when the market interest rate at the time of issue was lower than the current market interest rate. The current market value will exceed the book value when the current market interest rate is lower than the market interest rate at the time of issue.

9.12   Accountants initially record assets at acquisition cost and then allocate this amount to future periods as an expense. Changes in the market value of most assets (except for use of the lower-of-cost-or-market method for inventories and the market value method for marketable securities and investments in securities) do not appear in the accounting records. Similarly, using the market interest rate at the time of issue to account for bonds results in an initial liability equal to the amount of cash received and a subsequent liability that reflects amortization of this initial amount. Changes in the market value of bonds do not appear in the accounting records.

9.13   Interest expense as a percentage of the book value of a liability at the beginning of a period equals the market interest rate at the time debt was issued. Accountants use this interest rate throughout the life of the debt under the effective interest method. The amount of interest expense will change if the book value changes each period. The latter occurs if the firm issues debt at an amount exceeding or less than par or if each periodic payment includes a repayment of a portion of the principal.

9.14   With bond financing, the firm borrows the entire principal, $1 million, for the entire term of the loan. With lease or mortgage financing, the firm repays part of the principal with each payment. Thus, the effective amount borrowed decreases over time and interest expenses should also decrease, even though the borrowings use the same rate.

9.15   Zero coupon bonds offer no cash payments to the investor until maturity. The issuer benefits by delaying cash payments. The issuer also gets a tax deduction for interest expense (that is, amortization of bond discount) during the period the bonds are outstanding even though it has no immediate cash outflow for interest. The investor locks in a yield at the time of purchase. The investor need not worry about having to invest periodic coupon payments during the life of the bonds. Thus, the investor avoids the risk of interest rate changes. The disadvantage to the investor is that the amortization of bond discount during the life of the bonds is taxable income even though the investor receives no cash. Most investors in zero coupon bonds do not pay taxes (for example, pension funds).

9.16   The call premium, which typically declines as bonds approach maturity, compensates bondholders for the loss of interest payments when a firm calls, or buys back, some of its outstanding bonds before the maturity date. The call premium protects the bondholder from redemption by the issuer if interest rates in the market decline by reasonably small amounts.

9.17   When market interest rates change, so do market values of bonds. When interest rates rise, bond prices decline, but book values of bonds remain unchanged. Firms can issue new bonds at current market rates and use the proceeds to retire outstanding bonds previously issued when rates were lower, and accountants record this transaction as a gain. The gain actually occurred as market rates rose and the burden of the debt fell. This is an unrealized holding gain in historical cost accounting. Because management can time bond retirements, management can time income recognition. This possibility explains in part the requirement that firms report gains and losses on bond retirements as extraordinary items in the income statement.

9.18   (McGee Associates; journal entries for payroll.)

a. Wage and Salary Expense............................. 700,000
        U.S. Withholding Taxes Payable.................. 126,000
        State Withholding Taxes Payable................ 35,000
        FICA Taxes Payable 42,000
        Wages and Salaries Payable....................... 497,000
    Amounts payable to and for employees.

    Wage and Salary Expense............................. 107,800
        FICA Taxes Payable 42,000
        FUTA Taxes Payable to U.S. Government..... 14,000
        FUTA Taxes Payable to State Government.... 7,000
        Payable to Profit Sharing Fund................... 28,000
        Vacation Liability..................................... 16,800
    Employer's additional wage expense; estimated
    vacation liability is $16,800 (= 1.20 X $14,000).

b. $807,800 = $700,000 + $107,800.

9.19   (PepsiCo; computations and journal entries for income taxes payable.)

Income Taxes at .35 X $1,900 million = $665.0 million.
Income Taxes at .35 X $2,010 million = $703.5 million.
Income Taxes at .35 X $1,940 million = $679.0 million.
Income Taxes at .35 X $1,950 million = $682.5 million.
Income Taxes at .35 X $2,000 million = $700.0 million.

9.19 continued.

   a. (Amounts in Millions)

      (1)   **Tax Returns**

Date	Estimated Taxes for Year	Cumulative Payments Due	Payment
4/15/Y1	$ 665.00	$ 166.25[a]	$ 166.25
6/15/Y1	703.50	351.75[b]	185.50
9/15/Y1	679.00	509.25[c]	157.50
12/15/Y1	682.50	682.50	173.25
12/31/Y1	700.00	--	--
3/15/Y2	700.00	700.00	17.50
			$ 700.00

[a]$1/4 \times \$665.0$ million. [b]$1/2 \times \$703.5$ million. [c]$3/4 \times \$679.0$ million.

      (2)   **Financial Statements**

Date	Tax Expense for Quarter	Cumulative Tax Expense
3/31/Y1	$ 166.25	$ 166.25
6/30/Y1	185.50	351.75
9/30/Y1	157.50	509.25
12/31/Y1	190.75	700.00
For Year...............	$ 700.00	

   b. (Amounts in Millions)

Year 1

March 31

Tax Expense...	166.25	
Taxes Payable...		166.25

April 15

Taxes Payable..	166.25	
Cash		166.25

June 15

Prepaid Taxes..	185.50	
Cash		185.50

June 30

Tax Expense...	185.50	
Prepaid Taxes		185.50

9.19 b. continued.

Sept. 15

Prepaid Taxes..	157.50	
Cash		157.50

Sept. 30

Tax Expense..	157.50	
Prepaid Taxes		157.50

Dec. 15

Prepaid Taxes..	173.25	
Cash		173.25

Dec. 31

Tax Expense..	190.75	
Prepaid Taxes		173.25
Taxes Payable..		17.50

Year 2

March 15

Taxes Payable...	17.50	
Cash		17.50

c. (Amounts in Millions)

Date	Cash	Prepaid Income Taxes	Income Taxes Payable		Tax Expense
Year 1					
March 31				166.25	166.25
April 15	166.25		166.25		
June 15	185.50	185.50			
June 30			185.50		185.50
Sept. 15	157.50	157.50			
Sept. 30			157.50		157.50
Dec. 15	173.25	173.25			
Dec. 31			173.25	17.50	190.75
		√ 0		17.50√	√ 700.00
Year 2					
March 15	17.50		17.50		

9.20   (Morrison's Cafeteria; journal entries for coupons.)

a. **January**

Cash	50,100	
Sales Revenue		48,000
Coupon Liability		2,100

Coupon Liability...	1,600	
Sales Revenue		1,600

February

Cash..	50,700	
Sales Revenue		48,500
Coupon Liability		2,200

Coupon Liability...	2,300	
Sales Revenue		2,300

March

Cash..	52,400	
Sales Revenue		50,000
Coupon Liability		2,400

Coupon Liability...	2,100	
Sales Revenue		2,100

b. The Coupon Liability account has a balance of $4,700 (= $4,000 + $2,100 − $1,600 + $2,200 − $2,300 + $2,400 − $2,100) on March 31.

9.21   (Abson Corporation; journal entries for service contracts.)

a. **1/31–3/31**

Cash...	180,000	
Service Contract Fees Received in Advance....		180,000

To record sale of 300 annual contracts.

3/31

Service Contract Fees Received in Advance.......	22,500	
Contract Revenues......................................		22,500

To recognize revenue on 300 contracts sold during the first quarter; 1.5/12 × $180,000.

1/01–3/31

Service Expenses...	32,000	
Cash (and Other Assets and Liabilities).........		32,000

9.21 a. continued.

4/01–6/30

Cash...	300,000	
Service Contract Fees Received in Advance....		300,000
To record sale of 500 annual contracts.		

6/30

Service Contract Fees Received in Advance.......	82,500	
Contract Revenues.....................................		82,500

To recognize revenue on 500 contracts sold and
300 contracts outstanding:
>   First Quarter:
>   3/12   × $ 180,000 = $45,000
>   Second Quarter:
>   1.5/12 × $ 300,000   =   37,500
> $82,500

4/01–6/30

Service Expenses...	71,000	
Cash (and Other Assets and Liabilities).........		71,000

7/01–9/30

Cash...	240,000	
Service Contract Fees Received in Advance....		240,000
To record sale of 400 annual contracts.		

9/30

Service Contract Fees Received in Advance.......	150,000	
Contract Revenues.....................................		150,000

To recognize revenue on 400 contracts sold and
800 contracts outstanding from prior sales.
>   First Quarter Sales:
>   3/12   × $180,000 = $ 45,000
>   Second Quarter Sales:
>   3/12   × $300,000 =   75,000
>   Third Quarter Sales:
>   1.5/12 × $240,000 =   30,000
>   = $ 150,000

7/01–9/30

Service Expenses...	105,000	
Cash (and Other Assets and Liabilities).........		105,000

9.21 continued.

b. Balances in Service Contract Fees Received in Advance Account:

January 1	--
Less First Quarter Expirations	$ (22,500)
Plus First Quarter Sales	180,000
March 31	$ 157,500
Less Second Quarter Expirations	(82,500)
Plus Second Quarter Sales	300,000
June 30	$ 375,000
Less Third Quarter Expirations	(150,000)
Plus Third Quarter Sales	240,000
September 30	$ 465,000
Less Fourth Quarter Expirations	(195,000)
Plus Fourth Quarter Sales	120,000
December 31	$ 390,000

OR

Contracts	X	Balance Remaining	X	$ 600	=	Amount
300	X	1.5/12	X	$ 600	=	$ 22,500
500	X	4.5/12	X	$ 600	=	112,500
400	X	7.5/12	X	$ 600	=	150,000
200	X	10.5/12	X	$ 600	=	105,000
						$ 390,000

9.22 (Maypool Corporation; journal entries for estimated warranty liabilities and subsequent expenditures.)

a. **Year 1**

Accounts Receivable	1,200,000	
Sales		1,200,000

Estimated Warranty Liability	12,000	
Cash		12,000

Expenditures actually made.

Warranty Expense	48,000	
Estimated Warranty Liability		48,000

$(.01 + .03) \times \$1,200,000$.

9.22 a. continued.

Year 2

Accounts Receivable	1,500,000	
Sales Revenue		1,500,000

Estimated Warranty Liability	50,000	
Cash		50,000

Expenditures actually made.

Warranty Expense	60,000	
Estimated Warranty Liability		60,000

$(.01 + .03) \times \$1,500,000.$

b. $\$46,000 = \$48,000 - \$12,000 + \$60,000 - \$50,000.$

9.23   (Global Motors Corporation; journal entries for estimated warranty liabilities and subsequent expenditures.)

a. **Year 1**

Cash	800,000	
Sales Revenue		800,000

Estimated Warranty Liability	22,000	
Cash		13,200
Parts Inventory		8,800

Warranty Expense	48,000	
Estimated Warranty Liability		48,000

$.06 \times \$800,000 = \$48,000.$

Year 2

Cash	1,200,000	
Sales Revenue		1,200,000

Estimated Warranty Liability	55,000	
Cash		33,000
Parts Inventory		22,000

Warranty Expense	72,000	
Estimated Warranty Liability		72,000

$.06 \times \$1,200,000 = \$72,000.$

9.23 a. continued.

Year 3

Cash..	900,000	
Sales Revenue		900,000

Estimated Warranty Liability	52,000	
Cash		31,200
Parts Inventory		20,800

Warranty Expense	54,000	
Estimated Warranty Liability		54,000

$.06 \times \$900,000 = \$54,000.$

b. $\$48,000 - \$22,000 + \$72,000 - \$55,000 + \$54,000 - \$52,000 = \$45,000.$

9.24   (Sung Company; journal entry for short-term note payable.)

a. **12/01**

Cash..	50,000	
Notes Payable		50,000

12/31

Interest Expense...	250	
Interest Payable..		250

$\$50,000 \times .06 \times 30/360 = \$250.$

1/30

Interest Expense...	250	
Interest Payable..		250

1/30

Notes Payable (Original Note).........................	50,000	
Interest Payable...	500	
Notes Payable (New Note)............................		50,000
Cash		500

> *Note:* Omitting the entries to the Notes Payable account above is also acceptable.

3/2

Notes Payable	50,000	
Interest Expense...	250	
Cash		50,250

9.24 continued.

b. The entry to complete the accrual of interest (30 days) is the first entry under both alternatives. It is:

Interest Expense.....................................	250	
Interest Payable...................................		250

(1) **1/30**

Notes Payable (Original Note)	50,000	
Interest Payable	500	
Cash..		50,500

(2) **1/30**

Notes Payable (Original Note)	50,000	
Interest Payable	500	
Notes Payable (New Note)......................		50,500

9.25 (Blaydon Company; amortization schedule for note where explicit interest differs from market rate of interest.)

a. **Amortization Schedule for a Three-Year Note with a Maturity Value of $40,000, Calling for 8-Percent Annual Interest Payments, Yield of 12 Percent per Year**

Year	Book Value Start of Year	Interest Expense for Period	Payment	Interest Added to (Subtracted from) Book Value	Book Value End of Year
(1)	(2)	(3)a	(4)	(5)	(6)
0					$ 36,157
1	$ 36,157	$ 4,339	$ 3,200	$ 1,139	37,296
2	37,296	4,476	3,200	1,276	38,572
3	38,572	4,628	43,200	(38,572)	-0-

a(3) = (2) X .12, except in Year 3 where it is a plug.

b.

Computer..	36,157	
Note Payable..		36,157

To record purchase.

Annual Journal Entry for Interest and Principal

Dr. Interest Expense..	Amount in Col. (3)	
Cr. Cash................		Amount in Col. (4)
Cr. Note Payable.....		Amount in Col. (5)*

*In third year, the firm debits Note Payable for $38,572.

9.26   (Skinner Corporation; computing the issue price of bonds.)

a.

Required Cash Flows	Present Value Factor for 6 Percent Discount Rate Compounded Semi-annually for 10 Years	Present Value of Required Cash Flows
$ 10,000,000 at End of 10 Years	.55368[a]	$ 5,536,800
$400,000 Every Six Months for 10 Years	14.87747[b]	5,950,988
Issue Price		$11,487,788

[a]Table 2, 3-percent column and 20-period row.
[b]Table 4, 3-percent column and 20-period row.

b.

Required Cash Flows	Present Value Factor for 8 Percent Discount Rate Compounded Semi-annually for 10 Years	Present Value of Required Cash Flows
$ 10,000,000 at End of 10 Years	.45639[a]	$ 4,563,900
$400,000 Every Six Months for 10 Years	13.59033[b]	5,436,132
Issue Price		$10,000,032[c]

[a]Table 2, 4-percent column and 20-period row.
[b]Table 4, 4-percent column and 20-period row.
[c]Difference from $10,000,000 due to rounding.

c.

Required Cash Flows	Present Value Factor for 10 Percent Discount Rate Compounded Semi-annually for 10 Years	Present Value of Required Cash Flows
$ 10,000,000 at End of 10 Years	.37689[a]	$ 3,768,900
$400,000 Every Six Months for 10 Years	12.46221[b]	4,984,884
Issue Price		$ 8,753,784

[a]Table 2, 5-percent column and 20-period row.
[b]Table 4, 5-percent column and 20-period row.

9.27   (Computing the issue price of bonds.)

   a. $1,000,000 × .23138[a] .... $ 231,380
       $60,000 × 15.37245[b]   922,347
           Issue Price... $1,153,727

       [a]Table 2, 5-percent column and 30-period row.
       [b]Table 4, 5-percent column and 30-period row.

   b. $75,000 × 17.29203[a] $1,296,902

       [a]Table 4, 4-percent column and 30-period row.

   c. $1,000,000 × .17411[a] .... $ 174,110

       [a]Table 2, 6-percent column and 30-period row.

9.28   (O'Brien Corporation; computing the issue price of bonds and interest
        expense.)

   a. $8,000,000 × .30656[a] $2,452,480
       $320,000 × 23.11477[b]   7,396,726
           Issue Price... $9,849,206

       [a]Table 2, 3-percent column and 40-period row.
       [b]Table 4, 3-percent column and 40-period row.

   b. .03 × $9,849,206 = $295,476.

   c. .03($9,849,206 + $295,476 – $320,000) = $294,740.

   d. Book Value: ($9,849,206 + $295,476 – $320,000 +
       $294,740 – $320,000).. $9,799,422

   e. $8,000,000 × .32523[a] $2,601,840
       $320,000 × 22.49246[b]   7,197,587
           Present Value... $9,799,427

       [a]Table 2, 3-percent column and 38-period row.
       [b]Table 4 3-percent column and 38-period row.

       The difference between the book value in Part d. and the present
       value in Part e. results from rounding present value factors.

9.29   (Robinson Company; computing the issue price of bonds and interest expense.)

     a. $5,000,000 × .37689[a] $1,884,450
         $200,000 × 12.46221[b] 2,492,442
           Issue Price $4,376,892

[a]Table 2, 5-percent column and 20-period row.
[b]Table 4, 5-percent column and 20-period row.

     b. .05 × $4,376,892 = $218,845.

     c. .05($4,376,892 + $218,845 − $200,000) = $219,787.

     d. $4,376,892 + $218,845 − $200,000 + $219,787 − $200,000 = $4,415,524.

     e. $5,000,000 × .41552[a] $2,077,600
         $200,000 × 11.68959[b] 2,337,918
           Present Value $4,415,518

[a]Table 2, 5-percent column and 18-period row.
[b]Table 4, 5-percent column and 18-period row.

The difference between the book value in Part *d*. and the present value in Part *e*. results from rounding present value factors.

9.30   (Florida Edison Company; using bond tables; computing interest expense.)

     a. $885,301; see Table 5, 10-year row, 12-percent column.

     b. $53,118 = .06 × $885,301.

     c. $53,305 = .06 × $888,419; see Table 5, 9.5-year row, 12-percent column.

     d. $926,399; see Table 5, 5-year row, 12-percent column.

     e. $55,584 = .06 × $926,399.

9.31   (Centrix Company; using bond tables.)

Refer to Table 6.

     a. $1,084,658; 25-year row; 11-percent column.

     b. $1,080,231; 20-year row; 11-percent column.

     c. $1,072,669; 15-year row; 11-percent column.

9.31 continued.

    d. $1,072,669; same answer is *not* coincidental.

    e. ($1,000,000 × .06) – ($1,004,739 – $1,000,000) = $60,000 – $4,739 = $55,261; 0.5-year row; 11-percent column.

    f. $934,707; 15-year row; 13-percent column.

    g. 10 percent compounded semiannually; scan 10-year row to find 112.46.

9.32   (Mendoza Corporation; journal entries for bond coupon payments and retirements.)

    a. **7/1/Year 7**

Interest Expense (.05 × $1,124,622)	56,231	
Bonds Payable (plug)	3,769	
Cash (.06 × $1,000,000)		60,000

        12/31/Year 7

Interest Expense[a]	56,043	
Bonds Payable (Plug)	3,957	
Cash (as above)		60,000

       [a].05 × ($1,124,622 – $3,769) = $56,043.

    b.

Bonds Payable ($1,116,896/2)	558,448	
Gain on Retirement (Plug)		108,743
Cash[a]		449,705

       [a]$500,000 × .899409 = $449,705 (value in a 14 percent market).

    c. It would appear as an extraordinary gain on the income statement.

9.33   (Womack Company; amortization schedule for bonds.)

    a.

$100,000 × .67556[a]	$ 67,556
$5,000 × 8.11090[b]	40,555
Issue Price	$ 108,111[c]

    [a]Table 2, 4-percent column and 10-period row.
    [b]Table 4, 4-percent column and 10-period row.
    [c]Also see Table 5.

9.33 continued.

b.

Six-Month Period	Liability at Start of Period	Interest at 4 Percent for Period	Coupon at 5% of Par	Increase in Book Value of Liability	Liability at End of Period
0					$ 108,111
1	$ 108,111	$ 4,324	$ 5,000	$ 676	107,435
2	107,435	4,297	5,000	703	106,732
3	106,732	4,269	5,000	731	106,001
4	106,001	4,240	5,000	760	105,241
5	105,241	4,210	5,000	790	104,451
6	104,451	4,178	5,000	822	103,629
7	103,629	4,145	5,000	855	102,774
8	102,774	4,111	5,000	889	101,885
9	101,885	4,075	5,000	925	100,960
10	100,960	4,040[a]	5,000	960	100,000
Total.................		$41,889	$50,000	$8,111	

[a]Does not equal .04 X $100,960 due to rounding.

c.   Book Value of Bonds: $10,363.

Bonds Payable...	10,363	
Extraordinary Loss on Bond Retirement.......		63
Cash		10,300

9.34   (Seward Corporation; amortization schedule for bonds.)

a. $100,000 X .74622[a].. $ 74,622
     $4,000 X 5.07569[b].. 20,303
     Issue Price.. $ 94,925

[a]Table 2, 5-percent column and 6-period row.
[b]Table 4, 5-percent column and 6-period row.

b.

Six-Month Period	Liability at Start of Period	Interest at 5 Percent for Period	Coupon at 4% of Par	Increase in Book Value of Liability	Liability at End of Period
0					$ 94,925
1	$ 94,925	$ 4,746	$ 4,000	$ 746	95,671
2	95,671	4,784	4,000	784	96,455
3	96,455	4,823	4,000	823	97,278
4	97,278	4,864	4,000	864	98,142
5	98,142	4,907	4,000	907	99,049
6	99,049	4,951	4,000	951	100,000
Total.................		$29,075	$24,000	$5,075	

9.34 continued.

    c. **January 2, Year 1**

Cash..	94,925	
Bonds Payable		94,925

      June 30, Year 1

Interest Expense..	4,746	
Interest Payable		4,000
Bonds Payable		746

      July 1, Year 1

Interest Payable...	4,000	
Cash		4,000

      December 31, Year 1

Interest Expense..	4,784	
Interest Payable		4,000
Bonds Payable		784

    d.

Bonds Payable (.20 X $98,142)...........................	19,628	
Loss on Retirement of Bonds...........................	772	
Cash		20,400

9.35   (Brooks Corporation; journal entries to account for bonds.)

    a.

$100,000 X .55368[a]..	$ 55,368
$4,000 X 14.87747[b]..	59,510
Issue Price...	$114,878

    [a]Table 2, 3-percent column and 20-period row.
    [b]Table 4, 3-percent column and 20-period row.

    b. **January 2, Year 2**

Cash..	114,878	
Bonds Payable		114,878

      June 30, Year 2

Interest Expense (.03 X $114,878)	3,446	
Bonds Payable..	554	
Cash		4,000

      December 31, Year 2

Interest Expense [.03 X ($114,878 – $554)]...........	3,430	
Bonds Payable..	570	
Cash		4,000

9.35 continued.

    c. Book Value: $114,878 – $554 – $570 = $113,754.
        Market Value:

$100,000 × .41552[a]	$ 41,552
$4,000 × 11.68959[b]	46,758
Total Market Value	$ 88,310

[a]Table 2, 5-percent column and 18-period row.
[b]Table 4, 5-percent column and 18-period row.

Bonds Payable	113,754	
Cash		88,310
Gain on Bond Retirement		25,444

9.36   (Central Appliance; allowance method for warranties; reconstructing transactions.)

    a. $720,000 = $820,000 (Goods Available for Sale) – $100,000 (Beginning Inventory).

    b. $700,000 = $820,000 (Goods Available for Sale) – $120,000 (Ending Inventory).

    c. $21,000 = $6,000 (Cr. Balance) + $15,000 (Dr. Balance).

    d. $20,000 = $5,000 (Required Cr. Balance) + $15,000 (Existing Dr. Balance).

    e.

Dr. Estimated Liability for Warranty Repairs	21,000	
Cr. Various Assets Used for Repairs		21,000

Repairs made during Year 2.

Dr. Warranty Expense	20,000	
Cr. Estimated Liability for Warranty Repairs		20,000

Expense recognition for Year 2.

Dr. Cost of Goods Sold	700,000	
Cr. Merchandise Inventory		700,000

Cost of goods sold is goods available for sale less ending inventory.

9.37   (Time Warner, Inc.; accounting for zero-coupon debt; see *The Wall Street Journal* for December 8, 1992.)

a. $483 million = $1,550 million/3.20714; see table 1, 6-percent column, 20-period row.

b. 5.8 percent = ($1,550/$500)$^{1/20}$ – 1 = 3.10$^{1/20}$ – 1. That is, for each dollar of the initial issue proceeds (of the $500 million), Time Warner must pay $3.10 (= $1,550/$500) at maturity of the notes. You can find the periodic interest rate to make $1.00 grow to $3.10 in 20 periods by trial and error or by using the exponential function on your computer or calculator. Note that you can state an equation to solve, as follows:

$$(1 + r)^{20} = 3.10; \text{ solve for } r.$$

You can see from Table 1 that 5.8 percent is approximately correct.

c. $28 million = .07 × $400 million.

d. $101.4 million. Ask, first, what must the book value of the notes be at the end of Year 19. Then, compute interest for the year on that amount. The book value of the loan at the end of Year 19 must be $1,448.6 (= $1,550/1.07) million. Interest for one year at 7 percent on $1,448.6 million is $101.4 (= .07 × $1,448.6 = $1,550.0 – $1,448.6) million. You can check this approach to finding the answer by noting that:

$$\$1,448.6 \times 1.07 = \$1,550.0.$$

9.38   (Aggarwal Corporation; accounting for long-term bonds.)

a. **Interest Expense**
First Six Months: .05 × $301,512 = $15,076.
Second Six Months: .05($301,512 + $15,076) = $15,829.
Book value of bonds on December 31, Year 4: $301,512 + $15,076 + $15,829 = $332,417.

b. **Book Value of Bonds on December 31, Year 3**
Interest:
$ 35,000 × 8.11090 = $ 283,882   (Table 4, 10 periods and 4%)
Principal:
$1,000,000 × .67556 =   675,560   (Table 2, 10 periods and 4%)
    Total........................ $ 959,442

Book Value of Bonds, December 31, Year 3.................... $ 959,442
Add Interest Expense for Year 4.................................. X
Subtract Coupon Payments during Year 4.................... (70,000)
Book Value of Bonds, December 31, Year 4.................... $ 966,336

Interest expense for Year 4 is $76,894.

9.38 continued.

   c. **Book Value of Bonds on July 1, Year 4**

Book Value of Bonds, December 31, Year 3......................	$1,305,832
Plus Interest Expense for First Six Months of Year 4: .03	
X $1,305,832..	39,175
Subtract Coupon Payment during First Six Months of	
Year 4..	(45,000)
Book Value of Bonds, July 1, Year 4	$1,300,007
Book Value of One-Half of Bonds..................................	$ 650,004

Bonds Payable..	650,004	
Cash		526,720
Gain on Bonds Retirement		123,284

   d. **Interest Expense for Second Six Months**

      .03 X $650,004 = $19,500.

9.39   (Wal-Mart Stores; accounting for long-term bonds.)

   a.

.06 X $83,758,595..	$ 5,025,516
.06($83,758,595 + $5,025,516 – $4,500,000)......................	5,057,047
	$10,082,563

   b.

Interest Expense..	$10,082,563
Interest Payable...	9,000,000
Increase in Bonds Payable.......................................	$ 1,082,563
Book Value, January 31, Year 11...............................	83,758,595
Book Value, January 31, Year 12...............................	$84,841,158

   c. Present Value = Maturity Value X Present Value Factors.
      $162,395,233 = Maturity Value X (4 percent, 11 periods).
      $175,646,684 = Maturity Value X (4 percent, 9 periods).
      Maturity Value = $250,000,000.

   d. The book value equals the par value, so the initial market yield is the stated interest yield of 9.25 percent compounded semiannually.

9.40   (IBM Credit Corporation; comparison of straight-line and effective interest methods of amortizing bond discount.)

   a. $58,173,000. See Table 2, 14-period column, 7-percent row, where the factor is .38782.

      .38782 X $150,000,000 = $58,173,000.

   b. $4,072,110 = $58,173,000 X .07.

9.40 continued.

   c. $\$6,559,071 = (\$150,000,000 - \$58,173,000)/14.$

       $\$2,623,628 = .40 \times \$6,559,071.$

   d. $\$87,754,890 = \$150,000,000 - \$58,173,000 - \$4,072,110$
                   $= \$150,000,000 - (1.07 \times \$58,173,000).$

   e.   Issuers like not having to pay the cash for coupons during the life of the issue, but this fact is reflected in the original issue price of the bonds, so it is hard to justify this as being an economic advantage.

       Some purchasers like zero coupon bonds, because there is no need to consider uncertainty about future interest rates and the reinvesting of interest coupons. If one wants a fixed sum some years in the future, then zero coupon notes may be a more useful instrument than coupon bonds. Investment advisors understand this advantage. Another advantage to the purchaser, but one not so well understood by the press, accountants, and even some investment bankers, is the extra call protection in a zero coupon note. Because the issuer can call the bonds at par value (and no other cash interest payments will occur over the entire life of the bond), it will never pay the issuer to call them unless interest rates drop to zero. Thus, the lender has more protection than in a callable coupon-bearing bond against interest rate declines. Of course, such protection has a price, and the lack of an "option" feature to the issuer may account for much of the apparently lower cost of borrowing via zero coupon notes.

       As to the loophole, the Treasury might take offense that the tax rules, generally cash-based, allow the current deduction and current tax savings for an item whose cash flows occur seven years in the future. Note from the preceding part that the only cash effect of the interest and related tax transactions is IBMCC's saving $2,623,628 in income tax payments it would otherwise have made.

       The Wall Street Journal story indicated, however, that the Treasury had in mind as a "loophole" the $2,486,961 difference between the $6,559,071 interest deduction resulting from using the straight-line method and the $4,072,110 interest computed "correctly" with the effective interest method. Using the straight-line method resulted in cash savings in taxes of $994,784 (= .40 × $2,486,961) as compared to the effective interest method.

       The Tax Equity and Fiscal Reform Act (TEFRA) of 1982 did indeed change the tax law so that issues must amortize original-issue discount for tax purposes using the effective interest method, not the straight-line method.

       However, the Treasury position overlooks the symmetry in the tax treatment of zero coupon bonds to the issuer and the holder. While the issuer is entitled to deduct interest on a straight-line basis, the holder is taxable on a straight-line basis. The Treasury

9.40 e. continued.

might respond to such arguments by noting that the issuer is generally a taxable entity, while the holder of zero-coupon notes is often tax-exempt (a pension fund, for example).

If we choose to interpret the words "interest expense" in a precise mathematical fashion, the mathematics of compound interest seems to favor the effective interest method, as does Accounting Principles Board *Opinion No. 21.* The straight-line method is easier to compute, but the availability of low cost computing largely obviates this advantage. An alternative point of view, of course, is that the words "interest expense" mean whatever Congress and the courts define them to mean, insofar as taxes are concerned.

A more important economic issue is the symmetry of the tax laws. If both lender and borrower are taxed at the same rate, the total proceeds to the Treasury are the same under either method, so long as the lender and borrower are treated symmetrically. Of course, the *incidence* of the tax will be affected, holding all other things constant (i.e., in a partial equilibrium analysis). Switching to the effective interest method for both parties would shift taxes from the lender to the borrower. In a general equilibrium analysis, however, the subsequent readjustment of bond prices is much harder to compute. If, on the other hand, many of the lenders are tax exempt, revenues to the Treasury would be increased by the effective interest method, because it raises the present value of the borrower's tax liability. But again, the ultimate equilibrium that would be obtained after such a change is not readily apparent, at least to us.

9.41   (Quaker Oats Company; managing income and the debt-equity ratio through bond retirement.)

a. $25,200,000 = .63 × $40,000,000 of cash must be raised to retire old issue.

Dollars in Thousands

Cash..	25,200	
Bonds Payable—9 Percent...........................		25,200
Issue of new bonds.		
Bonds Payable—5 Percent.............................	40,000	
Cash..		25,200
Gain on Bond Retirement (Extraordinary		
Item)...		14,800
Income Tax Expense.....................................	5,920	
Cash..		5,920
.40 × $14,800.		

9.41 continued.

b. Income increases by $8,880,000 [= (1 − .40) × $14,800,000], or by about 110 percent (= $8,880/$8,000) to about $15 million. Retained Earnings increases by $8,880,000.

c. Debt-equity ratio ($ in 000):

$$\frac{\$\,5{,}000 + \$\,25{,}200}{\$\,5{,}000 + \$\,25{,}200 + \$\,35{,}000 + \$\,8{,}880} = \frac{\$\,30{,}200}{\$\,74{,}080} = 40.8\%.$$

9.42 (FNB/OOPS; accounting for bonds in a troubled-debt restructuring.)

a. Present value of newly-promised cash flows at 20 percent, compounded semiannually = $2,563,903.

Present value of 50 semiannual payments of $1 discounted at 10 percent per period = 9.91481; see Table 4, 50-period row, 10-percent column. 9.91481 × $250,000	$2,478,703
Present value of $1 paid 50 periods hence, discounted at 10 percent per period = .00852; see Table 2, 50-period row, 10-percent column. .00852 × $10,000,000	85,200
	$2,563,903

b. Present value of newly-promised cash flows at 12 percent, compounded semiannually = $4,483,365.

Present value of 50 semiannual payments of $1 discounted at 6 percent per period = 15.76186; see Table 4, 50-period row, 6-percent column. 15.76186 × $250,000	$3,940,465
Present value of $1 paid 50 periods hence, discounted at 6 percent per period = .05429; see Table 2, 50-period row, 6-percent column. .05429 × $10,000,000	542,900
	$4,483,365

c. FNB would recognize a loss of $7,436,097 (= $10,000,000 − $2,563,903) under the first method. This would be followed by interest revenue of $12,500,000 (= 50 × $250,000) from cash receipts plus interest revenue from amortization of discount of $7,436,097. Total income under the first method would be $−7,436,097 for write down in 1990 plus $12,500,000 for cash receipts plus $7,436,097 for interest revenue from amortization; total income equal to $12,500,000.

9.42 c. continued.

Under the second method, FNB would recognize a loss of $5,516,635 (= $10,000,000 − $4,483,365). This would be followed by interest revenue of $12,500,000 (= 50 X $250,000) from cash receipts plus interest revenue from amortization of discount of $5,516,635. Total income under the second method would be $12,500,000 (= $−5,516,635 + $12,500,000 + $5,516,635).

Under the third method, income over the next twenty years would be $12,500,000 (= 50 X $250,000) for cash receipts.

Over long enough time spans, accounting income is equal to cash receipts. But note that the timing of income recognition varies drastically as a function of the treatment chosen.

d. We prefer the first method, because we think the troubled-debt restructuring results from an arm's length transaction. FASB *Statement No. 114*, however, requires the use of the second method.

9.43   (Discounting warranty obligations.)

a. **Year 1**
    Warranty Expense... 2,000,000
        Estimated Warranty Liability.................... 2,000,000

    Year 2
    Estimated Warranty Liability........................ 500,000
        Cash and Other Accounts......................... 500,000

    Year 3
    Estimated Warranty Liability........................ 600,000
        Cash and Other Accounts......................... 600,000

    Year 4
    Estimated Warranty Liability........................ 900,000
        Cash and Other Accounts......................... 900,000

b. The present value of the future cost amounts on December 31, Year 1, discounted as 10 percent, is $1,626,594, computed as follows:

Year 2: $500,000 X .90909... $ 454,545
Year 3: $600,000 X .82645...   495,870
Year 4: $900,000 X .75131...   676,179
        Total.. $1,626,594

9.43 b. continued.

Year 1

Warranty Expense	1,626,594	
Estimated Warranty Liability		1,626,594

Year 2

Interest Expense	162,659	
Estimated Warranty Liability		162,659

.10 × $1,626,594 = $162,659.

Year 2

Estimated Warranty Liability	500,000	
Cash and Other Accounts		500,000

Year 3

Interest Expense	128,925	
Estimated Warranty Liability		128,925

.10($1,626,594 + $162,659 − $500,000) = $128,925.

Year 3

Estimated Warranty Liability	600,000	
Cash and Other Accounts		600,000

Year 4

Interest Expense	81,818	
Estimated Warranty Liability		81,818

.10($1,626,594 + $162,659 − $500,000 + $128,925 − $600,000) = .10 × $818,178 = $81,818.

Year 4

Estimated Warranty Liability	899,996	
Interest Expense	4	
Cash and Other Accounts		900,000

There is a rounding error of $4 in the Estimated Warranty Liability account at the end of Year 4. Interest expense for Year 4, therefore, increases by $4.

c. The firm must first acquire for cash the goods and services provided under the warranty plan. Thus, even though customers will receive goods and services, the firm must expend cash at some point. To be consistent with monetary liabilities, accounting would discount these amounts to their present value.

9.44   (Effects on statement of cash flows.)

    a.   The journal entry to record this transaction is:

Cash..	100,000	
Bonds Payable		100,000

The debit to the Cash account results in an increase of $100,000 in Line (9). Issuing debit is a financing activity, so Line (6) increases by $100,000.

    b.   The journal entry for this transaction is:

Building..	100,000	
Bonds Payable		100,000

The transaction does not affect the Cash account, so Line (9) does not change. This transaction does not affect net income, so Line (1) does not change. This transaction does not appear in the statement of cash flows but in a note to the financial statements.

    c.   The journal entry to record this transaction is:

Bonds Payable..	100,000	
Cash		90,000
Extraordinary Gain on Bond Retirement.......		10,000

The Cash account decreases, so Line (9) decreases by $90,000. Retiring bonds is a financing activity, so Line (7) increases by $90,000. The extraordinary gain increases net income, so Line (1) increases by $10,000. Because this gain does not provide an operating source of cash, Line (3) increases by $10,000 to offset the gain and result in a zero net effect on cash flow from operations.

9.44 continued.

d. The journal entry for this transaction is:

Bonds Payable... 100,000
Extraordinary Loss on Bond Retirement........... 5,000
   Cash 105,000

The Cash account decreases, so Line (9) decreases by $105,000. Calling bonds is a financing activity, so Line (7) increases by $105,000. The extraordinary loss reduces net income, so Line (1) decreases by $5,000. Because this loss does not use an operating cash flow, Line (2) increases by $5,000 to offset the loss and result in a zero net effect on cash flow from operations.

e. The journal entry to record this transaction is:

Interest Expense (= .06 X $90,000) 5,400
   Cash (= .05 X $100,000) 5,000
   Bonds Payable 400

The Cash account decreases by $5,000, so Line (9) decreases by $5,000. Net income decreases by $5,400 for interest expense, so Line (1) decreases by $5,400. Because the firm uses only $5,000 cash for this expense, Line (2) increases by $400 for the portion of the expense that does not use cash.

f. The journal entry to record this transaction is:

Interest Expense (= .06 X $90,000) 5,250
Bonds Payable... 750
   Cash (= .06 X $100,000) 6,000

The Cash account decreases by $6,000, so Line (9) decreases by $6,000. Net income decreases by $5,250, so Line (1) decreases by $5,250. Because the firm uses more cash than the amount of interest expense, Line (3) increases by $750. The total effect on cash flow from operations is $6,000 (= $5,250 + $750).

9.45   (Rhodes Company; preparing statement of cash flows.) A T-account
        work sheet for Rhodes Company appears after the statement of cash
        flows.

RHODES COMPANY
Statement of Cash Flows
Year 2

Operations:
    Net Income... $ 53,000
    Addbacks and Additions:
        Depreciation Expense 48,000
        Loss on Bond Retirement....................... 3,000
        Bad Debt Expense.................................. 9,000
        Increase in Accounts Payable................. 11,000
    Subtractions:
        Gain on Sale of Equipment .... (4,900)
        Cash Used for Debt Service Exceeding
            Interest Expense............................... (5,000)
        Increase in Accounts Receivable............. (15,900)
        Increase in Inventories.......................... (12,000)
Cash Flow from Operations............................ $ 86,200
Investing:
    Sale of Property, Plant and Equipment .... $ 19,900
    Acquisition of Property, Plant and Equip-
        ment.. (57,300)
Cash Flow from Investing.............................. (37,400)
Financing:
    Issue of Bonds....................................... $ 50,000
    Retirement of Bonds................................. (73,000)
    Dividends... (30,000)
Cash Flow from Financing............................. (53,000)
Change in Cash... $ (4,200)
Cash, January 1, Year 2 47,000
Cash, December 31, Year 2............................ $ 42,800

Supplementary Information

Rhodes Company issued $11,000 of common stock during Year 2 to
acquire property, plant and equipment.

9.45 continued.

Cash

√ 47,000

Operations

(1)	53,000	4,900	(5)
(4)	48,000	5,000	(9)
(7)	3,000	15,900	(12)
(10)	9,000	12,000	(13)
(14)	11,000		

Investing

(5)	19,900	57,300	(6)

Financing

(8)	50,000	30,000	(2)
		73,000	(7)

√ 42,800

Accounts Receivable				Allowance for Un-collectible Accounts				Inventory		
√	80,000					1,200	√	√	110,000	
(12)	15,900	8,900	(11)	(11) 8,900		9,000	(10)	(13)	12,000	
√	87,000					1,300	√	√	122,000	

Property, Plant and Equipment				Accumulated Depreciation				Accounts Payable		
√	474,000					189,800	√		70,000	√
(3)	11,000	60,100	(5)	(5) 45,100		48,000	(4)		11,000	(14)
(6)	57,300									
√	482,200					192,700	√		81,000	√

Bonds Payable				Common Stock				Retained Earnings		
		195,000	√			100,000	√		155,000	√
(7)	70,000	50,000	(8)			11,000	(3)	(2) 30,000	53,000	(1)
(9)	5,000									
		170,000	√			111,000	√		178,000	√

CHAPTER 10

LIABILITIES: OFF-BALANCE-SHEET FINANCING, LEASES, DEFERRED INCOME TAXES, RETIREMENT BENEFITS, AND DERIVATIVES

Questions, Exercises, Problems, and Cases: Answers and Solutions

10.1   See the text or the glossary at the end of the book.

10.2   One premise underlying this statement is that the notes provide sufficient information to permit the analyst to make an informed judgment about the nature of the obligation or commitment and its associated risks. Current disclosures of off-balance-sheet commitments aggregate similar transactions, making an informed judgment about individual items difficult. Even if the disclosure permitted an informed judgment, the question arises as to whether information processing costs for analysts would decrease if firms actually recognized these items as liabilities. The counter argument to recognition of off-balance-sheet liabilities is that they differ in their risk characteristics relative to liabilities appearing on the books; thus disclosure in the notes is more appropriate than recognition in the balance sheet.

10.3   Using an executory contract to achieve off-balance-sheet financing results in the recognition of neither an asset (for example, leased assets) nor a liability (for example, lease liability) on the balance sheet. Using an asset sale with recourse results in a decrease in an asset (for example, accounts receivable) and an increase in cash. In both cases, no liability appears on the balance sheet.

10.4   The party with the risks and rewards of ownership effectively owns the asset, whatever the legal niceties. The asset should appear on the balance sheet of the owner. The capital lease criteria attempt to state unambiguously who has economic ownership.

10.5   The distinction depends upon which criteria of the lease made it a capital lease. The major difference is that at the end of a lease term the asset reverts to the lessor in a capital lease, whereas at the end of the installment payments, the asset belongs to the purchaser. The criteria for capitalizing a lease are such that the expected value of the asset when it reverts to the lessor is small, but misestimates can occur. In most other respects, capital leases and installment purchases are similar in economic substance.

10.6   The differences are minor. The lessee's asset is Leasehold on the one hand and Actual Asset (Plant or Fixed Assets) on the other. The liability will have different titles. The effect on income and balance sheet totals is the same for both transactions.

10.7   Expenses are gone assets. The measure of expense over the life of a lease is the total outflow of cash to discharge the obligation. The accounting for leases, either operating or capital, does not change the total cash outflow, only the timing of the recognition of asset expirations.

10.8   Disagree. Operating Lease: Rent revenue for the lessor will equal rent expense for the lessee on an operating lease, but lessor also has depreciation expense on leased assets. Capital Lease: Interest revenue for the lessor should equal interest expense for the lessee on a capital lease. The lessor recognizes its cost to acquire or manufacture the leased asset as cost of goods sold under a capital lease. The lessor also recognizes revenue under a capital lease equal to the "selling price" of the lease asset on the date of signing the lease.

10.9   Deferred tax accounting matches against pre-tax book income each period the income taxes a firm has to pay currently plus (minus) the income taxes the firm expects to pay (save) in the future when revenues and expenses that appear in book income now appear in tax returns later.

10.10   This statement is incorrect. In order for deferred taxes to be a loan, there must be a receipt of cash or other goods or services at the inception of the loan and a disbursement of cash or other goods or services at the maturity date. The entries for deferred taxes are as follows:

When Timing Differences Originate:

Income Tax Expense..	X	
Deferred Tax Liability.....................................		X

When Timing Differences Reverse:

Deferred Tax Liability..	X	
Income Tax Expense		X

There are no cash or other asset flows involved and, therefore, no loan.

Another approach is to raise the question: How would cash flows have differed if a firm used the same methods of accounting for book as it used for tax? The response is that cash flows would have been the same even though deferred income taxes would have been eliminated. Thus, recognizing or not recognizing deferred taxes has no incremental effect on cash or other asset flows and, therefore, cannot represent a loan.

10.11   The Congress defines the manner in which firms calculate taxable income and income taxes payable. Corporations pay the income taxes each year that the income tax law legally requires them to pay. The amount shown for Deferred Tax Liability is not a liability. It may become a liability if the firm earns taxable income in the future. It represents the cumulative tax savings from using different methods of accounting for financial reporting and income tax purposes. The Congress and the FASB permit such differences in accounting methods because the objectives of income taxation and financial reporting differ. The income taxation system attempts to raise revenues in an equitable manner. Generally accepted accounting principles attempt to measure operating performance and financial position. If the Congress feels that it should not permit such differences, it should legislate either (1) that firms prepare their financial statements in conformance with the accounting methods used for tax purposes, or (2) that they compute taxable income in accordance with the accounting methods used for financial reporting purposes. Both approaches result in eliminating the Deferred Tax Liability account. Given the differences in objectives of the two reporting systems, it seems undesirable for Congress to take either of the actions indicated above. Congress should merely recognize that Deferred Tax Liability is not a liability but the result of accountants' attempts to obtain meaningful measures of operating performance over time.

10.12   Unlike Accounts Payable or Bonds, which "roll over" and new obligations replace them, the deferred tax liability does not arise from specific transactions. A firm computes taxes on operations as a whole, not on specific transactions. The analyst should attempt to ascertain when the firm is likely to pay the deferred taxes. Then the analyst should use the present value of those payments as the amount of the debt. If, as is likely, a stable or growing firm is never likely to pay the deferred taxes (for example, as with deferred taxes arising from depreciation charges for a growing firm), then the present value of the payments is zero, and the analyst should exclude the "liability" from the amount of debt. (This results in larger shareholders' equity.)

10.13   Deferred tax assets (liabilities) arise when a firm recognizes revenue (expense) earlier for tax purposes than book purposes or expenses (revenues) later for tax purposes than for book purposes. Deferred tax assets (liabilities) provide for lower (higher) taxable income in the future relative to book income and, therefore, future tax savings (costs).

10.14   The difference arises for two principal reasons: tax rate differences and permanent differences. The income tax rate on state, municipal and foreign income likely differs from the statutory U.S. tax rate. Also, firms recognize various revenues and expenses for book purposes that never appear (for example, interest on state and municipal bonds) or appear in smaller amounts (for example, dividends received from domestic subsidiaries) in taxable income.

10.15   The matching convention suggests that firms recognize as expenses each period all costs actually incurred currently or expected to be incurred in the future to generate the current period's revenues. Employees provide labor services each period in return for both current compensation (salary, health care benefits) and compensation deferred until retirement (pensions, health care benefits). The absence of deferred compensation arrangements would presumably lead employees to demand higher current compensation to permit them to fund their own retirement plans. Thus, firms must match current compensation and the present value of deferred compensation against the current period's revenues.

10.16   Laws require firms to contribute funds to an independent trustee to manage on behalf of employees. The employer cannot use these funds for its general corporate purposes. Firms must, however, report some underfunded pension obligations on the balance sheet as a liability.

10.17   One defines outputs (defined benefit) whereas the other defines inputs (defined contribution). Actuaries can design both to have the same expected costs with the same payment patterns by the company.
        Immediate funding for defined-contribution plans transfers all accounting problems subsequent to funding to the plan trustee. The defined-benefit plan could similarly transfer obligations to the pension fund by immediate cash payments, but the company would ultimately be responsible for making up any shortages caused by deviations of earnings or mortality from expectations.

10.18   Pension fund assets appear when a firm funds its pension plan faster than it expenses it. Pension fund liabilities appear when a firm expenses its pension plan faster than it funds it.

10.19   A derivative is a hedge when the firm holding the derivative bears a risk such that the change in the value of the derivative just offsets the change in the value of the firm as time passes and the firm bears the risk.

        A derivative is not a hedge when changes in its fair value do not offset other changes in firm value occurring at the same time.

10.20   A *fair-value hedge* is a hedge of an exposure to changes in the fair value of a recognized asset or liability or of an unrecognized firm commitment. A *cash-flow hedge* is a hedge of an exposure to variability in the cash flows of a recognized asset or liability, such as variable interest rates, or of a forecasted transaction, such as expected future foreign sales.
        The following part is not in the text. When a fair-value hedge qualifies as effective, the gain or loss on the hedging instrument appears currently in earnings along with the related loss or gain on the hedged item. When a cash-flow hedge qualifies as effective, the gain or loss on the hedging instrument will be deferred and reported as part of comprehensive income. The deferred gain or loss appears in current

10.20 continued.

earnings in the same period in which the hedged forecasted transaction or cash flows affects earnings, such as when the inventory purchased as part of a forecasted transaction is sold. See *SFAS No. 133*.

10.21 When the firm has a cash-flow hedge. Then the value of the firm stays the same, but no accounting asset nor liability changes in value to offset the change in the value of the derivative.

10.22 (Cypres Appliance Store; using accounts receivable to achieve off-balance sheet financing.)

a. (1) **January 2, Year 2**

Cash..	89,286	
Bank Loan Payable.............................		89,286
To record bank loan.		

December 31, Year 2

Cash..	100,000	
Accounts Receivable............................		100,000
To record collections from customers.		

Interest Expense (= .12 X $89,286)..............	10,714	
Bank Loan Payable	89,286	
Cash...		100,000
To record interest expense on loan for Year 2 and repayment of the loan.		

(2)

Cash..	89,286	
Loss from Sale of Accounts Receivable	10,714	
Accounts Receivable............................		100,000
To record sale of accounts receivable; alternative title for the loss account is interest expense.		

b. Both transactions result in an expense of $10,714 for Year 2 for this financing. Both transactions result in an immediate increase in cash. Liabilities increase for the collateralized loan, whereas an asset decreases for the sale.

c. Cypres Appliance Store must attempt to shift credit and interest rate risk to the bank. The bank should have no rights to demand additional receivables if interest rates increase or uncollectible accounts appear. Likewise, Cypres Appliance Store should have no rights to buy back the accounts receivable if interest rates decline. The bank of course will not both lend on the receivables and purchase the receivables at the same price because it incurs different amounts of risk in each case.

10.23   (P. J. Lorimar Company; using inventory to achieve off-balance sheet financing.)

a.   (i)   **January 2, Year 5**

Cash...	300,000	
Bank Loan Payable.............................		300,000
To record bank loan.		

December 31, Year 5

Interest Expense (= .10 × $300,000).............	30,000	
Bank Loan Payable.............................		30,000
To record interest expense for Year 5.		

December 31, Year 6

Cash...	363,000	
Sales Revenue....................................		363,000
To record sale of tobacco inventory.		

Cost of Goods Sold.................................	200,000	
Inventory..		200,000
To record cost of tobacco inventory sold.		

Interest Expense (= .10 × $330,000).............	33,000	
Bank Loan Payable	330,000	
Cash..		363,000
To record interest expense for Year 6 and repayment of loan.		

(ii)   **January 2, Year 5**

Cash...	300,000	
Sales Revenue....................................		300,000
To record "sale" of tobacco to bank.		

Cost of Goods Sold.................................	200,000	
Inventory..		200,000
To record cost of tobacco "sold".		

b.   Both transactions result in a total of $100,000 income for the two years combined. The collateralized loan shows $163,000 gross profit from the sale in Year 6 and interest expense of $30,000 in Year 5 and $33,000 in Year 6. The "sale" results in $100,000 gross profit in Year 5. Cash increases by $300,000 in both transactions. Liabilities increase for the collateralized loan, whereas an asset decreases for the sale.

10.23 continued.

    c. P. J. Lorimar Company must shift the risk of changes in storage costs for Year 5 and Year 6 and the selling price for the tobacco at the end of Year 6 to the bank. The firm should not guarantee a price or agree to cover insurance and other storage costs. Of course, the bank will not both lend on the inventory and "purchase" the inventory for $300,000 because it incurs different amounts of risk in each case.

10.24   (Boeing and American; applying the capital lease criteria.)

    a. This lease is a capital lease because the lease period of 20 years exceeds 75 percent of the expected life of the aircraft. The lease does not meet any other capital lease criteria. The aircraft reverts to Boeing at the end of 20 years. The present value of the lease payments when discounted at 10 percent is $51.1 million ($6 million X 8.51356), which is less than $54 million = 90 percent of the fair market value of $60 million.

    b. This lease is a capital lease because the present value of the lease payments of $54.8 million (= $7.2 million X 7.60608) exceeds 90 percent of the $60 million fair market value of the aircraft.

    c. The lease is not a capital lease. The present value of the required lease payments of $36.9 million (= $5.5 million X 6.71008) is less than $54 million = 90 percent of the market value of the aircraft. The life of the lease is less than 75 percent of the expected useful life of the aircraft. The purchase option price coupled with the rental payments provides Boeing with a present value of all cash flows exceeding the usual sale price of the aircraft of $62.4 million [= ($5.5 million X 6.71008) + ($55 million X .46319)], so there does not appear to be a bargain purchase option.

    d. This lease is not a capital lease. The present value of the minimum required lease payments is $50.9 million (= $6.2 million X 8.20141). The fee contingent on usage could be zero, so the calculations exclude it. The life of the lease is less than 75 percent of the useful life of the aircraft. The aircraft reverts to Boeing at the end of the lease period.

10.25   (FedUp Delivery Services; preparing lessee's journal entries for an operating and a capital lease.)

    a. This lease is a capital lease because the present value of the lease payments of $22,581 (= $750 X 30.10751) exceeds 90 percent of the market value of the leased asset (.90 X $24,000 = $21,600). The life of the lease is less than 75 percent of the life of the leased property and the property reverts to GM at the end of the lease period, so the lease fails these criteria for a capital lease.

10.25 continued.

   b. **Time of Signing Lease**
No Entry.

End of Each Month

Rent Expense...	750	
Cash..		750

To record monthly rental expense and payment.

   c. **Time of Signing Lease**

Asset—Leasehold......................................	22,581	
Liability—Present Value of Lease Obligation.		22,581

To record capital lease.

End of First Month

Interest Expense (= .01 × $22,581).....................	225.81	
Liability—Present Value of Lease Obligation....	524.19	
Cash..		750.00

To record interest expense and cash payment for first month; the book value of the lease liability is now $22,056.81 (= $22,581.00 – $524.19).

Depreciation Expense	627.25	
Accumulated Depreciation.........................		627.25

To record depreciation expense for the first month of $627.25 (= $22,581/36).

End of Second Month

Interest Expense (= .01 × $22,056.81).................	220.57	
Liability—Present Value of Lease Obligation....	529.43	
Cash..		750.00

To record interest expense and cash payment for the second month.

Depreciation Expense	627.25	
Accumulated Depreciation.........................		627.25

To record depreciation expense for the second month.

10.26   (Baldwin Products; preparing lessee's journal entries for an operating lease and a capital lease.)

a.   This lease does not satisfy any of the criteria for a capital lease, so it is an operating lease. The leased asset reverts to the lessor at the end of the lease period. The life of the lease (3 years) is less than 75 percent of the expected useful life of the leased asset (5 years). The present value of the lease payments of $24,018 (= $10,000 X 2.40183) is less than 90 percent of the market value of the leased asset of $30,000.

b.   **December 31, of Each Year**

Rent Expense...	10,000	
Cash...		10,000

To record annual rent expense and cash payment.

c.   **January 2, Year 6**

Asset—Leasehold...	24,018	
Liability—Present Value of Lease Obligation.		24,018

To record capital lease.

December 31, Year 6

Interest Expense (= .12 X $24,018).....................	2,882	
Liability—Present Value of Lease Obligation....	7,118	
Cash...		10,000

To record interest expense and cash payment for Year 6. The book value of the lease liability is now $16,900 (= $24,018 – $7,118).

Depreciation Expense or Work-in-Process Inventory ($24,018/3)	8,006	
Accumulated Depreciation......................		8,006

To record depreciation expense for Year 6.

December 31, Year 7

Interest Expense (= .12 X $16,900).....................	2,028	
Liability—Present Value of Lease Obligation....	7,972	
Cash...		10,000

To record interest expense and cash payment for Year 7. The book value of the lease liability is now $8,928 (= $16,900 – $7,972).

Depreciation Expense or Work-in-Process Inventory..	8,006	
Accumulated Depreciation......................		8,006

To record depreciation expense for Year 7.

10.26 c. continued.

December 31, Year 8

Interest Expense (= .12 × $8,928)....................	1,072	
Liability—Present Value of Lease Obligation....	8,928	
Cash...		10,000

To record interest expense and cash payment for Year 8. Interest expense does not precisely equal .12 × $8,928 due to rounding.

Depreciation Expense on Work-in-Process Inventory...	8,006	
Accumulated Depreciation......................		8,006

To record depreciation expense for Year 8.

d. Operating Lease Method: Rent Expense (= $10,000 × 3).... $ 30,000

Capital Lease Method: Interest Expense (= $2,882 + $2,028 + $1,072) .... $ 5,982

Depreciation (= $8,006 × 3)... 24,018

  Total Expenses .... $ 30,000

10.27 (Sun Microsystems; preparing lessor's journal entries for an operating lease and a capital lease.)

a. This lease is a capital lease. The life of the lease equals the expected useful life of the property. The present value of the lease payments of $12,000 [= $4,386.70 + ($4,386.70 × 1.73554)] equals the market value of the leased asset.

b. **Beginning of Each Year**

Cash..	4,386.70	
Rental Fees Received in Advance.................		4,386.70

To record cash received in advance from lessee.

End of Each Year

Rental Fees Received in Advance	4,386.70	
Rent Revenue		4,386.70

To record rent revenue for each year.

Depreciation Expense	2,400.00	
Accumulated Depreciation........................		2,400.00

To record annual depreciation (= $7,200/3).

10.27 continued.

   c. **January 2, Year 2**

Cash..	4,386.70	
Lease Receivable (= $4,386.70 × 1.73554).............	7,613.30	
Sales Revenue...		12,000.00
To record "sale" of work station..		

Cost of Goods Sold.......................................	7,200.00	
Inventory..		7,200.00
To record cost of work station "sold".		

December 31, Year 2

Lease Receivable (= .10 × $7,613.30)...................	761.33	
Interest Revenue.......................................		761.33
To record interest revenue for Year 2.		

January 2, Year 3

Cash..	4,386.70	
Lease Receivable.......................................		4,386.70
To record cash received at the beginning of Year 3. The book value of the receivable is now $3,987.93 (= $7,613.30 + $761.33 – $4,386.70).		

December 31, Year 3

Lease Receivable (= .10 × $3,987.93)...................	398.77	
Interest Revenue.......................................		398.77
To record interest revenue for Year 3. Interest revenue is slightly less than .10 × $3,987.93 due to rounding of present value factors. The book value of the receivable is now $4,386.70 (= $3,987.93 + $398.77).		

January 2, Year 4

Cash..	4,386.70	
Lease Receivable.......................................		4,386.70
To record cash received for Year 4.		

10.28   (Ingersoll-Rand; preparing journal entries for income tax expense.)

a. **Year 9**

Income Tax Expense	67,400	
Deferred Tax Liability	43,575	
Cash or Income Tax Payable		110,975

Year 10

Income Tax Expense	90,000	
Deferred Tax Liability	15,537	
Cash or Income Tax Payable		105,537

Year 11

Income Tax Expense	118,800	
Deferred Tax Liability		14,185
Cash or Income Tax Payable		104,615

b. Taxable income exceeds book income for Year 9 and Year 10 but taxable income was less than book income for Year 11. Ingersoll-Rand probably reduced its expenditures on new depreciable assets during Year 9 and Year 10 so that depreciation expense for financial reporting exceeded depreciation deducted in computing taxable income. Ingersoll-Rand increased its capital expenditures during Year 11 so that depreciation deducted in computing taxable income exceeded depreciation expense recognized for financial reporting.

10.29   (L.A. Gear; preparing journal entries for income tax expense.)

a. **Year 4**

Income Tax Expense	34,364	
Deferred Tax Asset	3,555	
Cash or Income Tax Payable		37,919

Year 5

Income Tax Expense	9,392	
Deferred Tax Asset	3,492	
Cash or Income Tax Payable		12,884

Year 6

Cash or Income Tax Receivable	17,184	
Deferred Tax Asset	5,543	
Income Tax Expense (Credit)		22,727

b. Book income and taxable income were both positive for Years 4 and 5. Taxable income exceeded book income. The deferred tax asset related to uncollectible accounts increased, suggesting an increased sales level for each year.

10.29 b. continued.

Book income and taxable income were both negative in Year 6. The loss for book purposes exceeded the loss for tax purposes. The increase in the deferred tax asset related to uncollectible accounts suggests increasing sales but decreasing profits on those sales.

10.30 (Sung Company; computations and journal entries for income taxes with both temporary and permanent differences.)

a. **Year 1**

Income Tax Expense (.40 × $560,000)................	224,000	
Deferred Tax Liability (.40 × $40,000)	16,000	
Income Tax Payable—Current (.40 × $600,000)..		240,000

Year 2

Income Tax Expense (.40 × $500,000)................	200,000	
Deferred Tax Liability (.40 × $50,000).............		20,000
Income Tax Payable—Current (.40 × $450,000)..		180,000

Year 3

Income Tax Expense (.40 × $620,000)................	248,000	
Deferred Tax Liability (.40 × $6,000)...............		24,000
Income Tax Payable—Current (.40 × $560,000)..		224,000

b. **Year 1**

Income Tax Expense [.40 × ($560,000 – $10,000)]..	220,000	
Deferred Tax Liability (.40 × $50,000)	20,000	
Income Tax Payable—Current (.40 × $600,000)..		240,000

Year 2

Income Tax Expense [.40 × ($500,000 – $10,000)]..	196,000	
Deferred Tax Liability (.40 × $40,000).............		16,000
Income Tax Payable—Current (.40 × $450,000)..		180,000

Year 3

Income Tax Expense (.40 × $610,000)................	244,000	
Deferred Tax Liability (.40 × $50,000).............		20,000
Income Tax Payable—Current (.40 × $560,000)..		224,000

10.31   (Beneish Company; deriving permanent and temporary differences from financial statement disclosures.)

a.

	Income Tax Expense	=	Income Taxes Currently Payable	+	Change in Deferred Tax Liability
	$78,000	=	$24,000	+	X
	X	=	$54,000		

Temporary Differences = Changes in Deferred Tax Liability/.40

= $54,000/.40

= $135,000

Because income tax expense exceeds income taxes payable, book income exceeded taxable income.

b.
Taxable Income: $24,000/.40	$ 60,000
Temporary Differences	135,000
Book Income before Taxes Excluding Permanent Differences	$ 195,000
Permanent Differences (Plug)	36,000
Book Income before Taxes (Given)	$ 159,000

The amortization of goodwill of $36,000 for book purposes and zero for tax purposes causes taxable income to exceed book income.

10.32 (Woodward Corporation; effect of temporary differences on income taxes.)

a.

	Year 1	Year 2	Year 3	Year 4
Other Pre-Tax Income.........	$ 35,000	$ 35,000	$35,000	$35,000
Income before Depreciation from Machine..................	25,000	25,000	25,000	25,000
Depreciation Deduction:				
.33 × $50,000......................	(16,500)			
.44 × $50,000......................		(22,000)		
.15 × $50,000......................			(7,500)	
.08 × $50,000......................				(4,000)
Taxable Income	$ 43,500	$ 38,000	$52,500	$56,000
Tax Rate...........................	.40	.40	.40	.40
Income Taxes Payable	$ 17,400	$ 15,200	$21,000	$22,400

b.

Financial Reporting	Year 1	Year 2	Year 3	Year 4
Book Value, January 1.........	$ 50,000	$ 37,500	$25,000	$12,500
Depreciation Expense	(12,500)	(12,500)	(12,500)	(12,500)
Book Value, December 31	$ 37,500	$ 25,000	$12,500	$ --
Tax Reporting				
Tax Basis, January 1...........	$ 50,000	$ 33,500	$11,500	$ 4,000
Depreciation Deduction........	(16,500)	(22,000)	(7,500)	(4,000)
Tax Basis, December 31........	$ 33,500	$ 11,500	$ 4,000	$ --

c.

Financial Reporting	Year 1	Year 2	Year 3	Year 4
Income before Depreciation..	$ 60,000	$ 60,000	$60,000	$60,000
Depreciation Expense ($50,000/4).........................	(12,500)	(12,500)	(12,500)	(12,500)
Pretax Income...................	$ 47,500	$ 47,500	$47,500	$47,500
Income Tax Expense	$ 19,000	$ 19,000	$19,000	$19,000

d.

	Year 1	Year 2	Year 3	Year 4
Income Tax Payable (from Part a.)—Cr.	$ 17,400	$ 15,200	$21,000	$22,400
Change in Deferred Tax Liability (Plug): Cr. if Positive Dr. if Negative	1,600	3,800	(2,000)	(3,400)
Income Tax Expense—Dr. ...	$ 19,000	$ 19,000	$19,000	$19,000

10.32 d. continued.

Year 1

Income Tax Expense	19,000	
Cash or Income Tax Payable		17,400
Deferred Tax Liability		1,600

Year 2

Income Tax Expense	19,000	
Cash or Income Tax Payable		15,200
Deferred Tax Liability		3,800

Year 3

Income Tax Expense	19,000	
Deferred Tax Liability	2,000	
Cash or Income Tax Payable		21,000

Year 4

Income Tax Expense	19,000	
Deferred Tax Liability	3,400	
Cash or Income Tax Payable		22,400

10.33   (Lilly Company; reconstructing information about income taxes.)

LILLY COMPANY
Illustrations of Timing Differences and Permanent Differences

	Financial Statements	Type of Difference	Income Tax Return
Operating Income Except Depreciation	$ 427,800 (6)	--	$ 427,800 (4)
Depreciation	(322,800) (g)	Timing	(358,800) (3)
Municipal Bond Interest	85,800 (5)	Permanent	--
Taxable Income	--		$ 69,000 (2)
Pretax Income	$ 190,800 (g)		
Income Taxes Payable at 40 Percent			$ 27,600 (g)
Income Tax Expense at 40 Percent of $90,000 = $160,000 – $70,000, Which Is Book Income Excluding Permanent Differences	(42,000) (g)		
Net Income	$ 148,800 (1)		

10.33 continued.

Order and derivation of computations:

(g) Given.
(1) $148,800 = $190,800 − $42,000.
(2) $69,000 = $27,600/.40.
(3) Timing difference for depreciation is ($42,000 − $27,600)/.40 = $36,000. Because income taxes payable are less than income tax expense, we know that depreciation deducted on tax return exceeds depreciation expense on financial statements. Thus, the depreciation deduction on the tax return is $358,800 = $322,800 + $36,000.
(4) $427,800 = $358,800 + $69,000.
(5) Taxable income on financial statements is $105,000 = $42,000/.40. Total financial statement income before taxes, including permanent differences, is $190,800. Hence, permanent differences are $190,800 − $105,000 = $85,800.
(6) $190,800 + $322,800 − $85,800 = $427,800. See also (4), for check.

10.34 (Mascagni Company; interpreting hedging transaction.)

Fair-value hedge. Mascagni Company has an asset on the balance sheet whose change in market value it is hedging.

10.35 (DaimlerChrysler Corporation; interpreting derivatives and hedging disclosures.)

a. The counterparty is the person who promises to pay DaimlerChrysler [DC] if the derivative entitles DC to receive funds. DC runs the risk that the counterparty who owes funds will not be able to pay That is counterparty credit risk. DC minimizes such risk by dealing only with high quality counterparties.

b. DC says it does not engage in transactions in the third, italicized, sentence of the note. It apparently uses all derivatives for hedging activities.

c. We cannot be sure, but it is likely that all hedges to deal with revenue variations are cash-flow hedges because revenues result from a series of future cash flows. If all revenues were committed to in advance by the purchaser, such as by paying all amounts in advance, then DC might engage in a fair-value hedge. Cost hedges could be either fair-value or cash-flow hedges, depending on the nature of the item hedged. Hedging a fixed purchase commitment is a fair-value hedge; hedging the cost of future labor services would be a cash-flow hedge.

d. Ever since Chapter 2, we have seen that the recorded cost of an asset includes all costs of the hedging derivative instrument as part of the dollar cost of the asset being acquired when the purchase price is denominated in some other currency.

10.36   (Fixed Issue Company; journal entries for hedging transactions.) (Dollar Amounts in Thousands)

a. **January 1**

Cash..	10,000	
Bonds Payable		10,000

June 30

Interest Expense (1/2 × .09 × $10,000).................	450	
Cash		450

Cash [1/2 × (.09 − .06) × $10,000].......................	150	
Interest Expense...		150

Loss on Revaluation of Bonds..........................	4,000	
Bonds Payable		4,000

Derivative Financial Asset.............................	3,800	
Gain on Derivative......................................		3,800

December 31

Interest Expense (1/2 × .09 × $10,000).................	450	
Cash		450

Cash [1/2 × (.09 − .07) × $10,000].......................	100	
Interest Expense...		100

Bonds Payable...	1,250	
Gain on Revaluation of Bonds.......................		1,250

Loss on Derivative Asset	1,100	
Derivative Financial Asset..........................		1,100

b. Fair-value hedge. Both the loss on the revaluation of the bond and the gain on the revaluation of the derivative asset appear in net income for the period. Because the derivative is not a perfect hedge, the loss and the gain do not fully offset each other. The hedge has been effective; in practice, we would not be surprised to see deviations of this magnitude in failure of the hedge to fully offset the gains and losses.

10.37   (Floating Issue Company; journal entries for hedging transactions.)
         (Dollar Amounts in Thousands)

   a. **January 1**
Cash..	9,000	
Bonds Payable		9,000

       June 30
Interest Expense (1/2 × .09 × $10,000).................	450	
Cash		450

Interest Expense [1/2 × (.09 – .06) × $10,000].......	150	
Cash		150

Other Equity Adjustment (Comprehensive Income)..	3,800	
Derivative Liability		3,800

       December 31
Interest Expense (1/2 × .06 × $10,000).................	300	
Cash		300

Interest Expense [1/2 × (.09 – .07) × $10,000].......	100	
Cash		100

Derivative Liability..	1,100	
Other Equity Adjustment (Comprehensive Income)		1,100

   b. Cash-flow hedge. One cannot tell from the data given how effective
       the hedge has been.

10.38   (Effects of leases on statement of cash flows.)

   a. The journal entry to record this transaction is:

Depreciation Expense.....................................	10,000	
Accumulated Depreciation		10,000

       Because this entry does not involve a debit or credit to the Cash
       account, Line (9) does not change. Depreciation expense reduces net
       income, so Line (1) decreases by $10,000. The recognition of
       depreciation expense does not affect cash, so Line (2) increases by
       $10,000.

   b. The journal entry for this transaction is:

Cash...	19,925	
Rent Revenue...		19,925

       The debit to Cash results in an increase of $19,925 in Line (9). The
       credit to Rent Revenue increases Line (1), net income, by $19,925.

10.38 continued.

    c. The journal entry to record this transaction is:

Rent Revenue 19,925
   Cash   19,925

The credit to Cash results in an decrease of $19,925 in Line (9). The debit to Rent Expense reduces Line (1), net income, by $19,925.

    d. The journal entry for this transaction is:

Leasehold Asset.. 100,000
   Lease Liability   100,000

This transaction does not involve a change in cash, so Line (9) does not change. The entry does not affect net income, so Line (1) does not change. This transaction is an investing and financing activity that would appear in the statement of cash flows but in a supplementary schedule or note to the financial statements.

    e. The journal entry to record this transaction is:

Interest Expense... 15,000
Lease Liability 4,925
   Cash   19,925

This entry results in a reduction in Cash, so Line (9) decreases by $19,925. Line (1) decreases by $15,000 for interest expense and Line (7) increases by $4,925 for the reduction in the lease liability. Thus, $15,000 of the reduction in cash appears in the operating section and $4,925 appears in the financing section of the statement of cash flows.

10.39   (Effects of income taxes on statement of cash flows.)

    a. The entry to record this event is:

Income Tax Expense (.4 × $200,000).................. 80,000
   Income Tax Payable (.4 × $150,000)................   60,000
   Deferred Tax Liability (.4 × $50,000)...............   20,000

This entry does not involve a change in Cash, so Line (9) does not change. The debit to income tax expense reduces Line (1), net income, by $80,000. Line (2) increases by $60,000 for the increases in a current operating liability. Line (2) also increases by $20,000 for the addback of an expense that does not use cash. Thus, the effect on cash flow from operations is zero.

10.39 continued.

    b. The journal entry for this event is:

Income Tax Expense (.4 X $300,000)	120,000	
Deferred Tax Asset (.4 X $40,000)	16,000	
Cash (.4 X $340,000)		136,000

This entry reduces Cash, so Line (9) decreases by $136,000. The recognition of income tax expense reduces Line (1), net income, by $120,000. Line (3) increases by $16,000 for an expense that used more cash than the amount of the expense.

    c. The journal entry and explanation for this part are the same as in Part *b.* above. Line (1) decreases by $120,000, Line (3) increases by $16,000, and Line (9) decreases by $136,000.

    d. The journal entry is:.

Cash	10,000	
Interest Revenue		10,000

Interest on municipal bonds is nontaxable, so recognition of income taxes on the interest revenue is inappropriate (a permanent difference). The Cash account increases, so Line (9) increases by $10,000. The recognition of interest revenue increases Line (1), net income, by $10,000.

10.40   (Wal-Mart Stores; financial statement effects of operating and capital leases.)

    a.

Interest Expense (= .11 X $1,694.2)	186.4	
Liability—Present Value of Lease Obligation		
(Plug)	18.3	
Cash (Given)		204.7

    b.

Rent Expense	249.3	
Cash		249.3

    c. **January 31, Year 9**

Asset—Leasehold	1,586.5	
Liability—Present Value of Lease Obliga-		
tion		1,586.5

To capitalize operating leases.

10.40 c. continued.

January 31, Year 10

Interest Expense (= .12 × $1,586.5).................	190.4	
Liability—Present Value of Lease Obligation..	58.9	
Cash..		249.3

To record interest expense and cash payment on capitalized operating leases.

Depreciation Expense.................................	105.8	
Accumulated Depreciation......................		105.8

To record depreciation expense on capitalized operating leases; $105.8 = $1,586.5/15.

10.41   (American Airlines; financial statement effect of operating and capital leases.)

(Amounts in Millions)

a.
Capital Lease Liability, January 31, Year 10......................	$2,233
Interest Expense for Year 11 (= .08 × $2,233)......................	179
Cash Payment for Year 11..	(268)
New Leases Signed during Year 11 (Plug)........................	259
Capital Lease Liability, January 31, Year 11......................	$2,403

b.
Leasehold Asset, January 31, Year 10.............................	$1,716
New Leases Capitalized during Year 11 (from Part c.)........	259
Depreciation Expense for Year 11 (Plug)	(97)
Leasehold Asset, January 31, Year 11.............................	$1,878

c.   **December 31, Year 11**

Interest Expense	179	
Liability—Present Value of Lease Obligation.......	89	
Cash..		268

Depreciation Expense or Work-in-Process Inventory..	97	
Accumulated Depreciation.......................		97

Asset—Leasehold...	259	
Liability—Present Value of Lease Obligation....		259

d.   **December 31, Year 11**

Rent Expense	946	
Cash..		946

10.41 continued.

   e. **December 31, Year 10**

Asset—Leasehold...	7,793	
Liability—Present Value of Lease Obligation....		7,793

To capitalize operating leases as if they were
capital leases.

December 31, Year 11

Interest Expense (= .10 × $7,793).........................	779	
Liability—Present Value of Lease Obligation.......	167	
Cash..		946

To record interest expense and cash payment
for capitalized operating leases.

Depreciation Expense or Work-in-Process In- ventory...	354	
Accumulated Depreciation.........................		354

To record depreciation for Year 11; ($354 =
$7,793/22).

Asset—Leasehold...	538	
Liability—Present Value of Lease Obligation....		538

To record present value of new leases; $7,793 + X
− $167 = $8,164; X = $538.

10.42   (Carom Sports Collectibles Shop; comparison of borrow/buy with operating and capital leases.)

   a. $100,000/3.79079 = $26,379.725 = $26,380.

Carom Sports Collectibles Shop Amortization Schedule

Year	Start of Year Balance	Interest (10%)	Payment	Reduction	End of Year Balance
1	$100,000	$ 10,000	$ 26,380	$ 16,380	$ 83,620
2	83,620	8,362	26,380	18,018	65,602
3	65,602	6,560	26,380	19,820	45,782
4	45,782	4,578	26,380	21,802	23,980
5	23,980	2,398	26,380	23,982	(2)

10.42 continued.

   b. (1) Asset—Computer System.
          Asset Contra—Accumulated Depreciation on Computer System.
          Liability—Bonds Payable and Interest Payable.

      (2) None.

      (3) Asset—Leasehold for Computer System.
          Asset Contra—Accumulated Amortization of Leasehold (not required.)
          Liability—Present Value of Lease Obligations.
          Liability Contra—Discount on Lease Obligations (required only if previous account shows gross rentals.

   c. $150,000 = $100,000 + (.10 \times $100,000 \times 5)$.

   d. (1) Operating: $131,900 = $26,380 \times 5$.
      (2) Capital: $131,900.

   e. The method of accounting for a lease affects only the timing of expenses, not their total. Expenses under Plan (1) are larger because the firm borrows $100,000 for the entire 5 years, whereas under Plan (2) it pays the loan with part of each lease payment; with smaller average borrowing, interest expense is smaller.

   f. (1) $30,000 = $20,000 depreciation plus $10,000 bond interest.
      (2) Operating-lease Method: $26,380.
          Capital-lease Method: $30,000 = $20,000 amortization +
                                               $10,000 lease interest.

   g. (1) $30,000.
      (2) Operating: $26,380.
          Capital: $22,400 (or $22,398) = $20,000 + $2,400.

10.42 g. continued.

CAROM SPORTS COLLECTIBLES SHOP SUMMARY
(Not Required)

	Year 1	Year 2	Year 3	Year 4	Year 5	Total
Plan 1						
Depreciation Expense	$20,000	$20,000	$20,000	$20,000	$20,000	$ 100,000
Interest Expense	10,000	10,000	10,000	10,000	10,000	50,000
Total	$30,000	$30,000	$30,000	$30,000	$30,000	$ 150,000
Plan 2 (Operating)						
Lease Expense	$26,380	$26,380	$26,380	$26,380	$26,380	$ 131,900
Plan 2 (Financing)						
Amortization Expense	$20,000	$20,000	$20,000	$20,000	$20,000	$ 100,000
Interest Expense	10,000	8,362	6,560	4,578	2,400*	31,900
Total	$30,000	$28,362	$26,560	$24,578	$22,400	$ 131,900

*Plug to correct for rounding errors. By computations, this number is $2,398 = $26,380/1.10.

10.43 (U.S. Airlines; financial statement effects of capitalizing operating leases.)

	American	Delta	United
a. $7,878/($7,878 + $3,380)	70.0%		
$3,121/($3,121 + $1,827)		63.1%	
$3,617/($3,617 − $267)			108.0%
b. ($7,878 + $8,164)/($7,878 + $8,164 + $3,380)	82.6%		
($3,121 + $7,307)/($3,121 + $7,307 + $1,827)		85.1%	
($3,617 + $10,645)/($3,617 + $10,645 − $267)			101.9%

c. The airlines have high debt ratios without including operating leases. Inclusion of the operating leases in liabilities probably violates debt covenants of these airlines.

d. The lease period probably runs for less than 75 percent of the useful life of their equipment or the lessor incurs the salvage value risk.

10.43 continued.

e. The airlines often operate at a loss and are unable to take advantage of depreciation deductions. The airlines hope to obtain lower lease payments by allowing the lessor to claim the depreciation deductions for tax purposes.

10.44 (Deere & Company; interpreting income tax disclosures.) (Amounts in Millions)

a. **Year 10**

Income Tax Expense......................................	182	
Deferred Tax Asset (= $82 – $77)........................	5	
Deferred Tax Liability (= $375 – $312).............		63
Income Tax Payable or Cash........................		124

b. Book income before income taxes exceeded taxable income because income tax expense exceeds income taxes currently payable. Also, the deferred tax accounts on the balance sheet experienced a net credit change of $58 million (= $63 – $5) during Year 10, suggesting larger book income than taxable income.

c. **Year 11**

Deferred Tax Asset (= $149 – $82)	67	
Deferred Tax Liability (= $342 – $375)................	33	
Income Tax Payable....................................		95
Income Tax Expense (Credit)......................		5

d. Book loss before income taxes was smaller than taxable income. Also, the deferred tax accounts on the balance sheet experienced a net debit change of $100 million (= $67 + $33) during Year 11, suggesting smaller book income (loss) than taxable income.

e. The decline in book income before income taxes between Year 10 and Year 11 suggests the possibility of a slowdown in sales growth. Revenue recognized for tax purposes using the installment method exceeds revenue recognized at the time of sale for book purposes, resulting in a decrease in the deferred tax liability relating to installment sales. The increase in the deferred tax assets relating to uncollectible accounts and sales rebates and allowances suggest weak economic conditions, causing Deere to increase its provisions for these items for book purposes.

f.

Change in Deferred Tax Liability Relating to Depreciable Assets (= $215 – $208)...	$ 7
Income Tax Rate...	÷ .35
Temporary Difference for Year 11...............................	$ 20
Book Depreciation...	209
Tax Depreciation...	$ 229

10.44 continued.

g. Deere must amortize goodwill for book purposes but cannot amortize goodwill for tax purposes (that is, goodwill is a permanent difference). The computation of income taxes on pretax book income at the statutory tax rates assumes that Deere receives a tax saving from recognizing goodwill. The addition for goodwill eliminates the tax saving included in the statutory tax rate computation on the first line of the tax reconciliation.

10.45 (Sun Microsystems; interpreting income tax disclosures.) (Amounts in Millions)

a. **Year 5**

Income Tax Expense...	67	
Deferred Tax Asset (= $150 – $142)...........................	8	
Deferred Tax Liability (= $7 – $14)	7	
Income Tax Payable or Cash (= $38 + $38 + $6)		82

b. Book income before income taxes was less than taxable income because there is a net debit change (= $8 + $7) in the deferred tax accounts on the balance sheet.

c. **Year 6**

Income Tax Expense...	88	
Deferred Tax Asset (= $174 – $150)...........................	24	
Deferred Tax Liability (= $27 – $7)		20
Income Tax Payable or Cash (= $28 + $60 + $4)		92

d. Book income before income taxes was less than taxable income because there is a net debit change (= $24 – $20) in the deferred tax accounts on the balance sheet.

e. **Year 7**

Income Tax Expense...	167	
Deferred Tax Asset (= $195 – $174)...........................	21	
Deferred Tax Liability (= $25 – $27)...........................	2	
Income Tax Payable or Cash (= $123 + $57 + $10) ...		190

f. Taxable income exceeds book income (loss) before income taxes. The deferred tax accounts on the balance sheet experienced a net debit change (= $21 + $2) during Year 7.

10.45 continued.

g. Sun probably decreased its capital expenditures during Year 7 because depreciation for book purposes exceeded depreciation for tax purposes (that is, the deferred tax liability relating to depreciation temporary differences decreased during Year 7).

10.46 (General Products Company; interpreting income tax disclosures.)

a. Book income was likely less than taxable income because the deferred tax accounts on the balance sheet experienced a net debit change during Year 3.

b. Book income was likely larger than taxable income because the deferred tax accounts on the balance sheet experienced a net credit change during Year 4.

c. The sales of products on account and under warranty plans increased continually during the three-year period. Estimated bad debt expense on each year's sales exceeded actual write-off of uncollectible accounts arising from the current and previous years' sales. Estimated warranty expense on products sold each year exceeded actual expenditures for warranties and products sold during the current and previous years.

d.

Change in Deferred Tax Liability Relating to Temporary Depreciable Assets (= $213 – $155).............................	$ 58
Income Tax Rate..	÷ .35
Excess of Tax Depreciation Over Book Depreciation	$ 165.7

10.47 (Equilibrium Company; behavior of deferred income tax account when a firm acquires new assets every year.)

Year	Units Acquired
1	1
2	1
3	1
4	1
5	1
6	1
7	1

TAX DEPRECIATION (ACRS)

	1	2	3	4	5	6	7
	$2,400	$3,840	$2,280	$1,440	$1,320	$720	$0
		2,400	3,840	2,280	1,440	1,320	720
			2,400	3,840	2,280	1,440	1,320
				2,400	3,840	2,280	1,440
					2,400	3,840	2,280
						2,400	3,840
							2,400

	1	2	3	4	5	6	7
a. Annual Depreciation	$2,400	$6,240	$8,520	$9,960	$11,280	$12,000	$12,000
b. Straight Line Depreciation = $2,000 per Machine per Year	2,000	4,000	6,000	8,000	10,000	12,000	12,000
c. Difference	$400	$2,240	$2,520	$1,960	$1,280	$0	$0
d. Increase in Deferred Tax (40%)	$160	896	$1,008	784	512	$0	$0
e. Balance of Deferred Income Taxes	$160	$1,056	$2,064	$2,848	$3,360	$3,360	$3,360

f. The Deferred Income Taxes account balance will remain constant at $3,360 so long as the firm continues this replacement policy. If asset prices increase or physical assets increase, or both, the Deferred Tax Liability will continue to grow.

10.48   (Shiraz Company; attempts to achieve off-balance-sheet financing.)

[The chapter does not give sufficient information for the student to know the GAAP answers. The six items are designed to generate a lively discussion.]

Transfer of Receivables with Recourse *SFAS No. 77* (1983) sets out the following criteria to treat a transfer of receivables with recourse as a sale: (1) the seller (Shiraz) surrenders control of the future economic benefits and risks of the receivables, and (2) the purchaser of the receivables (Credit Company) cannot require the seller to repurchase the receivables except as set out in the original provision, and (3) the seller can estimate its obligation under the recourse provision.

Shiraz Company retains control of the future economic benefits. If interest rates decrease, Shiraz can borrow funds at the lower interest rate and repurchase the receivables. Because the receivables carry a fixed interest return, Shiraz enjoys the benefit of the difference between the fixed interest return on the receivables and the lower borrowing cost. If interest rates increase, Shiraz will not repurchase the receivables. Credit Company bears the risk of interest rate increases because of the fixed interest return on the receivables. The control of who benefits from interest rate changes and who bears the risk resides with Shiraz Company. Shiraz Company also bears credit risk in excess of the allowance. Thus, this transaction does not meet the first two criteria as a sale. Shiraz Company should report the transaction as a collateralized loan.

Product Financing Arrangement *SFAS No. 49* (1981) provides that firms recognize product financing arrangements as liabilities if (1) the arrangement requires the sponsoring firm (Shiraz) to purchase the inventory at specified prices and (2) the payments made to the other entity (Credit Company) cover all acquisition, holding, and financing costs.

Shiraz Company agrees to repurchase the inventory at a fixed price, thereby incurring the risk of changing prices. The purchase price formula includes a fixed interest rate, so Shiraz enjoys the benefits or incurs the risk of interest rate changes. Shiraz also controls the benefits and risk of changes in storage costs. Thus, Shiraz treats this product financing arrangement as a collateralized loan.

Throughput Contract *SFAS Statement No. 49* (1981) treats throughput contracts as executory contracts and does not require their recognition as a liability. Note, however, the similarity between a product financing arrangement (involving inventory) and a throughput contract (involving a service). Shiraz Company must pay specified amounts each period regardless of whether it uses the shipping services. The wording of the problem makes it unclear as to whether the initial contract specifies a selling price (railroad bears risk of operating cost increases) or whether the selling price is the railroad's current charges for shipping services each period (Shiraz bears risk of operating cost increases). It seems

10.48 continued.

unlikely that the railroad would accept a fixed price for all ten years. Thus, it appears that Shiraz incurs a commitment to make highly probable future cash payments in amounts that cover the railroad's operating and financing costs. This transaction has the economic characteristics of a collateralized loan, even though GAAP permits treatment as an executory contract.

Construction Joint Venture The construction loan appears as a liability of the books of Chemical, the joint entity. Because Shiraz and Mission each own 50 percent of Chemical, neither company consolidates Chemical's financial statements with their own. (Chapter 13 discusses consolidated financial statements.) Thus, the loan will not appear on either Shiraz's or Mission's balance sheet by way of their accounting for their investment in Chemical.

GAAP treats the commitment to pay one-half of the operating and debt service costs as an executory contract, similar to the throughput contract. Even though the probability of making future cash payments is high, GAAP concludes that a liability does not arise until the firm receives future benefits from Chemical.

The only way that Shiraz will recognize a liability is if the debt guarantee gives rise to a loss contingency. If Mission defaults on its share of operating and debt service costs, the probability of Shiraz having to repay the loan increases sufficiently to warrant recognition of a liability. It is difficult to see the logic of GAAP in recognizing the full liability in this case while not recognizing one-half of the liability in situations described in the preceding paragraphs. In both cases, the probability of future cash outflows is high.

Research and Development Partnership *SFAS No. 68* (1982) requires firms to recognize financings related to research and development (R & D) as liabilities if (1) the sponsoring firm (Shiraz) must repay the financing regardless of the outcome of the R & D work, or (2) the sponsoring firm, even in the a absence of a loan guarantee, bears the risk of failure of the R & D effort.

Shiraz guarantees the bank loan in this case regardless of the outcome of the R &D effort and therefore must recognize a liability (satisfies first criterion above). It does not matter whether Shiraz has an option or an obligation to purchase the results of the R & D effort.

If Shiraz did not guarantee the bank loan, then the second criterion above determines whether Shiraz recognizes a liability. If Shiraz has the option to purchase the results of the R & D work, it does not bear the risk of failure and need not recognize a liability. If Shiraz has the obligation to purchase the results, it recognizes a liability for the probable amount payable. The problem does not make it clear whether the amount payable includes the unpaid balance of the loan or merely the value of the R & D work (which could be zero). It seems unlikely that the bank would lend funds for the R & D work without some commitment or obligation by Shiraz to repay the loan.

10.48 continued.

Hotel Financing Shiraz Company will recognize a liability for the hotel financing only if its debt guarantee satisfies the criteria for a loss contingency. It appears in this case that the probability of Shiraz having to make payments under the loan guarantee is low. The hotel is profitable and probably generating cash flows. In addition, the bank can sell the hotel in the event of loan default to satisfy the unpaid balance of the loan. Thus, Shiraz's loan guarantee is a third level of defense against loan default. If default does occur and the first two lines of defense prove inadequate to repay the loan in full, then Shiraz would recognize a liability for the unpaid portion.

CHAPTER 11

MARKETABLE SECURITIES AND INVESTMENTS

Questions, Exercises, Problems, and Cases: Answers and Solutions

11.1   See the text or the glossary at the end of the book.

11.2   Securities that a firm intends to sell within approximately one year of the date of the balance sheet appear as current assets. All other securities appear as noncurrent assets.

11.3   a.   Debt securities that a firm intends to hold to maturity (for example, to lock in the yield at acquisition for the full period to maturity) and has the ability to hold to maturity (for example, the firm has adequate liquid assets and borrowing capacity such that it need not sell the debt securities prior to maturity to obtain cash) appear as "debt held to maturity." All other debt securities appear in the "available for sale" category. The latter includes short-term investments in government debt securities that serve as a liquid investment of excess cash and short-and long-term investments in government and corporate debt securities that serve either as hedges of interest rate, exchange rate, or similar risks or as sources of cash at a later date to pay debt coming due.

b.   The classification as "trading securities" implies a firm's active involvement in buying and selling securities for profit. The holding period of trading securities is typically measured in minutes or hours instead of days. The classification as "available for sale" implies less frequent trading and usually relates to an operating purpose other than profit alone (for example, to generate income while a firm haws temporarily excess cash, to invest in a firm with potential new technologies). The holding period of securities available for sale is typically measured in days, months, or years.

c.   Amortized acquisition cost equals the purchase price of debt securities plus or minus amortization of any difference between acquisition cost and maturity value. Amortized acquisition cost bears no necessary relation to the market value of the debt security during the periods subsequent to acquisition. The market value of a debt security depends on the risk characteristics of the issuer, the provisions of the debt security with respect to interest rate, term to maturity, and similar factors, and the general level of interest rates in the economy.

11.3 continued.

    d. Unrealized holding gains and losses occur when the market value of a security changes while the firm holds the security. The unrealized holding gain or loss on trading securities appears in the income statement each period, whereas it appears in a separate shareholders' equity account each period for securities available for sale.

    e. Realized gains and losses appear in the income statement when a firm sells a security. The realized gain or loss on trading securities equals the selling price minus the market value of the security on the most recent balance sheet. The realized gain or loss on securities available for sale equals the selling price minus the acquisition cost of the security.

11.4   Firms acquire trading securities primarily for their short-term profit potential. Including the unrealized holding gain or loss in income provides the financial statement user with relevant information for assessing the performance of the trading activity. Firms acquire securities available for sale to support an operating activity (for example, investment of temporarily excess cash) instead of primarily for their profit potential. Deferring recognition of any gain or loss until sale treats securities available for sale the same as inventories, equipment and other assets. Excluding the unrealized gain or loss from earnings also reduces earnings volatility.

11.5   The realized gain or loss for a security classified as available for sale equals the selling price minus the acquisition cost of the security. The realized gain or loss for a trading security equals the selling price minus the market value on the date of the most recent balance sheet. GAAP allocate all of the income from a security classified as available for sale to the period of sale, whereas GAAP allocate this same amount of income on a trading security to all periods between purchase and sale.

11.6   The required accounting does appear to contain a degree of inconsistency. One might explain this seeming inconsistency by arguing that the balance sheet and income statement serve different purposes. The balance sheet attempts to portray the resources of a firm and the claims on those users by creditors and owners. Market values for securities are more relevant than acquisition cost or lower-of-cost-or-market for assessing the adequacy of resources to satisfy claims. The income statement reports the results of operating performance. One might argue that operating performance from investing in marketable securities available for sale is not complete until the firm sells the securities. Another argument for excluding at least unrealized gains on marketable securities from earnings is that it achieves consistency with the delayed recognition of unrealized gains on inventories, equipment, and other assets.

11.7   (Linderman Company; classification of derivative instrument.)

Does not qualify as a hedge of any kind because there is no effective matching of risks. Linderman will likely classify the securities as trading securities because such options usually expire within a few months, rarely having terms longer than one year.

11.8   a. These accounts are both shareholders' equity accounts and reflect the change in the market value of securities since acquisition.

        b. Dividend Revenue is an income statement account. It reflects the revenue recognized when a firm uses the market-value method. Equity in Earnings of Unconsolidated Affiliates is also an income statement account. It reflects the revenue recognized when a firm uses the equity method.

        c. Equity in Earnings of Unconsolidated Affiliate is an income statement account. It reflects the revenue earned by a minority, active investor in an investee accounted for using the equity method. Minority Interest in Earnings of Consolidated Subsidiary is an account appearing on the consolidated income statement of a parent and its majority-owned, active investee. It represents the external, minority interest in the earnings of the investee.

        d. Minority Interest in Earnings of Consolidated Subsidiary is an income statement account. It reflects the external, minority interest in the earnings of a majority-owned consolidated subsidiary. Minority Interest in Net Assets of Consolidated Subsidiary is a balance sheet account. It reflects the external, minority interest in the net assets of a consolidated subsidiary.

11.9   Dividends represent revenues under the market-value method and a return of capital under the equity method.

11.10   Under the equity method, the change each period in the net assets, or shareholders' equity, of the subsidiary appears on the one line, Investment in Subsidiary, on the balance sheet. When the parent consolidates the subsidiary, changes in the individual assets and liabilities that comprise the net asset change appear in the individual consolidated assets and liabilities. Likewise, under the equity method, the investor's interest in the investee's earnings appears in one line on the income statement, Equity in Earnings of Unconsolidated Subsidiary. When the parent consolidates the subsidiary, the individual revenues and expenses of the subsidiary appear in consolidated revenues and expenses.

11.11   If Company A owns less than, or equal to, 50 percent of Company B's voting stock, it is a minority investor in Company B. If Company A owns more than 50 percent of Company C, it is a majority investor in Company C. The entities holding the remainder of the voting stock of Company C are minority investors. Their minority interest appears on the consolidated balance sheet of Company A and Company C.

11.12   When the investor uses the equity method, total assets include the Investment in Subsidiary account. The investment account reflects the parent's interest in the *net* assets (assets minus liabilities) of the subsidiary. When the investor consolidates the subsidiary, total consolidated assets include all of the subsidiary's assets. Consolidated liabilities include the liabilities of the subsidiary. Thus, total assets on a consolidated basis exceed total assets when the investor uses the equity method.

11.13   (Classifying securities.)

   a.   Securities available for sale; current asset.

   b.   Debt securities held to maturity; noncurrent asset.

   c.   Securities available for sale; current asset.

   d.   Securities available for sale; noncurrent asset.

   e.   Trading securities; current asset.

   f.   Securities available for sale; noncurrent asset (although a portion of these bonds might appear as a current asset).

11.14   (Vermont Company; journal entries for holdings of marketable equity securities.)

8/21

Marketable Securities..	45,000	
Cash...		45,000

To record the cost of purchases in asset account:
(1,000 × $45) = $45,000.

9/13

No entry because September 13 is not the end of an accounting period.

9/30

Dividends Receivable..	500	
Dividend Revenue..		500

To record declaration of dividend as revenue.

11.14 continued.

10/25

Cash	500	
Dividends Receivable		500

To record receipt of dividend in cash.

12/31

Marketable Securities..	6,000	
Unrealized Holding Gain on Securities Available for Sale (SE)		6,000

To record increase in market price: 1,000 × ($51 – $45) = $6,000.

1/20

Cash (600 × $55)...	33,000	
Marketable Securities (600 × $45)........................		27,000
Realized Gain on Sale of Securities Available for Sale (IncSt) [600 × ($55 – $45)]...........................		6,000

To record sale of 600 shares of Texas Instruments.

Unrealized Holding Gain on Securities Available for Sale (SE) [600 × ($51– $45)]...........................	3,600	
Marketable Securities...............................		3,600

To eliminate changes previously recorded in the market value of Texas Instruments.

11.15 (Elson Corporation; journal entries for holdings of marketable equity securities.)

10/15/Year 4

Marketable Securities (Security A)........................	28,000	
Cash...		28,000

To record acquisition of shares of Security A.

11/02/Year 4

Marketable Securities (Security B)	49,000	
Cash...		49,000

To record acquisition of shares of Security B.

12/31/Year 4

Cash	1,000	
Dividend Revenue...		1,000

To record dividend received from Security B.

12/31/Year 4

Unrealized Holding Loss on Security A Available for Sale (SE)...	3,000	
Marketable Securities (Security A)...............		3,000

To record unrealized holding loss on Security A.

11.15 continued.

12/31/Year 4

Marketable Securities (Security B)	6,000	
Unrealized Holding Gain on Security B Available for Sale (SE)		6,000

To record unrealized holding gain on Security B.

2/10/Year 5

Cash	24,000	
Realized Loss on Sale of Securities Available for Sale ($24,000 – $28,000) (IncSt)	4,000	
Marketable Securities (Security A)................		28,000

To record sale of Security A.

Marketable Securities (Security A)........................	3,000	
Unrealized Holding Loss on Security A Available for Sale (SE)		3,000

To eliminate the effects of changes previously recorded in the market value of Security A.

12/31/Year 5

Cash	1,200	
Dividend Revenue..		1,200

To record dividend received from Security B.

12/31/Year 5

Unrealized Holding Gain on Security B Available for Sale (SE)...	2,000	
Marketable Securities (Security B) ($53,000 – $55,000)		2,000

To revalue Security B to market value.

7/15/Year 6

Cash	57,000	
Marketable Securities (Security B)....................		49,000
Realized Gain on Sale of Securities Available for Sale ($57,000 – $49,000) (IncSt)		8,000

To record sale of Security B.

Unrealized Holding Gain on Security B Available for Sale ($6,000 – $2,000) (SE)...........................	4,000	
Marketable Securities (Security B)		4,000

To eliminate the effects of changes previously recorded in the market value of Security B.

11.16   (Simmons Corporation; journal entries for holdings of marketable equity securities.)

6/13/Year 6

Marketable Securities (Security S).........................	12,000	
Marketable Securities (Security T)	29,000	
Marketable Securities (Security U)........................	43,000	
Cash...		84,000

To record acquisition of marketable equity securities as a temporary investment.

10/11/Year 6

Cash	39,000	
Realized Loss on Sale of Security U Available for Sale (IncSt)...	4,000	
Marketable Securities (Security U)...............		43,000

To record sale of Security U.

12/31/Year 6

Marketable Securities (Security S) ($13,500 – $12,000)	1,500	
Unrealized Holding Gain on Security S Available for Sale (SE)............................		1,500

To revalue Security S to market value.

12/31/Year 6

Unrealized Holding Loss on Security T Available for Sale (SE)...	2,800	
Marketable Securities (Security T) ($26,200 – $29,000)		2,800

To revalue Security T to market value.

12/31/Year 7

Marketable Securities (Security S) ($15,200 – $13,500)	1,700	
Unrealized Holding Gain on Security S Available for Sale (SE)............................		1,700

To revalue Security S to market value.

12/31/Year 7

Marketable Securities (Security T) ($31,700 – $26,200)	5,500	
Unrealized Holding Loss on Security T Available for Sale (from 12/31/Year 6 Entry) (SE)...		2,800
Unrealized Holding Gain on Security T Available for Sale (SE)............................		2,700

To revalue Security T to market value.

11.16 continued.

2/15/Year 8

Cash	14,900	
Marketable Securities (Security S).....................		12,000
Realized Gain on Sale of Security S Available		
for Sale ($14,900 − $12,000) (IncSt).....................		2,900
To record sale of Security S.		

Unrealized Holding Gain on Security S Available		
for Sale ($1,500 + $1,700) (SE)............................	3,200	
Marketable Securities (Security S).................		3,200
To eliminate the effects of changes previously re-		
corded in the market value of Security S.		

8/22/Year 8

Cash	28,500	
Realized Loss on Sale of Securities Available for		
Sale (Security T) ($28,500 − $29,000) (IncSt)	500	
Marketable Securities (Security T)		29,000
To record sale of Security T.		

Unrealized Holding Gain on Security T Available		
for Sale (SE)...	2,700	
Marketable Securities (Security T)		2,700
To eliminate the effects of changes previously re-		
corded in the market value of Security T.		

11.17   (Fischer/Black Co.; working backwards from data on marketable securities transaction.)

a. $20,000 = $17,000 + $3,000.

b $17,000, the amount credited to Marketable Securities in the journal entry which the student might think of as $20,000 original cost, derived above, less $3,000 of Unrealized Holding Loss.

c. $5,000 loss from the debit for Realized Loss.

11.18   (Canning/Werther; working backwards from data on marketable securities transaction.)

a. $14,000 = $17,000 proceeds − $4,000 realized gain + $1,000 loss previously recognized because they are trading securities.

b. $13,000 = $17,000 proceeds − $4,000 realized gain which is selling price less original cost because they are securities available for sale.

11.19   (Reconstructing events from journal entries.)

   a.   The market value of a marketable security is $4,000 less than its book value and the firm increases the Unrealized Holding Loss account on the balance sheet. Alternatively, the firm sold a security with a cumulative unrealized loss recorded on the books and must now eliminate the effects of changes previously recorded in the market values of the security sold.

   b.   A firm sells marketable securities for an amount that is $100 (= $1,200 – $1,300) less than was originally paid for them.

   c.   The market value of marketable securities is $750 more than its book value and the firm increases the unrealized holding gain account on the balance sheet.

   d.   A firm sells marketable securities for an amount that is $100 (= $1,800 – $1,700) more than was originally paid for them.

11.20   (Apollo Corporation; amount of income recognized under various methods of accounting for investments.)

   a. and b.
      $3.0 million = .15 X $20 million.

   c. $24 million = .30 X $80 million.

   d. $16 million = .30 X $80 million – $80 million/10.*

   *The equity method recognizes amortization of goodwill.

11.21   (Trusco; balance sheet and income effects of alternative methods of accounting for investments.)

Part	Investment	Net Income
a.	$40 million	$2 million
b.	$39 million	$2 million
c.	$45 million	$2 million
d.	$129 million[a]	$15 million[b]
e.	$165 million[c]	$11 million[d]

[a]$120 million + .30($50 million – $20 million) = $129 million.
[b].30 X $50 million = $15 million.
[c]$160 million + .30($50 million – $20 million) – ($40 million/10) = $165 million.
[d](.30 X $50 million) – ($40 million/10) = $11 million.

11.22 (Randle Corporation; journal entries to apply the market value method for long-term investments in securities.)

April 10, Year 1

Investment in Securities (M)...............................	37,000	
Cash...		37,000

July 11, Year 1

Investment in Securities (N)	31,000	
Cash...		31,000

September 29, Year 1

Investment in Securities (O)...............................	94,000	
Cash...		94,000

December 31, Year 1

Cash	7,900	
Dividend Revenue..		7,900

December 31, Year 1

Unrealized Holding Loss on Investments in Securities (SE)..	9,000	
Investment in Securities (M).........................		2,000
Investment in Securities (O)..........................		7,000

December 31, Year 1

Investment in Securities (N)	7,000	
Unrealized Holding Gain on Investment in Securities (SE)..		7,000

October 15, Year 2

Cash	43,000	
Investment in Securities (M)...........................		37,000
Realized Gain on Sale of Investment in Securities (IncSt)		6,000

October 31, Year 2 or December 31, Year 2

Investment in Securities (M)...............................	2,000	
Unrealized Holding Loss on Investment in Securities (SE)...		2,000

December 31, Year 2

Cash	5,600	
Dividend Revenue..		5,600

December 31, Year 2

Investment in Securities (N)	7,000	
Unrealized Holding Gain on Investment in Securities (SE)		7,000

11.22 continued.

December 31, Year 2

Investment in Securities (O).............................	2,000	
Unrealized Holding Loss on Investment in Securities (SE)		2,000

11.23   (Blake Company; journal entries to apply the market value method to long-term investments in securities.)

July 2, Year 4

Investment in Securities (G)	42,800	
Cash...		42,800

October 19, Year 4

Investment in Securities (H)	29,600	
Cash...		29,600

October 29, Year 4

Cash	89,700	
Realized Loss on Sale of Investments in Securities (IncSt)..	4,000	
Investment in Securities (F).........................		93,700

October 29, Year 4 or December 31, Year 4

Investment in Securities (F).............................	2,500	
Unrealized Holding Loss on Investment in Securities (SE)		2,500

December 31, Year 4

Unrealized Holding Loss on Investment in Securities (SE)...	4,500	
Investment in Securities (G).........................		4,500

December 31, Year 4

Investment in Securities (H)	2,000	
Unrealized Holding Gain on Investment in Securities (SE)		2,000

February 9, Year 5

Investment in Securities (I)	18,100	
Cash...		18,100

September 17, Year 5

Cash	32,300	
Investment in Securities (H).........................		29,600
Realized Gain on Sale of Investment in Securities (IncSt)		2,700

11.23 continued.

September 17, Year 5 or December 31, Year 5

Unrealized Holding Gain on Investment in Securities (SE)..	2,000	
Investment in Securities (H)............................		2,000

December 31, Year 5

Unrealized Holding Loss on Investment in Securities (SE)..	1,400	
Investment in Securities (G)............................		1,400

December 31, Year 5

Investment in Securities (I)	2,600	
Unrealized Holding Gain on Investment in Securities (SE)		2,600

11.24 (Wood Corporation; journal entries to apply the equity method of accounting for investments in securities.)

January 2

Investment in Securities (Knox)	350,000	
Investment in Securities (Vachi)..........................	196,000	
Investment in Securities (Snow)..........................	100,000	
Cash..		646,000

December 31

Investment in Securities (Knox)	35,000	
Investment in Securities (Vachi)..........................	12,000	
Investment in Securities (Snow).......................		4,800
Equity in Earnings of Affiliates		42,200

$(.50 \times \$70,000) + (.30 \times \$40,000) - (.20 \times \$24,000) = \$42,200.$

December 31

Cash	19,800	
Investment in Securities (Knox).......................		15,000
Investment in Securities (Vachi)......................		4,800

$(.50 \times \$30,000) + (.30 \times \$16,000) = \$19,800.$

December 31

Amortization Expense..	3,000	
Investment in Securities (Vachi)......................		2,000
Investment in Securities (Snow).......................		1,000

$\$196,000 - (.30 \times \$520,000) = \$40,000; \$40,000/20 = \$2,000.$ $\$100,000 - (.20 \times \$400,000) = \$20,000;$ $\$20,000/20 = \$1,000.$

11.25 (Stebbins Corporation; journal entries to apply the equity method of accounting for investments in securities.)

a. **January 1, Year 1**

Investment in Securities (R)............................	250,000	
Investment in Securities (S)	325,000	
Investment in Securities (T)............................	475,000	
Cash		1,050,000

December 31, Year 1

Investment in Securities (R)............................	50,000	
Investment in Securities (S)	48,000	
Investment in Securities (T)........................		75,000
Equity in Earnings of Affiliates.....................		23,000

$(.25 \times \$200,000) + (.40 \times \$120,000) - (.50 \times \$150,000) = \$23,000.$

December 31, Year 1

Cash..	63,250	
Investment in Securities (R).........................		31,250
Investment in Securities (S).........................		32,000

$(.25 \times \$125,000) + (.40 \times \$80,000) = \$63,250.$

December 31, Year 1

Amortization Expense....................................	3,750	
Investment in Securities (R).........................		2,500
Investment in Securities (S).........................		1,250

$\$250,000 - (.25 \times \$800,000) = \$50,000; \$50,000/20 = \$2,500.$ $\$325,000 - (.40 \times \$750,000) = \$25,000;$ $\$25,000/20 = \$1,250.$ $\$475,000 - (.50 \times \$950,000) = 0.$

December 31, Year 2

Investment in Securities (R)............................	56,250	
Investment in Securities (S)	30,000	
Investment in Securities (T)............................	25,000	
Equity in Earnings of Affiliates.....................		111,250

$(.25 \times \$225,000) + (.40 \times \$75,000) - (.50 \times \$50,000) = \$111,250.$

December 31, Year 2

Cash..	64,500	
Investment in Securities (R).........................		32,500
Investment in Securities (S).........................		32,000

$(.25 \times \$130,000) + (.40 \times \$80,000).$

December 31, Year 2

Amortization Expense....................................	3,750	
Investment in Securities (R).........................		2,500
Investment in Securities (S).........................		1,250

11.25 continued.

b. Cash... 330,000
    Loss on Sale of Investments............................ 6,500
      Investment in Securities (S)......................... 336,500
    $325,000 + $48,000 − $32,000 − $1,250 + $30,000 −
    $32,000 − $1,250 = $336,500.

11.26   (Mulherin Corporation; journal entries under various methods of accounting for investments.)

a. **January 2**
    Investment in Hanson.................................. 320,000
    Investment in Maloney................................ 680,000
    Investment in Quinn.................................. 2,800,000
      Cash 3,800,000
    To record acquisition of investments.

    December 31
    Cash.. 6,000
      Dividend Revenue.................................... 6,000
    To record dividend from Hanson: .15 × $40,000 =
    $6,000.

    December 31
    Unrealized Holding Loss on Investment in Se-
      curities (SE) 15,000
        Investment in Hanson............................ 15,000
    To apply the market value method to the invest-
    ment in Hanson.

    December 31
    Investment in Maloney................................. 150,000
      Equity in Earnings of Maloney..................... 150,000
    To recognize share of Maloney's earnings; .30 ×
    $500,000 = $150,000.

    December 31
    Cash.. 54,000
      Investment in Maloney............................. 54,000
    To recognize share of Maloney's dividends; .30
    × $180,000 = $54,000.

    December 31
    Amortization Expense................................... 4,000
      Investment in Maloney............................. 4,000
    To amortize excess acquisition cost for Maloney;
    $680,000 − (.30 × $2,000,000) = $80,000; $80,000/20
    = $4,000.

11.26 a. continued.

December 31
Investment in Quinn.. 600,000
   Equity in Earnings of Quinn.......................   600,000
To recognize share of Quinn's earnings.

December 31
Cash... 310,000
   Investment in Quinn..................................   310,000
To recognize share of Quinn's dividends.

December 31
Amortization Expense.................................. 40,000
   Investment in Quinn..................................   40,000
$2,800,000 - $2,000,000 = $800,000; $800,000/20 = $40,000.

b. Common Stock (Quinn).................................. 200,000
     Additional Paid-in Capital (Quinn) 800,000
     Retained Earnings (Quinn)........................... 690,000
     Equity in Earnings of Quinn (Mulherin)........... 600,000
     Goodwill 760,000
       Investment in Quinn (Mulherin).................   3,050,000
     $2,800,000 + $600,000 - $310,000 - $40,000 = $3,050,000.

11.27 (CAR Corporation; consolidation policy and principal consolidation concepts.)

a. CAR Corporation should consolidate Alexandre du France Software Systems and R Credit Corporation or, under exceptional circumstances, use the market value method.

b. Charles Electronics.............................(.75 X $120,000) = $ 90,000
    Alexandre du France Software Systems.....(.80 X 60,000) =   48,000
    R Credit Corporation.............................(.90 X 144,000) =   129,600
       Total Income from Subsidiaries.............................. $ 267,600

c. Minority Interest shown under accounting assumed in problem:

    Charles Electronics ....(.25 X $120,000) = $ 30,000
    Alexandre du France Software Systems ....(None) =   --
    R Credit Corporation...(None) =   --
                                                     $ 30,000

CAR Corporation subtracts the minority interest in computing net income.

11.27 continued.

    d. Charles Electronics, no increase because already consolidated.

        Alexandre du France Software Systems increase by 80 percent of net income less dividends:

$$.80 \times (\$96,000 - \$60,000) = \$28,800.$$

        R Credit Corporation, no increase because equity method results in the same income statement effects as do consolidated statements. Net income of CAR Corporation would be:

$$\$1,228,800 = \$1,200,000 \text{ (as reported)} + \$28,800 \text{ (increase)}.$$

    e. Minority Interest shown if CAR Corporation consolidated all companies:

Charles Electronics	(.25 × $120,000) =	$ 30,000
Alexandre du France Software Systems	(.20 × 96,000) =	19,200
R Credit Corporation	(.10 × 144,000) =	14,400
		$ 63,600

11.28   (Clinton Corporation; equity method and consolidation elimination entries.) (Amounts in Millions.)

    a.

Investment in Stock of Dole Computer	500	
Cash		500
To record acquisition of shares of common stock.		

Investment in Stock of Dole Computer	100	
Equity in Earnings of Dole Computer		100
To accrue Dole Computer's earnings for the year.		

Cash or Dividends Receivable	30	
Investment in Stock of Dole Computer		30
To recognize dividends received or receivable.		

Amortization Expense	8	
Investment in Stock of Dole Computer		8

To amortize goodwill; $8 = ($500 − $420)/10.
Investment is now $562 = $500 + $100 − $30 − $8.

11.28 continued.

b.
Common Stock...	300	
Retained Earnings ($120 – $30)	90	
Equity in Earnings of Dole Computer...............	100	
Goodwill	72	
Investment in Stock of Dole Computer...........		562
To eliminate investment account.		

Accounts Payable..	3	
Accounts Receivable................................		3
To eliminate intercompany receivable and liability.		

11.29 (Hanna Company; equity method and consolidation elimination entries.)

a.
Investment in Stock of Denver Company...........	550,000	
Cash		550,000
To record acquisition of common stock.		

Investment in Stock of Denver Company...........	120,000	
Equity in Earnings of Denver Company.........		120,000
To accrue 100 percent share of Denver Company's earnings.		

Cash or Dividends Receivable.........................	40,000	
Investment in Stock of Denver Company		40,000
To accrue dividends received or receivable.		

b.
Common Stock...	200,000	
Retained Earnings ($350 – $40)	310,000	
Equity in Earnings of Denver Company	120,000	
Investment in Stock of Denver Company		630,000
To eliminate investment account; $630,000 = $550,000 + $120,000 – $40,000.		

11.30 (Joyce Company and Vogel Company; equity method and consolidation work sheet entries.)

a. **Joyce Company's Books**

(1)
Investment in Stock of Vogel Company......	420,000	
Cash...		420,000
To record acquisition of common stock.		

(2)
Accounts Receivable..............................	29,000	
Sales Revenue....................................		29,000
To record intercompany sales on account.		

11.30 a. continued.

(2)	Cost of Goods Sold..	29,000	
	Inventories...		29,000
	To record cost of intercompany sales.		

(3)	Advance to Vogel Company......................	6,000	
	Cash..		6,000
	To record advance to Vogel Company.		

(4)	Cash..	16,000	
	Accounts Receivable............................		16,000
	To record collections on account from Vogel Company.		

(5)	Cash..	4,000	
	Advance to Vogel Company..................		4,000
	To record collection of advance from Vogel Company.		

(6)	Cash..	20,000	
	Investment in Stock of Vogel Company...		20,000
	To record dividend from Vogel Company.		

(7)	Investment in Stock of Vogel Company......	30,000	
	Equity in Earnings of Vogel Company....		30,000
	To accrue 100 percent share of Vogel Company's net income.		

(8)	Amortization Expense	4,000	
	Investment in Stock of Vogel Company...		4,000
	To record amortization of goodwill; $4,000 = ($420,000 − $380,000)/10.		

Vogel Company's Books

(1) No entry.

(2)	Inventories..	29,000	
	Accounts Payable...............................		29,000
	To record intercompany purchase of materials on account.		

(3)	Cash..	6,000	
	Advance from Joyce Company..............		6,000
	To record advance from Joyce Company.		

(4)	Accounts Payable..................................	16,000	
	Cash..		16,000
	To record payment for purchases on account.		

11.30 a. continued.

    (5) Advance from Joyce Company 4,000
          Cash..   4,000
         To record repayment of advance.

    (6) Retained Earnings 20,000
          Cash..   20,000
         To record declaration and payment of divi-
         dend.

    (7) No entry.

b. Common Stock... 300,000
    Retained Earnings ($80,000 − $20,000).............. 60,000
    Equity in Earnings of Vogel Company 30,000
    Goodwill 36,000
      Investment in Stock of Vogel Company..........   426,000
    To eliminate investment account; $426,000 =
    $420,000 + $30,000 − $20,000 − $4,000.

    Accounts Payable....................................... 13,000
      Accounts Receivable................................   13,000
    To eliminate intercompany receivable and pay-
    able.

    Advance from Joyce Company........................ 2,000
      Advance to Vogel Company........................   2,000
    To eliminate intercompany advance.

11.31   (Laesch Company; working backwards to consolidation relations.)

    a. $80,000 = ($156,000 − $100,000)/.70.

    b.   72.7 percent = ($156,000 − $100,000)/$77,000.

    c. $56,000 = ($156,000 − $100,000).

11.32   (Dealco Corporation; working backwards from consolidated income statements.) (Amounts in Millions.)

    a. $56/$140 = 40 percent.

    b. $[.40 \times (1 − .20) \times \$140] = \$44.80$.

    c. $[1 − (\$42/\$280)] = 1 − .15 = 85$ percent.

11.33   (Alpha/Omega; working backwards from data which has eliminated intercompany transactions; requires Appendix 11.1.)

a. $90,000 = $450,000 + $250,000 – $610,000.

b. $30,000 is Omega's cost; $20,000 is Alpha's cost; $20,000 original cost to Alpha.

Markup on the goods sold from Alpha to Omega, which remain in Omega's inventory, is $10,000 (= $60,000 + $50,000 – $100,000).
Because Alpha priced the goods with markup 50 percent over its costs, the cost to Alpha to produce goods with markup of $10,000 is $20,000 and the total sales price from Alpha to Omega is $30,000 (= $10,000 + $20,000).

11.34   (Homer/Tonga; working backwards from purchase data to reconstruct pooling.)

a. $1,070,000 = $90,000 + $980,000.

b.   Journal entry for pooling:

Current Assets (Unchanged)............................	210,000	
Depreciable Assets (+ $1,070,000 – $210,000).......	860,000	
Liabilities (Unchanged)................................		90,000
Common Stock—Par (Unchanged)		150,000
Additional Paid-in Capital (Note 1)................		430,000
Retained Earnings (Unchanged)		400,000

Note 1. $430,000 = $1,070,000 (total assets) – $90,000 (liabilities) – $150,000 (common shares—par) – $400,000 (retained earnings).

11.35   (Water Company and Soluble Company; financial statement effects of purchase and pooling-of-interests methods.)

a.   (Amounts in Millions)

	(1) Purchase Method	(2) Pooling-of-Interests Method
Assets:		
Current Assets	$ 350	$ 350
Property, Plant and Equipment (Net)	650	600
Goodwill	100	--
Total Assets	$1,100	$ 950
Equities:		
Liabilities	$ 570	$ 570
Common Stock	380[a]	150[b]
Retained Earnings	150	230[c]
Total Equities	$1,100	$ 950

[a]$100 + $280 = $380.
[b]$100 + $50 = $150.
[c]$150 + $80 = $230.

b.   (Amounts in Millions)

	(1) Purchase Method	(2) Pooling-of-Interests Method
Precombination Net Income	$80	$80
Additional Depreciation Expense: $50/5	(10)	--
Goodwill Amortization: $100/20	(5)	--
Revised Projected Net Income	$65	$80

11.36   (Bristol-Myers and Squibb; financial statement effects of purchase and pooling-of-interests method.)

a.   (Amounts in Millions)

	(1) Purchase Method	(2) Pooling-of-Interests Method
Assets, Except Goodwill	$ 8,273	$8,273
Goodwill	11,469[a]	--
Total Assets	$19,742	$8,273
Liabilities	$ 3,325	$3,325
Shareholders' Equity	16,417[b]	4,948[c]
Total Equities	$19,742	$8,273

[a]$12,870 – $1,401 = $11,469.
[b]$3,547 + $12,870 = $16,417.
[c]$3,547 + $1,401 = $4,948.

11.36 continued.

b. (Amounts in Millions)

	(1) Purchase Method	(2) Pooling-of-Interests Method
Precombination Projected Consolidated Net Income	$1,748	$1,748
Goodwill Amortization:		
$11,469/10	(1,147)	--
Revised Projected Net Income	$ 601	$1,748

c. These firms will prefer the pooling-of-interests method because it results in higher future earnings and rates of return on assets and on shareholders' equity.

11.37 (Effects on statement of cash flows.)

a. The journal entry to record this transaction is as follows:

Marketable Securities	59,700	
Cash		59,700

Because this entry involves a credit to the Cash account, Line (9) decreases by $59,700. The purchase of marketable securities is an Investing activity, so Line (5) increases by $59,700. Note that Line (5) carries a negative sign, so increasing it reduces cash.

b. The journal entries to record this transaction are as follows:

Cash	47,900	
Marketable Securities		42,200
Realized Gain on Sale of Securities Available for Sale (IncSt)		5,700
Unrealized Holding Gain on Securities Available for Sale (SE)	1,800	
Marketable Securities ($44,000 − $42,200)		1,800

Because the first entry involves a debit to the Cash account, Line (9) increases by $47,900. The sale of marketable securities is an Investing activity, so Line (4) increases by $47,900. Because the Realized Gain on Sale of Securities Available for Sale account is an income statement account, Line (1) increases by $5,700. We show all of the cash proceeds of sale ($47,900) on Line (4). We double count cash in the amount of the gain if we do not eliminate $5,700 from the Operations section of the statement of cash flows. Thus, Line (3) increases by $5,700 to offset the realized gain. The net effect of the entries on Line (1) and Line (3) is zero. The second entry does not involve an income statement account or the Cash account and therefore would not appear on the statement of cash flows.

c.   The journal entries to record this transaction are as follows:

Cash...	18,700	
Realized Loss on Sale of Securities Available for Sale (IncSt)	6,400	
Marketable Securities.............................		25,100
Marketable Securities ($25,100 − $19,600)...........	5,500	
Unrealized Holding Loss on Securities Available for Sale (SE)...................................		5,500

Because the first entry involves a debit to the Cash account, Line (9) increases by $47,900. The sale of marketable securities is an Investing activity, so Line (4) increases by $47,900. Because the Realized Gain on Sale of Securities Available for Sale account is an income statement account, Line (1) increases by $5,700. We show all of the cash proceeds of sale ($47,900) on Line (4). We double count cash in the amount of the gain if we do not eliminate $5,700 from the Operations section of the statement of cash flows. Thus, Line (3) increases by $5,700 to offset the realized gain. The net effect of the entries on Line (1) and Line (3) is zero. The second entry does not involve an income statement account or the Cash account and therefore would not appear on the statement of cash flows.

d.   The journal entry is as follows:

Unrealized Holding Loss on Securities Available for Sale (SE).......................................	19,000	
Marketable Securities ($220,500 − $201,500)..		19,000

This entry does not involve a debit or credit to the Cash account, so Line (9) is not affected. This entry also does not affect an income statement account (the Unrealized Holding Loss on Securities Available for Sale account is a shareholders' equity account), so Line (1) is not affected. Thus, this entry does not appear on the statement of cash flows.

e.   The journal entry is as follows:

Marketable Securities.....................................	6,400	
Unrealized Holding Gain on Securities Available for Sale (SE).............................		6,400

For the same reasons given in Part d. above, this entry does not appear on the statement of cash flows.

11.37 continued.

f. The journal entry to record this transaction is:

Cash.. 7,000
   Dividend Revenue................................ 7,000

The Cash account increases, so Line (9) increases by $7,000. Net income increases, so Line (1) increases by $7,000.

g. The journal entry to record this event is:

Unrealized Holding Loss on Investment in
    Securities (SE)............................... 2,000
      Investments in Securities.................. 2,000

The Cash account does not change so there is no effect on Line (9). Net income does not change so there is no effect on Line (1). The firm would disclose this event in a supplementary schedule or note if the amount was material.

h. The journal entry to record this transaction is:

Cash (.40 X $10,000)................................. 4,000
Investment in Affiliate [.40($25,000 – $10,000)]... 6,000
   Equity in Earnings of Affiliate (.40 X $25,000).. 10,000

The Cash account increases in the amount of the dividend, so Line (9) increases $4,000. Net income on Line (1) increases by $10,000 for the equity in earnings. Because the firm recognizes more revenue ($10,000) than the cash received ($4,000), it must increase Line (3) by $6,000 to convert net income to cash flow from operations.

i. The journal entry to record this event is:

Equity in Loss of Affiliate (.40 X $12,500)............ 5,000
   Investment in Affiliate............................. 5,000

There is no effect on the Cash account so Line (9) does not change. Net income decreases for the share of the loss so Line (1) decreases by $5,000. Because the loss does not use cash, Line (2) increases by $5,000 when converting net income to cash flow from operations.

j. The journal entry to record this event is:

Amortization Expense.................................. 2,000
   Investment in Affiliate............................. 2,000

There is no effect on the Cash account so Line (9) does not change. Net income on Line (1) decreases for amortization expense. Because the amortization expense does not reduce cash, Line (2) increases by $2,000 when converting net income to cash flow from operations.

11.38 (Effect of errors involving marketable securities and accounts receivable on financial statement polices.)

		Rate of Return on Assets	CFO/ Average Current Liabilities	Debt Equity Ratio
a. Unrealized Holding Loss on Securities Available for Sale (Shareholders' Equity) .... Marketable securities	X	$\frac{\text{NO}}{\text{O/S}}$ = U/S	$\frac{\text{NO}}{\text{NO}}$ = NO	$\frac{\text{NO}}{\text{O/S}}$ = U/S
b. Bad Debt Expense.............. Allowance for Uncollectible Accounts	X	$\frac{\text{O/S}}{\text{O/S}}$ = O/S	$\frac{\text{NO}}{\text{NO}}$ = NO	$\frac{\text{NO}}{\text{O/S}}$ = U/S
c. Allowance for Uncollectible Accounts............ Accounts Receivable	X	$\frac{\text{NO}}{\text{NO}}$ = NO	$\frac{\text{NO}}{\text{NO}}$ = NO	$\frac{\text{NO}}{\text{NO}}$ = NO
d. Advances from Customers............ Accounts Receivable	X	$\frac{\text{NO}}{\text{O/S}}$ = U/S	$\frac{\text{NO}}{\text{O/S}}$ = U/S	$\frac{\text{O/S}}{\text{O/S}}$ = O/S
e. Interest Receivable............ Interest Revenue	X	$\frac{\text{U/S}}{\text{U/S}}$ = U/S	$\frac{\text{NO}}{\text{NO}}$ = NO	$\frac{\text{NO}}{\text{U/S}}$ = O/S

Note: This problem asks only for the net effect of each error on the three financial ratios. The journal entries and the numerator and denominator effects appear to show the reason for the net effect.

11.39 (Effect of errors on financial statements.)

	Assets	Liabilities	Shareholders' Equity	Net Income
a.	U/S	No	U/S	U/S
b.	O/S	No	O/S	No
c.	O/S	No	O/S	O/S
d.	O/S	No	O/S	O/S
e.	No	No	No	No
f.	O/S	O/S	No	No
g.	No	No or U/S[a]	O/S or No[a]	O/S

[a]Depending on classification on Balance Sheet of minority interest.

11.40 (Dostal Corporation; journal entries and financial statement presentation of marketable equity securities.)

a. **2/05/Year 1**

Marketable Securities (Security A)...................	60,000	
Cash		60,000

8/12/Year 1

Marketable Securities (Security B)..................	25,000	
Cash		25,000

12/31/Year 1

Marketable Securities (Security A) ($66,000 – $60,000)...	6,000	
Unrealized Holding Gain on Security A Available for Sale (SE).........................		6,000

Unrealized Holding Loss on Security B Available for Sale (SE)..	5,000	
Marketable Securities (Security B) ($20,000 – $25,000)		5,000

Note: The two entries on December 31, Year 1 could be combined into a single entry.

1/22/Year 2

Marketable Securities (Security C)	82,000	
Cash		82,000

2/25/Year 2

Marketable Securities (Security D)	42,000	
Cash		42,000

3/25/Year 2

Marketable Securities (Security E)...................	75,000	
Cash		75,000

11.40 a. continued.

6/05/Year 2

Cash..	72,000	
Marketable Securities (Security A)................		60,000
Realized Gain on Sale of Securities Available for Sale (IncSt)................................		12,000
Unrealized Holding Gain on Security A Available for Sale (SE)..	6,000	
Marketable Securities (Security A)............		6,000

6/05/Year 2

Cash..	39,000	
Realized Loss on Sale of Securities Available for Sale (IncSt)..	3,000	
Marketable Securities (Security D)............		42,000

12/31/Year 2

Marketable Securities (Security B) ($23,000 – $20,000)...	3,000	
Unrealized Holding Loss on Security B Available for Sale (SE).........................		3,000

12/31/Year 2

Unrealized Holding Loss on Security C Available for Sale (SE)..	3,000	
Marketable Securities (Security C) ($79,000 – $82,000)...		3,000

12/31/Year 2

Marketable Securities (Security E) ($80,000 – $75,000)...	5,000	
Unrealized Holding Gain on Security E Available for Sale (SE).........................		5,000

Note: The three entries on December 31, Year 2 could be combined into a single entry.

b. **Balance Sheet on December 31, Year 1**

Marketable Securities at Market Value........................	$	86,000
Net Unrealized Holding Gain on Securities Available for Sale ($6,000 – $5,000)	$	1,000

Footnote

Marketable Securities on December 31, Year 1 had an acquisition cost of $85,000 and a market value of $86,000. Gross unrealized gains total $6,000 and gross unrealized losses total $5,000.

11.40 continued.

   c. **Balance Sheet on December 31, Year 2**

Marketable Securities at Market Value......................... $ 182,000

Net Unrealized Holding Loss on Securities Available for
   Sale .... -0-

Footnote

Marketable Securities on December 31, Year 2 had an acquisition cost of $182,000 and a market value of $182,000. Gross unrealized gains total $5,000 and gross unrealized losses total $5,000. Proceeds from sales of marketable securities totaled $111,000 during Year 2. These sales resulted in gross realized gains of $12,000 and gross realized losses of $3,000. The net unrealized holding loss on securities available for sale changed as follows during Year 2:

Balance, December 31, Year 1 .... $ 1,000 Cr.

Unrealized Gain on Securities Sold .... (6,000) Dr.

Change in Net Unrealized Loss on Securities Held at
   Year End ($3,000 − $3,000 + $5,000)....................... <u>5,000</u> Cr.

Balance, December 31, Year 2 .... $ --

11.41   (Rice Corporation; journal entries and financial statement presentation of marketable equity securities.)

   a. **3/05/Year 1**

Marketable Securities (Security A)....................	40,000	
Cash		40,000

5/12/Year 1

Marketable Securities (Security B)....................	80,000	
Cash		80,000

12/31/Year 1

Marketable Securities (Security A) ($45,000 − $40,000)...	5,000	
Unrealized Holding Gain on Security A Available for Sale (SE)..........................		5,000

12/31/Year 1

Unrealized Holding Loss on Security B Available for Sale (SE).......................................	10,000	
Marketable Securities (Security B) ($70,000 − $80,000)		10,000

Note: The two entries on December 31, Year 1 could be combined into a single entry.

11.41 a. continued.

3/22/Year 2

Marketable Securities (Security C)	32,000	
Cash		32,000

5/25/Year 2

Marketable Securities (Security D)	17,000	
Cash		17,000

5/25/Year 2

Marketable Securities (Security E)..................	63,000	
Cash		63,000

10/05/Year 2

Cash...	52,000	
Marketable Securities (Security A)................		40,000
Realized Gain on Sale of Securities Available for Sale (IncSt)................................		12,000
Unrealized Holding Gain on Security A Available for Sale (SE).......................................	5,000	
Marketable Securities (Security A)		5,000

10/05/Year 2

Cash...	15,000	
Realized Loss on Sale of Securities Available for Sale (IncSt)	2,000	
Marketable Securities (Security D).............		17,000

12/31/Year 2

Marketable Securities (Security B) ($83,000 – $70,000)...	13,000	
Unrealized Holding Loss on Security B Available for Sale (SE)..........................		13,000

12/31/Year 2

Unrealized Holding Loss on Security C Available for Sale (SE) ($27,000 – $32,000)...............	5,000	
Marketable Securities (Security C).............		5,000

12/31/Year 2

Marketable Securities (Security E) ($67,000 – $63,000)...	4,000	
Unrealized Holding Gain on Security E Available for Sale (SE)..........................		4,000

Note: The three entries on December 31, Year 2 could be combined into a single entry.

11.41 continued.

    b. **Balance Sheet on December 31, Year 1**
        Marketable Securities at Market Value......................... $ 115,000
        Net Unrealized Holding Loss on Securities Available for
          Sale ($5,000 – $10,000) .... $ (5,000)

        Footnote
        Marketable Securities on December 31, Year 1 had an acquisition cost of $120,000 and a market value of $115,000. Gross unrealized gains total $5,000 and gross unrealized losses total $10,000.

    c. **Balance Sheet on December 31, Year 2**
        Marketable Securities at Market Value......................... $ 177,000
        Net Unrealized Holding Gain on Securities Available for
          Sale .... $ 2,000

        Footnote
        Marketable Securities on December 31, Year 2 had an acquisition cost of $175,000 and a market value of $177,000. Gross unrealized gains total $7,000 (= $3,000 + $4,000) and gross unrealized losses total $5,000. Proceeds from sales of marketable securities totaled $67,000 during Year 2. These sales resulted in gross realized gains of $12,000 and gross realized losses of $2,000. The net unrealized holding loss on securities available for sale changed as follows during Year 2:

        Balance, December 31, Year 1 .... $ (5,000) Dr.
        Unrealized Gain on Securities Sold .... (5,000) Dr.
        Change in Net Unrealized Loss on Securities Held at
          Year End ($13,000 – $5,000 + $4,000)...................... <u>12,000</u> Cr.
        Balance, December 31, Year 2 .... <u>$ 2,000</u> Cr.

11.42   (Zeff Corporation; reconstructing transactions involving marketable securities.)

Cash		Marketable Securities	
√ 14,000		√ 187,000	
			10,000 (1)
		(2) 1,000	3,000 (1)
	20,000 (3)	(3) 20,000	
		√ 195,000	

11.42 continued.

Net Unrealized Holding Gain on Securities Available for Sale			Realized Gain on Sale of Securities Available for Sale	
	12,000 √			
(1) 3,000				4,000 (1)
	1,000 (2)			
	10,000 √			4,000 √

(1) Sale of marketable securities during Year 2.
(2) Revaluation of marketable securities on December 31, Year 2.
(3) Purchase of marketable securities during Year 2.

11.43   (Sunshine Mining Company; analysis of financial statement disclosures for marketable equity securities.) (Amounts in Thousands)

a. $10,267 loss = $11,418 − $21,685.

b. $2,649 gain = $8,807 − $6,158.

c. $12,459 gain = $21,685 − $6,158 − $3,068.

d.   None. The unrealized holding loss on current marketable securities of $2,466 (= $4,601 − $7,067) and the unrealized holding gain on noncurrent marketable securities of $2,649 (= $8,807 − $6,158) appear in the shareholders' equity section of the balance sheet.

11.44   (Callahan Corporation; effect of various methods of accounting for marketable equity securities.)

a.   **Trading Securities**

	Year 1	Year 2
Income Statement:		
Dividend Revenue...................................	$ 3,300	$ 2,200
Unrealized Holding Gain (Loss):		
($54,000 − $55,000).............................	(1,000)	--
($15,000 − $14,000).............................	--	1,000
Realized Holding Gain (Loss) ($14,500 + $26,000) − ($16,000 + $24,000).................	--	500
Total...	$ 2,300	$ 3,700
Balance Sheet:		
Current Assets:		
Marketable Securities at Market Value...	$ 54,000	$ 15,000

11.44 continued.

b. **Securities Available for Sale (Current Asset)**

	Year 1	Year 2
Income Statement:		
Dividend Revenue..	$ 3,300	$ 2,200
Realized Holding Gain (Loss): [$40,500 –		
($18,000 + $25,000)]................................	--	(2,500)
Total...	$ 3,300	$ (300)
Balance Sheet:		
Current Assets:		
Marketable Securities at Market Value...	$ 54,000	$ 15,000
Shareholders' Equity:		
Net Unrealized Holding Gain (Loss) on Securities Available for Sale:		
($54,000 – $55,000)..............................	(1,000)	--
($15,000 – $12,000)..............................	--	3,000

c. Same as Part *b.* except that the securities appear in the noncurrent assets section of the balance sheet.

d.

	Trading Securities	Securities Available for Sale Current Assets	Noncurrent Assets
Year 1...........................	$2,300	$3,300	$3,300
Year 2...........................	3,700	(300)	(300)
Total....................	$6,000	$3,000	$3,000

The unrealized gain on Security I of $3,000 (= $15,000 – $12,000) at the end of Year 2 appears in income if these securities are trading securities but in a separate shareholders' equity account if these securities are securities available for sale (either a current asset or a noncurrent asset). Total shareholders' equity is the same. Retained earnings (pretax) are $3,000 larger if these securities are trading securities and the unrealized holding gain account is $3,000 larger if these securities are classified as securities available for sale.

11.45 (Citibank; analysis of financial statement disclosures related to marketable securities.) (Amounts in Millions)

a.

Cash...	37,600	
Realized Loss on Sale of Securities Available for Sale...	113	
Realized Gain on Securities Available for Sale..		443
Marketable Securities.............................		37,270[a]

[a]$14,075 + $37,163 – $13,968 = $37,270.

11.45 a. continued.

Marketable Securities......................................	262		
Unrealized Holding Loss on Securities			
Available for Sale ($37,270 – $37,008).........		262	

b.
Balance, December 31, Year 10	$	447 Cr.
Net Unrealized Holding Loss on Securities Sold (from		
Part *a*.)..		262 Cr.
Increase in Net Unrealized Holding Gain on Secur-		
ities Held on December 31, Year 11 (Plug)		518 Cr.
Balance, December 31, Year 11	$	1,227 Cr.

c.
Interest and Dividend Revenue	$	1,081
Net Realized Gain on Securities Sold from Market		
Price Changes Occurring During Year 11:		
($37,600 – $37,008)..		592
Net Unrealized Holding Gain on Securities Held on		
December 31, Year 11 (from Part *b*.)		518
Total Income	$	2,191

d. Citibank sold marketable securities during Year 11 which had net unrealized holding losses of $262 million as of December 31, Year 10. The sale of these securities at a gain suggests that market prices increased substantially ($592 million) during Year 11. The substantial increase in the net unrealized holding gain of $518 lends support to this conclusion about market price increases. Citibank could have increased its income still further by selecting securities for sale that had unrealized holding *gains* as of December 31, Year 10. If prices continued to increase on such securities during Year 11 prior to sale, the realized gain would have been even larger than the reported realized gain of $330 million (= $443 – $113).

11.46 (Using contra and adjunct accounts for securities available for sale.)

a. One does not have to keep track of the individual holding gains and losses on each separate security. Rather, at the end of the period, one computes the market value of the securities on hand, their acquisition cost and subtracts the second from the first. If the number is positive, then that number represents a cumulative holding gain and will be the required debit balance in both the asset contra/adjunct account and in the owners' equity contra/adjunct account. (If the difference is negative, then the absolute value of the number will be the required credit balance in those accounts.) The adjusting entry then merely adjusts the existing balance in the account to the required balance. The student need keep track only of the original cost of the securities held as available for sale.

11.46 continued.

    b.   **End of Year 1**

Current Asset Contra/Adjunct.........................	200	
Owners' Equity Contra/Adjunct (Unrealized Gains on Holdings of Securities Available for Sale)..		200

        End of Year 2

Cash..	120	
Owners' Equity Contra/Adjunct (Unrealized Gains on Holdings of Securities Available for Sale)..	350	
Marketable Securities..............................		100
Realized Gain on Sale of Securities Available for Sale.......................................		20
Marketable Securities Contra/Adjunct.......		350

11.47   (Rockwell Corporation; journal entries and consolidation work sheet entries for various methods of accounting for intercorporate investments.)

    a.

Investment in Stock of Company R..................	648,000	
Cash		648,000
To record acquisitions of shares of Company R.		

Cash and Dividends Receivable.......................	48,000	
Dividend Revenue.....................................		48,000
To record dividends received or receivable.		

Unrealized Holding Loss on Investment in Securities (SE)	24,000	
Investment in Stock of Company R............		24,000
To write down investment in stock of Company R account to market value; $24,000 = $648,000 − $624,000.		

    b.

Investment in Stock of Company S	2,040,000	
Cash		2,040,000
To record acquisitions of shares of Company S.		

Investment in Stock of Company S	360,000	
Equity in Earnings of Company S..................		360,000
To accrue share of Company S's earnings; $360,000 = .30 × $1,200,000.		

Cash and Dividends Receivable.......................	144,000	
Investment in Stock of Company S		144,000
To record dividends received or receivable.		

11.47 b. continued.

Amortization Expense	24,000	
Investment in Stock of Company S		24,000

To record amortization of goodwill implicit in purchase price; $24,000 = (\$2,040,000 - \$1,800,000)/10$.

c.

Investment in Stock of Company T	6,000,000	
Cash		6,000,000

To record acquisitions of shares of Company T.

Investment in Stock of Company T	1,200,000	
Equity in Earnings of Company T		1,200,000

To accrue earnings of Company T; $1,200,000 = 100\% \times \$1,200,000$.

Cash and Dividends Receivable	480,000	
Investment in Stock of Company T		480,000

To record dividends received or receivable.

d.

Common Stock	2,400,000	
Retained Earnings ($3,600,000 - \$480,000)	3,120,000	
Equity in Earnings of Company T	1,200,000	
Investment in Stock of Company T		6,720,000

To eliminate investment account on consolidation work sheet.

e.

Common Stock	2,400,000	
Retained Earnings	4,320,000	
Investment in Stock of Company T		6,720,000

To eliminate investment account on consolidation work sheet.

f.

Investment in Stock of Company T	6,600,000	
Cash		6,600,000

To record acquisitions of shares of Company T.

Investment in Stock of Company T	1,200,000	
Equity in Earnings of Company T		1,200,000

To accrue earnings of Company T.

Cash and Dividends Receivable	480,000	
Investment in Stock of Company T		480,000

To record dividends received or receivable.

Amortization Expense	60,000	
Investment in Stock of Company T		60,000

To record amortization of goodwill implicit in purchase price; $60,000 = (\$6,600,000 - \$6,000,000)/10$.

11.47 continued.

g. Common Stock.. 2,400,000
   Retained Earnings ($3,600,000 – $480,000) 3,120,000
   Equity in Earnings of Company T..................... 1,200,000
   Goodwill   540,000
      Investment in Stock of Company T...............   7,260,000
   To eliminate investment account on consolida-
   tion work sheet; $7,260,000 = $6,600,000 +
   $1,200,000 – $480,000 – $60,000.

11.48   (Peak Company and Valley Company; preparing a consolidation work
         sheet.)

   a. See next page.

   b. Common Stock (Valley)...................................   5
      Retained Earnings (Valley)...........................   41
      Equity in Earnings of Valley Company (Peak)....   10
      Goodwill (= $20,000 – 1/10 X $20,000)   18
         Investment in Stock of Valley Company
         (Peak)...   74

      Initial Goodwill was $20,000 = $70,000 – $50,000.

11.48 continued.

a.

PEAK COMPANY AND VALLEY COMPANY
Consolidation Work Sheet
(Amounts in Thousands)

	Peak Company Debit	Peak Company Credit	Valley Company Debit	Valley Company Credit	Adjustments and Eliminations Debit	Adjustments and Eliminations Credit	Consolidated Debit	Consolidated Credit
Cash......................	$ 13		$ 6				$ 19	
Accounts Receivable	42		20			$ 8 (2)	54	
Investment in Stock of Valley Company............	56		--			56 (1)	--	
Other Assets...............	143		85				228	
Cost of Goods Sold..........	320		90				410	
Selling and Administrative Expenses..............	44		20				64	
Income Tax Expense........	12		5				17	
Accounts Payable..........		$ 80		$ 25	(2) $ 8			$ 97
Bonds Payable..............		50		30				80
Common Stock..............		10		5	(1) 5			10
Retained Earnings..........		80		41	(1) 41			80
Sales Revenue..............		400		125				525
Equity in Earnings..........		10		--	(1) 10			--
Totals.................	$ 630	$ 630	$ 226	$ 226	$64	$64	$ 792	$ 792

(1) To eliminate the investment account.
(2) To eliminate intercompany receivables and payables.

11.49 (Company P and Company S; preparing a consolidation work sheet.)

a.

COMPANY P AND COMPANY S
Consolidation Work Sheet
(Amounts in Thousands)

	Company P Debit	Company P Credit	Company S Debit	Company S Credit	Adjustments and Eliminations Debit	Adjustments and Eliminations Credit	Consolidated Debit	Consolidated Credit
Receivables	$ 60		$ 40			$ 12 (3)	$ 88	
Investment in Stock of Company S	272		--			272 (1)	--	
Other Assets	496		352				848	
Cost of Goods Sold	1,160		496			40 (2)	1,616	
Other Expenses	280		112				392	
Accounts Payable		$ 72		$ 48	(3) $ 12			$ 108
Other Liabilities		88		72				160
Common Stock		160		80	(1) 80			160
Retained Earnings		316		160	(1) 160			316
Sales Revenue		1,600		640	(2) 40			2,200
Equity in Earnings of Company S		32		--	(1) 32			--
Totals	$2,268	$2,268	$1,000	$1,000	$ 324	$ 324	$2,944	$2,944

(1) Eliminate investment account.
(2) Eliminate intercompany sales.
(3) Eliminate intercompany receivables and payables.

11.49 continued.

b.

COMPANY P AND COMPANY S
Consolidated Statement of Income
and Retained Earnings
For Year 2

Sales Revenue	$2,200,000
Expenses:	
Cost of Goods Sold	$1,616,000
Other Expenses	392,000
Total	$2,008,000
Net Income	$ 192,000
Less Dividends Declared	(40,000)
Increase in Retained Earnings for Year 2	$ 152,000
Retained Earnings, December 31, Year 1	356,000[a]
Retained Earnings, December 31, Year 2	$ 508,000

[a]$316,000 retained earnings on December 31, Year 2 + $40,000 dividend declared during year 2.

COMPANY P AND COMPANY S
Consolidated Balance Sheet
December 31, Year 2

Assets

Receivables	$ 88,000
Other Assets	848,000
Total	$ 936,000

Equities

Accounts Payable	$ 108,000
Other Liabilities	160,000
Common Stock	160,000
Retained Earnings	508,000
Total	$ 936,000

11.50 (Ely Company and Sims Company; preparing a consolidation work sheet.)

ELY COMPANY AND SIMS COMPANY
Consolidation Work Sheet
(Amounts in Thousands)

	Ely Company Debit	Ely Company Credit	Sims Company Debit	Sims Company Credit	Adjustments and Eliminations Debit	Adjustments and Eliminations Credit	Consolidated Debit	Consolidated Credit
Cash..........	$ 12,000		$ 5,000				$ 17,000	
Accounts Receivable......	25,000		15,000			$ 7,500 (2)	32,500	
Investment in Sims Company Stock..........	78,000		--			78,000 (1)	--	
Other Assets..........	85,000		80,000				165,000	
Goodwill..........	--		--		$18,000 (1)		18,000	
Current Liabilities..........		$ 45,000		$ 40,000	7,500 (2)			$ 77,500
Common Stock..........		50,000		10,000	10,000 (1)			50,000
Retained Earnings..........		105,000		50,000	50,000 (1)			105,000
Totals..........	$200,000	$200,000	$100,000	$100,000	$85,500	$85,500	$232,500	$232,500

(1) Eliminate investment account.
(2) Eliminate intercompany obligations.

11.51 (Company S and Company J; preparing a consolidation work sheet subsequent to year of acquisition.)

COMPANY S AND COMPANY J
Consolidation Work Sheet
December 31, Year 2
(Amounts in Thousands)

	Company S Debit	Company S Credit	Company J Debit	Company J Credit		Adjustments and Eliminations Debit	Adjustments and Eliminations Credit		Consolidated Debit	Consolidated Credit
Cash..............	$ 36.00		$ 26.00						$ 62.00	
Accounts and Notes Receivable........	180.00		50.00						213.60	
Inventories.........	440.00		250.00				$ 16.40 (2)		690.00	
Investment in Stock of Company J........	726.00		--				726.00 (1)		--	
Plant Assets........	600.00		424.00						1,024.00	
Accounts and Notes Payable.........		$ 110.00		$ 59.00	(2)	$ 16.40				$ 152.60
Other Liabilities......		286.00		22.00						308.00
Common Stock.........		1,200.00		500.00	(1)	500.00				1,200.00
Capital Contributed in Excess of Stated Value....		--		100.00	(1)	100.00				
Retained Earnings........		386.00		69.00	(1)	69.00				386.00
Goodwill..........					(1)	57.00			57.00	
Totals...........	$1,982.00	$1,982.00	$ 750.00	$ 750.00		$ 742.40	$ 742.40		$2,046.60	$2,046.60

(1) Eliminate investment account; all amounts given except plug for Goodwill.
(2) Eliminate intercompany obligations.

11.52 (Hatfield Corporation and McCoy Corporation; effect of purchase and pooling-of-interests methods on financial statements.)

a. HATFIELD CORPORATION AND McCOY CORPORATION
Consolidated Balance Sheet
January 1, Year 8

	(1) Purchase Method	(2) Pooling-of-Interests Method
Assets at Historical Cost	$ 3,500	$3,500
Asset Revaluation	400	--
Goodwill	200	--
Total Assets	$ 4,100	$3,500
Liabilities	$ 1,500	$1,500
Common Stock ($1 Par)	150[a]	150[a]
Additional Paid-in Capital	1,750[b]	750[c]
Retained Earnings	700	1,100[d]
Total Equities	$ 4,100	$3,500

[a]$100,000 + (50,000 × $1) = $150,000.
[b]$400,000 + (50,000 × $27) = $1,750,000.
[c]$400,000 + ($100,000 + $300,000 − $50,000) = $750,000.
[d]$700,000 + $400,000 = $1,100,000.

b. HATFIELD CORPORATION AND McCOY CORPORATION
Consolidated Income Statement
First Year After Merger

	(1) Purchase Method	(2) Pooling-of-Interests Method
Sales	$14,000	$14,000
Other Revenues	125	125
Total Revenues	$14,125	$14,125
Expenses Except Income Taxes	(11,125)	(11,125)
Taxable Income	$ 3,000	$ 3,000
Tax Expense at 40%	(1,200)	(1,200)
Amortization of Increased Asset Costs	(80)[a]	--
Amortization of Goodwill	(20)[b]	--
Net Income	$ 1,700	$ 1,800
Earnings per Share	$11.33[c]	$12.00[c]

[a]$400,000/5 = $80,000.
[b]$200,000/10 = $20,000.
[c]Based on 150,000 shares.

11.53   (Coke and Pepsi; effect of intercorporate investment policies on financial statements.)

   a.   Coke as Reported: [$1,364 + (1 − .34)($231)]/$9,280 = 16.3%.
        Coke's Bottlers: [$290 + (1 − .34)($452)]/$11,110 = 5.3%.
        Coke and Bottlers
           Consolidated: [$1,364 + (1 − .34)($231 + $452) + .51($290)]/$18,675
                                = 10.5%.

        Pepsi as Reported: [$1,091 + (1 − .34)($689)/$15,637 = 9.9%.

   b.   Coke as Reported: ($4,296 + $1,133)/$9,280 = 58.5%.
        Coke's Bottlers: ($2,752 + $4,858)/$11,110 = 68.5%.
        Coke and Bottlers
           Consolidated: ($7,048 + $5,991)/$18,675 = 69.8%.

        Pepsi as Reported: ($3,264 + $7,469)/$15,637 = 68.6%.

   c.   The rate of return on assets using reported amounts suggests that Coke is considerably more profitable than Pepsi. This measure of the rate of return on assets includes Coke's 49 percent interest in the earnings of its bottlers but does not include Coke's 49 percent interest in the assets of these bottlers. Coke's rate of return on assets with its bottlers consolidated includes 100 percent of the net income and assets of these bottlers. Thus, Coke appears only slightly more profitable than Pepsi during Year 8.

        Coke's liabilities to assets ratio is less than the corresponding ratio for its bottlers. On a comparable measurement basis with Pepsi, Coke has slightly more debt in its capital structure instead of approximately 14.7 percent less debt as indicated by the reported amounts [14.7% = (68.6% − 58.5%)/68.6%].

   d.   Coke's intercorporate investment policy permits it to report higher profitability and lower debt ratios than if it held a sufficient ownership percentage to consolidate its bottlers. Coke's 49 percent ownership probably permits it to exert control over its bottlers because (1) the remaining 51 percent is widely-held by many individuals and institutions, and (2) Coke maintains exclusive contracts with its bottlers that tie their success to Coke's success. Thus, one might argue that consolidation reflects the economic reality of the relationship better than use of the equity method.

11.54　(Agee Electronics; preparing statement of cash flows.)　A T-account work sheet appears on the page following the statement of cash flows.

AGEE ELECTRONICS
Statement of Cash Flows
For Year 5

Operations:	
Net Income	$ 320
Depreciation Expense	350
Bad Debt Expense	45
Loss on Sale of Investments in Securities	40
Gain on Sale of Marketable Securities	(30)
Gain on Sale of Equipment	(40)
Decrease in Inventories	50
Increase in Other Current Liabilities	110
Increase in Accounts Receivable	(235)
Increase in Prepayments	(50)
Decrease in Accounts Payable	(30)
Cash Flow from Operations	$ 530
Investing:	
Sale of Marketable Securities	$ 145
Sale of Investments in Securities	70
Sale of Equipment	80
Acquisition of Marketable Securities	(125)
Acquisition of Property, Plant and Equipment	(480)
Cash Flow from Investing	$ (310)
Financing:	
Income in Bank Borrowing	$ 60
Issue of Common Stock	60
Payment of Dividends	(285)
Cash Flow from Financing	$ (165)
Change in Cash	$ 55
Cash, December 31, Year 4	130
Cash, December 31, Year 5	$ 185

11.54 continued.

Cash

√	130		

Operations

Net Income	(1)	320	30	(4)	Gain on Sale of Marketable Securities
Bad Debt Expense	(7)	45			
Loss on Investment in Securities	(8)	40	40	(11)	Gain on Sale of Equipment
Decrease in Inventories	(15)	50	235	(14)	Increase in Accounts Receivable
Depreciation	(19)	350			
Increase of Current Liabilities	(22)	110	50	(16)	Increase in Prepayments
			30	(20)	Decrease in Accounts Payable

Investing

Sale of Marketable Securities	(4)	145	125	(13)	Purchase of Marketable Securities
Sale of Investments	(8)	70			
Sale of Equipment	(11)	80	480	(18)	Purchase of PP&E

Financing

Bank Loan	(21)	60	285	(3)	Dividend Paid
Issue Common Stock	(23)	60			
√		185			

Marketable Securities				Accounts Receivable				Allowance for Uncollectible Accounts			
√	270			√	770					40	√
		115	(4)			35	(6)	(6)	35	45	(7)
(12)	15	5	(5)	(14)	235						
(13)	125										
√	290			√	970					50	√

11.54 continued.

Inventories			Prepayments			Investments in Securities		
√	620		√	120		√	460	
		50 (15)	(16)	50		(9)	40	110 (8)
								10 (17)
√	570		√	170		√	380	

Property, Plant and Equipment			Accumulated Depreciation			Accounts Payable		
√	2,840				1,210	√		490	√
(10)	140	150 (11)	(11)	110				
(18)	480				350 (19)	(20)	30	
√	3,310				1,450	√		460	√

Bank Loans Payable			Dividends Payable			Other Current Liabilities		
		820	√			60	√		90	√
		60 (21)	(3)	285	305 (2)			110 (22)
		880	√			80	√		200	√

Long-Term Debt			Common Stock			Additional Paid-In Capital		
		510	√			100	√		460	√
		140 (10)			50 (23)			10 (23)
		650	√			150	√		470	√

Unrealized Holding Gain—Marketable Securities			Unrealized Holding Loss—Investment in Securities			Retained Earnings		
		40	√	√	120				1,510	√
(5)	5					40 (9)	(2)	305	320 (1)
		15 (12)	(17)	10				
		50	√	√	90				1,525	√

11.55　(Cherry Corporation; preparing a statement of cash flows.)

a.

	Cash			
√	287,000			

Operations

(1)	496,000	144,000	(4)	
(2)	5,000	7,000	(6)	
(5)	9,000	100,000	(15)	
(7)	1,200	162,000	(16)	
(10)	3,000	17,000	(20)	
(14)	4,000			
(17)	66,600			
(19)	100,000			

Investing

(6)	46,000	72,000	(3)	
(7)	3,200	81,000	(8)	
		15,000	(9)	
		10,000	(18)	

Financing

(21)	54,000	17,000	(13)	
√	450,000			

Accounts Receivable—Net				
√	550,000			
(15)	100,000	5,000	(2)	
√	645,000			

Inventories			
√	298,000		
(16)	162,000		
√	460,000		

Investments—Roy Co.				
√	39,000			
		39,000	(6)	
√	0			

Investments—Zuber Co.				
√	0			
(3)	111,300			
(4)	144,000	9,000	(5)	
√	246,300			

Plant Assets				
√	381,000			
(8)	81,000	22,000	(7)	
(9)	15,000			
√	455,000			

Accumulated Depreciation				
		144,000	√	
(7)	17,600	66,600	(17)	
		193,000	√	

11.55 a. continued.

	Patents (Net)		
√	19,000		
(18)	10,000	3,000	(10)
√	26,000		

		Dividends Payable	
		0	√
		181,000	(12)
		181,000	√

	Accounts Payable		
		70,000	√
		100,000	(19)
		170,000	√

		Accrued Liabilities	
		41,800	√
(20)	17,000		
		24,800	√

	Long-Term Bonds Payable		
		133,000	√
(13)	17,000	4,000	(14)
		54,000	(21)
		174,000	√

		Common Stock	
		700,000	√
		24,000	(3)
		28,000	(11)
		752,000	√

	Additional Paid-in Capital—Common		
		9,600	√
		4,800	(3)
		5,600	(11)
		20,000	√

		Preferred Stock	
		53,000	√
		7,000	(3)
		60,000	√

	Additional Paid-in Capital—Preferred		
		2,500	√
		3,500	(3)
		6,000	√

		Retained Earnings	
		420,100	√
(11)	33,600	496,000	(1)
(12)	181,000		
		701,500	√

11.55 a. continued.

Explanation of entries in work sheet (not required):

(1) Net income of $496,000.
(2) Bad debt expense of $5,000.
(3) Issue of preferred shares totaling $10,500 (= 3,500 × $3), issue of common shares totaling $28,800 (= 2,400 × $12), and expenditure of $72,000 cash in the acquisition of 45 percent of Zuber, $111,300 = $10,500 + $28,800 + $72,000.
(4) Share of earnings of Zuber; $144,000 (= .45 × $320,000).
(5) Reduce investment for dividends declared by Zuber; $9,000 (= .45 × $20,000).
(6) Gain on sale of Roy; $7,000 (= $46,000 − $39,000).
(7) Loss on sale of plant; $1,200 (= $22,000 − $17,600 − $3,200).
(8) Acquire new plant for $81,000.
(9) Acquire new plant (major improvements) for $15,000; plug in Plant Assets account.
(10) Amortization of patents; $3,000.
(11) Stock dividend; .04 × 70,000 × $12 = $33,600.
(12) Dividends declared; $181,000 (= $145,000 + $36,000).
(13) Retire bonds at book value.
(14) Amortization of bond discount of $4,000 does not use cash.
(15) Plug for net increase in receivables.
(16) Plug for net increase in inventories.
(17) Plug for net increase in accumulated depreciation; an addback for expense not using cash.
(18) Acquire new patents (net) for $10,000; plug in Patents (Net) account.
(19) Plug for net increase in accounts payable.
(20) Plug for net decrease in accrued liabilities.
(21) Plug for issue of new bonds.

11.55 continued.

b.   CHERRY CORPORATION
                         Statement of Cash Flows
                             For Year 6

Operations:
    Net Income .... $ 496,000
    Additions:
        Bad Debt Expense   5,000
        Loss on Sale of Plant Asset................   1,200
        Amortization of Patent.....................   3,000
        Amortization of Discount..................   4,000
        Depreciation Expense......................   66,600
        Increase in Accounts Payable...........   100,000
    Subtractions:
        Equity in Undistributed Earnings......   (135,000)
        Gain on Sale of Investment...............   (7,000)
        Increase in Accounts Receivable.......   (100,000)
        Increase in Inventories...................   (162,000)
        Decrease in Accrued Liabilities.........   (17,000)
Cash Flow from Operations..................... $ 254,800
Investing:
    Sale of Investment in Roy Company ...... $ 46,000
    Sale of Plant Asset............................   3,200
    Acquisition of Investment in Zuber
        Company.......................................   (72,000)
    Acquisition of Plant Assets...................   (81,000)
    Major Repairs to Plant Assets ....   (15,000)
    Acquisition of Patent ....   (10,000)
Cash Flow from Investing......................   (128,800)
Financing:
    Issue of Bonds .... $ 54,000
    Redemption of Bonds ....   (17,000)
Cash Flow from Financing......................   37,000
Net Change in Cash .... $ 163,000
Cash, January 1, Year 6   287,000
Cash, December 31, Year 6.................... $ 450,000

Supplementary Information
During Year 6 Cheery Corporation acquired 45 percent of the
common stock of Zuber Company for $111,300, comprising $72,000
cash, $10,500 of preferred stock, and $28,800 of common stock.

11.56 (Interaction of regulation and accounting rules for financial institutions, particularly banks.)

Effects of Changing Market Value of Assets on a Bank's Activities
Bank Has Capital Ratio of 5 Percent

Step [1]: Market Value of Assets Increases, Also Increasing Owners' Equity
Step [2]: Bank Increases Lending to Maintain Capital (Leverage) Ratio at 5 Percent
Step [3]: Market Value of Original Bank Decreases, Decreasing Owners' Equity
Step [4]: Bank Decreases Lending to Maintain Capital (Leverage) Ratio at 5 Percent
Operating Income Excludes Gains and Losses in Market Value of Assets Held

Balance Sheet — *Original Bank, before Market Value Changes*

Assets			Equities			Partial Income Statement			Rate of Return On:	
				Liabilities:		Revenues as % of Assets				
	$1,000	Original		Borrowings	$950	7.0%	$70.0			
						Interest Expense				
						5.5%	(52.3)			
				Owners' Equity		Operating Expense % of Assets				
				Contributed Capital	50	0.4%	(4.0)			
				Retained Earnings	0					
				Total Owners' Equity ...	$50	Fixed costs	(1.0)		Assets	1.3%
									Owners'	
	$1,000		Totals		$1,000	Operating Income .	$12.8		Equity ...	25.5%

Market Value of Assets Increases 4.0%

Assets			Equities			Partial Income Statement			Rate of Return On:	
				Liabilities:		Revenues as % of Assets				
	$1,000	Original		Original Borrowings	$950	7.0%	$140.0			
						Interest Expense				
[1]	40	Market Value Increase				5.5%	(105.1)			
[2]	960	New Lending	[2]	New Borrowing	960	Operating Expense % of Assets				
				Owners' Equity:		0.4%	(8.0)			
				Contributed Capital	50	Fixed costs	(1.0)			
			[1]	Retained Earnings	40					
				Total Owners' Equity ...	$90				Assets	1.3%
									Owners'	
	$2,000		Totals		$2,000	Operating Income .	$26.0		Equity ...	28.8%

Market Value of Assets Decreases -4.0%

Assets			Equities			Partial Income Statement			Rate of Return On:	
				Liabilities:		Revenues as % of Assets				
	$1,000	Original		Original Borrowings	$950	7.0%	$14.0			
						Interest Expense				
[3]	(40)	Market Value Decline				5.5%	(10.5)			
[4]	(760)	Reduce Lending	[4]	Reduce Borrowing	(760)	Operating Expense % of Assets				
				Owners' Equity:		0.4%	(0.8)			
				Contributed Capital	50	Fixed costs	(1.0)			
			[3]	Retained Earnings	(40)					
				Total Owners' Equity ...	$10				Assets	2.4%
									Owners'	
	$200		Totals		$200	Operating Income .	$4.8		Equity ...	48.0%

CHAPTER 12

REPORTING EARNINGS, COMPREHENSIVE INCOME, AND SHAREHOLDERS' EQUITY

Questions, Exercises, Problems, and Cases: Answers and Solutions

12.1 See the text or the glossary at the end of the book.

12.2 The FASB suggests that the distinction between performance-related (subject to significant influence by management) and non-performance-related (subject to external influences not controllable by management) items drives the exclusion. The real reason, however, we suspect, has to do with the volatility of some of the items of other comprehensive income. Including all holding gains and losses on securities held in earnings will cause reported earnings to fluctuate (in response to fluctuations in market prices) more than it would otherwise. Many, probably most, managers prefer to report stable earnings in contrast to fluctuating earnings. All else equal, the less risky the earnings stream—that is, the less volatile are reported earnings—the higher will be the market price of the firm's shares.

12.3 The common shareholder would not likely receive an amount equal to the amounts in the common shareholders' equity accounts. The amounts in these accounts reflect acquisition cost valuations for assets. The firm might sell assets for more or less than their book values, with the common shareholders thereby receiving more or less than the amount in the common shareholders' equity accounts. Furthermore, the bankruptcy and liquidation process requires legal and other costs not now reflected on the balance sheet. The asset sales must generate sufficient cash to pay these costs before the common shareholders receive any residual cash.

12.4 Ordinarily, the shareholders of a corporation have no personal responsibility for the debts of the corporation. By endorsing the note, the president of the corporation becomes personally liable in case the corporation defaults. If the firm was a partnership, the president as a general partner would be personally liable for this debt in any case, as well as other liabilities of the partnership. The personal endorsement may, however, provide a higher priority claim against personal assets.

12.5 Firms have issued securities in recent years (for example, convertible bonds and redeemable preferred stock) that have both debt and equity characteristics. A clear distinction between liabilities and shareholders'

12.5 continued.

> equity no longer exists. Firms might list various claims against a firm's assets in decreasing order of priority in the case of bankruptcy with no distinction between liabilities and shareholders' equity. Alternatively, firms might create a third category that includes securities with both debt and equity characteristics and include it between liabilities and shareholders' equity on the balance sheet.

12.6 There is no reason to expect a newly organized firm to issue common shares at a price more than par value except to take advantage of some state laws which permit the distribution of Additional Paid-in Capital. The firm may issue additional shares of an old issue at more than par value in order to effect adjustments between old and new shareholders. If the company has been successful, new shareholders may have to contribute more than the amount contributed (par) by the original shareholders who invested when the business had not yet established its profitability.

12.7 The par value of preferred, rather than the amount contributed, serves as a basis for measuring the dividend rate and the amount of preference as to assets in event of liquidation. The par value of common stock may have legal significance in certain states, but it has no economic significance. Firms declare dividends based on the number of common shares outstanding, not on the par value of the common stock.

12.8 The three provisions provide different benefits and risks to the issuing firm and the investor and should sell at different prices. Callable preferred stock should sell for less than convertible preferred stock. The issuing firm gains benefits with an option to call, or repurchase, the preferred stock and must thereby accept a lower issue price. The investor gains benefits with an option to convert into capital stock and must pay a higher price. The mandatory redemption requirement makes the preferred stock more like debt than shareholders' equity. Its market price depends on market interest rates for similar maturity debt (versus the 4 percent yield on the preferred stock) and the rank-ordering priority of the preferred stock in bankruptcy.

12.9 The question addresses the tradeoff between relevance and reliability frequently encountered in accounting. Financial statement users desire information that helps them assess the economic value of firms. Information about the value of options is relevant information for this purpose. The measurement of the value of options is subject to varying degrees of subjectivity. Reliability decreases as subjectivity increases. Likewise, the usefulness of relevant information decreases as reliability decreases.

12.10 All three items permit their holder to acquire shares of common stock at a set price. Their values depend on the difference between the market price and the exercise price on the exercise date and the length of the exercise period. Firms grant stock options to employees, grant stock rights to current shareholders and either sell stock warrants on the open market or attach them to a debt or preferred stock issue. The issuance of stock options and stock rights does not result in an immediate cash inflow, whereas the issuance of a stock warrant usually does. Accountants credit a Stock Warrant account if the value of the stock warrant is objectively measurable. At the time of exercise of all these items, the accountant records the cash proceeds as a capital contribution.

12.11 The managers of a firm have knowledge of the plans and risks of the firm that external investors may not possess. Although laws prevent firms from taking advantage of this "inside information," inclusion of gains from treasury stock transactions in net income might motivate firms to buy and sell treasury stock to improve reported earnings. Excluding these gains from net income removes this incentive. Also, the accounting for the acquisition of treasury stock (that is, a reduction from total shareholders' equity) has the same effect on shareholders' equity as a retirement of the capital stock. The reissue of the treasury stock for more than its acquisition cost does not result in a gain any more than the issue of common stock for more than par value represents a gain.

12.12 Most firms acquire treasury stock with the intention of reissuing the stock upon the exercise of stock options or warrants or the conversion of debt or preferred stock into common stock. Thus, treasury stock typically does not remain as treasury stock for an extended period. The fallacy in this explanation is that firms destroy the stock certificates underlying shares purchased as treasury stock, the same as for retired stock, and issue new stock certificates to purchasers of the treasury stock, the same as for newly issued stock.

12.13 The president is right, but the shareholders may prefer that the firm pay a cash dividend rather than force the shareholders to sell off some shares to raise funds. The president's point is that they do not lose out in any fundamental sense by not receiving dividends, since their equity in the firm increases (absolutely, not proportionately) as a result and, presumably, the market price of the shares increases. Furthermore, shareholders save a set of personal income taxes. The statement is somewhat self-serving, but this process does simplify raising additional capital.

12.14 Yes. Earnings do not necessarily indicate the availability of idle cash funds for distribution. The corporation may have insufficient cash to meet maturing obligations, additional working capital requirements in connection with increasing accounts receivable and inventory replacement, replacements of equipment, or other such expenditures.

12.15   As the Retained Earnings account has grown, so has the firm's net assets. The firm has likely invested these assets in plant, not in cash and temporary marketable securities. The firm is unlikely to have cash in the amount of the increase in retained earnings available for paying dividends. If the firm had regularly declared stock dividends (to capitalize into the contributed capital accounts amounts permanently invested in plant assets), then the balance in the Retained Earnings account might better indicate the ability to pay cash dividends. But then, of course, the Retained Earnings account would have a smaller balance.

12.16   In the case of a cash dividend, the shareholder now holds the investment in two parts—cash and stock certificates. The sum of the cash and the book value of the stock after the dividend declaration equals the book value of the stock before the firm declared the dividend. It is common to speak of a cash dividend as income, but it is merely the conversion of a portion of the shareholder's investment into a different form. In a sense, the shareholder earns income on the investment when the corporation earns its income. Because of the realization test for income recognition in accounting, however, the shareholders do not recognize income (except under the equity method discussed in Chapter 13) until the firm distributes cash. A stock dividend does not even improve the marketability of the investment, although when a firm issues preferred shares to common shareholders or vice versa, shareholders may view the situation as similar to a cash dividend. The stock dividend capitalizes a portion of retained earnings.

12.17   An error in previously-issued financial statements results from oversights or errors which the firm should not have made given reasonable diligence in accessing available information at the time. Accountants restate the previously-issued financial statements to correct the error. A change in an accounting estimate results from *new* information that suggests that the original estimate was inaccurate as judged *ex post*. Accountants adjust for changes in estimates during the current and future periods instead of restating previously-issued financial statements.

12.18   Prior-period adjustments are direct debits or credits to Retained Earnings for information resolving uncertainty from earlier accounting periods. Some accountants suspect that if management were allowed to use prior-period adjustments for the resolution of past uncertainty, all "bad" news would find its way into the financial statements via prior-period adjustments, never having appeared in the income statement originally issued for any period. For example, firms might take an optimistic view with respect to the depreciable life of assets, showing low periodic depreciation charges in each year's income statement. When the firm discovers that the assets will last a shorter time than projected, there is a direct debit to Retained Earnings and a credit to Accumulated Depreciation for the catch-up. These accountants think that all losses

12.18 continued.

> (gains are seldom a problem; why?) should appear in income as discipline for managements that might wish to report favorably on their own performances.

12.19   *Comprehensive income* includes all causes of changes in owners' equity accounts for a period, other than transactions with owners. It includes all operating items, recurring and non-recurring, extraordinary items, results of continuing and discontinued operations, all holding gains and losses—realized or not, foreign exchange gains and losses, all pension adjustments.   It excludes 'gains and losses' on treasury share transactions, as these are transactions with owners.

In contrast, *other comprehensive income* refers to the components of comprehensive income *not* considered earnings. The primary example discussed in this book is unrealized holding gins and losses on securities available for sale, but the text mentions holding gains and losses on cash flow hedges, foreign exchange gains and losses and some pension adjustments. We have tried and failed to find an abstraction that will distinguish earnings from other comprehensive income. For the moment, one must rely on fiat—a list specified by the FASB. The FASB has attempted to distinguish earnings as performance related (subject to significant influence by management) from other comprehensive income as non-performance related (subject to external influences not controllable by management), but this distinction really does not work well. Consider, for example, that gains and losses on fair value hedges are earnings but on cash flow hedges and foreign exchange positions are not. Holding gains and losses
   • on trading securities are earnings, but,
   • on securities available for sale are not.
This item measures a flow for a period.

Accumulated other comprehensive income measures a balance at the start or end of a period—ending balance is beginning balance plus *other comprehensive income* for the period.

Accumulated comprehensive income would refer to the sum of Retained Earnings and Accumulated Other Comprehensive Income at any balance sheet date, but so far neither the FASB nor the analysts' community has expressed interest in this subtotal of owners' equity.

12.20   (Journal entries to record the issuance of capital stock.)

a. Cash... 625,000
      Common Stock (= 25,000 X $10) 250,000
      Additional Paid-in Capital (= 25,000 X $15)...... 375,000

b. Cash... 1,000,000
      Preferred Stock.. 1,000,000

12.20 continued.

   c. Land.. 180,000
        Common Stock (= 12,000 × $1)....................... 12,000
        Additional Paid-in Capital (= 12,000 × $14)...... 168,000

The market value of the stock seems a better indicator of the value of the land than either the assessed value or the asking price.

   d. No entry.

   e. Cash.. 180,000
        Common Stock (= 3,000 × $10)....................... 30,000
        Additional Paid-in Capital (= 3,000 × $50)........ 150,000

   f. Bonds Payable... 300,000
        Common Stock (= 10,000 × $10) 100,000
        Additional Paid-in Capital 200,000

   g. Bonds Payable... 300,000
      Loss on Conversion of Bonds........................... 50,000
        Common Stock (= 10,000 × $10) 100,000
        Additional Paid-in Capital (= 10,000 × $25)...... 250,000

12.21   (Journal entries for the issuance of common stock.)

   a. Inventory 250,000
      Land 160,000
      Building.. 1,200,000
      Equipment... 390,000
        Common Stock (= 40,000 × $15)..................... 600,000
        Additional Paid-in Capital 1,400,000

   b. Cash... 500,000
        Redeemable Preferred Stock 500,000

   c. Cash (= 20,000 × $18)..................................... 360,000
      Common Stock Warrants (= 20,000 × $2)............ 40,000
        Common Stock (= 20,000 × $1)....................... 20,000
        Additional Paid-in Capital 380,000

   d. Preferred Stock (= 20,000 × $100)...................... 2,000,000
        Common Stock (= 50,000 × $10)..................... 500,000
        Additional Paid-in Capital 1,500,000

12.22   (Vertovec Corporation; journal entries for employee stock options.)

a. **December 31, Year 3**
No entry.

October 15, Year 5

Cash..	375,000	
Common Stock (= 15,000 × $10)		150,000
Additional Paid-in Capital (= 15,000 × $15)......		225,000

November 30, Year 6

Cash..	125,000	
Common Stock (= 5,000 × $10)		50,000
Additional Paid-in Capital (= 5,000 × $15)........		75,000

b. **December 31, Year 3**

Compensation Expense...................................	100,000	
Common Stock Options (= 20,000 × $5)............		100,000

October 15, Year 5

Cash..	375,000	
Common Stock Options (= 15,000 × $5)	75,000	
Common Stock (= 15,000 × $10)		150,000
Additional Paid-in Capital		300,000

November 30, Year 6

Cash..	125,000	
Common Stock Options (= 5,000 × $5)................	25,000	
Common Stock (= 5,000 × $10)		50,000
Additional Paid-in Capital		100,000

12.23   (Haskins Corporation; journal entries for stock warrants.)

February 26, Year 6

Cash	120,000	
Common Stock Warrants (= 40,000 × $3).............		120,000

June 6, Year 7

Cash (= 30,000 × $40)	1,200,000	
Common Stock Warrants (= 30,000 × $3).................	90,000	
Common Stock (= 30,000 × $5)		150,000
Additional Paid-in Capital.............................		1,140,000

February 26, Year 8

Common Stock Warrants (= 10,000 × $3).................	30,000	
Additional Paid-in Capital.............................		30,000

12.24   (Higgins Corporation; journal entries for convertible bonds.)

    a. **1/02/Year 1**
       Cash.. 1,000,000
          Convertible Bonds Payable   1,000,000
       To record the issue of convertible bonds.

       1/02/Year 5
       Convertible Bonds Payable............................... 1,000,000
          Common Stock—$1 Par   40,000
          Additional Paid-in Capital   960,000
       To record conversion using book value of bonds.

    b. **1/02/Year 1**
       Cash 1,000,000
          Convertible Bonds Payable..........................   685,140.50
          Additional Paid-in Capital..........................   314,859.50
       Issue of 10-percent semiannual coupon con-
       vertible bonds at a time when the firm could
       issue ordinary 10-percent bonds for $685,140.50
       when the market interest rate is 15 percent
       compounded semiannually.

         Supporting Computations
         $50,000 × 12.59441..................................... $629,720.50
         $1,000,000 × .05542.....................................   55,420.00
            Issue Price... $685,140.50

       Also see Table 6 at the back of the book.

12.25   (Huerta Corporation; journal entries for treasury stock transactions.)

    a. Treasury Stock.. 240,000
          Cash (= 8,000 × $30)...................................   240,000

    b. Cash (= 3,000 × $32)... 96,000
          Treasury Stock (= 3,000 × $30).......................   90,000
          Additional Paid-in Capital   6,000

    c. Treasury Stock.. 190,000
          Cash (= 5,000 × $38)...................................   190,000

    d. Land.. 200,000
          Treasury Stock [= (5,000 × $30) + (1,000 ×
             $38)]..   188,000
          Additional Paid-in Capital   12,000

    e. Cash (= 4,000 × $36).. 144,000
       Additional Paid-in Capital 8,000
          Treasury Stock (= 4,000 × $38).......................   152,000

12.26   (Melissa Corporation; journal entries for treasury stock transactions.)

a.   Treasury Stock... 120,000
           Cash (= 10,000 × $12)   120,000

b.   Bonds Payable.. 72,000
           Treasury Stock (= 6,000 × $12)   72,000

c.   Treasury Stock... 300,000
           Cash (= 20,000 × $15)   300,000

d.   Land... 540,000
           Treasury Stock [= (4,000 × $12) + (20,000 ×
               $15)]..   348,000
           Common Stock (= 6,000 × $5)   30,000
           Additional Paid-in Capital...........................   162,000

12.27   (Uncertainty Corporation; journal entries to correct errors and adjust
         for changes in estimates.)

a.   Retained Earnings 12,000
           Patent (or Accumulated Amortization)..........   12,000
       To correct error from neglecting to amortize
       patent during previous year.

b.   Accumulated Depreciation............................. 7,000
           Retained Earnings.....................................   7,000
       To eliminate the balance in accumulated depre-
       ciation relating to the machine sold and convert
       a $4,000 loss on the sale to a $3,000 gain.

c.   Depreciation Expense 50,000
           Accumulated Depreciation   50,000
       Book value on January 1, Year 13 is $1,600,000
       [= $2,400,000 – ($80,000 × 10)]. The revised
       annual depreciation is $50,000 (= $1,600,000/32).

d.   Bad Debt Expense... 10,000
           Allowance for Uncollectible Accounts   10,000
       To adjust the balance in the allowance account
       to the amount needed to cover estimated un-
       collectibles.

12.28   (Journal entries for cash dividends.)

a.   Retained Earnings 4,600
           Dividends Payable—Preferred Stock..............   4,600
       2,300 shares at $2.

12.28 continued.

b.	Retained Earnings...		30,000	
	Dividends Payable—Common Stock..............			30,000
	10,000 shares at $3.			

c.	Dividends Payable—Preferred Stock................		4,600	
	Cash			4,600

d.	Dividends Payable—Common Stock		30,000	
	Cash			30,000

12.29 (Journal entries for dividends.)

a.	Retained Earnings...		16,000	
	Dividends Payable—Preferred Stock..............			16,000
	Dividend of $2.50 per share on 6,400 shares.			

b.	Dividends Payable—Preferred Stock................		16,000	
	Cash			16,000

c.	Retained Earnings...		250,000	
	Common Stock			250,000

d. No entry.

12.30 (Watt Corporation; journal entries for dividends.)

a.	**March 31, Year 6**			
	Retained Earnings......................................		10,000	
	Dividends Payable.....................................			10,000
	$10,000 = 20,000 × $.50.			

b.	**April 15, Year 6**			
	Dividends Payable......................................		10,000	
	Cash			10,000

c.	**June 30, Year 6**			
	Retained Earnings (= 2,000 × $20)		40,000	
	Common Stock (= 2,000 × $15)			30,000
	Additional Paid-in Capital...........................			10,000

d.	**September 30, Year 6**			
	Retained Earnings......................................		11,000	
	Dividends Payable.....................................			11,000
	$11,000 = 22,000 × $.50.			

e.	**October 15, Year 6**			
	Dividends Payable......................................		11,000	
	Cash			11,000

12.30 continued.

    f. **December 31, Year 6**

Additional Paid-in Capital	165,000	
Common Stock (= 11,000 X $15)		165,000

12.31   (Effects on statement of cash flows.)

    a. The journal entry to record this transaction is:

Cash..	200,000	
Common Stock		200,000

The Cash account increases, so Line (9) increases by $200,000. Issuing common stock is a financing activity, so Line (6) increases by $200,000.

    b. The journal entry to record this transaction is:

Common Stock..	50,000	
Additional Paid-in Capital	25,000	
Cash		75,000

The Cash account decreases, so Line (9) decreases by $75,000. Repurchasing common stock is a financing activity, so Line (7) increases by $75,000.

    c. The journal entry to record this transaction using the book value method is:

Convertible Bonds Payable..............................	100,000	
Common Stock		10,000
Additional Paid-in Capital..........................		90,000

The journal entry to record this transaction under the market value method is:

Convertible Bonds Payable..............................	100,000	
Loss on Conversion of Bonds...........................	140,000	
Common Stock		10,000
Additional Paid-in Capital..........................		230,000

The Cash account does not change under either method of recording the transaction. The transaction does not appear on the statement of cash flows when the firm uses the book value method. When the firm uses the market value method, net income on Line (1) decreases for the loss. Line (2) increases to add back the loss to net income since it does not affect cash. The firm reports this financing transaction in a supplementary schedule or note.

12.31 continued.

d. The journal entry to record this transaction is:

Cash.. 15,000
Additional Paid-in Capital 5,000
   Treasury Stock 20,000

The Cash account increases, so Line (9) increases by $15,000. Issuing treasury stock is a financing transaction, so Line (6) increases by $15,000.

e. The journal entry to record this transaction is:

Retained Earnings.. 300,000
   Common Stock 1,000
   Additional Paid-in Capital.......................... 299,000

Because this transaction does not affect the Cash account, it does not appear in the statement of cash flows.

f. The journal entry to record this transaction is:

Retained Earnings.. 70,000
   Dividends Payable..................................... 70,000

Because this transaction does not affect the Cash account, it does not appear in the statement of cash flows.

g. The journal entry to record this transaction is:

Dividends Payable.. 70,000
   Cash 70,000

The Cash account decreases, so Line (9) decreases by $70,000. Paying dividends is a financing activity, so Line (8) increases by $70,000.

h. The journal entry to record this transaction is:

Cash.. 20,000
   Common Stock 1,000
   Additional Paid-in Capital.......................... 19,000

The Cash account increases, so Line (9) increases by $20,000. Issuing common stock under a stock rights plan is a financing activity, so Line (6) increases by $20,000.

12.32   (Wilson Supply Company; transactions to incorporate and run a business.)

a. **1/02**

Cash..	9,000	
Common Stock—$30 Stated Value.................		9,000

300 shares × $30 = $9,000.

b. **1/06**

Cash..	60,000	
Common Stock—$30 Stated Value.................		60,000

2,000 shares × $30 = $60,000.

c. **1/08**

Cash..	400,000	
Preferred Stock—Par		400,000

4,000 shares × $100 = $400,000.

d. **1/09**

No entry.

e. **1/12**

Inventories..	50,000	
Land..	80,000	
Building...	210,000	
Equipment	120,000	
Preferred Stock—Par		100,000
Common Stock—Stated Value....................		360,000

f. **7/03**

Retained Earnings......................................	20,000	
Dividends Payable on Preferred Stock............		20,000

$100 × (.08/2) × (4,000 + 1,000) shares = $20,000.

g. **7/05**

Cash..	825,000	
Common Stock—$30 Stated Value.................		750,000
Additional Paid-in Capital.........................		75,000

25,000 shares × $33 = $825,000.

h. **7/25**

Dividends Payable on Preferred Stock................	20,000	
Cash		20,000

i. **10/02**

Retained Earnings......................................	39,300	
Dividends Payable on Common Stock		39,300

$1 × (300 + 2,000 + 12,000 + 25,000) shares = $39,300.

12.32 continued.

    j. **10/25**

Dividends Payable on Common Stock................	39,300	
Cash		39,300

12.33   (Hutchins Company; transactions to incorporate and run a business.)

    a. No formal entry is required.

    b. **July 8, Year 1**

Cash..	240,000	
Common Stock		240,000
6,000 shares issued at $40 per share.		

    c. **July 9, Year 1**

Accounts Receivable.....................................	20,000	
Inventories..	30,000	
Land..	40,000	
Buildings...	50,000	
Equipment	20,000	
Common Stock		160,000
4,000 shares issued at $40 per share.		

    d. **July 13, Year 1**

Cash..	80,000	
Preferred Stock—Par		80,000

    e. **Dec. 31, Year 1**

Income Summary..	75,000	
Retained Earnings.......................................		75,000

    f. **Jan. 4, Year 2**

Retained Earnings..	31,600	
Dividends Payable on Preferred Stock............		1,600
Dividends Payable on Common Stock		30,000
800 × $2 = $1,600; 10,000 × $3 = $30,000.		

    g. **Feb. 1, Year 2**

Dividends Payable on Preferred Stock..............	1,600	
Dividends Payable on Common Stock................	30,000	
Cash		31,600

    h. **July 2, Year 2**

Retained Earnings..	1,600	
Dividends Payable on Preferred Stock............		1,600

    i. **Aug. 1, Year 2**

Dividends Payable on Preferred Stock..............	1,600	
Cash		1,600

12.34   (Conrad Company; reconstructing transactions involving shareholders' equity.)

a. $30,000 par value/$10 per share = 3,000 shares.

b. $3,600/180 = $20 per share.

c.   300 – 180 = 120 shares.

d.   If the Additional Paid-in Capital is $15,720, then $15,000 [= 3,000 × ($15 – $10)] represents contributions in excess of par value on original issue of 3,000 shares. Then, $720 (= $15,720 – $15,000) represents the credit to Additional Paid-in Capital when it reissued the treasury shares.

   The $720 represents 120 shares reissued times the excess of reissue price over acquisition price:

$$120(\$X - \$20) = \$720, \text{ or } X = \$26.$$

The shares were reissued for $26 each.

e.   (1)   Cash (3,000 × $15) 45,000
            Capital Stock ($10 Par Value).................   30,000
            Additional Paid-in Capital   15,000

     (2)   Treasury Shares 6,000
            Cash (300 × $20)...................................   6,000

     (3)   Cash (120 × $26)...................................... 3,120
            Treasury Shares (120 × $20)   2,400
            Additional Paid-in Capital   720

     (4)   Cash... 5,000
            Securities Available for Sale..................   3,000
            Realized Gain on Sale of Securities
               Available for Sale (Income Statement)..   2,000

     (5)   Securities Available for Sale 1,000
            Unrealized Holding Gain on Securities
               Available for Sale (Balance Sheet,
               Component of Other Comprehensive
               Income...   1,000

f.   Realized gain appears in Income (Earnings) Statement and the Unrealized Gain appears in Statement of Comprehensive Income or in reconciliation of Accumulated Other Comprehensive Income.

12.35 (Shea Company; reconstructing transactions involving shareholders' equity.)

a. $100,000 par value/$5 per share = 20,000 shares.

b. $33,600/1,200 = $28 per share.

c. 2,000 − 1,200 = 800 shares.

d. If the Additional Paid-in Capital is $509,600, then $500,000 [= 20,000 × ($30 − $5)] represents contributions in excess of par value on original issue of 20,000 shares. Then, $9,600 (= $509,600 − $500,000) represents the credit to Additional Paid-in Capital when it reissued the treasury shares.

The $9,600 represents 800 shares reissued times the excess of reissue price over acquisition price:

$$800(\$X - \$28) = \$9,600, \text{ or } X = \$40.$$

The shares were reissued for $40 each.

e. (1) Cash... 600,000
        Capital Stock ($5 Par Value)...................   100,000
        Additional Paid-in Capital   500,000

    (2) Treasury Shares 56,000
        Cash...   56,000

    (3) Cash... 32,000
        Treasury Shares..............................   22,400
        Additional Paid-in Capital   9,600
        800 × $40 = $32,000.

    (4) Cash... 12,000
        Realized Loss on Sale of Securities Avail-
        able for Sale (Income Statement)............   2,000
        Securities Available for Sale...............   14,000

    (5) Unrealized Holding Loss on Securities
        Available for Sale (Balance Sheet, Com-
        ponent of Other Comprehensive In-
        come...   7,000
        Securities Available for Sale..............   7,000
        Write down securities from $25,000 to
        $18,000.

f. Realized Loss appears in Income (Earnings) Statement and the Unrealized Loss appears in Statement of Comprehensive Income or in reconciliation of Accumulated Other Comprehensive Income.

12.36   (General Electric Company; dilutive effects of stock options.)

    a.   2.7 million shares × $77 = $207.9 million.

    b.   2.7 million shares × $54 = $145.8 million.

    c.   Shareholders are $62.1 million better off with a public issue than with a private issue. $207.9 million − $145.8 million = 2.7 million shares × ($77 − $54) = $62.1 million.

    d.   The unwary reader might mistakenly infer from GE's explanation that exercised options do not dilute the equity of other shareholders. Holders will not exercise options unless the market price at time of exercise exceeds the exercise price. At the time of exercise, the firm issues shares at a price less than it would realize if it issued the shares to the general public. The $62.1 million dilution in shareholders' equity is the realized amount of compensation expense that GE incurred when it granted the options. If GAAP permitted the firm to recognize compensation expense when it granted the options, the amount of expense would be the present value of the estimate of the eventual dilution or perhaps a measure of the services rendered by the employees. GE's shareholders are better off if the employees who were granted the options worked harder than they otherwise would have and produced more than $62.1 million of aftertax income since the time of the grant. Otherwise, shareholders were hurt.

12.37   (Jastern Company; accounting for detachable warrants.)

    a.   The warrants reduced the amount borrowed, but not the interest rate. In reality, see Part *b.* below, the Company borrowed $855,812 at an interest rate of 12 percent per year and issued detachable warrants for $144,188. One cannot ascertain whether or not this was a fair price for the option under the circumstances from the available data.

    b.

Present Value of $80,000 in arrears for 5 years discounted at 12% is 3.60478 × $80,000	$ 288,382
Present Value of $1,000,000 paid in 5 years discounted at 12% is .56743 × $1,000,000	567,430
Present Value of loan repayments is	$ 855,812

The remaining $144,188 must be for the option. Thus, the entry to reflect the economics of the situation is:

Cash	1,000,000	
Note Payable		855,812
Additional Paid-in Capital		144,188

12.37 b. continued.

At each interest payment date, the entry is:

Interest Expense.. 80,000 + X
  Cash   80,000
  Note Payable...   X
Where X is the increase in interest expense to
recognize increase in book value of the note.

End of Year	X = Increase in Note Payable[a]	Remaining Loan
0	--	$ 855,812
1	$22,697	878,509
2	25,421	903,930
3	28,472	932,402
4	31,888	964,290
5	35,710	1,000,000

[a]= $(.12 \times$ Amount in Last Column for Preceding Year$) -$ \$80,000, except in Year 5 where it is the amount required to give \$1,000,000 in last column.

c. Cash.. 400,000
     Common Stock—$5 Par   100,000
     Additional Paid-in Capital..........................   300,000
  20,000 × $5 = $100,000. 20,000 × ($20 – $5) =
  $300,000.

d. Yes. The firm could issue the same shares to other investors for $45 per share. This does not mean that shareholders were hurt by the entire transaction. They gambled with the lending-investor and "lost." If the option was fairly priced at $144,188, then all sides were treated fairly.

e. During the life of the loan, disclosure of the amount of the options outstanding and their exercise price would enable the reader of financial statements to see the potential dilution of earnings overhanging the company.

12.38 (Alex Corporation; comprehensive review of accounting for shareholders' equity.)

a.

BOOK VALUE PER SHARE
(Numerator is Total Book Value)

$\dfrac{\$2,250,000}{50,000} = \$45.00$ per share.

$\dfrac{\$2,250,000}{55,000} = \$40.91$ per share.

$\dfrac{\$2,250,000}{100,000} = \$22.50$ per share.

$\dfrac{\$2,125,000}{45,000} = \$47.22$ per share.

$\dfrac{\$2,175,000}{45,000} = \$48.33$ per share.

$\dfrac{\$2,300,000}{50,000} = \$46.00$ per share.

$\dfrac{\$2,225,000}{50,000} = \$44.50$ per share.

$\dfrac{\$2,200,000}{50,000} = \$44.00$ per share.

$\dfrac{\$2,325,000}{55,000} = \$42.27$ per share.

$\dfrac{\$2,500,000}{55,000} = \$45.45$ per share.

$\dfrac{\$2,400,000}{60,000} = \$40.00$ per share.

$\dfrac{\$2,400,000}{60,000} = \$40.00$ per share.

JOURNAL ENTRY

b.

(1) Retained Earnings 150,000
    Common Stock (5,000 × $10) 50,000
    Additional Paid-in Capital (5,000 × $20) 100,000

(2) Common Stock ($10 Par Value) 500,000
    Common Stock ($5 per Share) 500,000

(3) Treasury Stock 125,000
    Cash (5,000 × $25) 125,000

(4) Treasury Stock 75,000
    Cash (5,000 × $15) 75,000

(5) Cash (5,000 × $35) 175,000
    Treasury Stock (5,000 × $25) 125,000
    Additional Paid-in Capital 50,000

(6) Cash (5,000 × $20) 100,000
    Additional Paid-in Capital 25,000
    Treasury Stock (5,000 × $25) 125,000

(7) Cash (5,000 × $15) 75,000
    Additional Paid-in Capital 50,000
    Treasury Stock (5,000 × $25) 125,000

(8) Cash (5,000 × $15) 75,000
    Common Stock (5,000 × $10) 50,000
    Additional Paid-in Capital 25,000

(9) Cash (5,000 × $50) 250,000
    Common Stock (5,000 × $10) 50,000
    Additional Paid-in Capital 200,000

(10) Bonds Payable 150,000
    Common Stock (10,000 × $10) 100,000
    Additional Paid-in Capital 50,000

(11) Bonds Payable 150,000
    Loss on Conversion of Bonds 20,000
    Common Stock 100,000
    Additional Paid-in Capital 70,000

12.38 continued.

    c. (1) The acquisition of treasury shares, the declaration of dividends, and the incurrence of a net loss reduce total book value.

        (2) The issue of common shares for a price less than current book value per share (for example, under stock option plans), the acquisition of treasury shares for a price greater than current book value per share, and the sale or reissue of treasury shares at a price less than their acquisition cost (at a "loss") reduce book value per share.

12.39   (Neslin Company; reconstructing events affecting shareholders' equity.)

    a. (1) Issue of 20,000 shares of common stock at $52 per share for cash or other assets.

        (2) Acquisition of 4,000 shares of treasury stock for $55 per share.

        (3) Reissue of 3,000 shares of treasury stock for $48 per share.

        (4) Reissue of 1,000 shares of treasury stock for $60 per share.

        (5) Net income of $2,400,000 closed to Retained Earnings.

        (6) Securities available for sale on hand at year end have a market value of $1,050,000 greater than book value, but this represents a decline of $150,000 reported in Other Comprehensive Income.

        (7) Dividends declared of $10 per share.

b.

(1)
Cash	1,040,000	
Common Stock		200,000
Additional Paid-in Capital		840,000

(2)
Treasury Stock	220,000	
Cash		220,000

(3)
Cash	144,000	
Additional Paid-in Capital	21,000	
Treasury Stock		165,000

(4)
Cash	60,000	
Treasury Stock		55,000
Additional Paid-in Capital		5,000

(5)
Income Summary	2,400,000	
Retained Earnings		2,400,000

12.39 b. continued.

(6)   Unrealized Holding Gain on Holdings
       of Securities Available for Sale   150,000
       Securities Available for Sale   150,000

(7)   Retained Earnings..........................   1,200,000
       Cash or Dividends Payable   1,200,000

12.40   (Wal-Mart Stores; journal entries for changes in shareholders' equity.)

(1)   Income Summary...   1,291,024
       Retained Earnings   1,291,024

(2)   Retained Earnings.......................................   158,889
       Dividends Payable or Cash..........................   158,889

(3)   Cash..   3,820
       Common Stock   66
       Additional Paid-in Capital...........................   3,754

(4)   Additional Paid-in Capital   56,680
       Common Stock   56,680

(5)   Investment in Securities...............................   274,696
       Common Stock   1,037
       Additional Paid-in Capital...........................   273,659

(6)   Treasury Stock...   25,826
       Cash   25,826

(7)   Unrealized Gains on Holdings of Securities
       Available for Sale.....................................   57,086
       Securities Available for Sale   57,086

12.41   (Wellington Company; journal entries for changes in shareholders' equity.)

(1)   Income Summary...   210,500
       Retained Earnings   210,500

(2)   Retained Earnings.......................................   120,000
       Cash or Dividends Payable   120,000

(3)   Bonds Payable...   70,000
       Common Stock   6,270
       Additional Paid-in Capital...........................   63,730

12.41 continued.

(4)	Cash...	950	
	Common Stock		73
	Additional Paid-in Capital.............		877
(5)	Retained Earnings..........................	62,810	
	Common Stock		5,604
	Additional Paid-in Capital.............		57,206
(6)	Treasury Stock...............................	48,600	
	Cash		48,600
(7)	Cash...	40,530	
	Additional Paid-in Capital	2,170	
	Treasury Stock		42,700
(8)	Securities Available for Sale..........	44,400	
	Unrealized Loss on Holdings of Securities		
	Available for Sale		44,400

12.42 (Baiman Corporation; preparing a statement of cash flows.)

a.

		Cash			
√	45,000				

Operations

(1)	48,000	15,000	(9)
(4)	28,000	20,000	(10)
(5)	4,000		
(6)	3,000		
(12)	1,000		
(14)	7,000		

Investing

		37,000	(11)

Financing

(8)	12,000	39,000	(2)
(13)	4,000	25,000	(16)
(15)	38,000		
√	54,000		

12.42 a. continued.

Accounts Receivable—Net		
√	160,000	
(9)	15,000	
√	175,000	

Inventory		
√	115,000	
(10)	20,000	
√	135,000	

Property, Plant and Equipment			
√	265,000		
(3)	20,000	22,000	(5)
(11)	37,000		
√	300,000		

Accumulated Depreciation			
		120,000	√
(5)	18,000	28,000	(4)
		130,000	√

Accounts Payable		
	105,000	√
	1,000	(12)
	106,000	√

Dividends Payable		
	10,000	√
	4,000	(13)
	14,000	√

Bonds Payable		
	90,000	√
	3,000	(6)
	93,000	√

Convertible Bonds Payable		
		50,000	√
(7)	50,000		
		--	√

Deferred Income Taxes		
	20,000	√
	7,000	(12)
	27,000	√

Preferred Stock		
	60,000	√
	60,000	√

Common Stock (Par)		
	25,000	√
	4,000	(3)
	10,000	(7)
	8,000	(15)
	47,000	√

Additional Paid-in Capital		
	65,000	√
	16,000	(3)
	40,000	(7)
	2,000	(8)
	30,000	(15)
	153,000	√

Retained Earnings			
		55,000	√
(2)	39,000	48,000	(1)
		64,000	√

Treasury Stock			
√	15,000		
(16)	25,000	10,000	(8)
√	30,000		

12.42 continued.

b.

BAIMAN CORPORATION
Statement of Cash Flows
For Year 2

Operations:
Net Income	$ 48,000	
Addbacks and Additions:		
Depreciation Expense	28,000	
Loss on Sale of Equipment	4,000	
Amortization of Bond Discount	3,000	
Increase in Accounts Payable	1,000	
Increase in Deferred Income Tax		
Liability	7,000	
Subtractions:		
(Increase) in Accounts Receivable	(15,000)	
(Increase) in Inventories	(20,000)	
Cash Flow from Operations		$ 56,000
Investing:		
Acquisition of Property, Plant and		
Equipment	$ (37,000)	
Cash Flow from Investing		(37,000)
Financing:		
Issue of Common Stock	$ 38,000	
Reissue of Treasury Stock	12,000	
Reacquisition of Common Stock	(25,000)	
Dividends Paid ($39,000 – $4,000)	(35,000)	
Cash Flow from Financing		(10,000)
Net Change in Cash		$ 9,000
Cash, January 1, Year 2		45,000
Cash, December 31, Year 2		$ 54,000

Supplementary Information

1. Holders of convertible bonds with a book value of $50,000 exercised their option to convert their bonds into shares of common stock.

2. The firm issued common shares with a market value of $20,000 in the acquisition of a machine.

12.43   (Merck & Co.; treasury shares and their effects on performance ratios.)

a.   Cash..   714.1
    Treasury Stock 427.6
    Common Stock/Additional Paid-in Capital.....   286.5

The common shares were issued at an option price of $49.28 per share [= $714.1/(.307 + 14.183)]. The treasury shares issued were purchased for $30.15 per share (= $427.6/14.183). The difference of $19.13 per share (= $49.28 − $30.15) was credited to Additional Paid-in Capital. The remaining credits to Common Stock and Additional Paid-in Capital were for the amounts received for the .307 common shares issued.

Treasury Stock..   2,572.8
    Cash 2,572.8

These treasury shares were purchased for an average price of $93.75 per share (= $2,572.8/27.444).

b.

	Year 3/Year 4	Year 4/Year 5
Net Income:		
[($3,870.5/$3,376.6) − 1].............	+14.6%	
[($4,596.5/$3,870.5) − 1].............		+18.8%
Earnings per Common Share:		
[($3.20/$2.70) − 1].....................	+18.5%	
[($3.83/$3.20) − 1].....................		+19.7%

Earnings per share increases faster than net income because Merck reduces the number of shares outstanding each year by repurchasing shares of treasury stock.

c.

	Year 3	Year 4	Year 5
Book Value per Share:			
$11,735.7/(1,483.463 − 254.615).......	$9.55		
$11,970.5/(1,483.619 − 277.017).......		$9.92	
$12,613.5/(1,483.926 − 290.278).......			$10.57
Percentage Change:			
[($9.92/$9.55) − 1].......................	+3.9%		
[($10.57/$9.92) − 1].....................		+6.6%	

There are several reasons why book value per share increases more slowly than net income and earnings per share. First, dividends reduce shareholders' equity but not net income. Second, the repurchases of treasury shares reduce the numerator proportionally more than they reduce the denominator. The average repurchase price during Year 5 of $93.75 per share (see the answer

12.43 c. continued.

to Part *a*.) had the effect of reducing book value per share. Book value per share increased overall in Year 5 because of net income.

d.

	Year 3	Year 4	Year 5
[$3,376.6/.5($11,139.0 + $11,735.7)]	29.5%		
[$3,870.5/.5($11,735.7 + $11,970.5)]		32.7%	
[$4,596.5/.5($11,970.5 + $12,613.5)]			37.4%

e. No. Merck has purchased considerably more treasury shares than are needed for its stock option plans. Treasury shares do not receive dividends, so Merck does conserve cash. However, dividends have grown at approximately the same growth rate as net income. One purpose might have been to increase the return on common shareholders' equity. Cash generally earns a return of approximately 4 percent each year after taxes. By eliminating this low-yielding asset from the balance sheet, Merck's overall rate of return on common shareholders' equity increases. The market often interprets stock repurchases as a positive signal that management has inside information and thinks that the stock is undervalued. The positive signal results in an increase in the stock price. One can estimate the increase in market price by observing the average price at which Merck repurchased its shares each year:

Year 3: $1,570.9/33.377 = $47.07
Year 4: $2,493.3/38.384 = $64.96
Year 5: $2,572.8/27.444 = $93.75

Thus, the stock price doubled during the three-year period, whereas earnings increased by approximately 36 percent [= ($4,596.5/$3,376.6) – 1].

12.44 (Wendy's International; mandatorily redeemable preferred shares substitute for debt and help manage the debt/equity ratio.)

a. Wendy's prefers not to have even more debt on its Year 6 balance sheet than it already shows on its Year 5 balance sheet.

b. Wendy's consolidates Financial, so it eliminates in consolidation the intercompany debt issued by Wendy's to Financial and shows only Financial's issue to its purchases outside the consolidated entity. Wendy's shows mandatorily redeemable preferred shares, sometimes called *mezzanine financing*, on its balance sheet, not debt. The name *mezzanine* results from the SEC's rule requiring the issuer to segregate such items from other components of shareholder's equity, midway between (on the mezzanine between) liabilities and other shareholders' equity.

12.44 continued.

c.	**Year 6**	**Year 5**
Treat Preferred as Shareholders' Equity	($207.8 + $253.9)/$1,781.4 = 25.9%	($295.9 + $346.6)/$1,509.2 = 42.6%
Treat Preferred as Debt	($207.8 + $253.9 + $200.0)/$1,781.4 = 37.1%	($295.9 + $346.6)/$1,509.2 = 42.6%

12.45 (Kellogg Company; analysis of non-recurring transactions; introduction to constructive liabilities.)

a.

	Year 2		Year 3		Year 4	
Streamlining Charges ..	348.0		121.1		161.1	
Liability for Streamlining Costs...........		348.0		121.1		161.1
To record expense and set up liability.						
Liability for Streamlining Costs.................	254.0		160.8		163.5	
Cash		40.0		120.0		85.0
Other Assets Written Down or Written Off		214.0		40.8		78.5
To record cash spent to discharge some of the liability and to write off assets already on hand, now impaired or removed.						

One can combine these two entries as follows:

	Year 2		Year 3		Year 4	
Streamlining Charges ..	348.0		121.1		161.1	
Liability for Streamlining Costs..............			39.7			
Liability for Streamlining Costs.................		94.0			2.4	
Cash		40.0		120.0		85.0
Other Assets Written Down or Written Off		214.0		40.8		78.5

12.45 continued.

b.
Streamlining Charges..	144.1	
Liability for Stream-		
lining Costs...........		144.1
To record expense and		
set up liability.		

Liability for Streamlin-		
ing Costs.................	23.0	
Streamlining		
Charges............		23.0

Without the reversal, income for Year 3 would have been $23 smaller.

c. Without the reversal, income for Year 2 would have been $23 larger and income for Year 3 would have been $23 smaller. Income for the three years, as reported, and without the extra charge in Year 2, reversed in Year 3, are:

	Year 4	Year 3	Year 2
Net Earnings, as Reported.....................	$546.0	$531.0	$490.3
Net Earnings, Without Need for Re-versals...	$546.0	$508.0	$513.3

d. Kellogg reported smoothly growing earnings over the three-year period. Without the reversal, however, the pattern shows a dip from Year 2 to Year 3, before increasing in Year 4. Most analysts, all else equal, give higher valuations to firms reporting steadily rising income (such as Kellogg's actuals) than to yo-yo income (Kellogg with chargers and subsequent reversal). The ability to record charges, such as the retirement and severance costs where cash payments will be in the future and management has some discretion to affect the future amount, lowers the quality of earnings because it gives management the opportunity to manipulate income. Notice how a relative small reversal, $23 out of net income of about $500—an adjustment of less than 5 percent—gives a pattern of stable growth.

Our colleagues who study non-recurring charges tell us that Kellogg discloses more extensively than most. In Kellogg's defense, then, we can say that if it had wanted to manipulate income and hide from the reader the fact that they had, then they could have given less detail than they did give. They need not have given so much detail, detail which allows the analyst to do the unscrambling that the actual disclosures allow us to do. Still, we would bet that Kellogg's management, in choosing the $23 amount for the reversal, had its eye on the income pattern that resulted.

12.45 continued.

    e. If firms are allowed or required to record constructive liabilities, then hard-to-audit judgments will enter the financial statements of a sort that will allow management to manipulate the timing of income recognition.

        Kellogg's management surely has some discretion in timing, and probably in setting the number, of employee severances. It can use that discretion to alter incomes in small, but relatively powerful, ways. In the actual case of Kellogg, any reversal from Year 2 to Year 3 of about $3 [= ($513.3 − $508.0)/2] or more will result in removing the downward dip in income between Years 2 and 3 and replacing it with upward trend.

12.46 (Layton Ball Corporation; case introducing earnings-per-share calculations for a complex capital structure.)

    a. $\dfrac{\$9,500}{2,500} = \$3.80$ per share.

    b. 1,000 options $\times$ $15 = $15,000 cash raised.

$$\dfrac{\$15,000 \text{ new cash}}{\$25 \text{ per share}} = 600 \text{ shares.}$$

Total number of shares increases by 400 (= 1,000 − 600).

$$\dfrac{\$9,500}{2,500 + 400} = \$3.276 \text{ per share.}$$

    c. 2,000 warrants $\times$ $30 = $60,000 cash raised.

$$\dfrac{\$60,000 \text{ new cash}}{\$25 \text{ per share}} = 2,400 \text{ shares purchased.}$$

Total number of shares decreases by 400 (= 2,000 − 2,400).

$$\dfrac{\$9,500}{2,500 - 400} = \$4.524 \text{ per share.}$$

    d. Before taxes, each converted bond saves $41.66 2/3 in annual interest expense. After taxes, the savings in expense and increase in income is only $25 [= (1 − .40) $\times$ $41.66 2/3].

        There are 100 bonds outstanding; each is convertible into 10 shares. Thus, the new earnings per share figure is:

$$\dfrac{\$9,500 + \$25 \text{ savings per bond} \times 100 \text{ bonds}}{2,500 + 10 \text{ shares/bond} \times 100 \text{ bonds}} = \dfrac{\$12,000}{3,500 \text{ shares}} =$$

$3.429 per share.

12.46 continued.

    e.   The warrants are antidilutive and should be ignored if we seek the maximum possible dilution of earnings per share.

$$\frac{\$9,500 + \$2,500 \text{ (Increase from interest savings)}}{2,500 + 1,000 \text{ (bond conversion)} + 400 \text{ (option exercise)}} = \frac{\$12,000}{3,900} =$$

$3.077 per share.

    f.   Probably the *Wall Street Journal* should use the earnings per share that results in the maximum possible dilution. It should clearly ignore antidilutive securities. Do not conclude from the presentation in this problem that one can check the dilution characteristics of potentially dilutive securities one by one and know for sure which combination of assumed exercise and conversions lead to the minimum earnings per share figure. See S. Davidson and R. L. Weil, "A Shortcut in Computing Earnings per Share," *Journal of Accountancy*, December 1975, page 45.

12.47   (Case for discussion: value of stock options.)

The answer must be either *a.* or *b.* The cost per option cannot exceed one penny per share, for otherwise StartUp would merely buy the shares on the open market, rather than pay Goldman Sachs to relieve StartUp of the burden. The total cost of the options awarded to Bithead, then, cannot exceed $100 (= 10,000 shares × $.01 per share). We think the answer is likely to be in the range of $15–$40 for those shares, so we would answer *b.*

Within the last two decades, no subject has caused more controversy in accounting than the accounting for the cost of employee stock options. When it issued *SFAS No. 119* in 1995, FASB said that this issue threatened to end standard-setting in the private sector and that the debate had ceased to be rational.

Some firms, such as GE, grant to employees the right to buy a specified number of shares of the firm's stock at a fixed price, called the *exercise price*, usually the price on the day the firm awards the options to the employee, say $10 per share. The employee, typically, has several years to decide whether to exercise the option—that is, give up the option and cash in return for the shares. If the stock price rises above the exercise price, say to $18 per share, then the employee can give up the option and $10 in return for a share with current market value of $18.

Such options have value to employees who receive them and many companies, particularly the high-tech Silicon Valley companies, award such options as part of their compensation in hopes that the employer's shares will skyrocket in value, enriching the employee.

12.47 continued.

The accounting issue has been: how much should the employer firm, such as GE, charge to expense in the period when it awards an option to its employees. The FASB proposed a method for computing such amounts of expense and proposed requiring that firms report such amounts as expense. Some members of Congress pressured the FASB into not enacting its proposals.

William H. Scott, Jr. of Scientific Applications International Corporation of San Diego, has studied the costs to the issuing firm. He found that under a wide variety of conditions, the cost to the firm issuing an option exercisable at the market price on the date of grant is, for most firms, about 10–20 percent of the market value of the shares on the date of the grant. The cost to the firm of awarding the option can never exceed the market value of the share itself on the date of the award. This is true because the firm can always, on that day, go out into the market to buy a share for the current market price, building that share until the employee exercises the option.

At the height of the debate, chief financial officers (CFOs) from Silicon Valley lobbied against the FASB proposal. We believed that many of those CFOs did not understand the FASB proposal, nor its consequences. Consequently, at a private seminar on the subject at which one of us taught, we administered the question in the text to the Silicon Valley CFOs.

The Silicon Valley CFOs answered as follows: $a. = 3$, $b. = 3$, $c. = 6$, $d. = 8$, $e. = 5$, and $f. = 1$. That is, only six of the 26 participating got the answer right, which means that 20 of the 26 got it wrong. In the discussion following, we pointed out that these officers should probably understand the cost of options better than they did before arguing so hard against the proposed accounting. It's no wonder that a CFO would dislike the proposed accounting for options which the CFO thinks cost $10,000 when they actually cost no more than $100. About 25 percent of the Silicon Valley CFOs had beliefs that much in error.

CHAPTER 13

STATEMENT OF CASH FLOWS: ANOTHER LOOK

Problems and Cases: Answers and Solutions

13.1   (Effects of transactions on statement of cash flows.)

a. The journal entry to record this transaction is:

Retained Earnings	15,000	
Dividends Payable		3,000
Cash		12,000

The credit to the Cash account reduces Line (9) by $12,000. Paying dividends is a financing activity so Line (8) increases by $12,000.

b. The journal entry to record this transaction is:

Cash	75,000	
Bank Loan Payable		75,000

The debit to the Cash account increases Line (9) by $75,000. Borrowing is a financing activity so Line (6) increases by $75,000.

c. The journal entry to record this transaction is:

Cash	20,000	
Accumulated Depreciation	35,000	
Machinery		40,000
Gain on Sale of Machinery		15,000

The debit to the Cash account results in an increase in Line (9) of $20,000. Selling machinery is an investing activity so Line (4) increases by $20,000. The gain on the sale increases net income on Line (1) by $15,000. Because the full cash proceeds is an investing activity, Line (3) increases by $15,000 to subtract from net income a revenue that did not provide an operating source of cash.

13.1 continued.

    d. The journal entry for this transaction is:

Rent Expense..	28,000	
Cash...		28,000

The credit to the Cash account reduces Line (9) by $28,000. The recognition of rent expense reduces net income on Line (1) by $28,000. Paying rent is an operating transaction so the accountant makes no adjustment to net income when computing cash flow from operations.

    e. The journal entry to record this transaction is:

Marketable Securities..................................	39,000	
Cash...		39,000

The credit to the Cash account reduces Line (9) by $39,000. Purchasing marketable securities is an investing transaction so Line (5) increases by $39,000.

    f. The journal entry to record this transaction is:

Accumulated Depreciation............................	14,000	
Truck...		14,000

Because this transaction does not affect either the Cash account on Line (9) or net income on Line (1), it does not appear on the statement of cash flows.

    g. The journal entry to record this event is:

Unrealized Holding Loss of Marketable Secur- ities (SE)..	8,000	
Marketable Securities............................		8,000

Because this entry does not affect either the Cash account on Line (9) or net income on Line (1), it does not appear on the statement of cash flows. The firm discloses in a supplementary schedule or note the write down of marketable equity securities totaling $8,000.

13.1 continued.

h. The journal entry to record this transaction is:

Interest Expense..	15,000	
Bonds Payable..		500
Cash..		14,500

The credit to the Cash account results in a decrease in Line (9) of $14,500. The recognition of interest expense reduces net income on Line (1) by $15,000. Because the firm used only $14,500 of cash for this expense, Line (2) increases by $500 for the portion of the expense that did not use cash.

i. The journal entry for this event is:

Amortization Expense.................................	22,000	
Goodwill...		22,000

This entry does not involve the Cash account so Line (9) does not change. The recognition of amortization expense reduces net income on Line (1) by $22,000. Because this expense requires no cash outflow, Line (2) increases by $22,000 to convert net income to cash flow from operations.

j. The journal entry to record this transaction is:

Building...	400,000	
Note Payable		360,000
Cash..		40,000

The credit to the Cash account reduces Line (9) by $40,000. Acquiring a building is an investing transaction so Line (5) increases by $40,000. The firm discloses in a supplementary schedule or note the acquisition of a building by assuming a mortgage for $360,000.

k. The journal entry for this event is:

Bad Debt Expense..	32,000	
Allowance for Uncollectible Accounts.........		32,000

This entry does not involve the Cash account so Line (9) does not change. The recognition of bad debt expense reduces net income on Line (1) by $32,000. Because this expense does not use cash, Line (2) increases by $32,000 to convert net income to cash flow from operations.

13.1 continued.

1. The journal entry for this event is:

Allowance for Uncollectible Accounts.............. 28,000
    Accounts Receivable   28,000

This event does not affect the Cash account so Line (9) does not change. The event also does not affect net income so Line (1) does not change. Thus, the event would not normally appear in the statement of cash flows. An alternative acceptable answer is Line (2) increases by $28,000 and Line (3) increases by $28,000.

m. The journal entry to record this transaction is:

Cash... 15,000
    Equity in Earnings of Affiliate...................   12,000
    Investment in Securities   3,000

The debit to the Cash account results in an increase in Line (9) of $15,000. The recognition of equity in earnings increases net income on Line (1) by $12,000. Because the firm received $3,000 more cash than its equity in earnings, Line (2) increases by $3,000 when converting net income to cash flow from operations. An alternative acceptable answer for the increase in Line (2) of $3,000 is that Line (2) increases by $15,000 for the dividend received and Line (3) increases by $15,000 to subtract the equity in earnings.

n. The journal entries to record this transaction are:

Cash... 22,000
Realized Loss on Sale of Marketable Secur-
    ities (IncSt).. 3,000
        Marketable Securities............................   25,000

Marketable Securities................................. 2,000
    Unrealized Holding Loss on Marketable
        Securities (SE).......................................   2,000

The debit to the Cash account results in an increase in Line (9) of $22,000. Selling marketable securities is an investing transaction so Line (4) increases by $22,000. The recognition of a realized loss on the sale reduces net income on Line (1) by $3,000. Because the loss does not use cash, the accountant increases Line (2) by $3,000 to add back the loss to net income when converting net income to cash flow from operations.

13.1 continued.

o. The journal entry to record this transaction is:

Preferred Stock...	10,000	
Common Stock.......................................		2,000
Additional Paid-in Capital........................		8,000

This transaction affects neither the Cash account [Line (9)] nor net income [Line (1)]. Thus, it would not appear on the statement of cash flows. The firm discloses in a supplementary schedule or note the conversion of preferred stock into common stock totaling $10,000.

p. The journal entry to record this transaction is:

Legal Expense	5,000	
Land...		5,000

The transaction does not affect the Cash account so Line (9) does not change. The recognition of legal expense reduces net income on Line (1) by $5,000. Because this expense does not use cash, Line (2) increases by $5,000 to convert net income to cash flow from operations.

q. The journal entry for this transaction is:

Rental Fees Received in Advance....................	8,000	
Rent Revenue..		8,000

This entry does not affect the Cash account so Line (9) does not change. The recognition of rent revenue increases net income on Line (1) by $8,000. Because this revenue does not increase cash during the current period, Line (3) increases by $8,000 to convert net income to cash flow from operations.

r. The journal entry to record this event is:

Long-Term Debt..	30,000	
Current Portion of Long-Term Debt		30,000

This entry affects neither the Cash account [Line (9)] nor net income [Line (1)] and would therefore not appear on the statement of cash flows.

13.1 continued.

s. The journal entry to record this event is:

Contracts in Process....................................... 15,000
    Contract Revenue   15,000

This entry does not affect the Cash account so Line (9) does not change. The recognition of contract revenue increases net income on Line (1) by $15,000. Because this revenue does not result in a change in cash, Line (3) increases by $15,000 to convert net income to cash flow from operations.

t. The journal entry to record this transaction is:

Land... 50,000
    Donated Capital (SE).................................   50,000

This transaction affects neither the Cash account [Line (9)] nor net income [Line (1)] and therefore does not appear on the statement of cash flows. The firm discloses in a supplementary schedule or note the donation of land by a governmental agency totaling $50,000.

u. The journal entry to record this event is:

Unrealized Holding Loss on Investments in
    Securities (SE).. 8,000
        Investments in Securities.......................   8,000

This transaction affects neither the Cash account [Line (9)] nor net income [Line (1)] so would not appear on the statement of cash flows. The firm discloses in a supplementary schedule or note the write down of marketable equity investments totaling $8,000.

v. The journal entry to record the recognition of depreciation is:

Inventories 60,000
    Accumulated Depreciation........................   60,000

The journal entry to record the sale of the inventory items is:

Cost of Goods Sold 60,000
    Inventories   60,000

These entries do not affect the Cash account so Line (9) does not change. The recognition of cost of goods sold containing depreciation reduces net income on Line (1) by $60,000. Because this expense does not use cash, Line (2) increases by $60,000 to convert net income to cash flow from operations.

13.1 continued.

w. The journal entry to record this transaction is:

Warranty Expense	35,000	
Estimated Warranty Liability.....................		35,000

This entry does not affect the Cash account so Line (9) does not change. The recognition of warranty expense reduces net income on Line (1) by $35,000. Because this expense does not use cash, Line (2) increases by $35,000 to convert net income to cash flow from operations.

x. The journal entry to record this transaction is:

Estimated Warranty Liability	28,000	
Cash...		28,000

The credit to the Cash account reduces Line (9) by $28,000. Using cash to service a warranty is an operating transaction. This entry does not affect net income on Line (1) this period. Thus, Line (3) increases by $28,000 to convert net income to cash flow from operations.

y. The journal entry to record this event is:

Income Tax Expense....................................	80,000	
Deferred Tax Liability...................................	20,000	
Cash...		100,000

The credit to the Cash account results in a reduction in Line (9) of $100,000. The recognition of income tax expense reduces net income on Line (1) by $80,000. Because the firm used more cash this period than the amount of income tax expense, Line (3) increases by $20,000 when converting net income to cash flow from operations.

z. The journal entry to record this event is:

Loss from Writedown of Inventories................	18,000	
Inventories		18,000

This entry does not affect the Cash account so Line (9) does not change. The recognition of the writedown reduces net income on Line (1) by $18,000. Because the writedown did not use cash, Line (2) increases by $18,000 to convert net income to cash flow from operations.

13.2   (Effects of transactions on cash changes equation.)

a.

	ΔC	=	ΔL	+	ΔSE	–	ΔN$C
Financing	–$12,000	=	$3,000	+	–$15,000	–	$0

b.

	ΔC	=	ΔL	+	ΔSE	–	ΔN$A
Financing	+$75,000	=	$75,000	+	$0	–	$0

c.

	ΔC	=	ΔL	+	ΔSE	–	ΔN$A
Operations	+$15,000	=	$0	+	+$15,000	–	$0
Investing	+$20,000	=	$0	+	$0	–	$5,000
Operations	–$15,000					–	
Net	$20,000	=	$0	+	$15,000	–	$5,000

d.

	ΔC	=	ΔL	+	ΔSE	–	ΔNC$
Operations	–$28,000	=	$0	+	–$28,000	–	$0

e.

	ΔC	=	ΔL	+	ΔSE	–	ΔN$A
Investing	–$39,000	=	$0	+	$0	–	$39,000

f.

	ΔC	=	ΔL	+	ΔSE	–	ΔN$A
	$0	=	$0	+	$0	–	$14,000
						+	$14,000
Net	$0	=	$0	+	$0	+	$0

g.

	ΔC	=	ΔL	+	ΔSE	–	ΔN$A
	$0	=	$0	+	–$8,000	–	–$8,000

h.

	ΔC	=	ΔL	+	ΔSE	–	ΔN$A
Operations	–$14,500	=	$500	+	–$15,000	–	$0

i.

	ΔC	=	ΔL	+	ΔSE	–	ΔN$A
Operations	–$22,000	=	$0	+	–$22,000	–	$0
Operations	+$22,000	=	$0	+	$0	–	–$22,000
Net	$0	=	$0	+	–$22,000	–	–$22,000

j.

	ΔC	=	ΔL	+	ΔSE	–	ΔN$A
Investing	–$40,000	=	$360,000	+	$0	–	$400,000

k.

	ΔC	=	ΔL	+	ΔSE	–	ΔN$A
Operations	–$32,000	=	$0	+	–$32,000	–	$0
Operations	+$32,000	=	$0	+	$0	–	–$32,000
Net	$0	=	$0	+	–$32,000	–	–$32,000

l.

	ΔC	=	ΔL	+	ΔSE	–	ΔN$A
	$0	=	$0	+	$0	–	$28,000
		=				+	$28,000
Net	$0	=	$0	+	$0	–	$0

13.2 continued.

m.

	ΔC	=	ΔL	+	ΔSE	−	$\Delta N\$A$
Operations	$12,000	=	$0	+	$12,000	−	$0
Operations	$3,000	=	$0	+	$0	−	−$3,000
Net	$15,000	=	$0	+	$12,000	−	−$3,000

n.

	ΔC	=	ΔL	+	ΔSE	−	$\Delta N\$A$
Operations	−$3,000	=	$0	+	−$3,000	−	$0
Investing	+$22,000					−	−$25,000
Operations	+$3,000						
	$0	=	$0	+	$2,000	−	$2,000
Net	+$22,000	=	$0	+	−$1,000	−	−$23,000

o.

	ΔC	=	ΔL	+	ΔSE	−	$\Delta N\$A$
	$0	=	$0	+	$10,000	−	$0
					−$10,000	−	
	$0	=	$0	+	$0	−	$0

p.

	ΔC	=	ΔL	+	ΔSE	−	$\Delta N\$A$
Operations	−$5,000	=	$0	+	−$5,000	−	$0
Operations	+$5,000	=	$0	+	$0	−	−$5,000
Net	$0	=	$0	+	−$5,000	−	−$5,000

q.

	ΔC	=	ΔL	+	ΔSE	−	$\Delta N\$A$
Operations	+$8,000	=	$0	+	$8,000	−	$0
Operations	−$8,000	=	−$8,000	+	$0	−	$0
Net	$0	=	−$8,000	+	$8,000	−	$0

r.

	ΔC	=	ΔL	+	ΔSE	−	$\Delta N\$A$
	$0	=	$30,000	+	$0	−	$0
		=	−30,000				
Net	$0	=	$0	+	$0	−	$0

s.

	ΔC	=	ΔL	+	ΔSE	−	$\Delta N\$A$
Operations	+$15,000	=	$0	+	$15,000	−	$0
Operations	−$15,000	=	$0	+	$0	−	$15,000
Net	$0	=	$0	+	$15,000	−	$15,000

t.

	ΔC	=	ΔL	+	ΔSE	−	$\Delta N\$A$
	$0	=	$0	+	$50,000	−	$50,000

u.

	ΔC	=	ΔL	+	ΔSE	−	$\Delta N\$A$
	$0	=	$0	+	−$8,000	−	−$8,000

v.

	ΔC	=	ΔL	+	ΔSE	−	$\Delta N\$A$
Operations	−$60,000	=	$0	+	−$60,000	−	$0
Operations	+$60,000	=	$0	+	$0	−	−$60,000
Net	$0	=	$0	+	−$60,000	−	−$60,000

13.2 continued.

w.

	ΔC	=	ΔL	+	ΔSE	–	$\Delta N\$A$
Operations	–$35,000	=	$0	+	–$35,000	–	$0
Operations	+$35,000	=	$35,000	+	$0	–	$0
Net	$0	=	$35,000	+	–$35,000	–	$0

x.

	ΔC	=	ΔL	+	ΔSE	–	$\Delta N\$A$
Operations	–$28,000	=	–$28,000	+	$0	–	$0

y.

	ΔC	=	ΔL	+	ΔSE	–	$\Delta N\$A$
Operations	–$80,000	=	$0	+	–$80,000	–	$0
Operations	–$20,000	=	–$20,000	+	$0	–	$0
Net	–$100,000	=	–$20,000	+	–$80,000	–	$0

z.

	ΔC	=	ΔL	+	ΔSE	–	$\Delta N\$A$
Operations	–$18,000	=	$0	+	–$18,000	–	$0
Operations	+$18,000	=	$0	+	$0	–	–$18,000
Net	$0	=	$0	+	–$18,000	–	–$18,000

13.3   (Alcoa; working backwards from statement of cash flows.)

(2) Cash (Operations—Depreciation Expense Add-
back)... 664.0
  Accumulated Depreciation...................... 664.0

(3) Cash (Operations—Deferred Tax Addback)...... 82.0
  Deferred Income Tax Liability..................... 82.0

(4) Investment in Affiliates................................ 47.1
  Cash (Operations—Equity in Undistributed
  Earnings Subtraction) 47.1

(5) Cash (Investing—Sale of Marketable Secur-
&   ities)... 49.8
(11)   Cash (Operations—Gain on Sale of Mar-
  ketable Securities Subtraction)............. 20.8
  Marketable Securities 29.0

(6) Cash (Operations—Decrease in Accounts Re-
ceivable)... 74.6
  Accounts Receivable 74.6

(7) Inventories... 198.9
  Cash (Operations—Increase in Inventories). 198.9

(8) Prepayments 40.3
  Cash (Operations—Increase in Prepay-
  ments).. 40.3

13.3 continued.

(9) Cash (Operations—Decrease in Accounts Payable) 33.9
      Accounts Payable 33.9

(10) Other Current Liabilities............................. 110.8
      Cash (Operations—Decrease in Other Current Liabilities)...................................... 110.8

(12) Marketable Securities 73.2
      Cash (Investing—Acquisition of Marketable Securities) 73.2

(13) Property, Plant and Equipment...................... 875.7
      Cash (Investing—Acquisition of Property, Plant and Equipment)............................ 875.7

(14) Investments in Securities............................. 44.5
      Cash (Investing—Acquisition of Subsidiaries) 44.5

(15) Cash (Financing—Common Stock Issued to Employees)... 34.4
      Common Stock 34.4

(16) Treasury Stock 100.9
      Cash (Financing—Repurchase of Common Stock) 100.9

(17) Retained Earnings 242.9
      Cash (Financing—Dividends Paid to Shareholders)... 242.9

(18) Cash (Financing—Additions to Short-Term Borrowing)... 127.6
      Notes Payable....................................... 127.6

(19) Cash (Financing—Additions to Long-Term Borrowing)... 121.6
      Bonds Payable 121.6

(20) Bonds Payable... 476.4
      Cash (Financing—Payments to Long-Term Borrowing) 476.4

(21) Property, Plant and Equipment...................... 76.9
      Mortgage Payable................................... 76.9

13.3 continued.

 (22) Property, Plant and Equipment..................... 98.2
     Capitalized Lease Obligation 98.2

 (23) Convertible Bonds Payable............................ 47.8
     Common Stock..   47.8

13.4 (Ingersoll-Rand; working backwards from statement of cash flows.)

 (2) Cash (Operations—Depreciation Expense Add-
   back)... 179.4
     Accumulated Depreciation.......................   179.4

 (3) Cash (Investing—Sale of Property, Plant, and
 & Equipment 26.5
 (12)   Property, Plant and Equipment (Net) 22.9
     Cash (Operations—Gain on Sale
      Subtraction).......................................   3.6

 (4) Investment in Securities.............................. 41.5
     Cash (Operations—Equity in Earnings
      Subtraction) 41.5

 (5) Cash (Operations—Deferred Taxes Addback)... 15.1
     Deferred Income Taxes.............................   15.1

 (6) Cash (Operations—Decrease in Accounts Receivable).. 50.9
     Accounts Receivable 50.9

 (7) Inventories.. 15.2
     Cash (Operations—Increase in Inventories).   15.2

 (8) Other Current Assets 33.1
     Cash (Operations—Increase in Other Cur-
      rent Assets) 33.1

 (9) Accounts Payable....................................... 37.9
     Cash (Operations—Decrease in Accounts
      Payable)..   37.9

 (10) Cash (Operations—Increase in Other Current
   Liabilities).. 19.2
     Other Current Liabilities........................   19.2

 (11) Property, Plant and Equipment..................... 211.7
     Cash (Investing—Acquisition of Property,
      Plant and Equipment)...........................   211.7

13.4 continued.

(13)	Marketable Securities	4.6	
	Cash (Investing—Acquisition of Marketable Securities)		4.6
(14)	Cash (Investing—Advances from Equity Companies)	18.4	
	Advances from Equity Companies		18.4
(15)	Short-Term Debt	81.5	
	Cash (Financing—Repayment of Short-Term Debt)		81.5
(16)	Cash (Financing—Issue of Long-Term Debt)	147.6	
	Long-Term Debt Payable		147.6
(17)	Long-Term Debt Payable	129.7	
	Cash (Financing—Repayment of Long-Term Debt)		129.7
(18)	Cash (Financing—Issue of Common Stock under Option Plan)	47.9	
	Common Stock, Additional Paid-in Capital		47.9
(19)	Cash (Financing—Sale of Treasury Stock)	59.3	
	Treasury Stock, Additional Paid-in Capital		59.3
(20)	Retained Earnings	78.5	
	Cash (Financing—Dividends Paid)		78.5
(21)	Leasehold Asset	147.9	
	Capitalized Lease Obligation		147.9
(22)	Preferred Stock	62.0	
	Common Stock, Additional Paid-in Capital ...		62.0
(23)	Investments in Securities.............................	94.3	
	Common Stock, Additional Paid-in Capital ...		94.3

13.5   See solution to Problem 8.46.

13.6   See solution to Problem 9.45.

13.7   See solution to Problem 11.55.

13.8   See solution to Problem 12.42.

13.9   (Warren Corporation; preparing a statement of cash flows.)

a.

		Cash			
		√ 223,200			

Operations

Net Income	(5)	234,000	
Loss on Sale of Machinery	(1b)	15,600	
Amortize Patent	(2b)	5,040	
Decrease in Accounts Receivable	(7)	18,000	
Bad Debt Expense	(8)	2,400	
Decrease in Inventories	(9)	66,000	
Depreciation Expense	(11)	106,800	
Amortize Leasehold Improvements	(12)	10,800	
Increase in Accounts Payable	(13)	153,360	

Investing

Sale of Machinery	(1b)	57,600	463,200	(1a)	Acquisition of Machinery
			2,400	(2a)	Payment for Patent Defense
			180,000	(10)	Acquisition of Securities

Financing

			13,200	(3)	Retirement of Preferred Stock
			60,000	(15)	Provision for Current Portion of Serial Bonds

		√ 174,000	

13.9 a. continued.

Accounts Receivable		Allowance for Un-collectible Accounts		Inventory	
√ 327,600			20,400 √	√ 645,600	
	3,600 (6)	(6) 3,600	2,400 (8)		66,000 (9)
	18,000 (7)				
√ 306,000			19,200 √	√ 579,600	

Securities Held for Plant Expansion		Machinery and Equipment (Cost)		Accumulated Depreciation	
√ -0-		√ 776,400			446,400 √
(10) 180,000		(1a) 463,200	127,200 (1b)	(1b) 54,000	106,800 (11)
√ 180,000		√ 1,112,400			499,200 √

Leasehold Improvements		Allowance for Amortization		Patents	
√ 104,400			58,800 √	√ 36,000	
			10,800 (12)	(2a) 2,400	5,040 (2b)
√ 104,400			69,600 √	√ 33,360	

Accounts Payable		Dividends Payable		Bonds Payable (Current)	
	126,000 √		-- √		60,000 √
	153,360 (13)		48,000 (4)	(15) 60,000	60,000 (14)
	279,360 √		48,000 √		60,000 √

6-Percent Serial Bonds Payable		Preferred Stock		Common Stock	
	360,000 √		120,000 √		600,000 √
(14) 60,000		(3) 12,000			
	300,000 √		108,000 √		600,000 √

Retained Earnings	
	321,600 √
(4) 48,000	234,000 (5)
(3) 1,200	
	506,400 √

13.9 continued.

b.

WARREN CORPORATION
Statement of Cash Flows
For the Year Ending December 31, Year 5

Operations:

Net Income...	$ 234,000	
Loss on Sale of Machinery	15,600	
Depreciation	106,800	
Amortization of Leasehold Improvements..	10,800	
Amortization of Patents............................	5,040	
Bad Debt Expense	2,400	
Decrease in Accounts Receivable...............	18,000	
Decrease in Inventories.............................	66,000	
Increase in Accounts Payable....................	153,360	
Cash Flow from Operations		$ 612,000
Investing:		
Sale of Machinery....................................	$ 57,600	
Payment of Legal Fee for Patent Defense	(2,400)	
Acquisition of Securities for Plant Expan-		
sion..	(180,000)	
Acquisition of Machinery	(463,200)	
Cash Flow from Investing		(588,000)
Financing:		
Retirement of Serial Bonds	$ (60,000)	
Retirement of Preferred Stock	(13,200)	
Cash Flow from Financing		(73,200)
Net Change in Cash...................................		$ (49,200)
Cash, January 1, Year 5............................		223,200
Cash, December 31, Year 5		$ 174,000

13.10 (Roth Company; preparing a statement of cash flows.)

a.

Cash

		√ 37,950			

Operations

			3,600	(2)	Gain on Sale of Marketable Securities
Net Income	(1)	95,847			
Bond Discount Amortization	(6)	225			
Amortize Goodwill	(8)	180	16,050	(4)	Gain on Condemnation of Land
Depreciation	(11)	1,875			
Increase in Income Taxes Payable	(15)	51,924	37,500	(9)	Increase in Accounts Receivable
Deferred Taxes	(16)	504			
			26,250	(10)	Increase in Inventories
			8,820	(12)	Equity in Earnings
			5,835	(13)	Decrease in Accounts Payable

Investing

			122,250	(5)	Acquisition of Equipment
Sale of Marketable Securities	(2)	17,400			
Proceeds from Condemnation of Land	(4)	48,000			

Financing

Issuance of Bonds	(7)	97,500			
	√	131,100			

Marketable Securities				Accounts Receivable				Inventory		
√ 24,000				√ 36,480				√ 46,635		
	13,800 (2)		(9) 37,500				(10) 26,250			
√ 10,200				√ 73,980				√ 72,885		

Land				Building				Equipment		
√ 60,000				√ 375,000				√ -0-		
	31,950 (4)						(5) 122,250			
√ 28,050				√ 375,000				√ 122,250		

13.10 a. continued.

Accumulated Depreciation		
	22,500	√
	1,875	(11)
	24,375	√

Investment in 30-Percent Owned Co.			
√	91,830		
(12)	8,820	180	(8)
√	100,470		

Other Assets		
√	22,650	
√	22,650	

Accounts Payable			
		31,830	√
(13)	5,835		
		25,995	√

Dividends Payable		
	-0-	√
	12,000	(14)
	12,000	√

Income Taxes Payable		
	-0-	√
	51,924	(15)
	51,924	√

Other Liabilities		
	279,000	√
	279,000	√

Bonds Payable		
	71,550	√
	225	(6)
	97,500	(7)
	169,275	√

Deferred Income Taxes		
	765	√
	504	(16)
	1,269	√

Preferred Stock			
		45,000	√
(3)	45,000		
		-0-	√

Common Stock		
	120,000	√
	45,000	(3)
	165,000	√

Dividends Declared			
√	-0-		
(14)	12,000		
√	12,000		

Unrealized Holding Loss on Marketable Securities		
√	750	
√	750	

Retained Earnings		
	124,650	√
	95,847	(1)
	220,497	√

13.10 continued.

b.

ROTH COMPANY
Statement of Cash Flows
For the Three Months Ended March 31, Year 7

Operations:

Net Income...	$ 95,847	
Bond Discount Amortization......................	225	
Goodwill Amortization.............................	180	
Depreciation	1,875	
Deferred Income Taxes...........................	504	
Increase in Income Taxes Payable	51,924	
Gain on Sale of Marketable Securities........	(3,600)	
Gain on Condemnation of Land	(16,050)	
Equity in Earnings.................................	(8,820)	
Increase in Accounts Receivable...............	(37,500)	
Increase in Inventories...........................	(26,250)	
Decrease in Accounts Payable..................	(5,835)	
Cash Flow from Operations		$ 52,500
Investing:		
Proceeds from Sale of Marketable Securities..	$ 17,400	
Proceeds from Condemnation of Land........	48,000	
Acquisition of Equipment	(122,250)	
Cash Flow from Investing		(56,850)
Financing:		
Issue of Bonds.......................................	$ 97,500	
Cash Flow from Financing		97,500
Net Change in Cash..................................		$ 93,150
Cash, January 1 Year 7.............................		37,950
Cash, March 31, Year 7.............................		$ 131,100

Supplementary Information

Holders of the firm's preferred stock converted shares with a book value of $45,000 into shares of common stock.

13.11 (Biddle Corporation; preparing a statement of cash flows.)

a.

		Cash		
√	45,000			

Operations

Income from Continuing Operations	(14)	54,500	35,000	(7)	Increase in Accounts Receivable
Loss on Sale of Equipment	(4)	2,000	20,000	(8)	Increase in Inventories
Depreciation	(9)	10,000	5,000	(12)	Decrease in Accrued Liabilities
Amortization	(10)	1,500			
Increase in Accounts Payable	(11)	30,000			
Deferred Income Taxes	(13)	20,000			

Extraordinary Gain or Loss

Income from Extraordinary Items	(14)	6,000	6,000	(3)	Gain on Retirement of Bonds Net of Income Taxes

Investing

Sale of Equipment	(4)	9,500	42,500	(6)	Acquisition of Land

Financing

			19,000	(3)	Retirement of Bonds, Including Income Taxes
			1,000	(5)	Dividends
√	50,000				

Accounts Receivable—Net		Inventories		Land	
√ 70,000		√ 110,000		√ 100,000	
(7) 35,000		(8) 20,000		(2) 20,000	
				(6) 42,500	
√ 105,000		√ 130,000		√ 162,500	

Solutions 13-20 Harcourt, Inc.

13.11 a. continued.

Plant and Equipment			Accumulated Depreciation				Patents		
√ 316,500				50,000 √		√ 16,500			
	26,500 (4)	(4) 15,000		10,000 (9)				1,500 (10)	
√ 290,000				45,000 √		√ 15,000			

Accounts Payable		Accrued Liabilities			Deferred Income Taxes	
	100,000 √		105,000 √			50,000 √
	30,000 (11)	(12) 5,000				20,000 (13)
	130,000 √		100,000 √			70,000 √

Long-term Bonds		Common Stock		Additional Paid-in Capital	
	90,000 √		105,000 √		85,000 √
(3) 25,000			10,500 (1)		21,000 (1)
			9,500 (2)		10,500 (2)
	65,000 √		125,000 √		116,500 √

Retained Earnings		
	73,000	√
(1) 31,500	60,500 (14)	
(5) 1,000		
	101,000	√

13.11 continued.

b.
BIDDLE CORPORATION
Statement of Cash Flows
For the Year Ended December, Year 2

Operations:		
Income from Continuing Operations.........	$ 54,500	
Loss on Sale of Equipment	2,000	
Depreciation	10,000	
Amortization	1,500	
Deferred Income Taxes............................	20,000	
Increase in Accounts Payable...................	30,000	
Increase in Accounts Receivable...............	(35,000)	
Increase in Inventories...........................	(20,000)	
Decrease in Accrued Liabilities.................	(5,000)	
Cash Flow from Operations		$ 58,000
Investing:		
Sale of Equipment...................................	$ 9,500	
Acquisition of Land.................................	(42,500)	
Cash Flow from Investing		(33,000)
Financing:		
Retirement of Bonds...............................	$ (19,000)	
Dividends	(1,000)	
Cash Flow from Financing		(20,000)
Net Change in Cash....................................		$ 5,000
Cash, January 1, Year 2.............................		45,000
Cash, December 31, Year 2		$ 50,000

Supplementary Information
During Year 2, Biddle Corporation issued common stock with a market value of $20,000 in the acquisition of land.

13.12 (Plainview Corporation; preparing a statement of cash flows.)

a.

Cash		
√ 165,300		

Operations

Income from Continuing Operations	(1)	239,580	17,000	(5)	Gain on Sale of Marketable Securities
Loss from Fire	(6)	35,000	131,100	(12)	Increase in Inventories
Equity in Loss	(9)	17,920	1,400	(13)	Increase in Prepayments
Decrease in Accounts Receivable—Net	(11)	59,000	1,500	(18)	Decrease in Accrued Payables
Depreciation	(15)	79,900	500	(20)	Deferred Taxes
Increase in Accounts Payable	(16)	24,800			
Increase in Income Taxes Payable	(19)	66,500			

From Extraordinary Items

Loss on Retirement of Bonds	(21)	3,000	3,000	(1)	Extraordinary Loss

Investing

Sale of Marketable Securities	(5)	127,000	28,000	(8)	Acquisition of Machinery
Building Sold	(7)	4,000	103,400	(10)	Acquisition of Marketable Securities
Bond Sinking Funds Utilized	(14)	63,000			

Financing

Sale of Treasury Stock	(3)	6,000	130,000	(2)	Dividends
Issuance of Debentures	(22)	125,000	145,000	(17)	Payment of Note Payable—Current
			313,000	(21)	Retirement of Bonds

√ 142,100		

13.12 a. continued.

Marketable Securities	
√ 129,200	
(10) 103,400	110,000 (5)
√ 122,600	

Accounts Receivable—Net	
√ 371,200	
	59,000 (11)
√ 312,200	

Inventories	
√ 124,100	
(12) 131,100	
√ 255,200	

Prepayments	
√ 22,000	
(13) 1,400	
√ 23,400	

Bond Sinking Fund	
√ 63,000	
	63,000 (14)
√ -0-	

Investment in Subsidiary	
√ 152,000	
	17,920 (9)
√ 134,080	

Plant and Equipment—Net	
√ 1,534,600	
(6) 65,000	100,000 (6)
(8) 28,000	4,000 (7)
	79,900 (15)
√ 1,443,700	

Accounts Payable	
	213,300 √
	24,800 (16)
	238,100 √

Notes Payable—Current	
	145,000 √
(17) 145,000	
	-0- √

Accrued Payables	
	18,000 √
(18) 1,500	
	16,500 √

Income Taxes Payable	
	31,000 √
	66,500 (19)
	97,500 √

Deferred Income Taxes	
	128,400 √
(20) 500	
	127,900 √

6-Percent Mortgage Bonds	
	310,000 √
(21) 310,000	
	-0- √

8-Percent Debentures	
	-0- √
	125,000 (22)
	125,000 √

Common Stock	
	950,000 √
	83,500 (4)
	1,033,500 √

Additional Paid-in Capital	
	51,000 √
	16,700 (4)
	67,700 √

Unrealized Holding Gain on Marketable Securities	
	2,500 √
	2,500 √

Retained Earnings	
	755,700 √
(2) 130,000	236,580 (1)
(3) 3,000	
(4) 100,200	
	759,080 √

Treasury Stock	
√ 43,500	
	9,000 (3)
√ 34,500	

13.12 continued.

b.

PLAINVIEW CORPORATION
Statement of Cash Flows
For the Year Ended December, Year 5

Operations:

Income from Continuing Operations.........	$ 239,580	
Loss from Fire..	35,000	
Equity in Loss of Subsidiary	17,920	
Depreciation	79,900	
Gain on Sale of Marketable Securities........	(17,000)	
Deferred Income Taxes...........................	(500)	
Decrease in Accounts Receivable—Net.......	59,000	
Increase in Accounts Payable...................	24,800	
Increase in Income Taxes Payable	66,500	
Increase in Inventories...........................	(131,100)	
Increase in Prepayments	(1,400)	
Decrease in Accounts Payable...................	(1,500)	
Cash Flow from Operations		$ 371,200
Investing:		
Marketable Securities Sold.......................	$ 127,000	
Building Sold	4,000	
Bond Sinking Funds Utilized	63,000	
Acquisition of Marketable Securities..........	(103,400)	
Acquisition of Machinery	(28,000)	
Cash Flow from Investing...........................		62,600
Financing:		
Sale of Treasury Stock.............................	$ 6,000	
Issue of Debentures	125,000	
Dividends	(130,000)	
Retirement of Bonds...............................	(313,000)	
Payment of Short-Term Note....................	(145,000)	
Cash Flow from Financing.........................		(457,000)
Net Change in Cash.................................		$ (23,200)
Cash, January 1, Year 5............................		165,300
Cash, December 31, Year 5		$ 142,100

13.13 (UAL Corporation; preparing and interpreting the statement of cash flows.)

a. T-account work sheet for Year 9.

	Cash		
√	1,087		

	Operations		
(1)	324	106	(4)
(3)	517	147	(7)
(11)	56	39	(8)
(15)	42	67	(9)
(17)	12	49	(16)

	Investing		
(4)	1,199	1,568	(2)
(10)	40	957	(6)

	Financing		
(12)	325	110	(13)
(18)	4	98	(19)
√	465		

Marketable Securities			Accounts Receivable			Inventories	
√	--		√	741		√	210
(5)	85		(7)	147		(8)	39
(6)	957						
√	1,042		√	888		√	249

Prepayments			Property, Plant and Equipment			Accumulated Depreciation	
√	112		√	7,710			3,769 √
(9)	67		(2)	1,568	1,574 (4)	(4) 481	517 (3)
√	179		√	7,704			3,805 √

Other Assets			Accounts Payable		Short-Term Borrowing	
√	610			540 √		121 √
		40 (10)		56 (11)		325 (12)
√	570			596 √		446 √

13.13 a. continued.

Current Portion Long-Term Debt				Advances from Customers				Other Current Liabilities		
		110	√			619	√		1,485	√
(13)	110	84	(14)			42	(15)	(16) 49		
		84	√			661	√		1,436	√

Long-Term Debt				Deferred Tax Liability			Other Noncurrent Liabilities		
		1,418	√		352	√		715	√
(14)	84				12	(17)		4	(18)
		1,334	√		364	√		719	√

Common Stock			Unrealized Holding Gain on Marketable Securities			Retained Earnings		
	119	√		--	√		1,188	√
				85	(5)		324	(1)
	119	√		85	√		1,512	√

Treasury Stock		
√	14	
(19)	98	
√	112	

13.13 a. continued.

a. T-account work sheet for Year 10.

Cash

√	465	

Operations

(1)	101	286	(4)
(3)	560	25	(7)
(15)	182	74	(8)
(16)	390	30	(9)
(18)	4	44	(11)

Investing

(4)	1,697	2,821	(2)
		17	(6)
		35	(10)

Financing

(12)	1	84	(13)
(17)	230		
(19)	2		
(20)	5		
√	221		

Marketable Securities		Accounts Receivable		Inventories	
√ 1,042		√ 888		√ 249	
(5) 7		(7) 25		(8) 74	
(6) 17					
√ 1,066		√ 913		√ 323	

Prepayments		Property, Plant and Equipment		Accumulated Depreciation	
√ 179		√ 7,704			3,805 √
(9) 30		(2) 2,821	1,938 (4)	(4) 527	560 (3)
√ 209		√ 8,587			3,838 √

13.13 a. continued.

Other Assets		
√	570	
(10)	35	
√	605	

Accounts Payable		
	596	√
(11) 44		
	552	√

Short-Term
Borrowing

	446	√
	1	(12)
	447	√

Current Portion
Long-Term Debt

	84	√
(13) 84	89	(14)
	89	√

Advances from
Customers

	661	√
	182	(15)
	843	√

Other Current
Liabilities

	1,436	√
	390	(16)
	1,826	√

Long-Term Debt		
	1,334	√
(14) 89	230	(17)
	1,475	√

Deferred Tax
Liability

	364	√
	4	(18)
	368	√

Other Noncurrent
Liabilities

	719	√
	2	(19)
	721	√

Common Stock		
	119	√
	1	(20)
	120	√

Additional Paid-in
Capital

	48	√
	4	(20)
	52	√

Unrealized Holding
Gain on Marketable
Securities

	85	√
	7	(5)
	92	√

Retained Earnings		
	1,512	√
	101	(1)
	1,613	√

Treasury Stock		
√	112	
√	112	

13.13 continued.

b. Comparative Statement of Cash Flows for UAL Corporation
(Amounts in Millions)

	Year 9	Year 10
Operations:		
Net Income......	$ 324	$ 101
Depreciation Expense......	517	560
Deferred Income Taxes......	12	4
Gain on Sale of Property, Plant and Equipment......	(106)	(286)
(Increase) Decrease in Accounts Receivable......	(147)	(25)
(Increase) Decrease in Inventories......	(39)	(74)
(Increase) Decrease in Prepayments......	(67)	(30)
Increase (Decrease) in Accounts Payable......	56	(44)
Increase (Decrease) in Advances from Customers......	42	182
Increase (Decrease) in Other Current Liabilities......	(49)	390
Cash Flow from Operations......	$ 543	$ 778
Investing:		
Sale of Property, Plant and Equipment......	$ 1,199	$ 1,697
Acquisition of Property, Plant and Equipment......	(1,568)	(2,821)
Acquisition of Marketable Securities......	(957)	(17)
(Increase) Decrease in Other Noncurrent Assets......	40	(35)
Cash Flow from Investing......	$(1,286)	$(1,176)
Financing:		
Increase in Short-Term Borrowing......	$ 325	$ 1
Increase in Long-Term Borrowing......	--	230
Increase in Common Stock......	--	5
Decrease in Long-Term Borrowing......	(110)	(84)
Acquisition of Treasury Stock......	(98)	--
Increase in Other Noncurrent Liabilities......	4	2
Cash Flow from Financing......	$ 121	$ 154
Net Change in Cash......	$ (622)	$ (244)
Cash, January 1......	1,087	465
Cash, December 31......	$ 465	$ 221

13.13 continued.

c. During Year 9, cash flow from operations exceeded net income primarily because of the noncash expense for depreciation. Cash flows from operations and from the sale of property, plant and equipment were sufficient to finance capital expenditures. UAL Corporation used the excess cash flow as well as cash from additional short-term borrowing to repay long-term debt and reacquire treasury stock. It invested the remaining excess cash flow in short-term marketable securities. Although the balance in the cash account declined during Year 9, the combined balance in cash and marketable securities actually increased.

Net income declined in Year 10 relative to Year 9 but cash flow from operations increased. The increase occurred because UAL Corporation received increased cash advances from customers and stretched its other current liabilities. Cash flow from operations and from the sale of property, plant and equipment were insufficient to finance capital expenditures. UAL Corporation increased long-term borrowing and decreased the balance in its cash account to finance these capital expenditures.

One additional item to note for UAL Corporation is the significant turnover of aircraft each year. The airline sold older aircraft at a gain and replaced them with newer aircraft.

13.14   (Irish Paper Company; preparing and interpreting the statement of cash flows.)

a.   T-account work sheet for Year 9.

Cash

	√	374		

Operations

(1)	376	221	(7)
(6)	306	31	(8)
(9)	2	112	(10)
(12)	54	59	(11)
(14)	72	5	(17)
(18)	87		

Investing

(7)	5	92	(3)
(13)	8	775	(4)

Financing

(5)	449	59	(2)
		129	(16)
		201	(19)

	√	49		

Accounts Receivable			Inventories			Prepayments		
√	611		√	522		√	108	
(10)	112		(11)	59				54 (12)
√	723		√	581		√	54	

Investments in Affiliates			Property, Plant and Equipment			Accumulated Depreciation		
√	254		√	5,272				2,160 √
(3)	92	2 (9)	(4)	775	78 (7)	(7)	74	306 (6)
(8)	31							
√	375		√	5,969				2,392 √

Other Assets			Accounts Payable			Current Portion Long-Term Debt		
√	175				920 √			129 √
(7)	220	8 (13)			72 (14)	(16)	129	221 (15)
√	387				992 √			221 √

13.14 a. continued.

Other Current Liabilities			Long-Term Debt			Deferred Income Taxes		
		98 √			1,450 √			607 √
(17)	5		(15)	221	449 (5)			87 (18)
		93 √			1,678 √			694 √

Common Stock			Retained Earnings			Treasury Stock		
		629 √			1,331 √	√	15	
(19)	201		(2)	59	376 (1)			
		428 √			1,648 √	√	15	

a. T-account work sheet for Year 10.

Cash

√	49	

Operations

(1)	169		19	(8)
(7)	346		38	(9)
(10)	5		106	(11)
(14)	186		154	(12)
			10	(17)
			26	(18)

Investing

(3)	86		931	(4)
(8)	21		78	(13)

Financing

(5)	890		59	(2)
(19)	4		221	(16)
√	114			

Accounts Receivable			Inventories			Prepayments		
√	723		√	581		√	54	
(11)	106		(12)	154				
√	829		√	735		√	54	

13.14 a. continued.

Investments in Affiliates		
√ 375		
(9) 38	86 (3)	
	5 (10)	
√ 322		

Property, Plant and Equipment		
√ 5,969		
(4) 931	42 (8)	
(6) 221		
√ 7,079		

Accumulated Depreciation		
	2,392 √	
(8) 40	346 (7)	
	2,698 √	

Other Assets	
√ 387	
(13) 78	
√ 465	

Accounts Payable	
	992 √
	186 (14)
	1,178 √

Current Portion Long-Term Debt	
	221 √
(16) 221	334 (15)
	334 √

Other Current Liabilities	
	93 √
(17) 10	
	83 √

Long-Term Debt	
	1,678 √
(15) 334	890 (5)
	221 (6)
	2,455 √

Deferred Income Taxes	
	694 √
(18) 26	
	668 √

Common Stock	
	428 √
	4 (19)
	432 √

Retained Earnings	
	1,648 √
(2) 59	169 (1)
	1,758 √

Treasury Stock	
√ 15	
√ 15	

13.14 a. continued.

a. T-account work sheet for Year 11.

Cash

√	114		

Operations

(6)	353	142	(1)
(7)	34	30	(8)
(9)	32	2	(12)
(10)	159	45	(17)
(11)	164	7	(18)
(14)	136		

Investing

(7)	114	13	(3)
		315	(4)
		19	(13)

Financing

(5)	36	59	(2)
(19)	8	334	(16)
√	184		

Accounts Receivable			
√	829		
		159	(10)
√	670		

Inventories			
√	735		
		164	(11)
√	571		

Prepayments			
√	54		
(12)	2		
√	56		

Investments in Affiliates			
√	322		
(3)	13	32	(9)
(8)	30		
√	333		

Property, Plant and Equipment			
√	7,079		
(4)	315	222	(7)
√	7,172		

Accumulated Depreciation			
		2,698	√
(7)	74	353	(6)
		2,977	√

Other Assets		
√	465	
(13)	19	
√	484	

Accounts Payable		
	1,178	√
	136	(14)
	1,314	√

Current Portion Long-Term Debt		
	334	√
(16) 334	158	(15)
	158	√

13.14 a. continued.

Other Current Liabilities

		83 √	
(17)	45		
		38 √	

Long-Term Debt

		2,455 √	
(15)	158	36 (5)	
		2,333 √	

Deferred Income Taxes

		668 √	
(18)	7		
		661 √	

Common Stock

	432 √	
	7 (19)	
	439 √	

Retained Earnings

		1,758 √ √	
(1)	142		
(2)	59		
		1,557 √ √	

Treasury Stock

15	
	1 (19)
14	

b.

IRISH PAPER COMPANY
Statement of Cash Flows
(Amounts in Millions)

	Year 9	Year 10	Year 11
Operations:			
Net Income (Loss)	$ 376	$ 169	$ (142)
Depreciation Expense	306	346	353
Loss (Gain) on Sale of Property, Plant and Equipment	(221)	(19)	34
Equity in Undistributed Earnings of Affiliates	(29)	(33)	2
Increase (Decrease) in Deferred Income Taxes	87	(26)	(7)
(Increase) Decrease in Accounts Receivable	(112)	(106)	159
(Increase) Decrease in Inventories	(59)	(154)	164
(Increase) Decrease in Prepayments	54	--	(2)
Increase (Decrease) in Accounts Payable	72	186	136
Increase (Decrease) in Other Current Liabilities	(5)	(10)	(45)
Cash Flow from Operations	$ 469	$ 353	$ 652
Investing:			
Sale of Property, Plant and Equipment	$ 5	$ 21	$ 114
Acquisition of Property, Plant and Equipment	(775)	(931)	(315)
(Increase) Decrease in Investments in Affiliates	(92)	86	(13)
(Increase) Decrease in Other Assets	8	(78)	(19)
Cash Flow from Investing	$ (854)	$ (902)	$ (233)

13.14 b. continued.

Financing:

Issue of Long-Term Debt..................	$ 449	$ 890	$ 36
Sale of Common Stork or Treasury Stock...	--	4	8
Redemption of Long-Term Debt.........	(129)	(221)	(334)
Redemption of Common Stock Warrants.......................................	(201)	--	--
Dividends......................................	(59)	(59)	(59)
Cash Flow from Financing.................	$ 60	$ 614	$ (349)
Net Change in Cash	$ (325)	$ 65	$ 70
Cash, January 1..............................	374	49	114
Cash, December 31	$ 49	$ 114	$ 184

Supplementary Information

During Year 10, Irish Paper Company assumed a mortgage payable of $221 million in the acquisition of property, plant and equipment.

c. The pattern of cash flows for Year 9 is typical of a growing, capital-intensive firm. Cash flow from operations exceeds net income because of the addback of depreciation expense. Book income before taxes exceeds taxable income, resulting in a deferral of taxes payable. Accounts receivable and inventories increased to support the growth, while accounts payable increased to finance the increased inventories. Irish made significant capital expenditures during the year for which it had to rely in part on external debt financing.

The pattern of cash flows for Year 10 is similar to that for Year 9, again typical of a growing firm. In this case, however, cash flow from operations declines relative to Year 9 because of reduced net income. The reduced net income occurs in part because of a smaller gain on sale of property, plant and equipment and in part because of larger depreciation and administrative expenses. Irish financed its increased capital expenditures with additional long-term borrowing.

The pattern of cash flows for Year 11 is typical of a firm that stopped growing. Sales and net income declined, the result of under-utilizing manufacturing capacity. Cash flow from operations increased, however, because Irish collected receivables and decreased its investment in inventories. It also stretched its accounts payable. Cash flow from operations was more than sufficient to finance a reduced level of capital expenditures and repay long-term dept.

13.15   (Breda Enterprises, Inc.; preparing a statement of cash flows.)

BREDA ENTERPRISES, INC.
Statement of Cash Flows
For the Year Ended December 31, Year 6

Operations:		
Net Income (1)...	$ 90,000	
Adjustments for Noncash Transactions:		
Decrease in Merchandise Inventory (3)............	4,000	
Increase in Accounts Payable (3)	12,000	
Loss on Sale of Equipment (4).........................	13,000	
Depreciation Expense (4).................................	42,000	
Amortization of Leasehold Asset (5)	5,000	
Loss on Conversion of Bonds (8)	15,000	
Increase in Accounts Receivable (Net) (2).........	(10,600)	
Increase in Notes Receivable (2)......................	(15,000)	
Increase in Interest Receivable (2) [(.08 X		
$15,000) X (1/6)]	(200)	
Decrease in Advances from Customers (2).......	(2,700)	
Realized Gain on Marketable Securities (7)	(4,600)	
Amortization of Bond Premium (8)...................	(1,500)	
Cash Flow from Operations..............................		$ 146,400
Investing:		
Sale of Equipment (4).....................................	$ 25,000	
Sale of Marketable Securities (7).....................	9,100	
Purchase of Equipment (4) ($31,000 + $38,000 –		
$26,000)...	(43,000)	
Cash Flow from Investing.................................		(8,900)
Financing:		
Reduction of Lease Liability (5).......................	$ (2,400)	
Dividends (6)...	(24,000)	
Cash Flow from Financing...............................		(26,400)
Change in Cash		$ 111,100

13.16   (L.A. Gear; interpreting the statement of cash flows.)

a. The rate of increase in net income suggests that L.A. Gear grew rapidly during the three-year period. Increased investments in accounts receivable and inventories used operating cash flow. Increases in supplier credit did not fully finance the increased working capital investments, resulting in negative cash flow from operations.

b. During Year 7, L.A. Gear sold marketable securities and borrowed short term to finance the negative cash flow from operations. Accounts receivable and inventories convert into cash within one year, so short-term financing is appropriate. Selling marketable securities to help finance these working capital investments suggests that the revenue from these securities was less than the cost of additional short-term borrowing.

During Year 8, L.A. Gear relied on short-term borrowing to finance its working capital needs, matching the term structure of its financing with the term structure of its assets.

During Year 9, L.A. Gear issued additional common stock to finance its working capital needs. Several explanations for this switch in financing are possible. First, the proportion of debt in the capital structure may have reached a point after the borrowing in Year 8 that lenders considered the firm unduly risky, thereby raising the cost of additional borrowing. Second, L.A. Gear may have expected continuing rapid growth and wished to infuse a more permanent form of capital than short-term debt into the capital structure. Third, short-term borrowing rates might have increased significantly relative to long-term rates and L.A. Gear chose to access longer term sources of capital.

c. L.A. Gear is growing rapidly, so that new capacity additions exceed depreciation recognized on existing capacity.

d. L.A. Gear is not very capital intensive. The firm uses independent manufacturers in East Asia and markets its products through independent retailers. Thus, its property, plant and equipment serves primarily its administrative needs.

e. L.A. Gear has few fixed assets that might serve as collateral for such borrowing. The principal collateral is short-term, so lenders likely prefer to extend short-term financing.

13.17   (Campbell Soup Company; interpreting the statement of cash flows.)

   a.   Campbell uses suppliers and other creditors to finance its working capital needs. Consumer foods is a mature industry in the United States, so Campbell's modest growth rate does not require large incremental investments in accounts receivable and inventories.

   b.   (1) Capital expenditures have declined slightly each year, suggesting little need to add productive capacity.

        (2) Depreciation expense is a growing percentage of acquisitions of property, plant and equipment, suggesting slower growth in manufacturing capacity.

        (3) Substantial trading in marketable securities each year. Mature, profitable firms tend to accumulate cash beyond their operating needs and invest in marketable securities until they need cash.

        (4) Acquisition of another business in Year 8. Firms in mature industries grow by acquiring other firms. Campbell financed this acquisition in part by selling marketable securities.

   c.   (1) Increases in long-term debt approximately equal repayments of long-term debt, particularly for Year 7 and Year 8. Mature firms tend to roll over debt as long as they remain in the no-growth phase.

        (2) Campbell repurchased a portion of its common stock with excess cash.

        (3) Dividends have grown in line with increases in net income and represent approximately a 37 percent payout rate relative to net income.

CHAPTER 14

SIGNIFICANCE AND IMPLICATIONS OF ALTERNATIVE ACCOUNTING PRINCIPLES

Questions, Exercises, Problems, and Cases: Answers and Solutions

14.1 See the text or the glossary at the end of the book.

14.2 This question emphasizes the dual dimensions of the standard-setting process that standard-setting bodies must reconcile. Such bodies need a conceptual foundation to guide their selection of accounting principles if the resulting financial statements are to have internal consistency and external usefulness over time. Such bodies cannot simply respond to various preparers and users on each issue addressed and hope to achieve the consistency and usefulness objectives stated above. Standard-setting bodies must recognize, however, the political nature of the standard-setting process and communicate on an on-going basis with its various constituencies. Such bodies may need to convince one or more constituencies of the desirability of a particular standard.

14.3 This question gets to the issue of uniformity versus flexibility in generally accepted accounting principles. One might argue that when the economic effects of a transaction on two firms are the same, the firms should use the same accounting method for the transaction. The firms should not have latitude to choose from among several alternative methods. On the other hand, when the economic effects of a transaction on two firms are different, the firms should have latitude to use different accounting methods. GAAP should not compel the firms to use the same method and inaccurately report the economic effects. In both cases, the economic effects should drive the *degree* of uniformity versus flexibility.

14.4 Because most firms select accounting methods for tax purposes that minimize the present value of income tax payments, this proposal would likely result in greater uniformity in financial statements. However, one might question the usefulness and meaningfulness of the resulting financial statements. The Congress sets income tax laws to accomplish certain governmental policies and not necessarily to measure accurately the economic effects of various transactions.

14.5   This question relates to the use of the cash basis versus the accrual basis of accounting. Chapter 3 discussed the deficiencies of the cash basis of accounting as a periodic measure of operating performance and the benefits of the accrual basis (more timely recognition of revenue, better matching of expenses with associated revenues). One of the "costs" of the accrual basis, however, is that it requires the allocation of revenues and expenses to periods of time. These allocations are the subject content of generally accepted accounting principles.

14.6   This statement is correct with respect to the *amount* of net income. Conservatism and profit maximizations relate to the *timing* of its recognition. Analysts use net income as a measure of the operating performance of a firm over time. The timing of income recognition affects the trend in earnings and thus the strategy a firm follows in selecting its accounting methods.

14.7   Net income over long time periods equals cash inflows minus cash outflows from operating and investing activities. Alternative accounting principles affect merely the timing of revenue and expense recognition. One accounting principle may report high revenues and expenses in early years and another accounting principle may report high revenues and expenses in later years. The first accounting principle produces higher (or lower) earnings in each of the early years as well as cumulatively during each year. At some point, the second accounting principle produces higher (or lower) earnings in each year but the first method continues to report higher (or lower) cumulative earnings until earnings under the second accounting principle catch up.

14.8   Alternative accounting methods differentially affect the statement of cash flows. Cash flow differences generally occur when two firms use different methods of accounting on their tax returns. If the methods used by two firms on their tax returns are the same but on their financial statements are different, then their balance sheets and income statements will differ. Their statements of cash flows will differ under the indirect method only with respect to the adjustments made to convert net income to cash flow from operations. They will report identical amounts of cash flow from operations, however.

14.9   There are two responses to this question:

    1. If the market reacts quickly and unbiasedly, then *someone* does the analysis. Sophisticated security analysts who trade continually in the markets likely perform the financial statement analysis.

    2. There are settings outside of the organized securities markets where financial statement analysis is beneficial. These include banks lending to business customers, governments contemplating antitrust actions, labor unions considering negotiating strategy, and so on.

14.10   (Identifying generally accepted accounting principles.)

    a.   FIFO cost flow assumption.

    b.   Allowance method.

    c.   Equity method.

    d.   Capital lease method.

    e.   Weighted-average cost flow assumption.

    f.   Effective interest method.

    g.   Lower-of-cost-or-market valuation basis.

    h.   Direct write-off method.

    i.   Double-declining-balance method.

    j.   Market value method.

    k.   Percentage-of-completion method.

    l.   Allowance method.

    m.   LIFO cost flow assumption.

    n.   Operating lease method.

    o.   FIFO cost flow assumption.

    p.   Market value method.

    q.   Straight line method.

    r.   FIFO cost flow assumption.

    s.   Operating lease method.

    t.   LIFO cost flow assumption.

    u.   Capital lease method.

    v.   LIFO cost flow assumption.

14.11   (Identifying generally accepted accounting principles.)

    a. Direct write-off method of accounting for uncollectible accounts.

        Write off of an uncollectible account.

    b. Market value method of accounting for either marketable securities or long-term investments in securities.

        Receipt of a dividend in cash.

    c. Market value method for marketable securities.

        Writedown of marketable securities to market value.

    d. Equity method of accounting for long-term investments.

        Receipt of dividend from an investee.

    e. Allowance method of accounting for uncollectible accounts.

        Recognition of expected loss from uncollectible accounts.

    f. Operating method of accounting for leases by lessee.

        Payment of rent for rental services received this period.

    g. Equity method of accounting for long-term investments.

        Accrual of investor's share of investee's earnings.

    h. Allowance method of accounting for uncollectible accounts.

        Write off of an uncollectible account.

    i. Lower-of-cost-or-market valuation basis for inventories. In most cases, the debit entry is made to cost of goods sold.

        Write down of inventories to market value.

    j. Capital lease method of accounting for long-term leases by lessee.

        Payment of cash for interest and for reduction in principal of lease liability.

14.12   (Identifying generally accepted accounting principles.)

   a.   Lower-of-cost-or-market method.

   b.   LIFO.

   c.   FIFO.

   d.   Market value method.

   e.   Equity method.

   f.   Sum-of-the-years' digits.

   g.   Sum-of-the-years' digits.   Conservatism is defined in terms of *cumulative* reported earnings rather than earnings for a single year.

   h.   Capital lease method.

   i.   Capital lease method.

14.13   (West Company and East Company; impact of capitalizing and amortizing versus expensing when incurred.)

   a. and b. see following two pages.

   c.   When R & D costs are constant each year, the largest difference in R & D expense occurs in the first year. For Year 5 and thereafter, R & D expense is the same whether the firm expenses the costs when incurred or capitalizes and then amortizes them over five years. The amount shown on the balance sheet as Deferred R &D Costs increases each year for four years when the firm uses the deferral method but stabilizes beginning in Year 5. The cumulative earnings are $200 million greater under the deferral than the immediate expense procedure as long as R & D costs remain at $100 million per year.

   When R & D costs increase each year, the effects are different. R & D expense under the immediate expensing procedure continues to be larger than under the deferral method. Likewise, the amount shown on the balance sheet each year as Deferred R & D Costs continues to increase each year. The larger is the increase in R & D costs each year, the larger will be the difference in R & D expense and deferred R & D costs between the immediate expensing and deferral methods.

14.13 continued.

(Amounts in Millions)

a.

	Year					
	1	2	3	4	5	6
R & D Expense						
West Company	$100	$100	$100	$100	$100	$100
East Company:						
Year 1 Costs	$ 20	$ 20	$ 20	$ 20	$ 20	
Year 2 Costs		20	20	20	20	$ 20
Year 3 Costs			20	20	20	20
Year 4 Costs				20	20	20
Year 5 Costs					20	20
Year 6 Costs						20
Total Expense	$ 20	$ 40	$ 60	$ 80	$100	$100
Deferred R & D Costs						
West Company	$ 0	$ 0	$ 0	$ 0	$ 0	$ 0
East Company:						
Year 1 Costs	$ 80	$ 60	$ 40	$ 20		
Year 2 Costs		80	60	40	$ 20	
Year 3 Costs			80	60	40	$ 20
Year 4 Costs				80	60	40
Year 5 Costs					80	60
Year 6 Costs						80
Total Deferred Costs	$ 80	$140	$180	$200	$200	$200

14.13 continued.

b.

			Year			
	1	2	3	4	5	6
R & D Expense						
West Company	$100	$120	$140	$160	$180	$200
East Company:						
Year 1 Costs	$ 20	$ 20	$ 20	$ 20	$ 20	
Year 2 Costs		24	24	24	24	$ 24
Year 3 Costs			28	28	28	28
Year 4 Costs				32	32	32
Year 5 Costs					36	36
Year 6 Costs						40
Total Expense	$ 20	$ 44	$ 72	$ 104	$ 140	$ 160
Deferred R & D Costs						
West Company	$ 0	$ 0	$ 0	$ 0	$ 0	$ 0
East Company:						
Year 1 Costs	$ 80	$ 60	$ 40	$ 20		
Year 2 Costs		96	72	48	$ 24	
Year 3 Costs			112	84	56	$ 28
Year 4 Costs				128	96	64
Year 5 Costs					144	108
Year 6 Costs						160
Total Deferred Costs	$ 80	$ 156	$ 224	$ 280	$ 320	$ 360

14.14 (Humble Company and Huff Company; impact of alternative accounting principles on two firms.)

a.

Comparative Income Statements
For the Year Ending December 31, Year 1

	Humble Company		Huff Company	
	Financial Statement	Tax Return	Financial Statement	Tax Return
Sales Revenue	$2,700,000	$2,700,000	$2,700,000	$2,700,000
Expenses:				
Cost of Goods Sold	$1,239,000a	$1,239,000a	$1,221,000b	$1,221,000b
Depreciation on Equipment	500,000c	293,700	275,000	293,700
Sales Promotion	375,000	375,000	93,750	375,000
Selling, General and Administrative	150,000	150,000	150,000	150,000
Expenses before Income Taxes	$2,264,000	$2,057,700	$1,739,750	$2,039,700
Net Income before Income Taxes	$436,000	$642,300	$960,250	$660,300
Income Tax Expense	130,800d		288,075d	
Net Income	$305,200		$672,175	

a[$1,641,000 − (30,000 × $8.00) + (20,000 × $8.10)] = $1,239,000.

b$1,641,000 − (50,000 × $8.40) = $1,221,000.

c10/55 × $2,750,000 = $500,000.

dComputation of Income Tax Expense

Income Taxes Payable—Current:

Humble Company: .30 × $642,300	$	192,690
Huff Company: .30 × $660,300	$	198,090

Credits (Debits) to Deferred Income Taxes:

Humble Company: Dr. .30($293,700 − $500,000)		(61,890)
Huff Company: Cr. .30($293,700 − $275,000) + ($375,000 − $93,750)		89,985
Total Income Tax Expense	$ 130,800	$ 288,075

14.14 continued.

b.   Comparative Balance Sheet
                        December 31, Year 1

	Humble Company	Huff Company
Assets		
Cash...	$ 639,848	$ 635,528
Accounts Receivable	1,300,000	1,300,000
Merchandise Inventory	402,000	420,000
Equipment (at Acquisition Cost)............	2,750,000	2,750,000
Less Accumulated Depreciation	(500,000)	(275,000)
Deferred Sales Promotion Costs............	--	281,250
Deferred Tax Asset............................	61,890	--
Total Assets..................................	$4,653,738	$5,111,778
Equities		
Accounts Payable...............................	$ 310,000	$ 310,000
Income Taxes Payable........................	38,538	39,618
Deferred Tax Liability.........................	--	89,985
Common Shares...............................	500,000	500,000
Additional Paid-in Capital	3,500,000	3,500,000
Retained Earnings.............................	305,200	672,175
Total Equity..................................	$4,653,738	$5,111,778

14.14 continued.

c.

Comparative Statement of Cash Flows
For the Year Ended December 31, Year 1

	Humble Company	Huff Company
Operations:		
Net Income	$ 305,200	$ 672,175
Depreciation Expense	500,000	275,000
Portion of Income Tax Expense Not Currently Payable	--	89,985
Increase in Accounts Payable	310,000	310,000
Increase in Income Tax Payable	38,538	39,618
Excess of Cash Used for Sales Promotion over Amount Recognized as Expense	--	(281,250)
Excess of Income Tax Paid over Income Tax Expense	(61,890)	--
Increase in Accounts Receivable	(1,300,000)	(1,300,000)
Increase in Merchandise Inventories	(402,000)	(420,000)
Cash Flow from Operations	$ (610,152)	$ (614,472)
Investing:		
Acquisition of Equipment	(2,750,000)	(2,750,000)
Financing:		
Issue of Common Stock	4,000,000	4,000,000
Net Change in Cash	$ 639,848	$ 635,528
Cash, January 1	0	0
Cash, December 31	$ 639,848	$ 635,528

d.

Cash on December 31, Year 1: Humble Company	$ 639,848
Additional Income Taxes Currently Payable by Huff Company: $198,090 – $192,690	(5,400)
Portion of Additional Income Taxes Not Yet Paid: $39,618 – $38,538	1,080
Cash on December 31, Year 1: Huff Company	$ 635,528

14.15 (Brown Corporation; impact of two sets of alternative accounting principles on net income and cash flows.)

a.

BROWN CORPORATION
Income Statements Under Alternative Principles
For the Year Ending December 31, Year 1

	Set A		Set B	
	Financial Statement	Tax Return	Financial Statement	Tax Return
Sales Revenue	$ 504,000	$ 504,000	$ 504,000	$ 504,000
Expenses:				
Cost of Goods Sold	$ 335,250 [1]	$ 335,250 [1]	$ 315,750 [2]	$ 315,750 [2]
Depreciation on Equipment	22,500 [3]	16,073	11,250 [4]	16,073
Training	37,500	37,500	7,500	37,500
Selling, General and Administrative	60,000	60,000	60,000	60,000
Goodwill	3,750	--	1,875	--
Expenses before Income Taxes	$ 459,000	$ 448,823	$ 396,375	$ 429,323
Net Income before Income Taxes	$ 45,000	$ 55,177	$ 107,625	$ 74,677
Income Tax Expense—Current	16,553 [5]		22,403 [7]	
Income Tax Expense—Deferred	(1,928)[6]		10,447 [8]	
Net Income	$ 30,375		$ 74,775	

[1] (37,500 × $2.40) + (15,000 × $2.20) + (22,500 × $2.10) + (82,500 × $2.00) = $335,250.
[2] (150,000 × $2.00) + (7,500 × $2.10) = $315,750.
[3] .20 × $112,500 = $22,500.
[4] $112,500/10 = $11,250.
[5] .30 × $55,177 = $16,553.
[6] .30 × ($16,073 − $22,500) = −$1,928.
[7] .30 × $74,677 = $22,403.
[8] .30($16,073 − $11,250) + .30($37,500 − $7,500) = $1,447 + $9,000 = $10,447.

14.15 continued.

b.

BROWN CORPORATION
Cash Flow from Operations
For Year 1

	Set A	Set B
Net Income..	$ 30,375	$ 74,775
Additions:		
Depreciation Expense.........................	22,500	11,250
Goodwill Amortization	3,750	1,875
Excess of Income Tax Expense over		
Amount Currently Payable...............	--	10,447
Increase in Accounts Payable..............	30,200	30,200
Increase in Income Taxes Payable........	4,138	5,601
Subtractions:		
Excess of Cash Used for Training over		
Amount Reported as an Expense.......	--	(30,000)
Excess of Income Taxes Currently Pay-		
able over Income Tax Expense	(1,928)	--
Increase in Accounts Receivable...........	(120,000)	(120,000)
Increase in Merchandise Inventories....	(135,000)	(154,500)
Cash Used for Operations......................	$ (165,965)	$ (170,352)

c.

Cash Flow from Operations, Set A................................	$(165,965)
Additional Income Taxes Currently Payable Under Set	
B: $22,403 – $16,553	(5,850)
Portion of Additional Income Taxes Not Yet Paid:	
$5,601 – $4,138...	1,463
Cash Flow from Operations, Set B	$(170,352)

14.16   (Chicago Corporation; comprehensive review problem.)

a.

Balance, January 1, Year 2..	$100,000
Provision for Year 2...	120,000
Less Balance, December 31, Year 2.............................	(160,000)
Write-offs during Year 2..	$ 60,000

b.

	LIFO	FIFO
Beginning Inventory	$ 1,500,000	$ 1,800,000
Purchases...	5,300,000	5,300,000
Available for Sale.................................	$ 6,800,000	$ 7,100,000
Less Ending Inventory.........................	(1,800,000)	(1,700,000)
Cost of Goods Sold	$ 5,000,000	$ 5,400,000
Net Sales..	$13,920,000	$13,920,000
Less Cost of Goods Sold........................	(5,000,000)	(5,400,000)
Gross Profit..	$ 8,920,000	$ 8,520,000

14.16 continued.

c. The quantity of inventory increased because the LIFO ending inventory is larger than the LIFO beginning inventory. The prices of the inventory items decreased because the FIFO ending inventory is less than the FIFO beginning inventory despite an increase in quantity during the year.

d. None of the companies declared dividends during Year 2 because the changes (increases) in the investment accounts equal the amounts recognized as Chicago Corporation's equity in the earnings of these companies.

e.

Investment in Chicago Finance Corporation....	1,800,000	
Investment in Rosenwald Company................	125,000	
Investment in Hutchinson Company...............	75,000	
Equity in Earnings of Chicago Finance Corporation		1,800,000
Equity in Earnings of Rosenwald Company		125,000
Equity in Earnings of Hutchinson Company		75,000

f. Year 1: $4,000,000 \times 2/40 = \$200,000$.
Year 2: ($4,000,000 - \$200,000) \times 2/40 = \$190,000$.

g.

Cash...	400,000	
Accumulated Depreciation...........................	800,000	
Machinery and Equipment.......................		1,000,000
Gain on Sale of Machinery and Equipment..		200,000

h.

Interest Expense..	288,000	
Bonds Payable (= $3,648,000 - \$3,600,000$)		48,000
Cash (= $.06 \times \$4,000,000$)		240,000

i. Effective interest rate $\times \$3,600,000 = \$288,000$. The effective interest rate = 8 percent. Chicago Corporation issued these bonds for less than their face value because the coupon rate of 6 percent is less than the market interest rate at the time of issue of 8 percent.

j. Difference between book and taxable depreciation = $150,000/.30 = \$500,000$.

Because the Deferred Tax Liability account increased, tax depreciation must be $500,000 larger than depreciation for financial reporting.

14.16 continued.

    k. Cash... 1,000,000

             Treasury Shares.. 400,000

             Additional Paid-in Capital......................... 600,000

    l. Acquisition Cost....................................... $1,250,000

       Less Book Value.. (750,000)

       Accumulated Amortization.......................... $ 500,000

       Because the patent is being amortized at the rate of $125,000 per year, the patent was acquired four years before the balance sheet date (= $500,000/$125,000).

    m. If Chicago Corporation owns less than 20 percent of the common stock of Hutchinson Company, it must use the market-value method. Chicago Corporation would show the Investment in Hutchinson account at its market value of $200,000 (= $175,000 + $25,000) and show a $25,000 amount in the Unrealized Holding Gain on Investment in Securities account in the shareholders' equity section of the balance sheet. Hutchinson Company did not declare dividends during the year. Thus, net income of Chicago Corporation would decrease by the $75,000 equity in Hutchinson Company's earnings during Year 2 recognized under the equity method. Consolidated retained earnings would, therefore, be $75,000 less than as now stated. In the statement of cash flows, there would be $75,000 smaller net income and no subtraction of $75,000 for the equity in earnings of Hutchinson Company.

    n. Capitalized Lease Obligation 80,000

       Interest Expense.. 90,000

         Cash... 170,000

       Amortization of Leased Property Rights........... 150,000

         Accumulated Amortization....................... 150,000

       Total expense would be $240,000 (= $90,000 + $150,000).

    o. The income statement would show a $200,000 loss from the price decline, and retained earnings would be $200,000 less than as shown. The Inventories account would be shown at $1,600,000 instead of $1,800,000. There would be an addback for the loss on the statement of cash flows because the loss did not use cash.

14.16 continued.

p. Basic earnings per share $= \dfrac{\$4,400,000 - \$120,000}{1,600,000} = \$2.675.$

Fully diluted earnings per share $= \dfrac{\$4,400,000}{1,600,000 + ?} = \$2.20.$

The number of common shares that would be issued is 400,000.

q.

	Cash		
√	200,000		

	Operations		
(1)	4,000,000	100,000	(3)
(11)	1,000,000	300,000	(4)
(12)	125,000	1,800,000	(5)
(13)	75,000	125,000	(6)
(14)	150,000	75,000	(7)
(16)	60,000	200,000	(9)
(17)	130,000	20,000	(15)
(18)	50,000		
(19)	260,000		
(20)	48,000		
(23)	170,000		

	Investing		
(9)	400,000	100,000	(8)
		1,700,000	(10)

	Financing		
(24)	1,000,000	2,200,000	(2)
		968,000	(21)
		80,000	(22)
√	400,000		

	Accounts Receivable	
√	500,000	
(3)	100,000	
√	600,000	

	Merchandise Inventory	
√	1,500,000	
(4)	300,000	
√	1,800,000	

14.16 q. continued.

Prepayments	
√ 200,000	
√ 200,000	

Investment in Chicago Finance Corp.	
√ 2,200,000	
(5) 1,800,000	
√ 4,000,000	

Investment in Rosenwald Corp.	
√ 900,000	
(6) 125,000	
√ 1,025,000	

Investment in Hutchinson Corp.	
√ 100,000	
(7) 75,000	
√ 175,000	

Land	
√ 400,000	
(8) 100,000	
√ 500,000	

Building	
√ 4,000,000	
√ 4,000,000	

Machinery and Equipment	
√ 7,300,000	
(10) 1,700,000	1,000,000 (9)
√ 8,000,000	

Property Rights Under Lease	
√ 1,500,000	
√ 1,500,000	

Accumulated Depreciation	
	3,800,000 √
(9) 800,000	1,000,000 (11)
	4,000,000 √

Patent	
√ 875,000	
	125,000 (12)
√ 750,000	

Goodwill	
√ 1,125,000	
	75,000 (13)
√ 1,050,000	

Accounts Payable	
	400,000 √
	150,000 (14)
	550,000 √

Advances from Customers	
	660,000 √
(15) 20,000	
	640,000 √

Salaries Payable	
	240,000 √
	60,000 (16)
	300,000 √

14.16 q. continued.

Income Taxes Payable			
	300,000	√	
	130,000	(17)	
	430,000	√	

Rent Received in Advance			
	0	√	
	50,000	(18)	
	50,000	√	

Other Current Liabilities			
	200,000	√	
	260,000	(19)	
	460,000	√	

Bonds Payable			
	3,600,000	√	
	48,000	(20))	
	3,648,000	√	

Equipment

Mortgage Payable			
		1,300,000	√
(21)	968,000		
		332,000	√

Capitalized Lease Obligation			
		1,100,000	√
(22)	80,000		
		1,020,000	√

Deferred Tax Liability			
	1,400,000	√	
	170,000	(23)	
	1,570,000	√	

Convertible Preferred Stock			
	2,000,000	√	
	2,000,000	√	

Common Stock			
	2,000,000	√	
	2,000,000	√	

Additional Paid-in Capital			
	2,400,000	√	
	600,000	(24)	
	3,000,000	√	

Retained Earnings			
		2,800,000	√
(2)	2,200,000	4,400,000	(1)
		5,000,000	√

Treasury Stock			
√	1,400,000		
		400,000	(24)
√	1,000,000		

r. The total shareholders' equity of Chicago Corporation is not an accurate measure of the value or worth of the firm for the following reasons.

(1) The balance sheet does not include such resources of the firm as superior managerial expertise, a well-trained labor force, or goodwill.

14.16 r. continued.

(2) The balance sheet shows assets at acquisition cost (net of accumulated depreciation or amortization in some instances). These amounts will likely differ from the current replacement costs or net realizable value of these assets.

(3) The total liabilities of Chicago Corporation do not include uncapitalized long-term operating leases. The liabilities do include Deferred Tax Liability. However, if the firm continues to grow, it is questionable whether Chicago Corporation will have to pay these taxes.

(4) Chicago Corporation reports the long-term debt at the present value of the future cash flows discounted at the market rate on the date of issue. The current market values of these obligations may differ significantly from their book values.

s.(1) *For Narrowing:*

(1) Lead to better interfirm and interperiod comparisons of financial statement data.

(2) Make financial statements easier to understand, because the reader will not need to be familiar with as many accounting methods.

(3) Reduces opportunities for management to manipulate earnings by selecting or changing accounting principles.

s.(2) *For Continuing Present System:*

(1) Management should have the flexibility to select the methods which most fairly reflect the firm's financial position and results of operations. A narrowing of acceptable methods may result in some firms showing less fairly their financial position and results of operations.

(2) Investors may see through the effects of using different accounting methods, as suggested by efficient markets theory and as supported by empirical research, which suggests additional disclosures rather than greater uniformity.

(3) Because the specification of accounting principles is a political process, standard-setting bodies would probably encounter difficulties obtaining consensus on which currently acceptable methods to eliminate.

14.17   (Tuck Corporation; comprehensive review problem.)

a. Balance in Marketable Equity Securities on December
        31, Year 21... $ 125,000
    Less Cost of Marketable Equity Securities Sold ....   (35,000)
    Plus Decrease in Unrealized Holding Loss on Market
        able Securities..   4,000
    Plus Cost of Marketable Equity Securities Purchased......   ?
    Balance in Marketable Equity Securities on December
        31, Year 22... $ 141,000

The cost of marketable equity securities purchased is $47,000.

b. Cost of Marketable Equity Securities Sold....................... $ 35,000
    Less Loss on Sale of Marketable Equity Securities...........   (8,000)
    Sales Proceeds... $ 27,000

c. Balance in Allowance Account on December 31, Year 21. $ 128,800
    Plus Provision for Estimated Uncollectible Accounts ......   ?
    Less Write-offs of Specific Customers' Accounts.............   (63,000)
    Balance in Allowance Account on December 31, Year 22. $ 210,400

The provision for estimated uncollectibles is $144,600.

d.

	LIFO	Difference	FIFO
Beginning Inventory	$1,257,261	$ 430,000	$1,687,261
Purchases........................	2,848,054	--	2,848,054
Available.........................	$4,105,315	$ 430,000	$4,535,315
Less Ending Inventory........	(1,525,315)	(410,000)	(1,935,315)
Cost of Goods Sold	$2,580,000	$ 20,000	$2,600,000

e. Unrealized Holding Loss on Investments in
        Securities (SE)..   5,000
            Investments in Securities   5,000
    To recognize unrealized holding loss on invest-
    ments in securities.

f. Dividend revenue of $8,000. The unrealized loss of $5,000 (see Part
    e.) is not included in the calculation of net income for Year 22.

14.17 continued.

g. Investment in Davis Corporation 87,000
    Equity in Earnings of Unconsolidated
        Affiliates 87,000
    To recognize share of Davis Corporation's
    earnings in Year 22; .40 X $217,500 = $87,000.

   Cash 24,000
       Investment in Davis Corporation 24,000
   To recognize dividend received from Davis
   Corporation; .40 X $60,000 = $24,000.

   Investment in Davis Corporation 20,000
       Cash 20,000
   To record additional investment in Davis
   Corporation.

h. Cash 7,000
   Accumulated Depreciation 19,000
       Equipment 23,000
       Gain on Sale of Equipment 3,000

i. Present Value of Lease Payment Due at Signing at January 2, Year 10 .... $ 10,000
   Present Value of Nineteen Lease Payments Due on January 2 of Each Subsequent Year at 8 Percent; $10,000 X 9.6036 96,036
   Total .... $ 106,036

j. Balance in Rental Fees Received in Advance on December 31, Year 21 .... $ 46,000
   Plus Cash Received for Rentals during Year 22 .... ?
   Less Rental Fees Earned during Year 22 .... (240,000)
   Balance in Rental Fees Received in Advance on December 31, Year 22 .... $ 58,000

   Cash received during Year 22 totaled $252,000.

k. Balance in Estimated Warranty Liability on December 31, Year 21 .... $ 75,200
   Plus Estimated Warranty Cost Provision for Year 22 46,800
   Less Cost of Actual Warranty Services .... (?)
   Balance in Estimated Warranty Liability on December 31, Year 22 .... $ 78,600

   Warranty costs incurred during Year 22 totaled $43,400.

14.17 continued.

l.

First 6 Months: .025 × $1,104,650.00		$ 27,616.25
Second 6 Months: .025 × $1,102,266.25[a]		27,556.66
Total Interest Expense		$ 55,172.91

[a]$1,104,650.00 − ($30,000.00 − $27,616.25) = $1,102,266.25.

m.

Interest Expense	20,996	
Mortgage Payable	19,004	
Cash		40,000

To record mortgage interest and principal payment; $20,996 = .07 × ($262,564 + 37,383).

n.

Present Value of Payment on January 1, Year 23		$ 10,000
Present Value of Seven Remaining Lease Payments		
($10,000 × 5.20637)		52,064
Total		$ 62,064

o.

Capitalized Lease Obligation, December 31, Year 21		$ 62,064
Lease Payment on January 1, Year 23		(10,000)
Interest Expense for Year 22 (.08 × $52,064)		4,165
Total ($10,000 + $46,229)		$ 56,229

p.

Income Tax Expense	150,000	
Income Tax Payable		135,000
Deferred Tax Liability ($145,000 − $130,000)		15,000

q.

Income Tax Payable—Current, December 31, Year 21		$ 140,000
Provision for Current Taxes Payable (See Part p.)		135,000
Less Cash Payments Made during Year 21		(?)
Income Tax Payable—Current, December 31, Year 22		$ 160,000

Cash payments for income taxes during Year 21 were $115,000.

r.
$$\frac{\text{Deferred Tax Expense Relating to Depreciation}}{\text{Income Tax Rate}} = \frac{\$12,000}{.30} = \$40,000.$$

s.

Convertible Preferred Stock (5,000 × $100)	500,000	
Common Stock (25,000 × $10)		250,000
Additional Paid-in Capital		250,000

To record conversion of preferred into common stock.

14.17 continued.

t. Treasury Stock.. 8,800
    Cash...   8,800
    To record purchases of treasury stock.

    Cash.. 25,200
        Treasury Stock.......................................   21,600[a]
        Additional Paid-in Capital........................   3,600[b]
    To record the sale of treasury stock.

[a]1,800 shares $\times$ \$12 = \$21,600.

[b]Additional Paid-in Capital on December 31, Year 21...... \$ 130,000
  Plus Amount Arising from Conversion of Preferred
    Stock 250,000
  Plus Amount Arising from Issue of Common Stock...... 200,000
  Plus Amount Arising from Sale of Treasury Stock........   ?
  Additional Paid-in Capital on December 31, Year 22...... \$ 583,600

    The additional paid-in capital arising from the treasury stock sales is \$3,600.

14.17 continued.

u.

Cash

√	240,000		

Operations

(1)	300,000	87,000	(7)
(3)	8,000	15,000	(10)
(8)	24,000	3,000	(11)
(13)	56,000	4,827	(15)
(14)	2,000	78,400	(25)
(17)	2,911	268,054	(26)
(20)	15,000	4,000	(27)
(29)	57,600		
(30)	12,000		
(31)	3,400		
(32)	500		
(34)	20,000		

Investing

(3)	27,000	47,000	(5)
(11)	7,000	20,000	(9)
		1,373,600	(12)

Financing

(16)	828,409	119,500	(2)
(22)	600,000	19,004	(18)
(23)	25,200	5,835	(19)
(28)	100,000	8,800	(24)
(33)	5,000		
√	280,000		

Marketable Securities—Net

√	125,000			
		35,000	(3)	
(4)	4,000			
(5)	47,000			
√	141,000			

Accounts Receivable—Net

√	1,431,200	
(25)	78,400	
√	1,509,600	

14.17 u. continued.

Inventories		Prepayments	
√ 1,257,261		√ 28,000	
(26) 268,054		(27) 4,000	
√ 1,525,315		√ 32,000	

Investment in Thayer—Net		Investment in Hitchcock	
√ 92,000		√ 120,000	
	5,000 (6)	(10) 15,000	
√ 87,000		√ 135,000	

Investment in Davis		Land	
√ 215,000		√ 82,000	
(7) 87,000			
(9) 20,000	24,000 (8)		
√ 298,000		√ 82,000	

Building		Equipment	
√ 843,000		√ 497,818	
		(12) 1,373,600	23,000 (11)
√ 843,000		√ 1,848,418	

Leasehold		Accumulated Depreciation and Amortization	
√ 98,182			376,000 √
		(11) 19,000	56,000 (13)
√ 98,182			413,000 √

Goodwill—Net		Notes Payable	
√ 36,000			100,000 √
	2,000 (14)		100,000 (28)
√ 34,000			200,000 √

Accounts Payable		Rental Fees Received in Advance	
	666,100 √		46,000 √
	57,600 (29)		12,000 (30)
	723,700 √		58,000 √

14.17 u. continued.

Estimated Warranty Liability

	75,200	√
	3,400	(31)
	78,600	√

Interest Payable on Notes

	1,500	√
	500	(32)
	2,000	√

Dividends Payable

	25,000	√
	5,000	(33)
	30,000	√

Income Taxes Payable—Current

	140,000	√
	20,000	(34)
	160,000	√

Bonds Payable

		1,104,650	√
(15)	4,827	828,409	(16)
		2,911	(17)
		1,931,143	√

Mortgage Payable

		299,947	√
(18)	19,004		
		280,943	√

Capitalized Lease Obligation

		62,064	√
(19)	5,835		
		56,229	√

Deferred Tax Liability

	130,000	√
	15,000	(20)
	145,000	√

Convertible Preferred Stock

		700,000	√
(21)	500,000		
		200,000	√

Common Stock

	1,000,000	√
	250,000	(21)
	400,000	(22)
	1,650,000	√

Additional Paid-in Capital

	130,000	√
	250,000	(21)
	200,000	(22)
	3,600	(23)
	583,600	√

Unrealized Holding Loss on Marketable Securities

√	25,000		
		4,000	(4)
√	21,000		

14.17 u. continued.

Unrealized Holding Loss on Investment in Securities				Retained Earnings			
√	16,000					277,000	√
(6)	5,000		(2)	119,500		300,000	(1)
√	21,000					457,500	√

Treasury Stock			
√	27,000		
(24)	8,800	21,600	(23)
√	14,200		

References to T-Account Entries

(1) Net Income.
(2) Dividends declared by Tuck Corporation.
(3) Sale of marketable securities.
(4) Recovery of unrealized holding loss on marketable securities.
(5) Purchase of marketable securities.
(6) Write down of investment in Thayer Corporation to market value.
(7) Tuck's share of Davis Corporation's earnings.
(8) Tuck's share of Davis Corporation's dividends.
(9) Additional investment in Davis Corporation.
(10) Tuck's share of Hitchcock's earnings ($102,000 – $87,000).
(11) Sale of equipment at a gain.
(12) Acquisition of equipment.
(13) Depreciation expenses.
(14) Amortization of goodwill.
(15) Interest on 6-percent bonds.
(16) Issue of 8-percent bonds.
(17) Interest on 8-percent bonds.
(18) Payment of principal on mortgage.
(19) Payment of principal on lease obligation ($10,000 – $4,165).
(20) Deferred tax liability.
(21) Conversion of preferred stock.
(22) Issue of common stock.
(23) Sale of treasury stock.
(24) Purchase of treasury stock.
(25) Increase in accounts receivable.
(26) Increase in inventories.
(27) Increase in prepayments.
(28) Increase in notes payable.
(29) Increase in accounts payable.
(30) Increase in rental fees received in advance.
(31) Increase in estimated warranty liability.
(32) Increase in interest payable.
(33) Increase in dividends payable.
(34) Increase in income taxes payable—current.

14.18   (Champion Clothiers, Inc.; selecting accounting methods.)

The objectives of the case are as follows:

1.   To illustrate the impact of alternative accounting methods on the financial statements.

2.   To illustrate the wide array of avenues open to a firm to manage reported earnings.

3.   To consider the arguments for and against managing earnings.

Techniques for Managing Earnings

The techniques for managing earnings fall into three categories: (1) selection of accounting methods (LIFO versus FIFO, accelerated versus straight-line depreciation, purchase versus pooling of interests), (2) application of accounting methods (nature of LIFO pools, depreciable lives of plant assets, amortization period on pension obligation), and (3) timing of asset acquisitions and dispositions (maintenance and advertising, sale of marketable securities and land).

LIFO versus FIFO. Remaining on LIFO is probably the best choice here because of the potential tax savings. Most firms now use LIFO for financial reporting as well, so that lack of comparability with one's competitors is not an issue. As discussed later, a number of research studies have shown that investors look through the accounting numbers to the underlying economics of accounting choices. Evidence indicates that the stock market penalizes firms that select FIFO in order to report higher earnings (at the expense of paying more taxes). There are sufficient disclosures in the annual report to convert a LIFO firm to a FIFO basis if an analyst feels it is a more appropriate cost flow assumption. Thus, a firm can realize the tax benefits of LIFO and disclose sufficient information so that the analyst can compute FIFO earnings.

Nature of LIFO Pools. It is obvious that broader pools are preferable for tax purposes in order to minimize the probability of dipping into an old, lower priced layer. The consistency requirement between tax and financial reporting for LIFO dictates remaining with broader pools for financial reporting as well. If a firm practices earnings management, it is preferable to use avenues that do not have negative economic consequences.

14.18 continued.

Depreciable Lives and Depreciation Method. Unlike LIFO, there is no consistency requirement between tax and financial reporting with respect to depreciation. Thus, a firm must choose on other grounds. A firm might use economic reality as the criterion. On this basis, the depreciable life would be the economic life of the assets. The depreciation method selected would be one that mirrored the economic decline in the usefulness of the assets. Unfortunately, the firm cannot observe or predict either of these items very accurately. The choice comes down to whether the firm wishes to portray a conservative or a nonconservative image to investors. The vast majority of publicly-held firms take the nonconservative position and write off depreciable assets over their estimated economic lives using the straight-line method. This is the position we would take.

Purchases versus Pooling of Interests. The position we would take here is that the accounting method used should not drive the economics of the transaction or the way the firm structures it. However, if the economics are the same regardless of whether the firm uses purchase or pooling, we opt for pooling because of its positive earnings effects. Without additional information, it is difficult to judge all of the important economic effects in this case. If the firm issues 40 percent of the stock to the public and 10 percent to the shareholders of Green Trucking, the Champion family will have a 50 percent interest in the firm. This should be sufficient to maintain effective control. It is not clear whether the company already has sufficient cash to structure the deal as a cash/purchase method transaction or whether the Champion family will have to inject more cash. Also, the treatment of the transaction for tax purposes is unclear. If one can make the heroic assumption that the economics are the same, we would opt for pooling in this case.

Amortization Period for Pension Obligation. There is no necessity that the firm fund the prior service obligation over the same period that it amortizes it to expense. Assuming that the economics (funding) will not change, we would opt for the longer amortization period to increase earnings.

Delay of Maintenance Expenditures. The firm can take this action to improve earnings in the short run, but it catches up later. Delaying the expenditure until 2001 will depress 2001 earnings. Delaying the maintenance indefinitely could affect the operational efficiency of the assets involved. We would tend not to use this avenue if other options were available to obtain the desired earnings per share.

14.18 continued.

Delay of Advertising Expenditures. The desired timing of the advertising campaign should be the deciding factor here. Because the post-Christmas timing seems set, we would not argue for delaying it. We might approach the firm's auditor about the possibility of capitalizing the advertising expenditure in 2000 and writing it off as an expense in 2001, the year of expected benefit. Auditors are reluctant to do this on intangibles such as advertising, but it is worth a try. The problem with this, however, is that this treatment of the expenditure negatively affects 2001 earnings.

Sale of Marketable Securities. The securities were probably purchased as a temporary investment of excess cash. If the firm could invest the sales proceeds in another investment alternative with equivalent returns and risk after considering transaction costs, we might use this avenue for propping up earnings for 2000. However, if the firm held the marketable securities for longer term purposes and viewed them as a desirable long-term investment, we would not likely sell them.

Sale of Land. As long as the firm still viewed the parcels as attractive locations for future stores, we would not sell them at this time.

The president of Champion is concerned with the *trend* in earnings per share. Several of the choices require retroactive restatements of prior years' earnings per share (LIFO versus FIFO, accelerated versus straight-line depreciation, purchase versus pooling of interests). These restatements affect the trend line of the desired level of earnings per share for 2000.

Assuming that the firm changes its depreciable life, depreciation method, corporate acquisition method, and pension obligation amortization period, earnings per share for 1997 through 2000 would be as follows:

	1997	1998	1999	2000
As Reported or Expected	$ 1.20	$ 1.38	$ 1.60	$ 1.65
Depreciable Lives	--	--	--	+ .04
Depreciation Method	+ .05	+ .06	+ .07	+ .08
Corporate Acquisition Period	+ .02	+ .04	+ .06	+ .10
Pension Amortization Period	--	--	--	+ .05
Revised	$ 1.27	$ 1.48	$ 1.73	$ 1.92

14.18 continued.

Earnings per share increased approximately 16 percent per year between 1997 and 1999. Maintaining this growth rate requires 2000 earnings per share to be approximately $2.02. We would be inclined to get some of the additional ten cents per share needed from the sale of marketable securities as long as there were no negative economic consequences of doing so. We would probably stop at this point and report earnings per share of $1.92. Using other avenues would probably have negative economic consequences.

Arguments For and Against Managing Earnings

The arguments for and against managing earnings vary both as to their underlying logic and to the evidence that is brought to bear in support of the position. The section presents the arguments in as unbiased a manner as possible so that readers can make up their own minds.

Capital Market Efficiency. The major argument against managing earnings is that capital markets are efficient, in the sense that market prices adjust quickly and *in an unbiased manner* to publicly-available information, and that earnings management is therefore a waste of valuable managerial time. An expanding number of theoretical and empirical studies have provided support for the efficiency of capital markets. For example, several studies have examined the effects of changes in accounting methods on stock prices. Researchers have shown that changes in accounting methods that have no real or economic effects (that is, those that do not affect cash flows) have little affect on stock prices. Using information from the financial statements and notes, the stock market at the aggregate level distinguishes changes with real effects from those that do not have real effects and reacts accordingly.

Proponents of earnings management acknowledge this recent work but counter with three observations. First, all of the empirical work on market efficiency has looked at the aggregate market (for example, all stocks traded on the New York Stock Exchange). There are numerous examples of cases where the market priced the securities of particular firms at a particular point in time inefficiently. Proponents of this view point to examples where the market prices of particular firms' shares decreased dramatically after the effects of using specific accounting procedures were carefully analyzed and reported in the financial press.

Second, the empirical work on market efficiency has focused for the most part on publicly-available information. There is little or no evidence to suggest that the market is able to access "inside" or nonpublic information. Information about the effects of changes in accounting methods is available in the financial statements and notes and has been studied empirically. However, information about management's efforts to manage the timing of asset acquisitions or dis-

14.18 continued.

positions is usually not disclosed separately and consequently has not been adequately studied.

Third, proponents of earnings management note that most of the empirical work on capital market efficiency has focused on equity securities traded on the New York Stock Exchange. Researchers have not tested adequately the efficiency of other capital markets (for example, the over-the-counter-market as well as short-term credit and long-term debt markets).

Proponents of earnings management would conclude that capital markets are not necessarily perfectly efficient in all cases. If by managing earnings the firm can take advantage of these inefficiencies and obtain capital at a lower cost than if earnings management were not practiced, then the shareholders of the firm are better off.

Opponents of earnings management might accept the notion that some degree of inefficiency exists in capital markets. They would then argue, though, that capital resources get allocated in a less than socially-optimal way if, because of earnings management, certain firms receive more resources than would otherwise be the case.

Management Incentives and Survival. Because over long enough time periods net income equals cash inflows minus cash outflows from operating and investing activities, some corporate managers acknowledge that earnings management is not particularly beneficial in the long run. They point out, however, that the long run is made up of a series of short-run periods in which shareholders' make decisions to retain or to fire management. Shareholders, they would argue, do not want to see wide, unexpected fluctuations in earnings from year to year. Earnings management is necessary to smooth out these fluctuations and create the impression that management has operations under control. Corporate managers also observe that all firms practice earnings management and that management's survival dictates that they do so to maintain the firm's position relative to other firms. They further point out that researchers have not yet provided sufficient and convincing evidence for not managing earnings. Opponents of earnings management, primarily academic researchers, point to an expanding number of studies that call into question the perceived benefits of earnings management. Whether the two viewpoints are ultimately reconcilable depends on the results of continuing research on the relation between accounting numbers and stock prices.

14.19   (Petite-Mart, Inc.; identifying quality of earnings issues.)

a.   Schedule 14.1 of this solution manual presents a common-size income statement for Petite-Mart, Inc. for fiscal Year 6, Year 7, and Year 8 based on its reported amounts. The discussion that follows suggests possible quality of earnings issues.

Cost of Goods Sold—LIFO matches current costs against revenues as long as a firm does not dip into LIFO layers. LIFO, therefore, provides a better indication of the ongoing profitability of a firm than FIFO. FIFO includes varying amounts of holding gains and losses depending on the rate of changes in acquisition costs each period. Petite-Mart, Inc., however, dipped into LIFO layers during fiscal Year 8 and, thereby reduced its cost of goods sold by $916 million. Sales declined between fiscal Year 7 and fiscal Year 8, so unexpected demand would not seem to explain the LIFO liquidation. The cost of goods sold to sales percentage increased slightly during the previous two years. Perhaps still further expected increases in this percentage led management to intentionally delay replacing inventory items, thereby, boosting net income. Without the LIFO liquidation, cost of goods sold would have been $35,176 million (= $34,260 million + $916 million) and the cost of goods sold to sales percentage would have been 70.0 percent (= $35,176 million/$50,234 million).

Depreciation Expense—The increase in depreciable lives for equipment from five to eight years decreased depreciation expense by $1,583 million. The equipment in a retail clothing store likely includes display counters, computers, and security devices. The desire of clothing retailers to maintain attractive stores would seem to suggest that an eight-year life for display counters is somewhat long. Changes in technologies would likely lead to obsolescence of computers and security devices prior to eight years. Thus, the change in depreciable life appears driven by a desire to increase earnings. Expenditures on equipment increased more rapidly than sales during the three-year period. Depreciation expense as a percentage of sales increased significantly between fiscal Year 6 and fiscal Year 7. Perhaps management anticipated still further increases in this expense percentage in future years and desired to dampen its effect. If the company had continued to use a five-year depreciable like, depreciation expense would have been $4,995 million (= $3,412 million + $1,583 million).

Another issue regarding depreciation is the company's policy of continuing to depreciate the building over 20 years after learning of the health and safety regulations. One must at least wonder whether a shorter life is more appropriate. The company may, however, have adequately dealt with the issue by recognizing the asset impairment loss.

14.19 a. continued.

Advertising Expense—Advertising expense as a percentage of sales decreased from 4.1 percent in fiscal Year 7 to 3.7 percent in fiscal Year 8. Given the decreased sales, one must wonder why the firm did not at least maintain the percentage, if not the amount, of spending. The advertising expense percentage was approximately 4 percent in fiscal Year 6 and fiscal Year 7, which appears to be the more recurring level.

Uncollectible Accounts and Sales Returns—This expense as a percentage of sales was approximately 2 percent during fiscal Year 6 and fiscal Year 7 and then dropped to 1.4 percent in fiscal Year 8. An analysis of the allowance accounts reveals the following:

Allowance for Uncollectible Accounts and Sales Returns

	Year 6	Year 7	Year 8
Balance, Beginning of Fiscal Year.....	$1,438	$1,785	$2,010
Plus Provision for Year...................	994	1,010	703
Less Write-Offs and Sales Returns.....	(647)	(785)	(954)
Balance, End of Fiscal Year..............	$1,785	$2,010	$1,759

Actual write-offs and sales returns increased during the three-year period. The provision for fiscal Year 6 and fiscal Year 7 exceeded the write-offs and returns as one would expect. One view is that management intentionally reduced the provision in Year 8 to boost earnings. An alternative view is that such a reduction is warranted because the balance in the allowance account is too large. Consider the following analysis:

Accounts Receivable

January 31:	Year 5	Year 6	Year 7	Year 8
Accounts Receivable (Net)..........	$8,000	$8,560	$9,159	$8,782
Plus Balance in Allowance Account...................................	1,438	1,785	2,010	1,759
Accounts Receivable (Gross)......	$9,438	$10,345	$11,169	$10,541
Balance in Allowance Account as a Percentage of Gross Accounts Receivable	15.2%	17.3%	18.0%	16.7%

There is some evidence here that a reduction in the provision might be appropriate.

Asset Impairment Charge—The *need* for recognizing an asset impairment charge arose from new regulations and, therefore, was not under the control of management. The *timing* of recognition was, however, under management's control. Operating income as

14.19 a. continued.

a percentage of sales would be 9.3 percent (= 4.6% + 4.7%) without the impairment loss. Thus, operating profitability declined between fiscal Year 7 and fiscal Year 8. Management might have attempted to get analysts to take their eye off the reasons for the decline in the operating income percentage without the restructuring charge by posting the large impairment loss. The charge is clearly nonrecurring. The analyst should, therefore, eliminate it and its tax effect when assessing ongoing profitability.

Gain on Sale of Land—The gain on the sale of land is likewise nonrecurring and in this case, peripheral to the firm's principal business activities. The analyst should eliminate it when assessing profitability. Given the other means used by the firm to increase earnings in fiscal Year 8 one wonders whether the sale of the land at a gain was motivated by valid business reasons instead of propping up earnings.

Capitalized Interest Costs—GAAP requires firms to capitalize interest cost during the construction period of self-constructed assets. It seems unlikely that the firm would have spent $1,840 million on new construction to enable it to capitalize $147 million of interest costs. Thus, this action does not appear motivated by earnings management.

b. Schedule 14.2 of this solution manual presents revised income statements in both dollar amounts and common-size percentages for fiscal Year 6, Year 7, and Year 8. We make adjustment for the LIFO liquidation, change in depreciable lives of equipment, advertising expense, uncollectible accounts and sales returns provision, asset impairment charge, and gain on sale of land.

c. Petite-Mart, Inc. shows a clear pattern of declining profitability. The deterioration occurs primarily because of increases in the cost of goods sold and depreciation expense percentages. Given the fashion orientation of its product line, one wonders about product obsolescence and failure to adapt to new fashion trends. The increased depreciation percentage results primarily from rapid increases in equipment. Perhaps the firm invested in new computer equipment for customer checkout and inventory control reasons. Such technologies are essential for remaining competitive in today's retailing environment.

14.19 a. continued.

Schedule 14.1
COMMON-SIZE INCOME STATEMENT FOR PETITE-MART, INC.

	Year 6	Year 7	Year 8
Sales	100.0%	100.0%	100.0%
Cost of Goods Sold	(68.0)	(68.1)	(68.2)
Depreciation Expense	(6.5)	(7.9)	(6.8)
Selling and Administrative:			
Advertising Expense	(4.0)	(4.1)	(3.7)
Bad Debt and Sales Returns Expense	(2.0)	(1.9)	(1.4)
Other Selling and Administrative	(9.0)	(8.7)	(9.4)
Asset Impairment Charge	--	(4.7)	--
Operating Income	10.5%	4.6%	10.5%
Gain on Sale of Land	--	--	1.4
Interest Expense	(2.4)	(2.2)	(2.1)
Income before Income Taxes	8.1%	2.4%	9.8%
Income Tax Expense	(2.8)	(.8)	(3.3)
Net Income	5.3%	1.6%	6.5%

14.19 b. continued.

Schedule 14.2
REVISED INCOME STATEMENTS FOR PETITE-MART, INC.

	Year 6		Year 7		Year 8	
Sales.................	$49,680	100.0%	$53,158	100.0%	$50,234	100.0%
Cost of Goods Sold...............	(33,782)	(68.0)	(36,200)	(68.1)	(35,176)[a]	(70.0)
Depreciation Expense.........	(3,235)	(6.5)	(4,167)	(7.9)	(4,995)[b]	(10.0)
Selling and Administrative:						
Advertising....	(1,987)	(4.0)	(2,179)	(4.1)	(2,060)[c]	(4.1)
Bad Debt and Sales Returns.........	(994)	(2.0)	(1,010)	(1.9)	(954)[d]	(1.9)
Other Selling and Administrative......	(4,472)	(9.0)	(4,625)	(8.7)	(4,723)	(9.4)
Operating Income	$ 5,210	10.5%	$ 4,977	9.3%	$ 2,326	4.6%
Interest Expense.............	(1,172)	(2.4)	(1,187)	(2.2)	(1,042)	(2.1)
Income before Income Tax....	$ 4,038	8.1%	$ 3,790	7.1%	$ 1,284	2.5%
Income Tax Expense.............	(1,373)	(2.8)	(1,289)[e]	(2.4)	(437)[f]	(.8)
Net Income........	$ 2,665	5.3%	$ 2,501	4.7%	$ 847	1.7%

[a]$34,260 + $916 = $35,176.

[b]$3,412 + $1,583 = $4,995.

[c].041 × $50,234 = $2,060.

[d].019 × $50,234 = $954.

[e].34 × $3,790 = $1,289.

[f].34 × $1,284 = $437.

APPENDIX A

COMPOUND INTEREST: CONCEPTS AND APPLICATIONS

Questions, Exercises, Problems, and Cases: Answers and Solutions

A.1   See the text or the glossary at the end of the book.

A.2   Rent paid or received for the use of the asset, cash.

A.3   In simple interest, only the principal sum earns interest. In compound interest, interest is earned on the principal plus amounts of interest not paid or withdrawn.

A.4   There is no difference; these items refer to the same thing.

A.5   The timing of the first payment for an annuity due is *now* (at the beginning of the first period) while that for an ordinary annuity is at the *end* of the first period. The future value of an annuity due is computed as of one year after the final payment, but for an ordinary annuity is computed as of the time of the last payment.

A.6   The discount rate that sets the net present value of a stream of payments equal to zero is the implicit rate for that stream.

(1) Guess a rate.

(2) Compute the net present values of the cash flows using the current guess.

(3) If the net present value in (2) is less than zero, then increase the rate guessed and go to Step (2).

(4) If the net present value in (2) is greater than zero, then reduce the rate guessed and go to Step (2).

(5) Otherwise, the current guess is the implicit rate of return.

The process will converge to the right answer only if one is systematic with the guesses, narrowing the range successively.

A.7   Present values increase when interest rates decrease and present values decrease when interest rates increase.

A.8   6 percent. The present value will be larger the smaller the discount rate.

A.9   (Effective interest rates.)

    a. 12 percent per period; 5 periods.

    b. 6 percent per period; 10 periods.

    c. 3 percent per period; 20 periods.

    d. 1 percent per period; 60 periods.

A.10   a. $100 × 1.21665 = $121.67.

    b. $500 × 1.34587 = $672.94.

    c. $200 × 1.26899 = $253.80.

    d. $2,500 × (1.74102 × 1.74102) = $7,577.88

$$(1.02)^{56} = (1.02)^{28} \times (1.02)^{28}.$$

    e. $600 × 1.43077 = $858.46.

A.11   a. $100 × .30832 = $30.83.

    b. $250 × .53063 = $132.66.

    c. $1,000 × .78757 = $787.57.

A.12   a. $100 × 14.23683 = $1,423.68.

    b. $850 × 9.89747 = $8,412.85.

    c. $400 × 49.96758 = $19,987.03.

A.13   a. DM5,000 × 3.20714 × 1.06 = DM16,998.

    b. DM5,000 × 10.06266 × 1.25971 = DM63,380.

A.14   a. Fr150,000 × .62741 = Fr94,112.

    b. Fr150,000 × .54027 = Fr81,041.

A.15   a. $4,000 × 6.97532 = $27,901.

        b. $4,000 × 7.33593 = $29,344.

A.16   a.   ¥45,000,000/10.63663 = ¥4.23 million.

        b.   ¥45,000,000/12.29969 = ¥3.66 million.

A.17   a.   90,000 lira × 14.20679 × 1.05 = 90,000 × (15.91713 − 1.0) lira = 1,342,542 lira.

        b.   90,000 lira × 18.53117 × 1.10 = 90,000 × (21.38428 − 1.0) lira = 1,834,585 lira.

A.18   a.   £145,000/4.62288 = £31,366.

        b.   £145,000/4.11141 = £35,268.

A.19   a.   (10) $100 × T(1, 5, 4).

                (11) $100 × T(2, 30, 4).

                (12) $100 × T(3, 13, 1.5).

                (13)   DM5,000 × T(1, 20, 6) × T(1, 1, 6) =
                        DM5,000 × T(1, 20, 6) × 1.06 =
                        DM5,000 × T(1, 21, 6)—but this is not in the tables.

                (14)   Fr150,000 × T(2, 8, 6).

        b.   (15) $4,000 × T(3, 6, 8).

                (16)   ¥45,000,000/T(3, 8, 12).

                (17)   90,000 lira × T(3, 11, 10) × 1.10 =
                        90,000 lira × T(3, 11, 10) × T(1, 1, 10).

                (18)   £145,000/T(4, 6, 12).

        c.   Asking questions about compound interest calculations on examinations presents a difficult logistical problem to teachers. They may want the students to use compound interest tables, but not wish to incur the costs of reproducing them in sufficient numbers for each student to have a copy. They may not wish to give an open book test. This device is useful for posing test questions about compound interest. The device is based on the fact that teachers of accounting are not particularly interested in testing their students' ability to do arithmetic. Teachers want to be sure that students know how to use the tables and calculating devices efficiently in combination. Such a combination suggests that the human do the thinking and the calculator do the multiplications and divisions.

A.20   a. $1,000(1.00 + .94340) + $2,000(4.21236 − .94340) + $2,500(6.80169 − 4.21236) = $14,955.

       b. $1,000(1.00 + .92593) + $2,000(3.99271 − .92593) + $2,500(6.24689 − 3.99271) = $13,695.

       c. $1,000(1.00 + .90909) + $2,000(3.79079 − .90909) + $2,500(5.75902 − 3.79079) = $12,593.

A.21   a. $3,000 + ($3,000/.06) = $53,000.

       b. $3,000 + ($3,000/.08) = $40,500.

A.22   a. $3,000/(.06 − .02) = $75,000.

       b. $3,000/(.08 − .02) = $50,000.

       c.   [$3,000/(.06) − .02)] × .79209 = $59,406.75.

       d.   [$3,000/(.08 − .02)] × .73503 = $36,751.50.

A.23   a. $60,000 + ($60,000/.1664) = $420,577. $(1.08)^2 − 1 = .1664$.

       b. $60,000 + ($60,000/.2544) = $295,850. $(1.12)^2 − 1 = .2544$.

A.24   7.00 percent. Note that $100,000/$55,307 = 1.80809. See Table 4, 2-period row and observe 1.80809 in the 7-percent column.

A.25   12 percent = $($140,493/$100,000)^{1/3} − 1$.

A.26   a.   16 percent = $($67,280/$50,000)^{1/2} − 1$.

       b.

Year (1)	Book Value Start of Year (2)	Interest for Year = (2) × .16 (3)	Amount (Reducing) Increasing Book Value (4)	Book Value End of Year = (2) + (3) + (4) (5)
1	$50,000	$8,000		$ 58,000
2	58,000	9,280	$ (67,280)	-0-

A.27 (Berman Company; find implicit interest rate; construct amortization schedule.)

a. 14.0 percent.

$$\text{Let } x = \frac{\$8,000}{(1 + r)} + \frac{\$8,000}{(1 + r)^2} + \frac{\$8,000}{(1 + r)^3} + \frac{\$100,000}{(1 + r)^3} = \$86,000$$

If r = 14.0 percent, then x = $18,573 + $67,497 − $86,000 = $70.

If r = 14.1 percent, then x = $18,542 + $67,320 − $86,000 = $138.

b.

Year (1)	Book Value Start of Year (2)	Interest for Year = (2) X .14 (3)	Payment End of Year (Given) (4)	Amount (Reducing) Increasing Book Value = (3) − (4) (5)	Book Value End of Year = (2) + (5) (6)
1	$ 86,000	$12,040	$ 8,000	$ 4,040	$ 90,040
2	90,040	12,605	8,000	4,605	94,645
3	94,645	13,250*	108,000	(94,750)	(105)
OR 3	94,645	13,355*	108,000	(94,645)	-0-

*Interest would actually be recorded at $13,355 (= $108,000 − $94,645) so that the book value of the note reduces to zero at its maturity.

A.28 a. Terms of sale of 2/10, net/30 on a $100 gross invoice price, for example, mean that the interest rate is 2/98 for a 20-day period, because if the discount is not taken, a charge of $2 is levied for the use of $98. The $98 is used for 20 days (= 30 − 10), so the number of compounding periods in a year is 365/20 = 18.25. The expression for the exact rate of interest implied by 2/10, net 30 is $(1 + 2/98)^{(365/20)} - 1 = 1.020408^{18.25} - 1 = 44.59\%$.

b. Table 1 can be used. Use the 2-percent column and the 18-period row to see that the rate implied by 2/10, net 30 must be at least 42.825 percent (= 1.42825 − 1).

A.29 (Present value of a perpetuity).

$30,000 + ($10,000/.01) = $1,030,000.

A.30 Present value of future proceeds = .72845($35,000) + C = $35,000; where C represents the present value of the foregone interest payments. Table 2, 16-period row, 2-percent column = .72845.

C = $35,000 − $25,495.75 = $9,504.25.

A.31   a.   Will: $24,000 + $24,000(3.31213) = $103,488.72 (Preferred).

Dower Option: $300,000/3 = $100,000.

b.   Will: $24,000 + $24,000(3.03735) = $96,896.40.

Dower Option: $300,000/3 = $100,000 (Preferred).

A.32   Present value of deposit = $3.00.

Present value of $3.00, recorded 20 periods, have discounted at .50 percent per period = $3.00 × .90506 = $2.72.

Loss of $.28 (= $3.00 – $2.72) in foregone interest vs. Loss of $1.20 in price.

Net advantage of returnables is $.92.

A.33 $1.00(1.00 + .92456 + .85480 + .79051 + .73069) = $1.00 × 4.30036 = $4.30.

$4.30 – $3.50 = $.80.

A.34 $600/12 = $50 saved per month. $2,000/$50 = 40.0.

Present value of annuity of 1 discounted at 1 percent for 50 periods = 39.19612.

The present value of the annuity is $40 when the annuity lasts between 51 and 52 weeks. Dean Foods will recoup its investment in about one year.

A.35   a. $ 3,000,000 × 7.46944 = $22,408,320.

b. $ 3,000,000 × 7.36578 = $22,097,340
               500,000 × 1.69005 =   845,025
                                                  $22,942,365

c. $ 2,000,000 × 7.36578 = $14,731,560
            1,000,000 × 2.40183 =   2,401,830
               500,000 × 1.69005 =   845,025
                                                  $17,978,415

d. $17,978,410 × .20   = $ 3,595,682.

A.36 (Friendly Loan Company; find implicit interest rate; truth-in lending laws reduce the type of deception suggested by this problem.)

The effective interest rate is 19.86 percent and must be found by trial and error. The time line for this problem is:

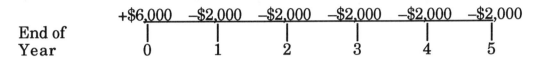

which is equivalent, at least in terms of the implied interest rate, to:

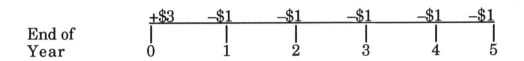

Scanning Table 4, 5-period column, one finds the factor 2.99061, which is approximately 3.00, in the 20-percent column, so one can easily see that the implied interest rate is about 20 percent per year.

A.37 (Black & Decker Company; derive net present value/cash flows for decision to dispose of asset.)

$40,698. The $100,000 is gone and an economic loss of $50,000 was suffered because of the bad purchase. The issue now is do we want to swap a larger current tax loss and smaller future depreciation charges for no tax loss now and larger future depreciation charges.

The new machine will lead to depreciation charges lower by $10,000 per year than the "old" machine and, hence, income taxes larger by $4,000. The present value of the larger taxes is $4,000 × 3.60478 (Table 4, 12 percent, 5 periods). Let S denote the proceeds from selling the old machine. The new current "outlay" to acquire the new machine is $50,000 − S − .40($100,000 − S) or $10,000 − .60S, so that for the new machine to be worthwhile:

$$\$10,000 - .60S < -\$14,419$$

OR

$$.6S > \$24,419$$

OR

$$S > \$40,698.$$

A.38   (Lynch Company/Bages Company; computation of present value of cash flows; untaxed acquisition, no change in tax basis of assets.)

a. $440,000 = $390,000 + $50,000 = $700,000 − $260,000.

b. $3,745,966 = $440,000 × 8.51356; see Table 4, 20-period column, 10-percent row.

A.39   (Lynch Company/Bages Company; computation of present value of cash flows; taxable acquisition, changing tax basis of assets.)

$4,258,199.   If the merger is taxable, then the value of the firm V satisfies:

(1)
$$V = 8.51356 \times [\$700,000 - .40(\$700,000 - V/20)]$$
$$V = \$5,959,492 - \$2,383,797 + .17027V, \text{ or}$$
$$.83972V = \$3,575,695, \text{ so}$$
$$V = \$4,258,199.$$

To understand (1), observe that:

$$V = \text{Value of firm}$$

$$V/20 = \text{New depreciation charge}$$

$$\$700,000 - V/20 = \text{New taxable income}$$

$$.40(\$700,000 - V/20) = \text{New income tax payable, so}$$

$$\$700,000 - .40(\$700,000 - V/20) = \text{New aftertax cash flow to be capitalized at 10 percent for 20 years using present value factor 8.51356.}$$

A.40 (Ragazze; analysis of benefits of acquisition of long-term assets.)

a. $270,831.

Dec. 31 Year	Cash Inflows Operating Receipts (1)	Salvage (2)	Cash Outflows Maintenance (3)	Test Runs (4)	Total (1) + (2) − (3) − (4) (5)	Present Values at 12% Factor (6)	Cash Flow (7)
0				$20,000	($20,000)		($ 17,857)
1	$130,000		$ 60,000		70,000	0.89286	55,804
2	130,000		60,000		70,000	0.79719	49,825
3	130,000		60,000		70,000	0.71178	44,486
4	130,000		60,000		70,000	0.63552	39,720
5	130,000		100,000		30,000	0.56743	15,199
6	130,000		100,000		30,000	0.50663	13,570
7	130,000		100,000		30,000	0.45235	12,116
8	130,000	$30,000			160,000	0.40388	57,968
9						0.36061	$ 270,831

(7) = (5) X (6).

b. $78,868 = $250,000/3.16987.

A.41   (Valuation of intangibles with perpetuity formulas.)

    a. $50 million = $4 million/.08.

    b. Increase.

    c. $66 2/3 million = $4 million/(.08 − .02).

    d. Increase.

    e. Decrease.

A.42   See following page.

A.43 (Horrigan Corporation; Perpetuity Growth Model Derivation of Results to Appendix to Chapter 5.) (Dollar and Shares Outstanding Amounts in Millions)

End of Year	Present Value Factor for End of Year 4 [Table 2]	Excess Cash to Owners [Column 5 on Page 274]	Present Value Dollars for End of Year 4 [Column 6 on Page 274]
4	1.00000		
5	0.83333	$ 7.0	$ 5.8
6	0.69444	24.0	16.7
7	0.57870	55.0	31.8
8	0.48225	109.0	52.5
9	0.40188	204.0	82.0
9	0.40188	2,856.0 = 1.12 × $204/(.20 − .12)	1,147.8
		Sum of Above..............................	$ 1,336.6
		Shares Outstanding	16.0
		Present Value per Share...............	$83.54

At the end of Year 9, the present value of a stream of $204 received in arrears, growing at 12 percent per year, with first cash flow equal to $204 × 1.12 = $228.48 is:

    = 1.12 × $204/(.20 − .12) = $228.48/.08 = $2,856.0

The calculations then reduce that $2,856.0 to present value at the end of Year 4.

(Gulf Coast Manufacturing; choosing between investment alternatives.)

	Basic Data Repeated from Problem		Present Value Computations			
	Lexus	Mercedes-Benz	Source [B]	Factor	Lexus	Mercedes-Benz
Initial Cost at the Start of Year 1.............	$ 60,000	$ 45,000		1.00000	$ 60,000	$ 45,000
Initial Cost at the Start of Year 4.............		48,000	T[2,3,.10]	0.75131		36,063
Trade-in Value						
End of Year 3		23,000	T[2,3,.10]	0.75131		(17,280)
End of Year 6 [Note A]	16,000	24,500	T[2,6,.10]	0.56447	(9,032)	(13,830)
Estimated Annual Cash Operating Costs, Except Major Servicing	4,000	4,500	T[4,6,.10]	4.35526	17,421	19,599
Estimated Cash Cost of Major Servicing						
End of Year 4	6,500		T[2,4,.10]	0.68301	4,440	
End of Year 2 and End of Year 5		2,500	T[2,2,.10]	0.82645		2,066
			T[2,5,.10]	0.62092		1,552
Sum of Present Values of All Costs............					$ 72,829	$ 73,170

Note A:
At this time Lexus is 6 years old; second Mercedes-Benz is 3 years old.

[B]T[i,j,r] means Table i (= Table 2 or Table 4) from the back of the book, row j, interest rate r.

a. Strategy L, buying one Lexus has lower present value of costs, but the difference is so small that we'd encourage the CEO to go with his whim, whatever it may be. Also, the relatively new theory of real options will likely prefer Strategy M because it gives the owner more choices at the end of the third year.

b. Depreciation plays no role, so long as we ignore income taxes. Only cash flows matter.